THE NEW
EUROPEAN UNION

Studies on the European Polity

BRENT NELSEN, SERIES EDITOR

The New European Union:
Confronting the Challenges of Integration
Steve Wood and Wolfgang Quaisser

The Europeans:
Political Identity in an Emerging Polity
David Michael Green

Sustaining European Monetary Union:
Confronting the Cost of Diversity
Tal Sadeh

Europe and the Middle East:
In the Shadow of September 11
Richard Youngs

THE NEW
EUROPEAN
UNION

Confronting the Challenges
of Integration

Steve Wood
Wolfgang Quaisser

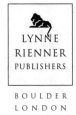

LYNNE
RIENNER
PUBLISHERS

BOULDER
LONDON

Published in the United States of America in 2008 by
Lynne Rienner Publishers, Inc.
1800 30th Street, Boulder, Colorado 80301
www.rienner.com

and in the United Kingdom by
Lynne Rienner Publishers, Inc.
3 Henrietta Street, Covent Garden, London WC2E 8LU

Library of Congress Cataloging-in-Publication Data
Wood, Stephen, 1961–
  The new European Union : confronting the challenges of integration / Steve
Wood and Wolfgang Quaisser.
      p. cm. — (Studies on the European polity)
  Includes bibliographical references and index.
  ISBN 978-1-58826-577-7 (hardcover : alk. paper) — ISBN 978-1-58826-553-1
(pbk. : alk. paper)
  1. European Union. 2. Europe—Economic integration. 3. Europe—Politics
and government. I. Quaisser, Wolfgang, 1955– II. Title.
  JN30.W665 2007
  341.242'2—dc22

                                                          2007025900

British Cataloguing in Publication Data
A Cataloguing in Publication record for this book
is available from the British Library.

Printed and bound in the United States of America

 The paper used in this publication meets the requirements
of the American National Standard for Permanence of
Paper for Printed Library Materials Z39.48-1992.

5 4 3 2 1

Contents

List of Illustrations   vii

Preface   ix

Map of the European Union, 2007   xiii

1   Setting the Stage   1
    A Short History of European Integration, 5
    Institutions and Policymaking, 8
    Stumbling Blocks and Unresolved Issues, 11

2   The Political Economy of Deepening and Widening   17
    Is There an Optimal Size of the Union? 18
    Eastern Enlargement, 21
    The Single Market, 23
    Labor Market Effects, 27
    Economic and Monetary Union, 31
    The Lisbon Agenda, 34
    The EU Budget and Financial Redistribution, 37
    Is a European Economic and Social Model Still Possible? 41
    Conclusion, 47

3   States, Publics, and Europeanization   55
    Institutions, Integration, and Inertia, 56
    Decisionmaking Processes, 61
    Domestic Contexts, 63
    A Constitution for Europe? 65
    Overcoming Deadlock on the Constitutional Treaty, 70
    Conclusion, 74

4   **Key Policy Areas: Developments, Reforms, and Resistance**   81
Voting Power and Funding Distribution, 81
The CAP, 84
Regional Policy, 88
Budget and Financing Reform, 95
Environmental Policy, 101
Energy Policy, 104
Conclusion, 107

5   **Becoming a Global Actor**   115
Common Foreign and Security Policy (CFSP), 118
European Security and Defence Policy (ESDP), 120
National Military Forces and Defense Policies, 126
Armaments and Technology, 134
Financial Resources and Funding Mechanisms, 135
Transatlantic Relations and NATO, 140
China, 142
Energy Security, 143
Internal Security and Terrorism, 144
Conclusion, 145

6   **Dealing with the Neighbors**   155
The Limits of Ambiguity, 156
Democratization, Stabilization, and Security, 159
Interests, Values, and Power, 162
EU Public Opinion and the Shift from Future Members
   to "Friends," 166
The Eastern Flank, 169
The Southern Flank, 177
The Balkans, 181
Turkey, 182
Conclusion, 183

7   **Considering Europe's Future**   193
The EU in Crisis, 193
The EU as Lame Duck? 196
The Consequences of EMU, 197
British Europe or Core Europe? 198
Defense, Security, and the Fight Against Terrorism, 199
Wider Europe, Wider Responsibility, Wider Risk, 201
Conclusion, 205

List of Acronyms   211
Bibliography   215
Index   243
About the Book   253

Illustrations

Tables

1.1	The Ever Wider Union	3
1.2	Major Steps in European Integration	7
2.1	Peculiarities of the EU Club	19
2.2	Steps Toward Eastern Enlargement	22
2.3	Main Interest Groups in Budgetary Negotiations	38
3.1	Public Opinion on the Constitution and Related Issues	68
4.1	Major Indicators and Voting Power in the EU27	83
4.2	Financial Position of Selected EU States in the CAP	87
4.3	Regional Policy: Aims and Instruments	89
4.4	Cohesion for Growth and Employment Funding, 2007–2013	94
4.5	Qualitative Estimations in Different EU Policy Fields	97
4.6	Financial Framework for the Enlarged EU, 2007–2013	98
4.7	Proposed Objectives and Policy Instruments	99
5.1	ESDP Missions	124
5.2	Evolution of CFSP/ESDP and Concurrent EU/Global Affairs	127
5.3	External Relations Appropriations for 2005	136
5.4	The EU as a Global Partner: Financial Perspectives, 2007–2013	137
6.1	Evolution of EU Policy Toward Neighboring States	157
6.2	European Neighbourhood and Partnership Instrument	160
6.3	Evaluation of Political Rights and Civil Freedoms, 2005	161
6.4	Levels of Development in Democracy and the Market Economy, 2005	163
6.5	Support for Enlargements in EU Member States	168
6.6	EU Relations with Neighbors, October 2006	169

Figures

1.1	EU Institutions	9
2.1	The Optimal Size of a Club	20
2.2	Adjusted Optimal Size of the EU Club with Reforms	20
2.3	Development of Real GDP in Selected Transition Countries	25
2.4	Comparison of Labor Productivity and Labor Participation Rates	35
2.5	Agreed Compromise for the Financial Perspective, 2007–2013	40
2.6	Net Budgetary Position of Net Payer Countries	41
2.7	European Social Models: A Typology	44
2.8	Assignment of Economic Policies at National and EU Levels	46
3.1	Levels of Political and Economic Activity Affecting the EU	61
4.1	CAP Receipts by Selected Member States, 2004	88
4.2	Quality of Public Institutions and Degree of Corruption	92
4.3	Factors Influencing Structural Funds Performance	92
5.1	Zones of EU Relationships: Internal, Neighborhood, Global	116
5.2	The European Defence Agency	134
7.1	Future Scenario A: Reforms Fail	202
7.2	Future Scenario B: Clubs Within the Club	202
7.3	Future Scenario C: A Pan-European Identity	203
7.4	Future Scenario D: Vulnerability to External Forces	204
7.5	Future Scenario E: The Demise of the EU	205

Preface

To understand the contemporary condition of the European Union (EU) one must look into the past and with equanimity into the future. The inclusion of the United Kingdom, Denmark, and Ireland in 1973, followed by Greece in 1981 and Spain and Portugal in 1986, expanded the size and potential of the then European Community (EC). The addition of these new members increased the economic, societal, and cultural heterogeneity of the EC and the range of basic understanding of Europe as a political entity. Some countries, especially the UK during the Thatcher revolution, discarded old models of economic and social organization; others continued to feed on the fruits of past success. At the end of the 1980s, Europe was divided. Central and Eastern Europe experienced communism's economic, social, and ideological collapse, culminating in the disintegration of the Soviet bloc between 1989 and 1991. Only later did it become clear just how derelict the economies of those countries actually were. The Single Market initiative, of which Margaret Thatcher approved, and plans to introduce a common currency, of which she did not, were on the EC's agenda as the Iron Curtain fell. Political personalities who had provided the impulse for ventures intended to intensify cooperation and policy alignment among a group of twelve states had to sustain momentum in a totally new context. An impetus to again increase the group's membership joined the demands of deepening its integration.

"How will the EU develop?" is a question frequently asked since the enlargement of 2004 and the rejection by French and Dutch voters of the Constitutional Treaty in 2005. Doubts have plagued many Europeans at elite and popular levels because they have to define themselves anew in a rapidly changing world. Overcoming these concerns is not an abstract question about what form of institutional arrangements should or might be found for a supranational construction, but rather is about practical issues of ensuring effective cooperation and with it sustainable prosperity, peace, and security. Here one senses a paradoxical feature of European integration. It is an attempt to implement a unique and even revolutionary method of political organization and governance for a group of mostly conservative nation-states.

A positive scenario for the EU in 2025 might show an enormous economic power with a dependable common currency. In this version of the future, as aspirations entailed in the Lisbon Agenda foresaw, the EU has developed into the world's most dynamic and innovative economic space, with high growth and low unemployment. These achievements are founded on a solid political unity that has enabled the EU not only to cope with globalization but to become its leading driver and beneficiary. Economic dynamism functions simultaneously as a precondition and the outcome of preferences for the preservation or advancement of particular social, cultural, and environmental goals. The EU asserts itself on the world stage and proves itself capable, not only militarily, to shape global politics and policy in accordance with its own ideals and interests. Prosperity has strengthened both internal unity and the capacity to realize preferred options externally.

Such a vision is realistic and existential. It requires self-assertion by the EU as the institutional-political representative of Europe and is dependent on the generation of a common European will among the states and peoples that comprise the continent. Demographic trends, weak economic growth, immigration, terrorism, energy needs, political extremism, and other factors place Europe under intense pressure. They may threaten its demise. The situation is serious. Reference to the impressive successes of the 1990s can only partially ignite Europe's full potential. A sober appraisal of all these issues can assist in defining and addressing current and future tasks.

Against a background of past achievement and contemporary challenges, we analyze the economic, social, security-strategic, institutional, and political dimensions of European integration. The core question is how can the EU master the tension between deepening and widening in a globalizing context with all the multifarious demands, dangers, and opportunities that entails?

* * *

The authors would like to especially thank Lynne Rienner for her encouragement, suggestions, and great patience. Many thanks also go to the staff at Lynne Rienner Publishers. We express our gratitude to the Alexander von Humboldt (AvH) Stiftung for its award of a Friedrich-Bessel Prize to Steve Wood, who would in particular like to thank General Secretary Georg Schütte, President Wolfgang Frühwald, and Mercedes Barbón, all of the AvH. Steve Wood also thanks Andrzej Staniek for his help and insights at the Seehaus, Leib und Seele, and many other places; Volkhart Vincentz and other members of the Osteuropa Institut München; Wilfried von Bredow; Alex Coram; Olaf Mager; Joan Kahler; Richard Leaver; Reinhard Meier-Walser; May and Stan.

Wolfgang Quaisser thanks the Bavarian State Ministry of Science, Research and Arts for sponsoring the research project "Reforms and Interests in an Extended European Union" in the context of its Forost Research Program on Eastern Europe. He is also grateful to Heinrich Oberreuter, director of the Academy of Civic Education in Tutzing, for providing the opportunity to finish this book as part of the project "Globalization and Eastern Europe Enlargement: Germany's Social Market Economy Confronted with International Competition." The authors also thank Silke, Eva, Eric, and Jim.

European Union, 2007

1

Setting the Stage

Legend has it that Zeus, in the form of a bull, kidnapped Europa, the daughter of a Phoenician king. Millennia after the story was first told, what the mythical Europa lent her name to remains protean and elusive. In geographic terms, the Atlantic and Arctic Oceans provide clear physical borders to the west and north of the curiously shaped landmass that protrudes from Asia. To the south, it is less clear why some Mediterranean islands should be classed as European and not African or Asian. And although numerous accounts refer to the Ural Mountains and varying shores of the Black, Caspian, and Azov Seas as boundaries, the eastern limits of Europe are most indistinct of all.

The lack of a precise geographic designation meant that culture and history gained authority as defining what and where Europe was. The history of Europe has become "world history" because so much has been exported, if then transmuted. Today many Europeans identify with a particular national consciousness and associate "Europe" with remote bureaucratic directives from "Brussels." At the same time, with border fences removed and passport controls relaxed, they can experience incredible variety within a few hundred kilometers. Were they to be transported to another continent, they would soon recognize that they were no longer in Europe and regard themselves communally as Europeans. An understanding of Europe's philosophical and intellectual roots in antiquity, the expansion of the Roman Empire and its judicial tradition, the influence of Christianity and Judaism and the Enlightenment and humanism, the separation of church and state, the development of citizenship, waves of emigration and immigration, bloody internal conflicts, and common defense against external threats, is needed to acquire insight into contemporary Europe.

Though regional empires were established, since the fall of Rome no power has maintained an enduring rule over the continent. Competition and rivalry spurred technological and human progress and contributed to countless wars. The excesses of totalitarian ideologies and regimes brought Europe to the brink of annihilation and left it divided under the control of two external superpowers. It is against this background that Europe after the fall of the Berlin Wall is to be understood. Europe can only realize its potential through its diversity and peaceful competition among differing approaches to its organization.

The idea of Europe as a unified political or economic entity is more recent than conjecture or assumptions about its cultural and historical commonality.[1] Paralleling developments from the founding of the European Coal and Steel Community (ECSC) to the emergence of the European Union (EU) and beyond, the last half-century has seen an explosive growth in the study of the continent's integration.[2] What the EU is might be more contested than controversies and speculations about the character, the meaning, and the limits of Europe. In contrast to scholars, publicists, and politicians who emphasize political, geographical, historical, or cultural factors, there are others who argue that institutions and law are the decisive shapers of the EU's identity.[3] That view is aligned with a discourse, conveyed by the European Commission and other supporters of a multilevel, quasi-supranational governance system, in which the EU and Europe are often presented as synonymous. The objective is to generate identification with and trust in the EU as a whole, which will in turn encourage solidarity and cooperation among its parts. The influence of the EU as an interdependent community of member states, citizens, and institutions should then increase vis-à-vis an alternative configuration of more autonomous and self-interested nation-states.

The EU has grown from an original membership of six to twenty-seven member states. Six enlargements have occurred over the past half-century, the largest when ten new members joined in 2004 (see Table 1.1). Europe is not, however, the same as the EU, even if the latter is increasingly expected to take responsibility for shaping the former. Resistance to the EU reinforcing itself in such a role often accompanies these expectations, not least because there is no consensus on where the ultimate borders of either are. Reflecting the vagueness of the *Méthode Monnet*, the functionalist approach adopted by early practitioners of integration, neither the current EU nor its forerunners clearly specified what or where Europe is: its geographic or cultural limits or what a "European state" is or is not. It is not affirmed in the 1952 Paris treaty, the 1957 Rome Treaties, or the Treaty of Nice in 2000. Nor was it apparent in the proposed Constitutional Treaty (CT), or the "Berlin Declaration," signed at the fiftieth anniversary celebrations of the Rome Treaties.[4]

A combination of ambition, ambiguity, and irresolution has positioned the EU in a precarious situation. Presenting the EU as analogous with Europe, without defining what Europe is or is not, has encouraged a miscellany of states and peoples to aim at joining the EU. In some cases aspirations are based on claims to Europeanness that are perceived as unconvincing and are opposed. Concurrent to the entreaties of would-be members and disinterest or

Table 1.1   The Ever Wider Union

Original Member States (1958)	Enlargements					
	First (1973)	Second (1981)	Third (1986)	Fourth (1995)	Fifth (2004)	Sixth (2007)
Belgium	Britain	Greece	Spain	Austria	Czech Republic	Bulgaria
France	Denmark		Portugal	Finland		Romania
W. Germany	Ireland			Sweden	Cyprus	
Italy					Hungary	
Luxembourg					Estonia	
Netherlands					Latvia	
					Lithuania	
					Malta	
					Poland	
					Slovak Republic	
					Slovenia	

turbulence among current ones, the EU must cope with multiple intensifying pressures: global commercial and economic forces; reform in agricultural and regional policy and voting arrangements; security threats posed by terrorism or instability on its periphery and beyond; development policy and humanitarian aid; environmental and energy concerns; greater transparency and citizen democracy; and effective representation in the United Nations (UN), the World Trade Organization (WTO), and other forums.

Confronted with these circumstances, the EU has experienced a generalized crisis with many dimensions. Despite signs of an at least partial emergence from stagnation in key continental member states, the word "crisis" was still being used to characterize the EU's condition in March 2007.[5] By June in that year, some optimism had returned after the political leaders of the member states managed to hammer out a preliminary compromise on a "Reform Treaty" to replace the failed CT. At time of writing, the new treaty still had to be approved at another Intergovernmental Conference (IGC) during the Portuguese presidency of the EU. It would then require ratification and implementation by all member states. With these processes incomplete it is uncertain how much content of the rejected CT will actually be adopted in revised form. The outcome of negotiations on the Reform Treaty will potentially have great effect on the EU's strategies of deepening and widening. Yet even if the treaty outcome is ostensibly favorable, it is not clear that pursuing these strategies simultaneously can be successful—or what may happen if one or the other is not.[6]

A comprehensive shift to innovation and forward-looking policies, and away from a subsidization and redistribution mentality, is required. The EU must balance the powers of its institutions, clarify the competences of participating actors, and define new, apposite policy approaches. Doing those things presupposes a reorganization of the Union based on a stronger communal will. A gradual delineation of the EU into subgroups of states may be manageable; but it also may lead to fragmentation and unraveling. A more differentiated or à la carte EU, accompanied by doubts about whether either could function properly, could diminish European security.

Much hinges on whether new French president Nicolas Sarkozy can revitalize France and Germany's "Grand Coalition" government can encourage the economic recovery that appeared toward the end of 2006 to drive sustained growth and productivity. These two states are crucial. Improvement in their employment situations will reduce antipathy toward national political elites and to the EU. It may also temper aversions to recent and potential approaching enlargements.

In this book we examine the EU's successes, shortcomings, and issues that have arisen as a result of increasing membership, insufficient reform, and pressures from the world outside. Notwithstanding the contribution made by the EU and its forerunners to peace, prosperity, and democratization on the European continent, it cannot merely congratulate itself. Nor can its admirers continue to evoke historical successes as a sufficient response to the EU's critics. Under the geopolitical, institutional, and simple arithmetical conditions of earlier decades, it was far easier to balance a much narrower range of national and sectoral interests. Even then, there were examples of failure to reach a common position. Now the breadth of policy competence, proliferating national and group interests, and a growing influence of publics on the integration process, usually through pressure on member state governments, mean that it is harder to concur. "National interest" is often criticized as a nebulous term, but "European interest" is vaguer still.

Following this introduction, Chapter 2 analyzes economic themes and problems associated with trying to concurrently deepen and widen the EU. It reviews the transition in Central and Eastern Europe (CEE) that led to the accessions of first eight and then two more countries (CEECs) and their effects on the political economy of the EU. Chapter 3 examines the attempt to provide a constitutional foundation in an environment of popular dissatisfaction with aspects of EU development and associated renationalization trends. The disinclinations of member states to, in some instances at least, relinquish individual controls and integrate supranationally, limits their "Europeanization." Chapter 4 deals with reform pressures and options in agricultural and regional policy and budget financing. It also addresses the environment and energy, areas that have gained prominence in recent years. In Chapter 5 we appraise the EU's role as a global actor, including the Common Foreign and Security Policy (CFSP) and its component, the European Security and Defence Policy

(ESDP). The EU's wider neighborhood is the focus of Chapter 6. Successful interaction with its extended regional environment is essential if the EU is to sustain itself as a serious actor globally. Some neighbors want to enter the EU, and others want assistance; some present authentic problems, and others contain the potential to do so. In Chapter 7 we summarize these entwined contexts and consider scenarios that may confront the EU.

A Short History of European Integration

The contours of a Western European institutional system[7] are sketched in the early correspondence between French foreign minister Robert Schumann and indicative planner Jean Monnet.[8] At the center was a Franco-German compromise that began with the ECSC.[9] Reconciliation among these hereditary enemies was envisaged as the foundation of lasting peace and prosperity in Europe. French agricultural interests and pretence to world power status were balanced with the Federal Republic of Germany's (FRG's) desire for international rehabilitation and secure markets for its industrial goods. The others, it was noted, were "window dressing."[10] The failure of the European Defence Community (EDC) in 1954, largely because of Gaullist aversions to intrusions in this core area of national sovereignty, confirmed the North Atlantic Treaty Organization (NATO) as Western Europe's sole credible security entity during the Cold War. France's withdrawal from NATO's integrated command structure followed in 1966. The alliance embodied the benign hegemony of the United States, which maintained Western Europe as a comfortable, hermetic economic community. In many estimations NATO contributed as much to the peace project as the European institutions.

It was in a context of guaranteed welfare and security that the "European social model" impressed itself on the elite and popular consciousness. Certainly there was and is differentiation in the operation of particular examples: the French, Dutch, Italian, Scandinavian, or German. Nonetheless, the political sociology and related expectations that formed during the postwar period have, despite tremendous geopolitical and economic changes, maintained influence among European electorates. That philosophy is also entrenched among sections of the older, continental, political and bureaucratic cadres in Brussels. It is one reason why innovative response to global economic forces, most pertinently in France and Germany, has proved difficult.[11] Reform of inefficient economic and social models is, however, unavoidable.[12]

The Single European Act (SEA), the 1986 outcome of a grand bargain between the governments of Margaret Thatcher, Helmut Kohl, and François Mitterrand, and the drive of then Commission president Jacques Delors, was a significant move toward liberalizing markets and deepening economic integration.[13] In return for freer trade, Thatcher consented to the introduction of qualified majority voting (QMV), which opened possibilities for integration in other areas. Economic and Monetary Union (EMU), introduced by the Maastricht Treaty of 1992, advanced the process toward a unified economic space and culminated in the arrival of the euro in 1999. Thereafter, the concentration shifted to the political-security project of eastern enlargement. In May 2004, eight states from CEE, along with (Greek) Cyprus and Malta, acceded to the EU.

The liberalization process that began with the SEA, and was further stimulated by enlargement, faces opposition in the labor market, agricultural, and other policy areas. Regulations for financial sectors and services industries remain largely national. Resistance to liberal reforms is bound with the political sclerosis that has affected key member states. A related effect is that certain legislation, like the Stability and Growth Pact (SGP), has been flouted by states that previously insisted on it. All that is a manifestation of how, as institutions developed, member states adapted and continued to represent disparate political communities, rather than evolving into a superstate with a corresponding European nation or public. These developments support cogent arguments that nation-states have not withered away as integration progressed, but rather have been reinforced by it.[14] Despite the dismantling of border controls throughout most of the EU, the nation-state is still instinctively regarded as a protector against threats, as a provider of social security, as responsible for employment creation, for sending compatriots to war, for law and order, and for taxation. Europeans identify much more—politically, culturally, and emotionally—with "their" nation-states than with Europe or the EU. That fact links to a central debate in the discipline of international relations: the relation between material interests and affective identifications and their relative influence on politics and policies. Both sets of motivations affect the integration process (see Table 1.2).

Each new member state increases the range of interests to be accounted for and balanced. For the most part, that was manageable until the goal of reunification enshrined in the FRG's 1949 Basic Law was surprisingly and expeditiously fulfilled. The transformation of 1989–1991 not only changed political and institutional interactions but also recast historical and psychological aspects of the German relationship with European integration[15] and with *Mitteleuropa*.[16] Although it initially appeared that German reunification would unleash an enlarged powerhouse in the center of Europe, it brought problems, disadvantages, and costs as well as benefits, not only for (West) Germany but much of Western Europe. The Cold War's end exposed the discrepancy between Western Europe's economic power on the one hand and its political weakness and security dependence on the other. Those features are present in many studies of the EU's advent and progress.[17] Realists did not pay much attention to Europe as a world actor; they considered that the western half's integration was only possible in the bipolar context: a negative integration fac-

Table 1.2 Major Steps in European Integration

Project	Year	Character/Content	Achievements/Problems
Treaty of Rome	1957	Basic treaty proclaiming "ever closer union"	Foundation of the EEC (European Economic Community); vagueness about finalité
Single European Act (SEA)	1986	Partly liberalizes EU economic space	Breakthrough toward the Single Market; introduces qualified majority voting
Single Market (SM)	1992	Capital, goods, labor, services move freely	Success incomplete; services and finance industries still largely national
Treaty on European Union (EMU, CFSP)	Signed, 1992; in effect, 1993	Monetary policy administered by European Central Bank (ECB); foreign/security policy	Success with EMU, but criteria not adhered to by all; stability pact under pressure; CFSP involved sharp learning curve, developing institutional structures, funding shortage
European Security and Defence Policy (ESDP)	1999	Security and defense policy	Success in initial missions; some rival preferences and sensitivities about sovereignty; aversions to military EU; tension with NATO/United States
Euro	1999	Common currency	After initial fall, a solid value maintained
Enlargement	2004	Entry of ten, mainly CEECs, to the EU	Despite skepticism a successful project; much left to complete
Enlargement	2007	Bulgaria and Romania accede	Two of the least developed states in Europe; very reliant on the EU

tor in the form of the Soviet Union on the one hand and a protective umbrella and political leadership provided by the United States on the other.[18] In contrast, neo-functionalism emerged as a response to internal Western European developments. Its adherents believed that integration was driven by an expansive logic and would gradually extend from one area to others (the "spillover" concept). At times highly influential, neo-functionalism was criticized for its apolitical nature, and a leading proponent came to write of its "obsolescence."[19] Another school combined elements of realist power politics, liberal economic interests, and historical institutionalism to account for the EU's evolution.[20]

In comparison with work on integration, there has been less theory about reforms and how to implement them, though it is widely agreed in the academic literature that the EU needs an injection of initiative and flexibility.[21] As Lars-Erik Cederman declares, "The golden days of Jean Monnet's functional integration are definitely over."[22] Fundamentals are being reassessed. A narrow inward focus is no longer possible. At the same time, effective external action requires internal resolve and cohesion. Creating "strategic partnerships" implies new applications of "variable geometry" and obliges a (tacit) categorization of insiders and outsiders involving "identity trade-offs."[23] An example was the "Ring of Friends" formulation floated by then Commission president Romano Prodi, as a discursive precursor to a neighborhood strategy.[24]

Without ignoring the potential for intense institutionalization or socialization to influence bureaucratic as well as political actors, and thereby the integration process more broadly, in our view intergovernmentalism has best reflected where decisive power resides within the EU complex. It provides a persuasive explanation of how and why agreement or impasse on substantive initiatives in integration, such as the SEA, TEU, or EDC, have occurred and of wrangling over voting weight, budgetary contributions and redistribution, and foreign policy interests. In recent years growing popular influence on EU politics has joined intergovernmental interaction as a crucial factor. National electorates have demonstrated a capacity to make agreement between state executives more difficult and to derail or cause the revision of policy. Despite its role in generating cooperation and welfare, the EU has not acquired the affection of member populations or generated the communal will to enthusiastically support agendas of transformation or enlargement, especially in times of economic uncertainty. Here emotive elements have a role in determining the EU's current condition. A combination of deficient popular identification with the EU, and intergovernmental power struggles, resulted in some renationalization trends.

Institutions and Policymaking

A singular feature of the European project is its institutional architecture. Whether states are perceived as decisive, predominant, or otherwise, institutions have a special status, role, and interaction in the EU—even if they do not always achieve what their personnel and advocates might wish. Accompanying this configuration is a distinctive form of interinstitutional rivalry. It is manifested in power struggles between the Commission, with its formal right of initiative in communal policy; the European Parliament (EP), with claims to authority based on democratic representation; and the European Council (the heads of state and government), seconded in day-to-day business by the Council of Ministers (hereafter the Council) and the two Committees of Permanent Representatives (COREPERs).[25] The Constitutional Treaty was a recent focus for a familiar lament that politics—national politics—ignores or subverts a proper and necessary European vocation, whereby states and publics unselfishly adapt their preferences for the common good.[26] Though supported by the Commission and Parliament, the first draft of the treaty failed because national political elites could not agree. Coexistent with the EU's unique institutional arrangements, all states have particular interests and strive to acquire or retain a capacity to attain them. Notwithstanding multilevel governance structures, institutional power resides primarily in the voting system of the Council. After grueling negotiations, a compromise on a new double majority requirement to pass the CT (55 percent of states representing 65 percent of the EU population) was reached in 2004 to enable the second CT draft to move toward ratification. Another power center, national electorates, then made its presence felt.

Institutional peculiarities are partly responsible for criticism targeting a lack of transparency and public scrutiny. Disapproval is directed at the Commission's "unelected" bureaucratic influence and at the secrecy surrounding Council deliberations. Although the calculated imprecision of the Monnet system still operates, the member states are no less responsible.[27] The EP has gained in authority, though an authentic European party system and electorate are yet to emerge. Some scholars accentuate an expansion of "informal governance," which may counter the EP's objective to strengthen, with itself as the focus, formal democratic representation at the European level (see Figure 1.1).[28]

In regard to the EU's complex policy and financing arrangements, Loukas Tsoulakis argues that "the economist from Mars would find it hard to make

Figure 1.1   EU Institutions

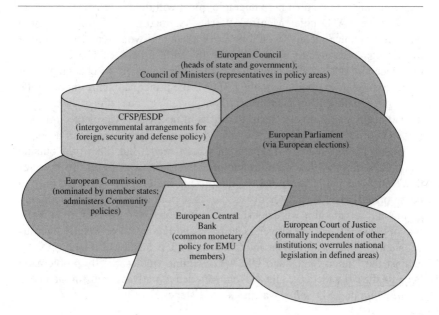

any sense of it. Rationality, as defined by economists, including those from outer space, does not always help much in understanding the ways of European integration." Perhaps no field has been so central to everyday EU affairs as the Common Agricultural Policy (CAP), and none has motivated such sustained demand for reform or abolition. Excepting those in receipt of subsidies or actors whose fortunes are partly dependent on its maintenance, the CAP is widely maligned. According to Tsoulakis, "The CAP is, undoubtedly, one of the best examples of the divorce between policy and economic rationality."[29] Problems already present were exacerbated by admitting several states whose economies featured large agricultural sectors. The arrival of poorer members also increased pressure on structural and cohesion funding, which had to be reformed. One inevitable result is that customary net receivers, such as Spain, Greece, and Ireland, will have their transfers reduced or become net payers.

Focused for decades on wealth redistribution, the EU is now compelled to develop programs that promote wealth generation. The Lisbon Agenda is the most ambitious, promoting high-quality, technological innovation. Its implementation and results have been disappointing, and the hoped-for extensive benefits have not ensued. The Single Market (SM) has been a success, though some areas are incomplete.[30] EMU and the introduction of its centerpiece, the euro, is an outstanding achievement.[31] If price stability and hard money goals have been successful, European employment strategies have failed. The euro's maintenance as a hard currency, after an initial fall vis-à-vis the US dollar, is opposed by some political forces. They argue for a relaxation of the criteria underpinning it to combat high unemployment within the eurozone.

Former NATO chief Manfred Wörner claimed, "The European Union without a defence identity would be incomplete and would condemn Europe to playing an essentially rhetorical role in world affairs."[32] The CFSP was introduced in 1993 and is central to the EU's adaptation to the changing global context. A newer component, the ESDP, is the principal manifestation of the EU's gradual transition from a "civilian power" to one with a capacity to defend itself against diverse security threats, if necessary by projected military force.[33] Foreign and security policy was the most evident location of a "capability-expectations gap."[34] Progress has been made, but the world outside sometimes intrudes in uncomfortable or dangerous ways. Tsoukalis observes that "many people have tended to take official rhetoric too seriously, only to be surprised when they later discovered that political union or a genuinely common foreign policy were not simply waiting around the corner."[35] In 2003, two of the CFSP's prime movers, Germany and France, traversed a dangerous course by allying with Russia and China in the UN Security Council (UNSC) against the United States and UK.[36] The timing was especially problematic because the rift widened while an Anglo-French initiative to transform an ESD *identity* into an ESD *policy* was in its early stages.[37]

Stumbling Blocks and Unresolved Issues

General efficiency in the functioning of a union approaching thirty members devolves in large part onto Council voting arrangements, which translate into political weight and room for national maneuver in the institutional context. Persisting differences of interest can mean the formation of blocking coalitions and the dilution or abandonment of initiatives. The rejection of the CT, which many politicians and analysts did not perceive as likely until it had become a fait accompli, left a practical and psychological hurdle. Even if some objectives in the CT may be reached via other routes, the ideal behind the enterprise has been undermined. Other questions, some linked to the 2005 referendum results, relate to the creation and distribution of resources. What are the preconditions for payments? Who can join? How will it all be funded?

The EU failed to grasp the opportunity for wholesale renovation presented by enlargement. The reasons include vested and competing interests in member states, the desire of governments to retain power and privileges domestically, including through populist appeals, and the underestimated category of national prestige, but the most important reason is a deficiency of common European will. The EU may espouse particular values, but it is not primarily a "value community." The EU is first a community of interests. When they are successfully balanced and pursued, then the sum of the parts can operate as a more or less efficient whole. The macro-objective of harmonization at the highest possible living standard within a secure environment is then facilitated.

To achieve that goal now requires a means of dealing with members that have a far lower per capita income and level of economic development than the EU average. Other neighbors are poorer still. In late 2004, as a Commission report and European Council summit to decide on opening membership negotiations with it approached, Turkey surged to the top of the EU's agenda.[38] For a brief period, it was overshadowed by events in Ukraine. Other states, weak, authoritarian, or undergoing transition to democracy, also make claims for assistance or accession. It is unlikely that all or perhaps any will have fulfilled the "Copenhagen criteria" in all respects.[39] Balkan countries will eventually be accepted for membership. If they and Turkey are, on what consistent grounds could the EU refuse others that might apply? Others include Armenia, Azerbaijan, Israel, a Palestinian state (or "authority"), Georgia, Moldova, Morocco, Tunisia, Egypt, Algeria, and even Russia, which in many estimations is culturally and historically the most "European" of all.[40] Belarus, "the last dictatorship in Europe," may also apply.

Possible further expansion of the EU raises a basic question: Who has legitimate claims to belong to "Europe," and thereby the EU, and who does not? It raises the issue of European solidarity, which links common identity, or a "we-feeling," with the financing of projects and the preparedness of some states and citizens to provide for others.[41] Although the EU has continued to expand in membership and policy scope, this solidarity is under more pressure than ever. Identity and interests can be barriers to unity. The generosity of richer member states, as well as those that have benefited greatly from resource redistribution, is tested. By comparison, the nonmembership of Switzerland and Norway indicates that they envisage more outlays and encumbrances than benefits. Both have held more than one referendum on EU entry, all resulting in "no" votes.

These themes are linked to a recurring criticism of the EU: its alleged democratic deficit. It was established and run by elites, even if it was inspired by the propensity of Europe's populations to engage in nationalist rivalries. One result is the continued absence of a pan-European public; another is ambivalence about features of the Brussels system. The impact of some developments, such as Turkey's bid for membership, was underestimated. While the December 2004 decision to open negotiations was made by the EU heads of state and government, some, including Jacques Chirac of France and Jan Peter Balkanende of the Netherlands, announced their countries would hold national referendums on the CT. Their decisions came after British prime minister Tony Blair announced that he would do so. Referendums granted citizens of those countries direct involvement in decisionmaking on a pivotal issue. The array of states wishing to join, reform pressures, and the scramble for funding will increase demands within member states' populations for a voice in determining the EU's agenda.

Meanwhile, defense, security, and foreign policy, fields in which progress has occurred in recent years, remain full of real and potential obstacles. And there are many other serious concerns. Two examples give some indication: first, the flow of people, many from Africa, attempting to enter the EU; and second, the need for an enormous supply of energy resources. The dispute between Russia and Ukraine in early 2006, which temporarily disrupted gas supplies to some EU states, exposed European sensitivities in this context. Political machinations may have greater significance for the security of continued EU access to energy resources than purely economic factors.

Extensive reforms are necessary for the EU to function at or near optimal capacity. It must not be afraid of competition. It must also generate a common political will: to act coherently and decisively; create wealth; defend itself, sometimes through crisis management and peace-ensuring missions in distant locations; and set limits on membership. Only then can Europe's potential be realized.

Notes

1. Cf. Pim den Boer, "Europe to 1914: The Making of an Idea," in Kevin Wilson and Jan van der Dussen, eds., *The History of the Idea of Europe* (London: Open

University/Routledge, 1995), 13. See also Norman Davies, *Europe: A History* (Oxford: Oxford University Press, 1996).

2. John Keeler, "Mapping EU Studies: The Evolution from Boutique to Boom Field, 1960–2001," *Journal of Common Market Studies* 43, no. 3 (2005): 551–582.

3. Franz Mayer and Jan Palmowski, "European Identities and the EU: The Ties That Bind the Peoples of Europe," *Journal of Common Market Studies* 42, no. 3 (2004): 573–598.

4. European Union, "Declaration on the Fiftieth Anniversary of the Signature of the Treaties of Rome," Berlin, 25 March 2007, www.eu2007.de/en/About_the_EU/Constitutional_Treaty/BerlinerErklaerung.html.

5. "Europe's Mid-life Crisis," *Economist,* 17 March 2007, p. 11.

6. Fraser Cameron, ed., *The Future of Europe: Integration and Enlargement* (London: Routledge, 2004); Bernard Steunenberg, ed., *Widening the European Union: The Politics of Institutional Change and Reform* (London: Routledge, 2002).

7. For more extensive coverage, see Desmond Dinan, *Europe Recast* (Boulder, CO: Lynne Rienner, 2004); Kjell Torbiörn, *Destination Europe: The Political and Economic Growth of a Continent* (Manchester: Manchester University Press, 2003).

8. *Jean Monnet–Robert Schumann: Correspondance 1947–1953* (Lausanne: Fondation Jean Monnet, 1986).

9. Ruprecht Vondran, "Die Montanunion war ein politischer Kompromiss," *Die Welt,* 22 July 2002, 12. The ECSC was retired at fifty, having "fulfilled its historical tasks."

10. Tony Judt, "Nineteen Eighty-Nine: The End of *Which* European Era?" *Dædelus* 123, no. 2 (1994): 1–19.

11. Wolfgang Munchau, *Das Ende der Sozialen Marktwirtschaft* (München: Hanser, 2006).

12. André Sapir, "Globalization and the Reform of European Social Models," *Journal of Common Market Studies* 44, no. 2 (2006): 369–390.

13. Andrew Moravcsik, "Negotiating the Single European Act: National Interests and Conventional Statecraft in the European Community," *International Organization* 45, no. 1 (1991): 19–56.

14. Alan Milward, *The European Rescue of the Nation-State,* 2nd ed. (London: Routledge, 2000); Loukas Tsoukalis, *What Kind of Europe?* (Oxford: Oxford University Press, 2003), 207.

15. Stephen Wood, *Germany, Europe, and the Persistence of Nations: Transformation, Interests, and Identity, 1989–1996* (Aldershot: Ashgate, 1998).

16. Steve Wood, *Germany and East Central Europe: Political, Economic and Socio-Cultural Relations in the Era of Eastern Enlargement* (Aldershot: Ashgate, 2004); Steve Wood, "A Common European Space? National Identity, Foreign Land Ownership and EU Enlargement: The Polish and Czech Cases," *Geopolitics* 9, no. 3 (2004): 588–607.

17. Cf. Stanley Hoffmann, *The European Sisyphus: Essays on Europe, 1964–1994* (Boulder, CO: Westview 1995); Karl Deutsch, *The Analysis of International Relations* (Englewood Cliffs, NJ: Prentice Hall, 1968); Leon Lindberg, *The Political Dynamics of European Economic Integration* (Stanford: Stanford University Press, 1963); Hedley Bull, "Civilian Power Europe: A Contradiction in Terms?" *Journal of Common Market Studies* 21, no. 1 (1982): 149–164; Milward, *The European Rescue.*

18. Kenneth Waltz, *Theory of International Politics* (Reading, MA: Addison Wesley, 1979). For a more recent view, see Robert Kagan, *Of Paradise and Power: America and Europe in the New World Order* (New York: Knopf, 2003).

19. Ernst Haas, *The Uniting of Europe: Political, Social and Economic Forces, 1950–57* (London: Stevens and Sons, 1958); Ernst Haas, *The Obsolescence of Regional Integration Theory* (Berkeley: Institute of International Studies, 1975). For a good coverage of theoretical approaches, see Ben Rosamond, *Theories of European Integration* (Houndmills: Macmillan, 2000).

20. Andrew Moravcsik, *The Choice for Europe: Social Purpose and State Power from Messina to Maastricht* (London: UCL Press, 1998).

21. Dimitris Chryssochoou, Michael Tsinisizelis, Stelios Stavridis, and Kostas Ifantis, *Theory and Reform in the European Union* (Manchester: Manchester University Press, 1999); Steunenberg, *Widening the European Union*.

22. Lars-Erik Cederman, "Political Boundaries and Identity Trade-Offs," in Lars-Erik Cederman, ed., *Constructing Europe's Identity: The External Dimension* (Boulder: Lynne Rienner, 2001), 1.

23. J. H. H. Weiler, Iain Begg, and John Peterson, eds., *Integration in an Expanding European Union: Reassessing the Fundamentals* (Oxford: Blackwell, 2003); Cederman, "Political Boundaries and Identity Trade-Offs"; Julie Smith and Charles Jenkins, eds., *Through the Paper Curtain: Insiders and Outsiders in the New Europe* (London: RIIA/Blackwell, 2003).

24. Romano Prodi, "A Wider Europe: A Proximity Policy as the Key to Stability," speech at the "Peace, Security and Stability: International Dialogue and the Role of the EU" conference, Brussels, December 2002.

25. Myrto Tsakatika, "Claims to Legitimacy: The European Commission Between Continuity and Change," *Journal of Common Market Studies* 43, no. 1 (2005): 193–220.

26. Dietrich von Kyaw, "The EU After the Agreement on a Constitutional Treaty," *European Foreign Affairs Review* 9, no. 4 (2004): 455–458; cf. Cindy Skach, "We, the Peoples? Constitutionalizing the European Union," *Journal of Common Market Studies* 43, no. 1 (2005): 149–170.

27. Craig Calhoun, "The Virtues of Inconsistency: Identity and Plurality in the Conceptualization of Europe," in Lars-Erik Cederman, ed., *Constructing Europe's Identity: The External Dimension* (Boulder, CO: Lynne Rienner, 2001), 35–56.

28. Thomas Christiansen and Simona Piattoni, eds., *Informal Governance in the European Union* (Cheltenham: Edward Elgar, 2003).

29. Tsoukalis, *What Kind of Europe?* 105.

30. This is sometimes referred to as the "Internal Market," the "single European Market," the "Common Market," or the "Binnenmarkt." .

31. Theo Hitris, *European Union Economics,* 5th ed. (Harlow: Pearson Education, 2003).

32. Cited in Philippe de Schoutheete, *The Case for Europe: Unity, Diversity, and Democracy in the European Union,* trans. Andrew Butler (Boulder, CO: Lynne Rienner, 2000), 83. See also James Gow, "EU Enlargement and Security: Turning the Inside Out," in Julie Smith and Charles Jenkins, eds., *Through the Paper Curtain: Insiders and Outsiders in the New Europe* (London: RIIA/Blackwell, 2003), 61–76.

33. Nicole Gnesotto, ed., *EU Security and Defence Policy: The First Five Years (1999–2004)* (Paris: ISS, 2004); Karen Smith, "The End of Civilian Power EU: A Welcome Demise or Cause for Concern?" *The International Spectator* 35, no. 2 (2002): 11–28.

34. Christopher Hill, "The Capability-Expectations Gap, or Conceptualising Europe's Foreign Policy," *Journal of Common Market Studies* 31, no. 3 (1993): 305–328.

35. Tsoukalis, *What Kind of Europe?* 206.

36. Hans-Peter Schwarz, "Elefanten und Biber," *Frankfurter Allgemeine Zeitung,* 20 May 2003, 8. An interesting account of the international dispute over Iraq and other relevant aspects of European, Russian, Chinese, and US foreign policy, combined with a theoretical argument against "soft balancing," is provided by Stephen Brooks and William Wohlforth, "Hard Times for Soft Balancing," *International Security* 30, no. 1 (2005): 72–108.

37. Jolyon Howorth, "France, Britain and the Euro-Atlantic Crisis," *Survival* 45, no. 4 (2003–2004): 173–192.

38. Wolfgang Quaisser and Steve Wood, *EU Member Turkey? Preconditions, Consequences, and Integration Alternatives* (München: Forost, 2004).

39. The Copenhagen criteria are conditions for membership of the EU as determined by the European Council in Copenhagen on 21–22 June 1993: "Membership requires that the candidate country has achieved stability of institutions guaranteeing democracy, the rule of law, human rights and respect for and protection of minorities, the existence of a functioning market economy as well as the capacity to cope with competitive pressure and market forces within the Union. Membership presupposes the candidate's ability to take on the obligations of membership including adherence to the aims of political, economic and monetary union." An additional criterion, especially in regard to Turkey's potential accession, stated that "the Union's capacity to absorb new members, while maintaining the momentum of European integration, is also an important consideration in the general interest of both the Union and the candidate countries." See Council of the European Union, European Council in Copenhagen, 21–22 June 1993: Conclusions of the Presidency SN 180/1/93 REV 1 (Copenhagen, 1993): 13.

40. Cf. Graeme Herd, "Russia and the European Union," and Christopher Preston, "Russia in the EU or the EU in Russia? Approaches to Kaliningrad," in Julie Smith and Charles Jenkins, eds., *Through the Paper Curtain: Insiders and Outsiders in the New Europe* (London: RIIA/Blackwell, 2003), 123–146 and 147–167, respectively.

41. Heinrich August Winkler, "Überdehntes Wir-Gerfühl," *Die Welt,* 28 December 2005, 25.

2

The Political Economy
of Deepening and Widening

A large part of EU development can be analyzed as the interplay of economics and politics in a tension field of simultaneous attempts to deepen integration and digest enlargements. "Deepening" is defined as the unifying of commodity, capital, and labor markets, as well as increasingly close coordination in economic, social, environmental, foreign, and other policy fields, organized around partly supranational institutions and regulations. "Widening" means to extend the EU and its *acquis communautaire*, the common legal basis of the EU to which all members have to accede, by including more states. In this chapter we examine these processes, and related problems, trade-offs, and tasks, during and after the accessions of 2004. Our analysis incorporates the effects of deepening and widening on the "social dimension," which is a significant political element in postwar Western Europe.

For the EU to be effective, it must have efficient common policies and political will at the national level to be more adaptive to global forces and structural change. Alongside specific challenges of enlargement, the EU has to retune or enliven the promotion of growth and employment. The SM has to be completed and a solid fiscal policy incorporated in EMU. The ambitious Lisbon Agenda aimed to make the EU the world's "most innovative knowledge-based economy." Advances in innovation and services are needed to raise productivity, create jobs, and engender rising incomes. If those things do not happen, some EU members may degenerate to industrial museums with underdeveloped service and high-tech sectors and persisting unemployment. The EU's future prosperity, perhaps its very existence, will be determined by whether it proceeds in one direction or the other. The issue is, can the EU act as a global economic player in the twenty-first century?[1]

Is There an Optimal Size of the Union?

Two integration paths, economic and political, can each be justified theoretically and remain closely connected. Economic integration has been the EU's main concentration but always required political initiatives to drive it. It was so for the ECSC, SM, and EMU. Coordinating core sectors, building a common market, and introducing a shared currency implies political agreement. An integrated market needs mutual understanding of how markets should function; the rules of competition, product standards and norms; and the institutions required for implementation and supervision.

In the 1990s the EU achieved some remarkable successes. The SM took shape, and EMU was introduced concurrent to the launching of an enlargement process that would include fifteen new members by 2007. Setbacks or slowdowns, however, have fostered skepticism about the concurrent pursuit of both directions. Although the EU grew to become an economic area comprising 28 percent of the world's gross domestic product (GDP) by 2005, its per capita GDP is 30 percent lower than that of the United States. Although the 2004 enlargement increased the population by 19 percent, total GPD grew by only 5.6 percent, and income differentials between regions increased tremendously.[2] Over 90 percent of the 2004 entrants' populations live in regions with a GDP per capita below 75 percent of the EU25 (the 25 member states of the EU at that time). Over two-thirds live in regions that are under half the average.[3] Without serious reforms, these and the further accessions of Bulgaria and Romania in 2007, Croatia shortly thereafter, then the Balkan states, and possibly Turkey, will cause an overextension, especially in structural funding and agricultural policy. Increasing heterogeneity provokes questions about the "optimal size" of the EU.[4] The problem might be approached by considering the EU as a club, more than a noncommittal league *(Staatenbund)* but less than a federal state *(Bundesstaat)* (see Table 2.1).[5]

The club aims to maximize welfare and security and has economic and social preferences, which differentiate it from an extended free trade area. Welfare is produced by success in the SM and EMU projects. Preferences are established by standards and expectations (products, security, environment, social, solidarity) and policies. These preferences are only justified when assumptions of neoclassical economic theory are not the sole basis for economic policy. Economic policy in the EU is largely determined by individual states, many of which are not noted for pursuing a direction consistent with neoclassical economic theory, that is, economic liberalism. When the EU had a smaller membership, under French de facto leadership, it was easier for it to concur on what became recognizable as Western European social democracy with generous welfare states, high taxes, redistribution, and a high level of government intervention in the economy. Pressure has intensified for member states and the EU as a whole to modify this form of economic governance in

Table 2.1   Peculiarities of the EU Club

Content	Characteristics/Objectives	Problem	Possible Solution
Identity	Between league of nations *(Staatenbund)* and federal state *(Bundesstaat)*. No clear definition of final shape/borders	Complicated to define because member states follow different concepts; heterogeneity	Question remains open whether a definition of end-state is necessary
Political	Democracy, human rights, social and environmental standards, solidarity, cultural identity, sustainable development	Preferences diversified in "nonessential" areas (social, environmental, cultural)	Basic democratic rights essential; minimum consensus in other areas
Economic	Single Market (SM), EMU, Stability and Growth Pact (SGP), Lisbon Agenda	In theory, there is no limit to SM if its rules are accepted; the EMU demands homogeneity; the Lisbon Agenda is difficult	Simplify SM; very sound preparation for EMU required
Institutions	Balance of power (Council, Commission, EP) favors intergovernmental Council; balance of competencies problem	Bargaining becomes more complex if decisionmaking is not streamlined (extended QMV); threat of gridlock	Implement elements of failed CT differently; work for a better balance between institutions
Policies	Agricultural and structural policies partially compensate "losers," function as side payments in bargaining game	Financial resources are limited. As more countries enter, the scope for bargaining shrinks	Policies redesigned to financial limits and heterogeneity
Operating principles	Harmonization or mutual recognition; coordination or system competition	Harmonization/ coordination more complex as membership increases	Simplify rules; make them flexible to fit scope and area

order to make itself more competitive globally. However, if the club becomes more liberal, its members become more mutually competitive. Solidarity then weakens and common policies with large amounts of public funding become harder to sustain. Only institutions and decisionmaking structures based on the subsidiarity principle will enable the club to function properly.[6] Institutions and policies are linked to "operating rules or principles," identified as "harmonization versus mutual recognition" or "policy cooperation versus system competition." The linkage can be further illustrated by reference to the method presented by Daniel Gros and Alfred Steinherr.[7] They consider clubs as associations of common interests. The optimal size is neither one unit nor all. Benefits arise from cooperation and are normally associated with *private,* not *public* goods (see Figure 2.1).

Figure 2.1   The Optimal Size of a Club

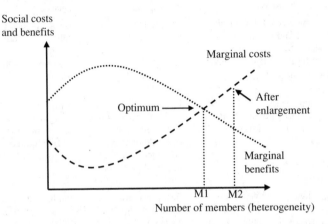

Source: Daniel Gros and Alfred Steinherr, *Economic Transition in Central and Eastern Europe* (Cambridge: Cambridge University Press, 2004).

Figure 2.2   Adjusted Optimal Size of the EU Club with Reforms

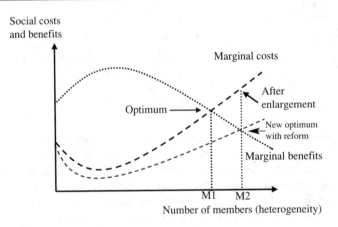

Source: Adapted from Daniel Gros and Alfred Steinherr, *Economic Transition in Central and Eastern Europe* (Cambridge: Cambridge University Press, 2004).

Figure 2.1 shows that, starting from a small number of members, the marginal benefits of incumbency increase as new members join, but at a critical point they begin to shrink and marginal costs begin to rise. Members benefit as the club grows, until the benefit curve meets the cost curve. Past that point, the costs of reaching agreement exceed the marginal benefits brought by new members. The club's optimal size may change if parameters are altered to shift the cost curve downward, as Figure 2.2 indicates. Arrangements foreseen in the CT could have done that. Under current circumstances, a "club of clubs" may emerge as the most likely outcome.[8]

Eastern Enlargement: Uniting the Continent by Widening the EU

Eastern enlargement was essentially a political project aimed at uniting a divided continent and securing lasting peace and freedom. The greatest challenge was less the creation of democratic structures—foundations for these already existed in the form of robust freedom movements—than ensuring their long-term viability. That required a reconfiguration of the CEECs into sound market economies. The integration of CEE was of strategic importance for the West: an unsuccessful economic transformation could trigger political crises and the rise of nationalist or even communist forces. The CEECs' economic backwardness and a vast increase in diversity for the EU made structural, institutional, and financial alignment difficult. To steer the process, it was necessary to make a long-term investment and link it to clearly formulated entry criteria. Support policies were needed to underpin the pre-accession phase while negotiations that would culminate in the comprehensive adoption of EU regulations were conducted.[9]

Eastern enlargement had four main objectives: (1) to overcome the political legacy of communism by instilling democratic and human rights standards held in the Western world and espoused by the EU in particular; (2) to bridge the economic and social gap with Western Europe by transformation to a market economy; (3) to remodel legal and policy frameworks in line with EU specifications to facilitate integration; and (4) to reform the institutions and policies of the EU itself to cope with enlargement. Although the entry criteria were drawn up and evaluated in a way that was not especially scientific, their fulfillment represented a benchmark of progress toward membership. The integration pattern was one whereby policies were implemented incrementally over a decade and half. Table 2.2 outlines the main stages from 1990 to 2007. Accession was the final step in a process during which certain member states, above all Germany, and the Commission steered the CEECs toward the goal. In addition to a general emphasis on trade liberalization, individual partnerships, technical and financial instruments, and political assistance were deployed. Yearly evaluations and ongoing negotiation proved a fairly sound reform anchor.

Nonetheless, weaknesses emerged. In some areas, entry criteria were vague and open to variable interpretations. Individual states were tempted to privilege narrow self-interests. Ultimately, a "big bang" enlargement occurred instead of a differentiated strategy. Because enthusiasm in the old EU was waning, differing entry dates with stricter conditionality would have eventual-

Table 2.2   Steps Toward Eastern Enlargement

Event	Date	Area
Provisional Agreement	1990	Trade
Europe Agreements	December 1991: trade policies implemented beginning of 1992	Trade and political dialogue; concrete support of enlargement process through assistance programs like Pologne-Hongrie: Assistance à la restructuration des économies (PHARE)
Copenhagen Council	December 1993	Economic criteria (market economy and ability to cope with EU competition)
Essen Council	December 1994	Decision on the "pre-accession strategy"
Cannes Council	June 1995	"White paper" as a guideline for preparation for accession
Madrid Council	December 1995	Advances provided by several initiatives
Agenda 2000, Berlin summit	March 1999	Preconditions to enlargement for EU15: reforms in structural and agricultural policy, access to financial resources
Enlargement negotiations	From 2000	Establishing *acquis communautaire* in accession countries
Nice IGC	December 2000, adopted 2001	Reforms of institutions and voting powers are deficient
Convention	2002–2003. Adapted in Brussels in 2004; rejected in referendums in France and Netherlands in 2005	Constitutional treaty on changes to institutions and decision-making; proposals in foreign and security policy, defense; Convention on Human Rights
"Big Bang" Enlargement	May 2004	Ten new member countries enter the EU
Second-Round CEECs	January 2007	Bulgaria and Romania enter the EU

Source: Alan Mayhew, *Re-creating Europe* (Cambridge: Cambridge University Press, 1998) and authors' formulation.

ly been realized. Though reservations existed concerning Bulgaria and Romania, they were, with extra conditions emphasized, accepted as members in 2007 because it had been promised years before.

The connection between institutional maturity and income levels provides some grounds for setting a measure of real economic convergence as a criterion of accession. Future enlargements will have tougher conditions, so the range of evaluation procedures should be expanded, the building of institutions stressed as imperative, and financial aid increased and accumulated before accession. Such measures can counter the situation whereby in the phase of highest adaptation costs, the least financial support flows in.

Membership does not guarantee good economic policy; nor does being rejected for membership guarantee a debacle. There were examples of policy failure in the old EU, but sanctions are weak. In some CEECs, reforms were delayed, and there were macroeconomic failures. These states received warnings from the Commission. In some cases, such as Hungary, the situation worsened well after accession. The quality of governments and national policy remains indispensable to improving economic performance. There is no unified European model and plenty of room for mistakes within the existing framework of rules and supervision. A central issue is the pace of convergence. The extent and duration of financial transfers depends on how long poorer members take to approach the per capita wealth of net payers. That is a yardstick by which to measure how economic integration, which influences the sustainability of the intertwined political project, has proceeded.

The Single Market

The SM concept, with its four freedoms—goods, capital, labor, and services—represents a core economic project. It is well founded in neoclassical economic theory in which integrated factor markets with no internal geographic limitations lead to efficiency and welfare gains. Since Delors's initiative in the 1980s, trade and intra-industrial specialization among member economies have increased. Sections of commodity markets were liberalized and became more competitive. The growth effects of the SM were overestimated in predictions of 4.5 to 7 percent of GDP, based on a steady state effect.[10] The Commission later estimated the cumulative welfare gain from 1992 to 2002 at €877 billion and that the EU's GDP was 1.8 percent higher than it would have been without the SM. The creation of about 2.5 million new jobs in that period was also attributed to the SM.[11]

On the downside, the integration of service and financial sectors was postponed, and public procurements lack competition. Capital markets are partly integrated but governed by different regulations from one member state to another. The banking sector has some common legal foundations but is in practice far from integrated. Instead, it is organized along national lines with national peculiarities. Only gradually are trans-European takeover bids emerging, and they often incite protests with xenophobic overtones. The Commission's attempt to liberalize services was restricted by some states because they feared sociopolitical consequences.[12] Networking industries like transportation, energy, and communication are still partly segmented by national regulations. Subsidies (open and hidden) in various branches distort cross-border competition. Thus, although the SM program is in general a success, it should not be overrated. Data on price convergence or trade intensity indicate that little further integration occurred after 1992.[13] One step forward was the Lamfalussy process for financial services,[14] but there were no major advances beyond it. Trade within the EU27, although at high levels compared to that in other economic zones, lacks momentum. Intra-EU trade shares declined slightly, and EU-induced intra-European trade is less than NAFTA-induced North American trade. Fifteen years after the removal of border controls, the EU is far from being a fully integrated economy.[15] Variations in product market regulation and the trend toward deregulation are similar to other Organization for Economic Cooperation and Development (OECD) countries. Protectionist reflexes have been reasserted.[16] A Commission study that appeared in early 2007 criticized the SM for not reaching its potential. Its contribution to the "transformation of the EU into a more dynamic, innovative and competitive economy" was viewed as "insufficient."[17]

Why, then, has intensification of market integration been limited? Has it been slowed by simultaneous widening of the EU? Theoretically, the SM has no geographical limitation. Nevertheless, borders play a role, and geography is important because trade intensity, with positive welfare effects, is usually higher among neighbors. Theories of custom unions suggest that regional economic integration needs a certain size before trade creation effects outweigh trade diversion effects.[18] Exactly what that size must be is hard to quantify. A customs union with two member countries makes little sense, especially if they are not very large because trade volume will be fairly limited. With six member countries, as the EU began with, a customs union is more justifiable. Free trade and flows of labor, capital, and goods in an extended economic area will stimulate specialization and equalization of prices. Growth and convergence of incomes will result. Regional economic integration is a second-best alternative to global liberalization, but it is easier to implement. Nonetheless, the EU is a large economic area, and if trade barriers are constantly reduced, the potential for benefits is evident.

In the case of eastern enlargement, economic relations with Western Europe were restored after the removal of trade barriers. CEECs' trade growth rates reached double digits and as much as 60 to 80 percent of total volume. Growth and employment effects for CEECs were estimated to be between 5 and 10 percent of their GDP (steady state effect), whereas for the old EU15, similar estimates only reached 0.2 percent.[19] For countries with more intensive economic relations, like Germany and Austria, welfare effects of up to 0.5 percent of GDP were calculated. A recent study suggests up to 1 percent for Germany, which has a high trade and current account surplus with the region (see Figure 2.3).[20]

There are, in mid-2007, no thorough ex-post analyses of integration effects related to the 2004 enlargement available. Early evidence of intensified trade suggests positive effects through the removal of remaining non-tariff restrictions.[21] Figure 2.3 indicates GDP development in selected transition countries from 1989 to 2007. Further convergence might be produced by knowledge spillovers.[22]

Figure 2.3   Development of Real GDP in Selected Transition Countries (1989 = 100)

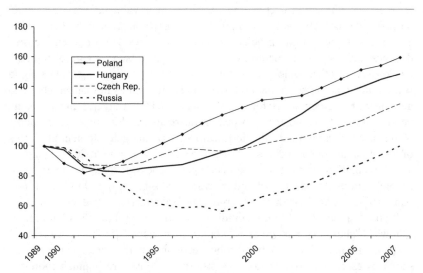

Source: European Commission, Directorate-General for Economic and Financial Affairs, *European Economy* 2006 (Brussels: European Commission, 2006); United Nations Economic Commission for Europe, *Economic Survey of Europe* 2/2005 (New York: United Nations, 2005); United Nations Economic Commission for Europe, "Towards a New European Model of a Reformed Welfare State: An Alternative to the United States Model" in *Economic Survey of Europe* 1/2005 (New York: United Nations, 2005), 105–114; and CES/ifo, *The EEAG Report on the European Economy 2007* (Munich: CES/ifo, 2007). Data for 2006 is estimated and for 2007 is a prognosis.

The institutional requirements of the SM are relatively modest, provided that the settings for a well-functioning market economy have been established nationally. Institutional sophistication and the level of development are interrelated. Cultural and historical aspects exert an influence. After forty years as planned economies, the transformation to fully fledged market economies has been a tremendous challenge for the CEECs, even with support from the EU and institutions like the International Monetary Fund (IMF) and the World Bank. In its 2004 evaluation, the Commission concluded that most countries had functioning market economies and thereby satisfied the first economic criterion for membership of the EU. The more advanced had ceased to regulate most prices and had realized a high degree of trade liberalization. Some prices, such as those for energy and rent, were still regulated. Market entry and exit are, from a legal standpoint, secured, but obstacles remain. That is especially true for market exit, where an avoidance of the practical implementation of bankruptcy laws was observed.

The second set of economic criteria aimed to ensure that acceding countries could cope with competitive pressures. Within the academic discipline of economics, "competitiveness" is a fairly vague term: it could relate to enterprises, industrial branches, or even to an entire national economy. Some economists have gone so far as to reject "competitiveness" as a valuable or even a useful term.[23] The EU stressed its importance, based on concerns that CEEC economies might run into problems operating in the SM. If or when industry declines, the specter of unemployment would exacerbate a range of political tensions. A sufficient endowment of human and physical capital was lacking in some states that joined in 2004. Others had shortcomings in management and administrative expertise. Before they joined in 2007, Bulgaria and Romania possessed real deficiencies in physical infrastructure and institutional capacity.

Small and medium-sized enterprises (SMEs) emerged as potential motors of growth and structural change. For some years leading up to 2004, Hungary and Slovenia were most advanced in competitiveness. Poland, however, faced problems in its oversized coal and metallurgical sectors. A 2006 Commission paper mentioned deficits there in large-scale privatization. State aid was twice as high as in the EU15.[24] OECD indicators show that product market regulation was higher in new member economies than in the EU15. A credible legal system, with incentives to support robust economic performance in the private sector, is essential. Privatization has progressed, but there is much room for improvement in corporate governance. Corruption is a major problem.

The *acquis communautaire* represented the hard criteria for institutions, requiring not only legal adjustments but the implementation of these rules in daily life. It included sensitive issues for both CEECs, such as foreign acquisition of property, and for some old member states, such as free movement of labor. In recent years the new members accelerated their transposition of directives into national legislation: by March 2006, they had codified 99 percent of the directives into law. In several fields, they have outperformed some EU15 states.[25] It is yet to be conclusively proved whether these regulations have been thoroughly implemented and are operating in practice. The EU missed an opportunity to streamline the *acquis* before 2004. Even when there were only nine members, certain limitations on harmonization were reached with the Cassis-de-Dijon case of 1979, which introduced a principle of mutual recognition. Consequently, different regulations coexist, and further harmonization is likely to be limited.[26] Competition between national systems (including in corporate taxation) will eventually determine which rules survive and which have to adjust. Some preferences will be overridden and member states forced to introduce more efficient regulations.[27] The "correct" equilibrium between harmonized minimum regulations and system competition is not easy to find in practice, even if in theory it does not set strict economic and institutional limits on enlargements.[28]

Labor Market Effects

The extension of the SM to countries with very different economic conditions has short- and medium-term adjustment costs that can reverse public acceptance. The liberalization of labor and services foreseen in the original project rested on the assumption of relatively homogeneous per capita incomes and economic structures. Diversity stimulates pressure on labor markets, including nontradable sectors affected by migration, and services, through the presence of firms from new members in the "national" markets of the EU15. Related apprehension motivated the insistence of some EU15 states on transition periods before new members could participate in full and free exchange. These concerns were reflected in the "no" voting in referendums on the CT. The potential of the SM is not only dependent on the capacity of institutions but the willingness of Europeans to accept periods of adjustment when money for compensating "losers" is limited.

Growing commodity trade and foreign direct investment (FDI) raised questions about a shift of jobs eastward and higher unemployment and lower wages or both, especially for unqualified labor, in the EU15. The Heckscher-Ohlin paradigm predicts that the economic integration of a relatively rich country and a poor country will lead to factor-price equalization: a downward shift in relative wages in the capital-rich country and an upward shift in the poorer country.[29] The opposite movement is predicted for the price of capital. Here a change in relative factor prices and not necessarily absolute prices (wages) is calculated because overall growth and welfare effects might compensate for wage decreases.[30]

Are stagnating real wages and high unemployment in some EU15 countries then caused by the integration of the CEECs? Consider the following optimistic scenario. Aggregate employment for all EU members will increase when the CEECs catch up with wage rates, per capita incomes, and levels of productivity. Distribution effects of trade will affect less qualified labor negatively, but the numbers are estimated to be minuscule relative to the total EU workforce. The CEECs' structures of production will transform, resulting in an increase in intra-industry trade, with positive growth effects for all. Although it might be expected that redistribution effects of an expanding intra-industry trade would register as marginal or neutral, differences in unit values between EU exports and CEEC imports in identical product categories indicate that vertical, intra-industry trade prevails. This reflects different factor contents of trade flows and will affect the distribution of income. The growth effects of a more thorough integration could offset such outcomes. Horizontal intra-industry trade will also increase. Because wages and overall employment are overlapped by other factors (such as globalization), it is hard to determine how strongly they are affected by intensified trade with the new entrants. Some studies suggest limited negative effects.[31] Even under the assumption of rigid labor markets and restricted immigration, other simulations predict positive employment outcomes for Germany because of the dynamic growth effects of the SM's extension.[32]

The next channel through which the mechanism of factor-price equalization operates is capital flows. With large differences in incomes from capital and wages, will capital movements, especially FDI into the CEECs, raise interest rates in the EU? It seems unlikely. The magnitude of transfers into CEE was too small to wield much influence over the price of capital. During the 1990s, there were FDI flows up to 3 percent of CEEC's GDPs, as accession perspectives reduced risk premiums on investments. These flows hardly affected the price of capital in Western Europe. Interest rates fell in most CEECs and assisted growth.[33] FDI showed a clear preference for strategic and market-oriented investments, although labor costs do play a role in FDI allocation.

Hans-Werner Sinn presents a different perspective by highlighting the contrast between Germany's sound export performance, notably with CEE, and its disappointing job performance.[34] He characterizes this phenomenon as a "bazaar economy," in which shrinking value-added content per export unit reflects a lower labor content of exports. The main reason for what he terms a "pathology" is high labor costs in Germany, which force German companies to outsource an increasing share of production.[35] Many supply industries with higher labor content are affected. Major industries can remain competitive and contribute to increasing exports, but they create jobs abroad rather than at home. A striking export performance is then accompanied by high unemployment. The transference of jobs to other countries begins to include more qualified positions, including jobs in tradable services, as human capital improves in the CEECs (and elsewhere) and as transportation facilities and communication technologies become cheaper and more sophisticated. Volkhart Vincentz estimates that from 1990 to 2001, German FDI created a maximum of 400,000 jobs in CEE as a result of labor cost considerations.[36]

Controversy arose in Germany over Sinn's "bazaar economy." The critique focused on three aspects: First, empirical evidence of shrinking value added in German exports is weak. Per unit, it might be true, but the overall balance is positive and total value added in exports is growing.[37] Second, there is no clear indication that branches heavily engaged in outsourcing have reduced jobs most. Since the mid-1990s, the German automobile industry has expanded its foreign engagement tremendously and is one of the few local industries to increase jobs in Germany. Third, it is methodologically difficult to precisely quantify the labor market effects of trade and investment.

Some large German enterprises operating in the global market were able to withstand pressures by reducing labor costs though outsourcing or moving parts of their production offshore. Because they were competitive, growth and restructuring enabled them to do so without large-scale retrenchments in Germany. SMEs, traditionally the biggest job-creating sector, have less opportunity for this type of adjustment, though even some of them try to bypass internal wage and add-on costs by outsourcing. German enterprises are competitive, but Germany's labor market is not. Growth and welfare effects of EU integration and global economic interaction have therefore not fully materialized. Homegrown problems are more responsible for high unemployment than enlargement and globalization. Neighbor Austria performed better in adjusting to and exploiting the opportunities of enlargement.

The last channel through which factor-price equalization can work is inward labor migration, whereby instead of jobs moving offshore, competition for jobs increases internally. It is a very sensitive topic. In the short term, migration was expected to have greater effects on the EU labor market than trade and investment. As Austria and Germany are contiguous to some CEECs and close to others, they were nominated as the main destinations. Most studies estimated long-term migration potential into the EU15 at 3 to 4 percent of the CEECs' population. That equates to an annual net migration of 170,000 to 250,000 persons from the eight CEECs and up to 400,000, if Bulgaria and Romania are included.[38] These figures correspond to earlier predictions that the numbers should halve within a decade.[39] Michael Fertig presented annual figures of 60,000 to 100,000 persons, whereas Sinn and his colleagues predicted somewhat larger flows stretching over a longer period. They calculated that 640,000 people would move to the EU15 and a large proportion thereof to Germany.[40] But that did not happen because Germany and some other EU15 states imposed transitional arrangements on labor movement, which allow states some flexibility to regulate inflows.

Herbert Brücker's estimates suggest that in 2004, a net migration of 156,000 people from the eight CEECs, or 226,000 with Bulgaria and Romania, would have occurred without restrictions. The restrictions are due to end five to seven years after the 2004 and 2007 enlargements. When that happens, the population from the eight CEECs in EU15 states will eventually grow to 1.7 million, or 2.4 million with Bulgaria and Romania.[41] Data for the first year of accession show that actual migration from these countries was much lower (100,000 to 150,000) than predicted. The UK and Ireland, which liberalized their labor markets immediately, registered higher flows than predicted, and there has been some negative public reaction. For Scandinavian countries, which also have no restrictions, the real inflow was less than the estimates. Other factors like language knowledge played a role in migration decisions. The figures show a decline in citizens from CEECs in Germany.[42]

Later studies indicate that East-West net flows do not cause serious threats to jobs and wages in the EU as a whole.[43] There are reasons that fears concerning the scope, scale, and effects of migration are exaggerated or misplaced. Several EU15 countries are expected to face a shortage of skilled labor. Migration from CEE may offset that, and as qualifications increase in CEE, it would become more important. A shortage in the qualified labor force is already a motive for FDI into the CEECs. There are also some shortages in the EU15 of less qualified workers (in restaurants, health care, home cleaning, and agriculture), which have special arrangements, especially for seasonal workers. Brücker points out that migration restrictions led to a failed allocation of resources and welfare losses. He argues for a rapid opening of the labor market.[44] If regulations do not change, the predicted welfare effects of enlargement may not materialize. A simulation model on the German economy shows that without migration restrictions, the overall growth effects of the eastern enlargement would be higher, but the reduction in unemployment would be slower.[45]

Whatever academic studies might conclude, many citizens and politicians in the EU15 worried that poorer people would relocate to Western Europe and alter ethnic compositions while burdening already stretched social welfare funds. Since trade in goods and services, as well as capital flows, are unlikely to lead to any short-term equalization of incomes, gaps in wages between regions are expected to persist for many years. Incentives known to promote labor migration, especially higher wages and nonwage compensation, will remain relevant. Economic models must take into account that permanent migration may lead to diverse costs for host countries.

The Commission's "service directive" confirmed an awareness of popular sensitivities about these issues.[46] This directive has nothing directly to do with enlargement, but its attempt to liberalize the market in services was rejected by Germany, Austria, and France. There is some justification to apply the home country principle, which means that a foreign service provider is governed by the given regulations of the country in which it operates, but the provider's national certification could be approved. Pressure in the sector has been observed in Germany and Austria, even though the "freedom" to provide services has been restricted to a few areas like construction, interior decorating, and gastronomy. Tradespeople are allowed to establish a one-person firm. A result was that the "Polish plumber" became a synonym for "unfair wage dumping," prominent in public discussions in France and Germany. Yet in mid-2005 it was reported that only 150 Polish plumbers were working in France.[47] There are, however, examples of unfair and illegal practices that deliver cheap and exploited labor for Western European firms. One is that of German abattoir workers being displaced by Poles, who had been hired for low wages—of which they were sometimes cheated—and under bad conditions. These experiences were part of the background to a discussion on the introduction of minimum wages that coincided with an election campaign in Germany.[48]

Economic and Monetary Union

EMU is the EU's second core economic project and represents a quantum leap in integration. Institutionally and politically, it is more complicated than the SM. For EMU members, decisionmaking power over monetary policy has been transferred to the supranational European Central Bank. Control over economic and fiscal policy remains at the national level, but members have an obligation to work toward stronger coordination. The SGP framework was intended to ensure that national governments abided by the Maastricht criteria concerning budget deficits, state debt, and inflation.[49] From the beginning, it was clear that EMU needs fiscal rules in order to avoid a weakening of the euro or an excessively restrictive monetary policy.[50] But the SGP has a weak institutional foundation because fiscal policy is ultimately controlled by national governments, which are held to account by national parliaments and electorates. Although the SGP was signed by governments, its democratic legitimacy is tenuous.[51]

The euro has been a success and is now the world's second most important currency. The ECB has been able to keep inflation rates down despite violations of the SGP. Some politicians and economists criticize an inflexible bias toward price stability and a neglect of growth.[52] This argument might not be fully convincing, but economic diversity and different adjustment paths and decisionmaking levels complicate the use of a pragmatic policymaking style that adapts to changes in business cycles, as Anglo-Saxon countries have deployed. Deficits, especially in EMU's initial main advocates, Germany and France, put the SGP under pressure and led to its softening. The relevant treaty-based commitment proved to be less than binding. The SGP calamity was a crisis at the center of the Union, containing the potential for further eruptions.[53] Some believed that monetary union was realizable only within the framework of a "political union," which is not in sight. Without such a foundation, the ECB has the difficult task of enforcing rules agreed on by the states in the Council and exerting some indirect influence on national fiscal policy.

If EMU is extended to new EU members, with the exception of smaller states such as Malta and Cyprus, more problems may arise concerning the functionality and rules of the ECB. Enlargement could impair the desired effects of monetary policy. Heterogeneity means exogenous shocks affect economies differently,[54] and it is not easy for monetary policymakers to steer a favorable course.[55] Although optimal size theories suggest restrictions on EMU membership, it has been politically determined that new EU members must strive to meet EMU conditions and join.[56] That should follow several years after a state enters the EU to allow sufficient nominal[57] and real convergence, which is required, for example, to reduce divergence in inflation rates between developed and transition countries related to variable productivity increases in the tradable and nontradable sectors.[58] Thus, "hard economics" sets some guidelines between EMU ins and outs when a high level of integration is needed to benefit most from an economy of scale. Participants should react to macroeconomic shocks (changes in trade direction, oil prices, interest rates, terms of trade) similarly, and flexible labor markets would be advantageous.[59]

The interrelationship between economic and political integration is especially strong between EMU members, more so than elites and publics realize. A serious economic or political crisis in a major state would have devastating consequences for other "club" members. Coordinated economic and especially fiscal policy is needed to sustain a strong currency. If common policy were to also encourage structural change and productivity, it would give the ECB more maneuverability to reduce interest rates. Less dramatic policy changes like reducing the workweek to thirty-five hours, as occurred in France, or different wage policies might provoke asymmetric shocks that impose adjustments on other EMU members. Some analysts argue that monetary union requires a certain budgetary redistribution in order to compensate for these shocks. Although that might be possible in national contexts, there is little or no political support for the eurozone as a whole. EMU cannot rely on a central budget with fiscal transfers and a stabilizing function during an economic downturn. Paul de Grauwe argues that without political union, or at a minimum a larger EU budget and closer policy coordination, EMU remains at risk.[60]

Macroeconomic policy is reasonably solid in most CEECs, although internal and external imbalances still pose threats. The Baltic states and the Slovak Republic have entered the present Exchange Rate Mechanism (ERM II), which requires that their currencies maintain value relative to the EU within specified narrow limits. The EMU criteria on inflation and interest rates have yet to be achieved by some new members. Levels of public debt and deficits generally fall in the range of acceptability, except for Poland, Hungary, and the Czech Republic. Various crises have demonstrated deficiencies in fiscal systems throughout most of CEE. A special problem is off-budget funds. Another important element is the structure of financial markets. In this respect, the CEECs have progressed to a respectable level. Hungary was most advanced in transforming its financial sector, primarily because much was bought or introduced by foreign firms, but it lacks fiscal discipline. Bulgaria, Romania, Croatia, and potentially Turkey would require sustained effort to overcome institutional shortcomings.[61] Most CEECs also have to cope with big gaps between saving and investment rates and, hence, current account deficits. The Maastricht criteria, especially those concerning fiscal deficits, are important for dealing with these imbalances. Their fulfillment should assist internal stability and provide incentive for capital inflows.[62]

Convergence has to occur in an environment in which levels of labor productivity vary significantly. Michael Frenkel and Christiane Nickel confirmed considerable differences in shocks and adjustment processes between CEECs and the eurozone, though they also found that these differences gradually declined over the period 1993–2001. Given that the CEECs are obliged to meet the conditions for adopting the euro, that decline can lead us to be cautiously optimistic.[63] Of these, only Slovenia joined EMU in 2007. Malta and Cyprus plan to in 2008. The others will have to wait several years.[64] The next likely candidates are the Baltic states, if they can further reduce inflation.[65] For smaller countries, the gains of joining a currency union are more transparent because such countries are more trade-dependent. They also have to align their monetary policy with large neighbors. There are signs, however, that some new members are not so concerned about entering EMU as soon as possible, having calculated that it may be politically more prudent to wait. That seems reasonable, since the three big CEECs have no clear incentives to incur the economic and political costs of EMU. Most politicians have a short-term time horizon, and the full benefits of joining may only appear in the long term. Although these countries have no opt-out clause, they may intentionally stay out of EMU for some years yet.[66]

Even though all ten CEECs initially constituted no more than 10 percent of total EU GDP and only one has joined EMU, the system has had to adjust. Reforms adopted in March 2003 envisage that after an extension of EMU, all members will have the right to present opinions at ECB Governing Council meetings, but only fifteen national central bank presidents and the six members of the ECB executive board, elected for eight-year terms, will be eligible to vote. Voting rights will rotate among members in groups. All members can help shape decisions, but the number of decisionmakers (twenty-one) will remain constant.[67] There are arguments for a reduction in the number of

Council seats and a changed allocation of regional voting rights. These measures would reduce regional bias and more accurately match ECB votes with the relative weight of national economies.[68]

The Lisbon Agenda

In 2000 the Lisbon Agenda, intended to make the EU the world's most dynamic knowledge-based economy by 2010, was launched. It was a policy reform strategy designed to encourage sustained growth and generate conditions for more and better jobs, social cohesion, and environmental awareness. It was based on three pillars: (1) promote economic integration through stronger coordination of EU and national policies; (2) increase the labor supply and tackle unemployment partly through a soft coordination of labor markets and pension reforms; and (3) restructure public spending toward research and development (R&D) and higher education in order to spur technological change and productivity. Theories of economic geography, which try to explain the regional location or relocation of industries and services, predict agglomeration effects built on externalities such as networks and infrastructure. These effects enable certain regions to become growth and innovation centers promoting high incomes and jobs. Other regions may gain through migration and spillover effects.[69] Though major examples might be located in Western Europe, several innovation centers are emerging in CEE. Good outcomes are expected in CEE because the starting base for the technology sector is low. Although neoclassical economic theory does not suggest Lisbon goals would cause major conflicts, divergences arise in a political economy context. Lisbon was the EU's political answer to slow growth, disappointing productivity performance, and high unemployment, especially as compared to the United States.[70] These conditions had provoked anxieties and unrest in some members and contributed to a weakening of the EU's authority.

Figure 2.4 shows that concerning productivity and the labor participation rate, the eurozone is performing worse than the United States and does not reach the Lisbon objectives. Some EU members, especially Scandinavian countries, the UK, and Ireland, have performed quite well. Lisbon was primarily aimed at sluggish continental economies.

Relevant problems are severe in countries like Germany, Italy, and France, which represent two-thirds of the Eurozone's GDP and have a decisive impact on the whole. They propelled integration over decades but have recently been bad examples. Their growth, productivity, and employment performance is disappointing. In overall competitiveness, the picture is more diverse. Germany's export performance is good, but it lags in the domestic market. Italy, Portugal, and France lost competitiveness and are confronted with export sector difficulties. For these and some new members, unemployment is the

Figure 2.4   Comparison of Labor Productivity and Labor Participatic

Labor productivity

120%

EU25
= 100%

60%

40%

Labor potential
is not sufficiently used
in Europe

Ireland:

United States

United Kingdom
Sweden
Denmark

Greece / Euro-
zone

Hungary
Czech
Poland   Republic

Turkey

Romania
Bulgaria

Lisbon objectives

40%   60%   65%   70%   Labor participation rate

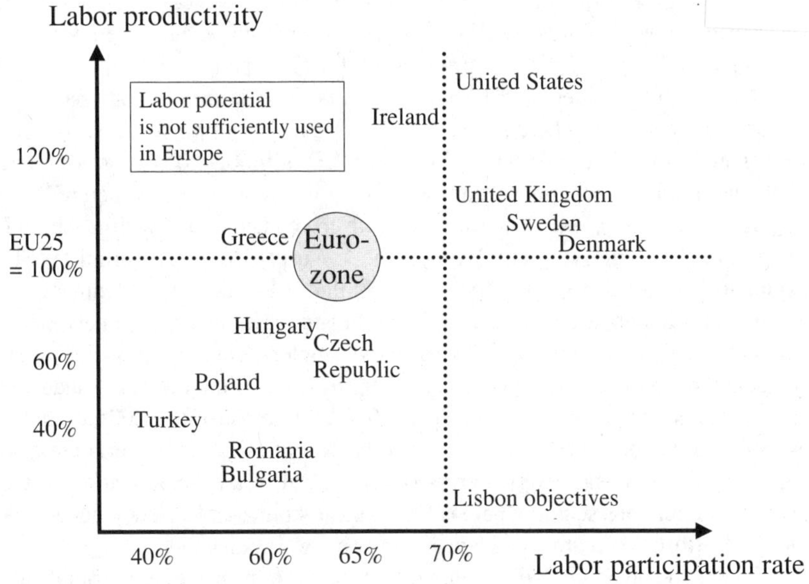

Source: Eurostat, "Structural Indicators, Population and Social Indicators, Economic
Indicators."

most pressing issue. Jobless growth is a phenomenon in CEE and some countries, above all Poland, are badly affected. Pressures for higher wages and welfare standards along EU15 lines could lead to wage gains moving ahead of
productivity growth. If that happens, social contracts needed to keep unit labor
costs at a competitive level, especially for exported products, will be threatened. Regarding the participation rate and technological indicators, CEECs are
not performing well. Nor are demographic trends, which indicate aging populations after 2010, very encouraging. The returns on integrating new members
into a successful Lisbon process would be high, as many could improve productivity by technological innovations and development of human capital.
FDI assisted some new members in improving their technological level, but
R&D spending by domestic firms and governments remains low.

The Lisbon Agenda's results have been modest at best, and aggregate
growth performance weakened from 2000, when it was adopted, up to 2005.[71]
That is unsurprising because measures undertaken in relation to its objectives
were insufficient. The Kok Report of November 2004 regarded the Lisbon
Agenda as a failure, and even Commission President José Manuel Barroso aired
similar views.[72] No substantial progress has been made in deepening economic

integration. In the areas of labor markets and tax or welfare reforms, coordination has been weak. Results are unsatisfactory for goals such as the degree of employment protection or the tax wedge, which is the amount of taxes and social security contributions, relative to wages, that is imposed on employers for each worker. This is especially so regarding work for older people.[73]

There is little evidence that Lisbon had a positive impact on national labor market policies, even where prescribed reforms had been pursued. No significant changes in public spending in favor of R&D or innovation occurred.[74] The depth and range of implementation concerning technology, infrastructure, education, employment, and labor markets differs considerably within the EU. Integration, an underlying aim, is lacking. A World Economic Forum (WEF) evaluation shows that among the EU15, Finland, Sweden, and Denmark are leading, and Italy and Greece are trailing. On similar indicators, the new member states perform even worse.[75] The speed of implementation also varies greatly. Denmark, Sweden, Austria, the Netherlands, and Finland have made the most progress, whereas Portugal, Spain, Italy, and most of the 2004 entrants, especially Poland, returned the worst results. Variations in subcriteria are also apparent. The UK and Sweden are most advanced in the liberalization of the telecommunications sector, whereas Denmark, Estonia, and Sweden undertook the most efforts to create an advanced "information society."[76]

It begs the question, having gained support from nearly every official side and being reformulated in 2005 to concentrate on growth and employment, why Lisbon did not deliver better outcomes.[77] Complexity of objectives and indicators may be responsible for implementation failures but does not reveal the roots of the problem. Political, rather than technical or economic shortcomings, seem a more plausible explanation. In the first years of the twenty-first century, many EU states had weak leaders, which made reform harder to enforce. Some politicians, disingenuously or otherwise, blamed integration, enlargement, and globalization for national difficulties. Populism encumbered attempts to progress beyond lethargy.[78] An "open method of coordination" did not provide the incentives for governments to launch reforms jointly. They oriented themselves more to domestic voters than to the Commission. Motivation to learn from best practice through nonbinding consultation and benchmarking was low.

The rationale for reform is also weak because positive externalities from supply-side policies are not evident. In the eurozone, the incentives to coordinate are stronger because productivity-oriented reforms give more room to monetary policy to reduce interest rates and encourage growth. A collective action problem remains because supply-side reforms may inflict short-term losses and conflicts that national governments are not willing to bear alone. The eurozone needs better coordination of structural and macroeconomic policies to build on complementarities.[79] Jean Pisani-Ferry suggests a concentration on areas where growth dividends can be expected. That does not imply liberalization across the board but a stronger focus on competition, the long-awaited community patent, completion of the SM for financial services, or the free cross-border provision of high-productivity services. It would require a removal of restrictions for the effective integration of new member states. Pisani-Ferry's strategy also needs to overcome the lack of incentives by using greater financial means and giving attention to cross-border externalities, such as migration or research and higher education. It presently appears that Lisbon Two is unlikely to succeed because it fails to recognize the shortcomings of its predecessor.

How, then, is it to be explained that in 2006 the EU economy grew by 2.9 percent, the Eurozone grew by 2.7 percent, and unemployment decreased to an average of 7.5 percent? Prospects for the next two years also seem brighter, though the EU will still have higher unemployment and lower labor participation rates than the United States.[80] Do these developments indicate that the Lisbon strategy is now paying off? Initial interpretations emphasize a cyclical upswing combined with an impressive improvement in the competitiveness of the German economy. Years of wage restraint and confined increases in unit labor costs are responsible for the latter. A resulting real exchange rate depreciation affecting expansionary impulses for foreign trade stimulated inward investment. Similar developments occurred earlier in the Netherlands and Denmark. Improvement in continental conditions was mainly caused by domestic demand. With the exception of Germany, the Netherlands, and Portugal, private consumption increased more than 2 percent everywhere. In Germany, where consumption had stagnated since 2002, it grew by 0.6 percent in 2006, and overall growth, driven by investment, should reach nearly 2 percent in 2007. Domestic economic policies and reforms are more important than the Lisbon strategy. It is by no means clear that major continental economies have really made a decisive breakthrough to sustained growth.[81]

The EU Budget and Financial Redistribution

Financial redistribution has been a central feature of EU integration. Agricultural and cohesion policies are the most expensive and disputed vehicles through which that has occurred. Based on solely economic considerations, integration does not require that they be maintained. Politically, continued integration depends on redistribution and a notional "solidarity." Theories of fiscal federalism and new political economy offer some explanation for the persistence of these policies.[82] Transfers are side payments to ensure that the whole project, which has produced welfare and security in other fields, is stabilized. There are threats to this rationale in a EU of twenty-seven or more. The will to provide side payments is diminishing because the objective of unifying the continent, in terms of a common commitment to democracy, has largely been reached. Less money for poorer states and regions, combined with increased economic and institutional competition for older and richer members, undermines the readiness of net payers to redistribute funds.

In response to financial issues, individual member states followed their self-interests, which reflected their net position. Table 2.3 shows four main interest constellations: (1) the net payers, who want to limit expenditures and avoid a worsening of their net positions; (2) net recipients among the EU15, who want to minimize a shifting of (principally structural) funding to new members; (3) new member states, which want to be fully integrated as soon as possible into funds-dispensing policies; (4) the UK alone. It has special rules for its rebate, which it intends to retain unless there is a fundamental reform of the budget and, in particular, CAP financing. Other net payers do not necessarily want to change the details of policies but are focused on their net position.

It must be noted that net receivers are only weak if the scope for politics is limited. They can, individually or in groups, engage in various issue linkage to entice or oblige net payers. Any ensuing quid pro quo means that formally discrete policy areas are subject to interference and "rules" can be perverted. The Commission tried to find technical solutions to reach a budget compromise. It proposed upper limits on expenditures in main policy fields, which implied real annual spending cuts, in order to finance enlargement. That was combined with schemes to phase out some funding streams. Structural funding for old EU members would decrease by 1 percent, and agricultural spending would increase only by a nominal 1 percent. In real terms, it meant a reduction of about 1 percent per year after inflation. The political determination of the schemes is evident. If existing rules, especially for objective one

Table 2.3   Main Interest Groups in Budgetary Negotiations

Groups of Countries	Main Interests	Power Position
Net payers (Germany, Netherlands, Sweden, Austria, UK,[a] France)	Reducing net payments	Strong power position as they represent ten countries combining the largest economies
Old net receivers (Spain Greece, Portugal, Ireland)	Avoiding reduced payments	Weak position: some would lose funds even without enlargement
New net receivers (CEECs)	Full integration into EU policies	Weak position: they are dependent on financial transfers
UK[a]	Retaining the rebate or fundamental reforms to EU policies	Weak: UK can only block; in the long run stronger if other net payers support the UK as costs rise

Note: a. The UK belongs in two categories.

funds, the major EU program to support less developed regions, were strictly applied, most regions in EU15 states would no longer be eligible for support. This is an example of the Commission having a formal right of initiative but in practice acting in response to expectations of particular interstate deals.

The communal position of the net payers was laid out in a 2004 letter in response to the Commission's proposal for a budget of 1.14 percent of EU gross national income (GNI). The net payers wanted a limit of 1 percent. They were united in the goal but not the route. Behind an apparently common front of refusal, the interests, motivations, and actions of individual states varied. Germany made it clear that it was no longer prepared to finance such a large share of costs. The Dutch were even more resistant, as they had become the highest net payers relative to GNI. In contrast, all net receiver states supported the Commission's proposal, especially new members who stressed their right to equal treatment. Old net receivers such as Spain, Greece, and Portugal emphasized that reduced funding for them should not be based on a so-called statistical effect. Under these circumstances, it was unlikely that the UK would allow serious alterations regarding its rebate. It was then an onerous task to reach a workable compromise.

The first serious attempt to reach a budget compromise for 2007–2013 came during the Luxembourg presidency, which presented a proposal in June 2004 for a total of €870 billion. Although some states initially joined the UK in rejecting it, what subsequently formed was a front of virtually all others against the UK. The British were late in bringing substantive argument to the table. Other net payers were unwilling to engage in a profound debate when the time remaining to construct a solid framework was short. During the UK presidency, negotiations were accompanied by disputes more petulant than usual. The Commission tried to break the budget deadlock by proposing a general correction mechanism, which would function as a rebate for all net payers. Commission calculations of the rebate's effects on financial flows in 2007–2013 indicated that existing net payers would be better off, except the UK, which would be substantially worse off. Again, there was little chance of the British accepting a decisive shift in the financial status quo (see Figure 2.5).

There has been no thorough restructuring of the budget. Rather, other lines have been added. For that reason, the Commission budget proposal was inflated and subsequently rejected. The eventual compromise was for a sum of €862 billion, €8 billion less than that proposed by the Luxembourg presidency. Differences of over €200 billion less than the sum suggested by the Commission (€1,075 billion) or over €100 billion of that submitted by the EP (€975 billion) were starker. The UK government finally agreed to reduce its rebate by €10.5 billion in combination with an increase in contributions from France, Germany, and Italy. Spending remains concentrated in agricultural policy and structural disbursements. Some headings were renamed, including those that represent Lisbon Agenda costs. That was a sleight-of-hand intend-

Figure 2.5   Agreed Compromise for the Financial Perspective, 2007–2013

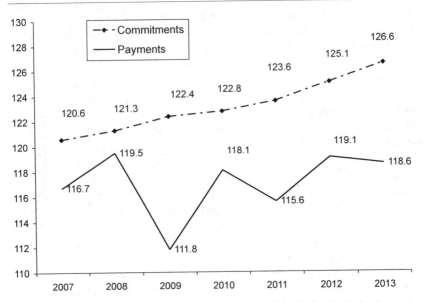

Source: Council of the European Union, Document 15915/05, CADREFIN 268, "Note from the Presidency to the European Council, Financial Perspective," Annex I, p. 33 (Brussels, 19 December 2005) at http://www.consilium.europa.eu/ueDocs/cms_Data/docs/pressData/en/misc/ 87677.pdf.
Note: Annual flows in €billion at 2004 constant prices.

ing to give an impression of change when nothing substantial had been changed. Despite the Commission's request for additional money, no plan was provided for specifically how and where it should be spent. Funds available are relatively small, though they will gradually increase. The budget negotiations betrayed little sense of "European public goods" as either existing or needing to be prioritized. The lack of substantial change was reflected in the outcomes (see Figure 2.6).

Despite proclamations that it would not again be the underwriter of last resort, Germany made the outcome in December 2005 possible. It is again the largest net payer in total and relative to its GNI (from 0.33 in 2004 to 0.42 percent in 2007–2013). The German contribution would have increased within the framework of the Commission's proposal (to 0.49 percent of GNI) and without a correction of the British rebate. The new *Länder* (the states of the present German Federal Republic that were part of the former German Democratic Republic, or East Germany) appear to be the main losers as they will receive €4 billion less than under the old financial arrangements. The UK budgetary position has worsened, but it obtained a commitment that policies will be subject to a thorough mid-term review. The Netherlands has been a

Figure 2.6 Net Budgetary Position of Net Payer Countries (% of GNI)

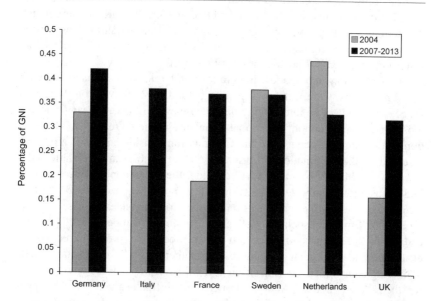

Source: European Commission, "Allocation of 2005 Expenditures by Member States" at http://ec.europa.eu/budget/library/documents/revenue_expenditure/agenda_2000/allocrep_2005_en.pdf and Council of the European Union, Interinstitutional File 2004/0170 (CNS) 2004/0171, "Proposal for a Council Decision on the System of the European Communities' Own Resources" (Brussels: 22 July 2004) at http://register.consilium.eu.int/pdf/en/04/st11/st11741.en04.pdf.

winner of the budget power play and will reduce its net transfers substantially. The Hague negotiated particularly hard because of a Euroskeptic mood in the country and the Dutch parliament's setting of a maximum possible financial contribution.

Is a European Economic and Social Model Still Possible?

The Rome Treaty establishing a European Economic Community contained provisions for the construction of a common market to be accompanied by social measures, though the formulations were vague, mentioning "coordination of social security regulation." Competencies in social affairs remained at the national level, and European policy has been to require unanimous Council decisions. In the 1970s these decisions were limited to social security for labor migrants and some employment programs in the framework of the European Social Funds (ESF). In 1980, ESF funding amounted to 4.3 percent of the budget.[83] In the early 1990s, planning for economic and monetary integration incorporated a discussion on flanking it with social policies. The perception was that increased mobility of factors of production needed common social policies to mitigate accelerated structural change. Harmonized social security would thus accompany a highly integrated market. In the Maastricht and Amsterdam Treaties, some competencies in social affairs shifted toward the European level, being partly subject to majority voting and to EP co-decision. ESF funding grew to 7 percent of the EU budget.

Globalization and market integration, and related dissatisfaction with social outcomes, were influential factors behind the "no" vote on the CT in France. One side of an intensifying debate argues that the European project is too biased toward economics and that social affairs should receive more attention. Prominent politicians and the Commission considered social affairs as essential for the legitimation of European integration. In many declarations the Commission has stressed that it will consider the social consequences of various measures in daily decisionmaking. The modification of the Bolkestein directive on the service sector was one of the most visible examples.

What "European social model" should or could then be pursued? At one end of the spectrum is Anglo-Saxon market liberalism, providing economic efficiency and low social protection; at the other end is a continental model, delivering equity but at costs in efficiency.[84] Most Europeans instinctively prefer their "own model." Many European intellectuals argue that Europe's approach should be clearly different from the US one and reflect greater sensitivity in social and ecological matters.[85] Global economic forces endanger this preference. Enlargement also threatens the possibilities for social harmonization, which means higher standards have to be extended across the continent. Doing so translates into high budgetary expenditures and/or higher labor costs and would slow catch-up processes. Despite the hardships, poorer new EU members realize they cannot succeed with, or fund, a high spending approach.

"European social model" is a term attributed to Jacques Delors.[86] But as André Sapir elaborates, there are not one but at least four different models. They cover differing geographic areas and are the result of history and tradition. The main features and outcomes of these models, which also contain internal variations, may be characterized as follows:[87]

1. The *Nordic model* (Denmark, Finland, Sweden plus the Netherlands) is characterized by the highest level of social protection expenditures, universal welfare provision, and extensive fiscal intervention in labor markets based on various "active" policy instruments. Strong labor unions ensure compressed wage structures. Protection against uninsurable labor market risks may be provided by employment legislation, preventing workers from being fired, or by unemployment benefits. Nordic countries prefer low employment protection (especially Denmark) but high unemployment benefits. Labor markets are flexible with high participation and low unemployment. High taxes are the price for generous social security systems. The tax system incorporates much

redistribution of incomes, causing a high degree of equalization and a low risk of becoming genuinely poor.

2. The *Anglo-Saxon model* is associated with the UK and Ireland. It provides social assistance, but only as a last resort. Transfers are mainly directed to people of working age. Some "active" policy instruments are used, especially for conditioning access to employment. The labor market is characterized by weak unions, wide wage differentiation, and a large low-wage sector. Employment protection and unemployment benefits are low and the labor market is flexible, but wages cannot drop below a set minimum in less qualified areas. Unemployment is low, and labor participation rates are relatively high. Income redistribution via taxes is classified as medium, but the poverty risk is high. Taxation in general, especially on labor, is low.

3. Continental countries (Austria, Belgium, France, Germany, and Luxembourg) use extensive insurance-based, nonemployment benefits, and old-age pensions. They have strong unions, though their influence is declining. The flexibility of the labor market is low and employment protection high. Social security systems are financed by contributions of employees and employers and increasingly by state subsidies. These countries have high taxation, especially on labor. Income redistribution and unemployment are comparatively high, and the labor participation rate is low.

4. Mediterranean states (Greece, Italy, Spain) concentrate social expenditures on old-age pensions and accept a large segmentation of entitlements and status. Employment protection is high, and provisions enable some of the working-age population to retire early. Participation rates are low, and unemployment rates high. Strong collective wage bargaining and compressed wage structures characterize these states. Labor market flexibility is low, as are unemployment benefits. No clear taxation pattern is identifiable, but income redistribution is low. The relative risk of poverty is high.[88]

CEECs might loosely form a fifth group. They do not represent a consistent model, although all have emerged from being planned economies with social security and full labor protection. They liberalized their labor markets and slowly reformed their social security systems. Weak unions and employer organizations arrived at decentralized wage bargaining partly mediated by the state. Similar to some Mediterranean countries, they have early retirement programs for state firms. Unemployment benefits are relatively easy to obtain but are very low. The tax on wages is high, and the state is still heavily burdened by social expenditures. In the private sector, which operates a large shadow economy, segments of the labor market are flexible but with low protection and a minimal social security net.

The Nordic and Anglo-Saxon models provide the best efficiency. They keep unemployment relatively low and produce high labor participation rates. These two models differ widely concerning equity, as Figure 2.7 indicates. According to André Sapir, both are sustainable. The Continental and

Figure 2.7   European Social Models: A Typology

| | | Efficiency | |
		Low	High
Equity	*High*	Continentals	Nordics
	Low	Mediterraneans	Anglo-Saxons

Source: André Sapir, "Globalisation and the Reform of European Social Models," *Bruegel Policy Brief* 1/2005, 1. Available at www.bruegel.org.

Mediterranean models are not, however, because they do not provide sufficient incentives to work. During times of rapid change, strict employment protection reduces overall employment and growth. Early pension schemes, introduced to reduce the pressure, or high unemployment benefits are hard to sustain in the face of fiscal deficits and demographic change. Larger shares of populations are recognizing that high unemployment and slow growth might jeopardize their pensions. The pressure to radically reform, or preferably phase out, the Continental and Mediterranean models is important as they represent nearly two-thirds of the EU25's GDP.

Some politicians, such as Jacques Chirac, demanded the preservation of a European social model, which in Chirac's case meant an adoption of the Continental (or French) version by others. In practice this would mean exporting comparative disadvantages, especially to new EU members. It would also mean losing ground in an ever more intense global competition. An inability to change will undermine the foundations of wealth in core EU states. Those reforms that are under way will take different paths according to national preferences. Sapir suggests that adherents of the Continental model may find it easiest to move toward the Nordic model, and retain a strong equity component, and Mediterranean countries could move toward the Anglo-Saxon model.[89] Attitudes within political parties are important. Conservative and liberal parties provide a more consistent picture across EU states, generally favoring flexible labor markets, but the political left, comprising social-democratic, socialist, and communist parties, is fragmented, from advocating traditional labor protection to fairly liberal approaches in Scandinavia.[90]

Many Europeans want to preserve a European social model, meaning some variation on or combination of the Continental, Mediterranean, and Nordic versions, as an alternative to Anglo-Saxon liberalism. They believe that, even if social welfare costs are streamlined, any such European model should provide comprehensive insurance against economic and social risks and broad health coverage. Environmental and social goals as well as relatively equal income distributions and the prevention of poverty would then remain high on the political agenda. This view holds that governments and public institutions should play an active role and that social partners (unions and employer representatives) should be engaged in wage formation, labor laws, and other aspects of public life. A larger role for the state implies that higher taxes are accepted. From this perspective, the Nordic model is regarded as a benchmark.[91]

Could the Nordic model then serve as a blueprint for Europe writ large? First, it is important to note that the starting point for the Scandinavian reforms had been a deep crisis of their social welfare system in the 1980s and early 1990s, featuring high fiscal deficits and unemployment. In Finland an additional external shock was caused by the crisis in the former Soviet Union. The positive element to these crises, as compared to the more creeping sort in France and Germany or the perpetual one in Italy, is that a change in mentality occurred. An important practical result is continuous fiscal consolidation. Substantial reforms in unemployment insurance and labor market policy were also made and led to much more flexible structures. In Denmark the "flexicurity system" only partly explains the success in the reduction in unemployment, especially of a structural nature. In contrast to Sweden, which had less spectacular results in this respect, the Danes reduced the generosity of unemployment benefits and set tougher requirements for claimants. The Scandinavians also encouraged liberal reforms in product market deregulation. These changes combined with the promotion of R&D, science, and education, which supported specialization in information technology and other high-tech sectors.[92] Whether the Scandinavian model might serve as a yardstick for big continental countries such as France and Germany is questionable because all models are the result of particular historical processes. Scandinavians are more willing to accept higher taxes and a greater role for the state as their experience includes efficient public services, which is not the case in other, and especially Mediterranean, states.[93]

Figure 2.8 indicates that the competencies to address these trade-offs are mainly situated at the national and not the EU level. The Amsterdam Treaty instituted basic social standards and a coordination of the employment policy, which is also the case for environmental and product regulations and health care. More extensive harmonization is unlikely to be reached. Enlargement exacerbated difficulties presented by existing diversity. The same is true for tax policy, whereby some CEECs, especially Baltic states, followed the example of Ireland and introduced low corporate taxes. Continental countries responded with complaints about unfair social and tax dumping. Social and tax policies are largely in the hands of national governments, and institutional competition is gradually forcing all EU states to introduce corporate tax

Figure 2.8   Assignment of Economic Policies at National and EU Levels

		National	*Union*
		Level	
Policy	*Micro*	Labor market regulation	Product and capital market regulation
	Macro	Fiscal policy Social policy	Monetary policy

Source: André Sapir, "Globalisation and the Reform of European Social Models," *Bruegel Policy Brief* 1/2005, 6. Available at www.bruegel.org.

reforms. Combined with other measures, such as a simplification of rules, these changes should lead to higher tax income. Underlying competition among systems might help create better institutional arrangements. Coordination is possible, but it has not delivered convincing results.

The 2004 directive (2004/38EC) on migration and inclusion into host-state social security systems demonstrated how difficult it is to agree on and institute EU-wide regulations. Concerns rose among Western Europeans that welfare conditions in CEE might motivate migration in their direction. Since the early 1990s, barriers on free movement and residency for EU citizens have been progressively lifted. That was considered fundamental to galvanizing a widespread sense of European citizenship. The new directive was more liberal regarding permanent migration and residency in other EU states. There is easier access to welfare benefits in host countries, but certain requirements remain. EU citizens who are not working and move to another EU state may only receive residency rights when proof of sufficient financial means and comprehensive health insurance is provided. For the first three months of residence, and longer for job seekers, new arrivals are excluded from access to social assistance programs.

Whether these regulations promote attempts to exploit more generous social welfare conditions is the subject of a vigorous debate. Since Directive 2004/38EC was not implemented until 2006, it is too early to give definitive answers. It is not likely to trigger substantial migration flows because migration is mainly driven by other motives. However, decisionmakers took a risk that may yet have consequences for national social security systems. The debate revealed how sensitive the balance of supranational and national competencies is, especially after enlargement increased the diversity of income levels and living conditions in general.[94]

Conclusion

Eastern enlargement was largely driven by political-strategic considerations but supported by positive integration effects that could only materialize if old and new EU member countries accepted the need for and consequences of structural change. As regards the SM, no serious conflict between widening and deepening is apparent if participants accept common rules and provide institutional settings for sustainable functioning market economies. New members fulfilled these preconditions.

Since enlargement, the SM and EMU have operated quite well but need to be consolidated.[95] In economic terms, the theoretical "boundlessness" of the SM presents it as an appropriate instrument for later extension to some of the EU's neighborhood, as it is already partly linked with the European Economic Area (EEA). Were that to happen, political considerations would set limits, as they have done to the present, because old and new member states alike confront vigorous global competition. The EU cannot become a fortress protecting exceptional welfare conditions and social or environmental standards ad infinitum, but it is not well prepared to cope with potent competitive forces.[96] Much of the pressure on labor markets and social welfare systems in the old EU15 stems from dynamic growing economies like China, India, and those in Southeast Asia. Blame is also attributed to cheaper costs in and increased competition from CEE. The market access, even with restrictions, that the CEECs acquired through EU accession is unwelcome in some sectors. Related concerns transformed into resentments toward enlargement, even if it is not a chief cause of unemployment problems in Western Europe. Similar reactions could be expected if the SM were to be extended to the EU's neighborhood. The ramifications of a shared currency go beyond the SM and demand closer economic and political coordination among EMU participants.

Insufficient coordination and a failure to install certain incentives in the EU budget undermined the Lisbon Agenda and will hamper Lisbon Two. An outdated focus on the CAP, cohesion and structural funds, and net financial positions stifles European potential. The cake is finite, and bargaining is tougher with an influx of poorer members. Options for using side payments are narrowing. A new approach is needed to cope with twenty-seven, thirty, or more members. Without revision, conflicts will sharpen, and the EU's legitimacy will be strained. A unified European social model cannot be used to mitigate unrest because harmonization is limited in this field. Nonetheless, it cannot be ignored that significant sections of national publics are concerned that competition may erode collective preferences and fear a "race to the bottom."

Some legislated minimum standards across the EU might ameliorate such an outcome.

Notes

1. Cf. Martin Hüfner, *Europa: Die Macht von morgen* (München: Hanser, 2006); Jean Pisani-Ferry, "The Accidential Player: The EU and the Global Economy," paper presented for the Indian Council for Research on International Economic Relations, New Delhi, 25 November 2005; Alberto Alesina and Francesco Giavazzi, *The Future of Europe: Reform or Decline* (Cambridge, Mass.: MIT Press, 2006).

2. World Bank, *World Development Indicators* (Washington, DC: July 2006); European Commission, Directorate-General of Economic and Financial Affairs, *European Economy. Statistical Annex,* Brussels, Spring 2006.

3. European Commission, *A New Partnership for Cohesion: Convergence, Competitiveness, Cooperation: Third Report on Cohesion,* Luxembourg, 2004, ix.

4. Daniel Gros and Alfred Steinherr, *Economic Transition in Central and Eastern Europe* (Cambridge: Cambridge University Press, 2004), 274–283.

5. James Buchanan, "An Economic Theory of Clubs," *Econometrica* 32, no. 1 (1965): 1–14, is the seminal work on the topic.

6. This principle holds that decisionmaking power and responsibility for related administration should lie with the most decentralized authority, for example, at the commune or regional level rather than the state or centralized EU ("Brussels") level.

7. Gros and Steinherr, *Economic Transition in Central and Eastern Europe*, 276–278.

8. Joachim Ahrens, Herman Hoen, and Renate Ohr, "Deepening Integration in an Enlarged EU: A Club-Theoretical Perspective," *Journal of European Integration* 27, no. 4 (2005): 417–439.

9. An informative account and good analysis is provided by Geoffrey Pridham, *Designing Democracy: EU Enlargement and Regime Change in Post-Communist Europe* (Basingstoke: Palgrave, 2005).

10. For example, Paolo Cecchini, *The European Challenge 1992: The Benefits of a Single Market* (Aldershot: Wildwood House, 1988). See also Michael Emerson et al., *The Economics of 1992: The EC's Commission Assessment of the Economic Effects of Completing the Internal Market* (Oxford: Oxford Univerity Press, 1988); Hans Jürgen Wagener, Thomas Eger, and Heiko Fritz, *Europäische Integration: Recht und Ökonomie, Geschichte und Politik* (München: Franz Vahlen, 2006).

11. European Commission, *The Internal Market: 10 Years Without Frontiers* SEC/2002/14/17, Brussels, 2002, ec.europa.eu/internal_market/10years/docs/working-doc/workingdoc_en.pdf.

12. Line Vogt, *The EU's Single Market: At Your Service?* Working Paper 449 (Paris: OECD, 2005).

13. Cf. Jürgen Kluge and Heino Fassbender, *Wirtschaftsmacht Europa* (Wien: Ueberreuter, 2003).

14. The Lamfalussy process aims to create a more efficient system for the EU institutions to prepare, adopt, and implement new legislation to integrate financial markets. See European Commission, "Financial Markets: Inter-institutional Monitoring Group Publishes First Report on 'Lamfalussy process,'" "Press Release IP/06/361, 22 March 2006, www.europa.eu/rapid/pressReleasesAction.do?reference=IP/06/361& format=HTML&aged=0&language=DE&guiLanguage=en.

15. Jean Pisani-Ferry, "Speeding Up European Reform: A Master Plan for the Lisbon Agenda," *CESifo Forum* 6, no. 2 (2005): 24.

16. George Parker, "Mandelson Attacks 'Populist' EU Protectionism," *Financial Times,* 7 February 2006.

17. Fabienne Ilzkovitz, Adriaan Dierx, Viktoria Kovacs, and Nuno Sousa, *Steps Towards a Deeper Economic Integration: The Internal Market in the Twenty-First Century,* European Economy Economic Papers 271 (Brussels: European Commission, January 2007), 76.

18. Cf. Paul Krugman and Maurice Obstfeld, *International Economics,* 2nd ed. (New York: HarperCollins, 1991), 213–238.

19. Cf. Fritz Breuss, *Macroeconomic Effects of EU Enlargement for Old and New Members,* Working Paper 142 (Vienna: WIFO, 2001); Wolfgang Quaisser and John Hall, *Towards Agenda 2007: Preparing the EU for Eastern Enlargement,* Working Paper 240 (München: Osteuropa Institut, 2002); CESifo, *Report on the European Economy 2004* (Munich: CESifo, 2004), 96–118.

20. Timo Baas, Herbert Brücker, and Elmar Hönekopp, "EU-Osterweiterung: Beachtliche Gewinne für die deutsche Volkswirtschaft," *IAB Kurzbericht* 6/2007 (Nürnberg: IAB/Bundesanstalt für Arbeit, March 2007).

21. Cf. European Commission, Directorate-General ECFIN, *European Economy Enlargement, Two Years After: An Economic Evaluation,* Occasional Paper 24 (Brussels: CEC, May 2006).

22. Cf. Jesus Crespo-Guaresma, Maria Antoinette Dimitz, and Doris Ritzberger-Grünwand, "The Impact of European Integration on Growth: What Can We Learn for EU Accession?" in Gertrude Tumpel-Gugerell and Peter Mooslechner, eds., *Economic Convergence and Divergence in Europe: Growth and Regional Development in an Enlarged European Union* (Cheltenham: Edward Elgar, 2003), 55–71.

23. Paul Krugman, "Competitiveness: A Dangerous Obsession," *Foreign Affairs* 73, no. 2 (1994): 28–45.

24. European Commission, *European Economy Enlargement, Two Years After,* 35–36.

25. Ibid., 6.

26. Horst Siebert, *Germany in the European Union: Economic Policy Under Ceded Sovereignty,* Working Paper 1217 (Kiel: Institute for World Economics, 2004); Siebert, *The World Economy,* 2nd ed. (London: Routledge, 2002).

27. Hans-Werner Sinn, *The New Systems Competition* (Oxford: Blackwell, 2003).

28. Charles Wyplosz, "The Challenge of a Wider and Deeper Europe," in Klaus Libscher et al., eds., *The Economic Potential of a Larger Europe* (Cheltenham: Edward Elgar, 2004), 8–33.

29. Krugman and Obstfeld, *International Economics,* 79–80.

30. Cf. Christian Dustman and Albrecht Glitz, *Immigration, Jobs and Wages: Theory, Evidence and Opinion* (London: Centre for Comparative European Policy Evaluation, 2005).

31. Cf. Tito Boeri and Herbert Brücker, *The Impact of Eastern Enlargement on Employment and Labour Markets in the EU Member States* (Brussels: CEC, 2001).

32. Baas et al., "EU-Osterweiterung: Beachtliche Gewinne," 4.

33. Claudia Buch, *Capital Mobility and EU Enlargement,* Working Paper 908 (Kiel: IWE, 1998).

34. Hans-Werner Sinn, *Ist Deutschland noch zu retten?* (Berlin: Ullstein, 2005).

35. Hans-Werner Sinn, "Basar-Ökonomie Deutschland, Exportweltmeister oder Schlußlicht?" *ifo Schnelldienst* 6 (special edition), March 2005.

36. Volkhart Vincentz, "Deutsche Direktinvestitionen in Osteuropa weiter rück-

läufig—Arbeitsplatzeffekte geringer als befürchtet," *Kurzinformationen und Analysen* 3 (München: Osteuropa Institut, April 2002).

37. Statistisches Bundesamt, *Volkswirtschaftliche Gesamtrechnung. Input-Output-Rechnung. Importabhängigkeit der deutschen Exporte 1991, 1995, 2000 und 2002* (Wiesbaden: SBA, 2004).

38. Patricia Alvarez-Plata, Herbert Brücker, and Boriss Siliverstovs, *Potential Migration from Central and Eastern Europe into the EU-15: An Update. Report for the Commission* (Brussels: CEC, 2003).

39. Boeri and Brücker, *The Impact of Eastern Enlargement on Employment and Labour Markets;* Thomas Bauer and Klaus Zimmermann, *Assessment of Possible Migration Pressure and Its Labour Market Impact Following EU Enlargement to Central and Eastern Europe* (Bonn: IZA, 1999).

40. Michael Fertig, "The Economic Impact of EU Enlargement: Assessing the Migration Potential," *Empirical Economics* 26, no. 4 (2001): 707–720; Hans-Werner Sinn, G. Flaig, M. Werding, S. Münz, N. Düll, and H. Hoffmann, *EU Erweiterung und Arbeitskräftemigration: Wege zu einer schrittweisen Annäherung der Arbeitsmärkt* (München: ifo, 2001).

41. Herbert Brücker, "EU-Osterweiterung: Übergangsfristenführen zu Umlenkung der Migration nach Großbritannien und Irland," *DIW-Wochenbericht* 22 June 2005, 355–356.

42. Brücker, "EU-Osterweiterung: Übergangsfristenführen," 358.

43. Cf. Barbara Dietz, "Ost-West-Migration nach Deutschland im Kontext der EU-Erweiterung," *Aus Politik und Zeitgeschichte* B nos. 5–6 (4 February 2004); Thomas Bauer, Barbara Dietz, Klaus Zimmermann, and Eric Zwintz, "German Migration: Development, Assimilation, and Labour Market Effects," in Klaus Zimmermann, ed., *European Migration: What Do We Know?* (Oxford: Oxford University Press, 2005): 197–261; Herbert Brücker, "EU-Osterweiterung Effekte der Migration," *DIW-Wochenbericht* 17 April 2004; N. Diez Guardia and K. Pichelmann, *Labour Migration Patterns in Europe: Recent Trends, Future Challenges,* Economic Papers 256 (Brussels: ECFIN, September 2006).

44. Tibo Boeri and Herbert Brücker, *Migration, Coordination Failures and EU Enlargement,* Discussion Paper 1600 (Bonn: IZA, May 2005); Brücker, "EU-Osterweiterung: Übergangsfristenführen zu Umlenkung der Migration."

45. Baas, Brücker, and Hönekopp *EU-Osterweiterung: Beachtliche Gewinne,* 6.

46. "Chancen für offene Dienstleistungsmärkte sinkt, führende SPD-Politiker warnen vor Konsequenzen—EU-Kommission schließt Scheitern der geplanten Richtlinie nicht aus," *Handelsblatt,* 22 February 2005, 5; S. Kafasack, "Der Zug der osteuropäischen Arbeiter ist noch nicht angekommen, Kaum verläßliche Statistiken, Erfahrungen deuten nicht auf Massenbewegung hin," *Frankfurter Allgemeine Zeitung,* 10 September 2005, 16.

47. "Ein polnischer Klempner gegen die französische Angst, Polen begegnet den Feindbildern mit feinem Humor," *Frankfurter Allgemeine Zeitung,* 2 July 2005, 14.

48. *Informationsdienst des Institut der deutschen Wirtschaft Köln* 31, September 2005, 6–7.

49. The Maastricht criteria are those that apply to EMU as determined in the Treaty on European Union. The key criteria are a debt-to-GDP ratio of no more than 60 percent; a deficit of no more than 3 percent of GDP; an inflation rate no more than 1.5 percent over the average of the three most price-stable member states; and a long-term interest rate that is no more than 2 percent above the three most stable member states in the previous year.

50. Cf. Iain Begg et al., "Reforming Fiscal Policy Coordination Under EMU:

What Should Become of the Stability and Growth Pact?" *Journal of Common Market Studies* 42, no. 5 (2004): 1023–1059; Montserrat Ferré, "Should Fiscal Authorities Co-operate in a Monetary Union with Public Deficit Targets?" *Journal of Common Market Studies* 43, no. 3 (2005): 539–550.

51. Paul de Grauwe, "Enlargement of the Euro Area: On Monetary and Political Union," *CESifo Forum* 7, no. 4 (2006): 8.

52. Cf. Peter Bofinger, *Wir sind besser als wir glauben: Wohlstand für alle* (München: Rowohlt, 2005); "Die EZB überzeugt mich nicht," interview with Robert Mundell, *Cicero,* March 2007, 84.

53. Ralph Rotte and Sascha Derichs, *Krise and Ende des Europäischen Stabilitäts- und Wachstumspakt,* aktuelle analysen 39 (München: Hanns-Seidel-Stiftung, 2005).

54. Michael Frenkel and Christiane Nickel, "How Symmetric Are the Shocks and the Shock Adjustment Dynamics Between the Euro Area and Central and Eastern European Countries?" *Journal of Common Market Studies* 43, no. 1 (2005): 53–74.

55. Alistair Dieppe, Keith Küster, and Peter McAdam, "Optimal Monetary Rules for the Euro Area: An Analysis Using the Area-Wide Model," *Journal of Common Market Studies* 43, no. 3 (2005): 507–537.

56. Robert Mundell, "A Theory of Optimum Currency Areas," *American Economic Review* 51, no. 4 (1961): 657–665; Francesco Paolo, "What Is European Economic and Monetary Union Telling Us About the Properties of Optimum Currency Areas?" *Journal of Common Market Studies* 43, no. 3 (2005): 607–635.

57. A minimum two-year period in the exchange rate mechanism (ERM) should first occur.

58. Cf. Krugman and Obstfeld, *International Economics,* 397–398.

59. De Grauwe, "Enlargement," 4.

60. Ibid., 10.

61. Friedrich Heinemann, Sebastian Hauptmeister, Michael Knogler, Dan Stegarescu, and Volkhart Vincentz, *Analyse ausgewählter Aspekte der Haushaltseinnahmen und–ausgaben sowie von außerbudgetären Fonds und Eventualverbindlichkeiten in den neuen Mitgliedsstaaten* (Bonn/München: ZEW/Osteuropa Institut München, February 2006). See also Friedrich Heinemann, Sebastian Hauptmeister, Michael Knogler, Dan Stegarescu, and Volkhart Vincentz, *Transparenz und Nachhaltigkeit der Haushaltspolitik in den neuen EU-Staaten* (Baden-Baden: Nomos, 2006).

62. Michael Bolle and Oliver Pamp, "It's Politics, Stupid—EMU Enlargement Between an Economic Rock and a Political Hard Place," *CESifo Forum* 7, no. 4 (2006): 26–28.

63. Frenkel and Nickel, "How Symmetric Are the Shocks and Shock Adjustment Dynamics?"

64. Cf. Thomas Meyer and Hanns Jacobsen, "Ever Closer Monetary Union? Euro Goes Central Europe," *Welt Trends* 51 (Summer 2006): 137–146.

65. *FAZ-net,* "Estland verzichtet auf frühen Beitritt," 12 March 2006, www.faz-net.

66. Bolle and Pamp, "It's Politics," 27.

67. Hermann Remsperger, "Comments on the Enlargement of the EU and EMU," speech at Johannes Gutenberg University, Mainz, 6 July 2005, www.bundesbank.de/download/presse/reden/2005/20050606remsperger.en.php.

68. Helge Berger, "Unfinished Business? The ECB Reform Ahead of the Euro Area Enlargement," *CESifo Forum* 7, no. 4 (2006): 39–40.

69. Paul Krugman, *Geography and Trade* (Cambridge, MA: MIT, 1991).

70. Cf. Jan Sevjnar, "Structural Reforms and Competitiveness—Will Europe Overtake America?" in Gertrude Tumpel-Gugerell and Peter Mooslechner, eds., *Structural Challenges for Europe* (Cheltenham: Edward Elgar, 2004): 35–59.

71. Pisani-Ferry, *Speeding Up European Reform.*

72. High-Level Group, chaired by Wim Kok, *Facing the Challenge: The Lisbon Strategy for Growth and Employment* (Luxembourg: European Communities, 2004).

73. The percentage of total tax and social security contributions in the gross cost of labor.

74. Pisani-Ferry, *Speeding Up European Reform,* 22; Daniele Archibugi and Alberto Coco, "Is Europe Becoming the Most Dynamic Knowledge Economy in the World?" *Journal of Common Market Studies* 43, no. 3 (2005): 433–459.

75. World Economic Forum, *Growth Competitiveness Report, 2005/2006* (Geneva: WEF, 2006).

76. A ranking is provided by Aurore Wanlin, *The Lisbon Scorecard VI: Will Europe's Economy Rise Again?* (London: Centre for European Reform, 2006), 1–52.

77. Influenced by the report of an "Independent High-Level Study Group." See André Sapir et al., *An Agenda for a Growing Europe: Making the EU Economic System Deliver* (Brussels: CEC, 2003).

78. Jean Pisani-Ferry, "Deutschlands Wette mit Europa," *Handelsblatt,* 22 November 2005, 9. Gilles Raveaud argues that although the employment component of the Lisbon Strategy came to dominate at the expense of anything else, "better" jobs were not created. See Gilles Raveaud, "The European Employment Strategy: Towards More and Better Jobs?" *Journal of Common Market Studies* 45, no. 2 (2007): 411–434.

79. Pisani-Ferry, *Speeding Up European Reform,* 28.

80. CES/ifo/European Economic Advisory Group, *The EEAG Report on the European Economy 2007,* Munich, 2007, 15–21; *Economist,* "Special Report on the European Union," 17 March 2007, 6–9.

81. CES/ifo/European Economic Advisory Group, *EEAG Report 2007,* 21; *Economist,* "Special Report on the European Union," 8.

82. Cf. Carsten Hefeker, *Ressourcenverteilung in der EU: Eine polit-ökonomische Perspektive,* Discussion Paper 252 (Hamburg: HWWA, November 2003).

83. Patrick Thalacker, "Ein Sozialmodell für Europa? Die EU-Sozialpolitik nach der Erweiterung," *Gesellschaft-Wirtschaft-Politik* (February 2002): 165–181.

84. CES/ifo/European Economic Advisory Group, *EEAG Report 2007,* 3.

85. Jürgen Habermas and Jacques Derrida, "Nach Dem Krieg: Die Wiedergeburt Europas," *Frankfurter Allgemeine Zeitung,* 31 May 2003, reprinted as, "What Binds Europeans Together," in Daniel Levy, Max Pensky, and John Torpey, eds., *Old Europe, New Europe, Core Europe: Transatlantic Relations After the Iraq War* (London: Verso, 2005).

86. Ruth Adam, "Ein Wirtschafts- und Sozialmodell für Europa? Untersuchung eines instrumentellen Begriffs," *CAP aktuell,* München, 25 October 2005.

87. Based on André Sapir, "Globalisation and the Reform of European Social Models," *Policy Brief,* January 2005, 6, www.bruegel.org; European Commission, *Employment in Europe, 2006,* Brussels, 2007, 103–107; Wolfgang Schröder, "Arbeitsbeziehungen in Mittel- und Osteuropa: Weder wilder Osten noch europäisches Sozialmodell," *Politikinformationen Osteuropa* 119 (Bonn: Friedrich Ebert Stiftung, June 2004).

88. Sapir, "Globalisation," 5–6.

89. Ibid., 10.

90. Marius Busemeyer, Christian Kellermann, Alexander Petring, and Andrej Stuchlik, "Politische Positionen zum Europäischen Wirtschafts- und Sozialmodell— Eine Landkarte der Interessen" (Bonn: Friedrich Ebert Stiftung, August 2006).

91. United Nations Economic Commission for Europe, "Towards a New European Model of a Reformed Welfare State: An Alternative to the United States Model," in *Economic Survey of Europe,* January 2005 (New York: United Nations, 2005), 105–114.

92. CES/ifo/European Economic Advisory Group, *EEAG Report 2007,* chapter 4, "Scandinavia: An Economic Miracle?" 82–120.

93. Ognian Hishow, "Das Wirtschafts- und Sozialmodell der nordischen EU-Mitglieder," SWP Aktuell 47 (Berlin: SWP, November 2005).

94. Wolfgang Ochel, "The EU Directive on Free Movement—A Challenge for the European Welfare State?" and Tanja El-Chekeh, Max Steinhardt, and Thomas Straubhaar, "Did the European Free Movement of Persons and Residence Directive Change Migration Patterns Within the EU? A First Glance," *CESifo Dice Report* 4, no. 4 (2006): 21–32 and 14–20, respectively.

95. Cf. Charles Wyplosz, "Gönnt Europa eine Pause," *Handelsblatt,* 24–26 June 2005, 9.

96. Sapir et al. *An Agenda for a Growing Europe;* Sapir, "Globalization and European Social Models."

3

States, Publics, and Europeanization

"Europeanization" is a concept or process that describes the transposition or subsuming of national policies and legislation by the EU and the impact of resulting reformulations within domestic polities. A range of rational institutionalist, constructivist, and neofunctionalist literature, some of it spanning nominal boundaries between them, has emphasized the role of institutions in Europeanization. The influence of states and publics is underplayed in much of this writing, though some scholars attribute more significance to them.[1] We contend that the institutions controlled by member states—the Council of Ministers and the European Council—have confirmed a predominant role in the EU's structure. Despite the potential for the social-institutional context to influence preference formation, decisionmaking in these forums is chiefly the outcome of bargaining, resulting from cost-benefit calculations and response to national electorates, economic interests, or foreign policy concerns.[2] Impetus could come from above or below the EU level. Governments may attempt to introduce European policy contrary to the wishes of domestic actors; publics or sectoral interests will sometimes deter governments from doing so; on other occasions, governments and national polities will be aligned.[3] Sufficient concord among states may result in delegation to the Commission.[4] The Council's centrality as a conduit for the pursuance of national aims at the EU level does not imply convergence or divergence of state preferences.

Even though this line of argument has a rationalist tone, it also comprises a "normative-affective" element. As Simon Bulmer and Claudio Radaelli note, "Europeanization is not simply about formal policy rules, but about less tangible aspects, such as beliefs and values."[5] The latter might reflect preferences for certain economic and social models or attachments to other national or regional particularities. Feelings of prestige or distinctiveness are also part of this affective sphere in which neither publics nor some political classes have been profoundly "Europeanized" or, more precisely, "EU-ized." A recent article by

Amitai Etzioni is instructive. He contends that the EU's evolution from a Step I to a Step II union, with an expanded level and scope of integration activity, has neither an appropriate institutional architecture nor a sense of itself as a "normative-affective" community. Implicit in Etzioni's argument is that a Step II union cannot survive indefinitely without suitable institutional frameworks *and* underpinning by a community identity of sufficient intensity.[6] When interests are conceptualized in large group contexts, rational and normative perceptions or assessments usually privilege nation-states over the EU or Europe.[7] Only when this order of priority is reversed can it be said that Europeans have been Europeanized. A European constitution, legitimated by popular imprimatur, would manifest the emergence of a European demos. These considerations form part of the backdrop to the following discussion.

Institutions, Integration, and Inertia

The EU is a conglomeration of many actors and variable interests, imperatives, and restraints. Nominally it has vast aggregate resources and expertise and a large influence in European and global affairs. Its unique combination of institutions is considered by many scholars as first enabling and then driving integration.[8] Following this interpretation, an institutional "fusion" can be credited with a major role in the EU's achievements and as the hope for the future.[9] It could also be held at least partly responsible for breakdown or inertia. The benefit of hindsight may establish that some institutions were ineffectual from an early stage but that it was disguised by the predominance of other actors.[10] Alternatively, while interinstitutional turf battles are a recurring feature, one institution may have always had or at some point attained greater influence over what occurs in the EU's political space.[11] George Tsebelis and Geoffrey Garrett contend that the balance of power among EC/EU institutions has shifted since 1957. In their view, the more veto players or blocking opportunities there are, the more scope there is for "bureaucracies and courts to move policy outcomes closer to their own preferences." They maintain that "if actors," that is, states, "operate under complete information . . . they will design institutions that best promote their preferences—subject to the constraint that every other actor will behave similarly."[12] Which institution is then best equipped and empowered to enable the EU to effectively deal with present and approaching challenges or, conversely, is most responsible for hindering it?

First, the Commission's right of initiative means that policy and rules expressed in the *acquis* may derive from its formulation of objectives and methods. Commission proposals are subject to modification or rejection by member states or the EP or both. In the mid- to late 1980s, the political skills and energy of Jacques Delors propelled the Commission to its zenith so far.

This period then was confronted by the geopolitical upheaval of 1989–1991, which motivated key member states to initiate a process of treaty revision that culminated in the TEU. As the 1990s progressed, the Commission's role as a quasi-executive came under threat. At certain periods, its influence was undermined, if not usurped. In the case of the CFSP, for example, the General Affairs and External Relations Council (GAERC) secretariat began as a "notetaker" before developing an identity and greater role because the member states did not want to delegate authority in this field to the Commission.[13] Had it been introduced, a simplified voting system might have reinvigorated the Commission's role.

Second, the authority of the European Court of Justice (ECJ) in the legal domain has lent it an integration-shaping and agenda-setting capacity, including for the SM. It also enjoys some scope for judicial activism. Much national legislation must conform to regulations and standards agreed on by all or a majority of member states and adjudicated by the Court. The Court's "supremacy doctrine" did not confer upon it the role of ultimate arbiter in regard to the proposed CT. Popular sovereignty proved a superior force in this case.[14] Neither the Court nor the body of law over which it presides can directly confront the main challenges facing member states or the EU as a collective.

Third, the EP has steadily acquired the rights of consultation, review, assent, and co-decision. Its roles include approval of the community budget and the appointment or dismissal of the Commission. Perhaps a future "Reform Treaty" will further increase the EP's power. Members of the European Parliament (MEPs) and other supporters are eager to obtain public attention for and promote loyalty to the institution. The powers that the EP presently has are largely restrictive in nature: they can be deployed to check the Council or Commission. Its aspirations to authority based on democratic accountability are undermined somewhat by decreasing turnouts in European elections and the lack of a pan-European political sociology or vigorous party system.

Even though they enjoy some initiating, shaping, and restraining capacities, these "supranational" institutions do not outrank the European Council/Council of Ministers tandem as the principal locus of power in the EU complex of multilevel governance.[15] Ben Crum argues, "All European political powers—legislative and executive—originate from the Member State governments assembled in the Council of Ministers." They command the initial allocation of powers, legislative processes, and through their administrations, the execution of European policies at the national level.[16] We, along with other scholars who have studied power distribution, presume that choices made at European Council meetings, or by delegated representatives, reflect the preferences of national political leaderships, having taken relevant considerations at the domestic, European, and international levels into account.[17] They can be measured along integrationist-independence or left-right dimensions of the EU's political space.[18] In their analysis of actor preferences in constitutional negotiations, Simon Hix and Cristophe Crombez applied a "mixed inductive/deductive" method, which produced, on the whole, an "intuitive set of ideal point estimates" for twenty-five member states, the Commission, and the EP. Conventional understandings of particular actors' preferences were largely confirmed on two axes of power allocation: centralization/decentralization of policy competences and majoritarian/consensual control. "Specifically," the authors declare:

> the United Kingdom is revealed as having a classic "intergovernmentalist" set of preferences—at the decentralization end of the vertical dimension, and towards the consensus side of the horizontal dimension. The position of France also accords with our expectations: pro-centralisation of policy competences, but in favour of intergovernmental institutions at the European level. Against these two, Belgium, the European Parliament and the Commission all reveal classic "Euro-federalist" preferences, with a centralization of power and majoritarian institutions.[19]

The record of a member state in voting with the majority does not necessarily prove it to be more or less integrationist. It may indicate that proposals put before the Council more often approximate the preferences of that state than those of some others, which may be due to a variety of reasons: diplomatic skill, privileged information, particular leverage, or being present at the creation. For the first forty years of European integration, France was adept at imposing its interests and practices, manifested in and assisted by the occupation of key positions by French officials.[20] France also registered a relatively low level of negative voting over the period 1995–2000. That may be because a status quo favored by French governments and its president (of any position on the political spectrum) was maintained. When this status quo was challenged, the reaction was to resist. At Nice in 2000, the refusal of France, then holding the EU presidency, to countenance a reweighting of votes in the Council to more accurately reflect Germany's relative population size was an exemplary indication of where decisive power resides. A subtler instance occurred toward the conclusion of the rancorous selection process to determine a successor to Romano Prodi as Commission president. Chirac was persuaded to accept José Manuel Barroso for the position because a Frenchman, Pierre de Boissieu, was reappointed as deputy secretary-general and, as Dinan puts it, "*de facto* head of the Council Secretariat—an indicator of where France thinks that institutional power in the EU lies."[21]

In this respect we concur with scholars like Andrew Moravcsik, Stanley Hoffmann, and Alan Milward who, although not disregarding the input of business, various lobbies, and institutional actors, stress the critical role of state interests in the formulation of grand bargains and shaping of the EU's constitutive features.[22] Opposing this broadly defined school, Stone Sweet's critique of what he terms Moravscik's "weak intergovernmentalism" is well made. Moravscik's approach, Stone Sweet argues, is not a theory of integration but rather a "theory of how governments interact with one another at specific moments in the process of integration."[23] It is precisely this type of interaction *or its absence* that is most crucial to progress or gridlock in the EU system. Neo-functionalism presumes that the EU is continually integrating through time and expanding or connecting the range of domains in which it does so. Our interpretation acknowledges periods without integration or integration that is minimalist. Beyond those areas already determined by treaty-based arrangements as the province of community policy, and even within them, the EU is not in a constant condition of integration. There are policy fields in which the EU has scarcely integrated at all, let alone in a perpetual sense. Breakthroughs into new areas or to overcome impasse require unanimous accord. The ordeal of reaching agreement on budgetary and other highly politicized issues has become more contentious. Some governments have been hamstrung domestically for reasons that do not necessarily derive from a community policy or directive. The "zone of discretion" enjoyed by either the Commission or the ECJ played no role in transforming the European Convention, and resulting draft CT, into a ratified statutory reality.[24] National politics and public dissatisfaction, not European law or supranational institutions, ultimately determined the outcome. It was one demonstration of the present limits of Europeanization.

Practical instances of supranationalism entail one or some member states being outvoted in QMV processes and having to accept a decision "above" an otherwise sovereign right to pursue their own preferences. It is sometimes overlooked that at the same time, a majority of member states have voted *for* a particular option. For it to become law and implemented as policy, there must be a majority or unanimity in favor of any initiative. Moreover, the veto option or "principle" introduced by the "Luxembourg Compromise" of 1966 remains critical despite the changes that have occurred since. There are few signs of a neo-functionalist revival. The supremacy of EU law in defined areas does not overcome the EU's major problems. The EU's judicial reality is subordinate to politics: within member states, among them, and globally.

Constructivist theory would contend that the EU's institutions are sites within which representatives of member states and community civil servants become socialized over time. Multiple actors and levels of governance are involved. The varying interests and preferences brought to these sites then undergo a process of transformation until a commonly accepted strategy, direction, response, quantity, and so on, is arrived at, formally agreed to, and instituted. In this understanding, a socially constructed consensus will be the outcome of deliberation, negotiation, and nonempirical influences among the parties that constitute the larger composite actor, the EU. The establishment and evolution of the EU to its present form shows that regular consensus and reshaping of individual interests and perspectives have occurred. There are, however, many instances of failure to reach unified positions across a range of policy domains and counter-evidence proving that interests often remain stubbornly national or sectoral. A real communal policy does not then emerge. Either a diluted compromise, possibly with opt-outs by some participants, or an abandonment of the project, or some form of pay-off to veto players may then occur. Constructivism accents the development of common methods and goals based on a convergence of normative understandings, encouraged by social and institutional contexts. Constructivism does not provide a consistently viable explanation of the EU because it does not adequately account for those occasions when consensus is blocked by one or more member states or when common norms, sometimes when most needed, are not manifested as pan-EU policy.

One initiative was the Open Method of Coordination (OMC), introduced at the Lisbon European Council in 2000 and intended to assist the simultaneously launched Lisbon Agenda. OMC aims to promote the workshopping of policy ideas and "ideational convergence" about best (and worst) practice and benchmarking.[25] OMC is consistent with constructivist and rationalist depictions and prescriptions. It is an intergovernmental arrangement and not grounded in or restricted by EU law—the lack of legal obligation being an incentive for an unencumbered exchange and quest for optimal policy design. OMC sounds plausible and promising as a noncoercive means of encouraging cooperation and ultimately positive results. OMC was not able to assist a better outcome at Nice later in 2000. The areas initially conceived for advancement by OMC (competitiveness, innovation, the knowledge economy, and high-tech industry) only marginally improved through 2007.

Contemporaneously, there has been a sustained attack on the *Méthode Monnet*, the incremental approach that relied on elite dominance, secrecy, and a favorable global environment to progress. Critics from across the political spectrum have called for an unambiguous division of competencies among institutions, clarity in the formulation of policies and legislation, and greater citizen involvement and influence. The EU's intention and route, at least for the next ten to twenty years, must be clarified, costs declared, and momentous decisions, such as enlargements, legitimated. A definitive *finalité* is not absolutely necessary. More important is *fonctionalité*, not in the neo-functionalist sense, but in the capacity to act. Preconditions, which give options and enable flexible response, must be met. Notwithstanding its high-profile advocates and apparent appeal for many EU scholars, federalism is not a likely outcome.[26]

Decisionmaking Processes

We presume that the broad objectives of the EU are to provide conditions for the generation of prosperity, the delivery of effective policy and resolution of possible conflicts, and the creation of a space of "freedom, security and justice," while moving toward an ever closer union of member states and populations. All decisionmaking procedures should contribute to those goals and be evaluated by their capacity to do so. The interinstitutional context has complex procedures governing decisionmaking, which manifest as a system of power sharing or of checks and balances. Member states are the critical actors, in both potentially negative (hindering objectives) and potentially positive (achieving objectives by overcoming hindrances) ways. External, or "supra-EU," factors have had great bearing on European integration, the form it takes and how deep or wide it extends. From the late 1940s, this top-down effect set the parameters within which other developments occurred. As Figure 3.1 indicates, in recent years bottom-up influences have assumed a greater role. These are less the expression of support for progressive goals within electorates than for the conservative retaining of privileges. They are not genuinely transnational in the sense of representing a unified pan-European orientation. Rather these pressures are filtered through national political, bureaucratic, and socioeconomic structures. As a result, it is important to distinguish between arenas of integration and of policymaking, the latter further divisible into policy-setting and policy-shaping.[27]

In formal terms, matters for deliberation in the Council are divided into

Figure 3.1   Levels of Political and Economic Activity Affecting the EU

Supra-EU level   World War II; Cold War; end of the Cold War; collapse of the Soviet Union; globalization; September 11; War on Terror

EU-level   Member state bargaining; institutional interactions; common projects; EP influence; EU law; lobbies

Domestic-level   Economic conditions and actors; sectoral and special interests; public opinion; party and coalition politics; historical-cultural factors

A-points, already de facto decided by COREPER, and B-points, matters on which COREPER did not reach consensus. A-points slightly outweigh B-points. For items governed by unanimity requirements, abstentions do not count as "no" votes. For QMV areas, abstentions have the effect of "no" votes.[28] A state's interest in pushing ahead with favored initiatives is balanced by the desire to safeguard against unfavorable developments resulting from other states doing the same. One proposition to overcome impasse was "enhanced cooperation," intended to enable groups of states that wish to move forward with a particular endeavor to do so without being restrained by others that do not. It requires the participation of at least eight member states. The more integration-friendly or ambitious states are the most likely candidates to proceed as part of this form of avant-garde. Skeptical attitudes, particularly in CEECs, reflect apprehensions that enhanced cooperation may be the initial manifestation of a two-speed or multiple-speed EU or an exclusive "core Europe."

The Nice system reflects an arbitrary, politically determined allocation of voting power among states, rather than a mathematical equivalence between EU citizens. The method proposed in the CT and projected for introduction in 2009 was simpler than its predecessor, though there were no guarantees that it would have always operated well. Two criteria, a majority of member states and a majority of the total EU population, were envisaged. They would have replaced the three criteria required for a qualified majority: a threshold of weighted votes, a majority of member states, and 62 percent of the total EU population. Vote weighting was to be dispensed with. Conscious of the increasing number of members and potential for blocking alliances, the proposed revision enabled many more permutations for reaching qualified majorities. They would be constituted by 55 percent of member states, including at least fifteen, that represented at least 65 percent of the EU population. The new system was also intended to avoid long negotiations on the allocation of votes before or during enlargements—which implied that others might occur. In response to criticism of shortcomings in popular democratic legitimacy and to concerns about publics losing interest, the proposed CT impressed the EU as a union of states and of peoples. One consequence was the referendums that decided the treaty's fate.

There were also special provisions governing voting in particular circumstances, first, where neither the Commission nor the Union minister for foreign affairs—the latter foreseen in the CT and not yet official—was the source of formal initiative. If, instead, one or some member states, acting in the Council or European Council, introduced a proposal, the qualified majority required is 72 percent of member states representing 65 percent of the total EU population. These specifications function in some areas of the CFSP and Justice and Home Affairs (JHA). Second, the CT aimed to reduce the opportunities for minorities to block initiatives by requiring that the blocking minority include at least four member states. Under the Nice system, three of the four largest states

(Germany, France, Italy, and the UK) could form a blocking minority. Third, for instances of very narrow qualified majorities, the Council would leave the discussion open (and not adopt the legislation) if 75 percent of the member states needed for a blocking minority (a minimum of four required) or 75 percent of the population necessary (a minimum of 35 percent of the total EU) requested the Council to do so. Additionally, replacement of a rotating six-month presidency with a two-and-a-half-year term was intended to "professionalize" the office and "facilitate consensual decisionmaking."[29] Some presidencies had become self-centered rather than focusing on EU achievement.

Some of the above proposals were scrapped, and some went back to the drawing board. Not all actors are displeased at the outcome. Some changes to the Nice arrangements had been fiercely opposed by Poland and Spain. Political elites, agricultural lobbies, and others angling for structural funding were not overly concerned by the failure of the CT and retention of the status quo. Even after both states had changes of government, there was continued dispute on the specifications of the double majority arrangements. Neither Spain nor Poland was content with a shift away from the Nice method to a simpler system.[30]

The situation after Nice (as before it) was one of overrepresentation, or malapportionment, in favor of small states. The absence of "allegiances to federation-wide political parties that might cut against pure regional self-seeking" indicates that the struggle over resources occurs between member states rather than having a transnational quality.[31] The introduction of the double majority would not have altered the strong linkage between national representation and redistribution. From the perspective of net payers with larger populations, above all Germany, the new voting system would have increased their weight in the Council. A presumed consequence is that the difference between payments and receipts for these net payers would decrease.

Despite the chorus urging a galvanizing of purpose, if the EU continues to require unanimity for any initiative to proceed, then "muddling through" will likely be a fairly accurate description of the next five or so years. Little else seems feasible under the present conditions. A consequence may be inability to respond to exigencies not yet apparent and potentially an unraveling of the entire project. If a more flexible system evolves, where there are clusters of sometimes overlapping mini-unions within the Union, then there are possibilities for differentiated progress. Logrolling and side payments will remain fundamental parts of the game.

Domestic Contexts

The EU has not been able to keep pace with some of the changes occurring around it. Divisions have hindered the reforms needed to enable a concerted and sustainable response to a panoply of demands. European initiatives must traverse a mélange of state "interests," sometimes the result of political egoism, or conceived in response to domestic lobbies or public opinion, and frequently expressed as disapproval of an actual or possible development. Sectoral interests pressure governments to maintain arrangements favorable to them. Differences in political and economic philosophy among national elites are also responsible for an inability to move forward on big issues or, if so, only in painstaking fashion and with the extraction of many quids pro quo.[32] Populations are disillusioned, because neither their own political systems nor that of the EU seems capable of solving persisting problems, above all unemployment and feeble or unsustained growth. Discontent was most apparent among some of the original six, rather than the designated "Euroskeptic," the UK, or the CEECs.[33] In Poland, the ascendancy of Jaroslaw and Lech Kaczyinski to prime minister and president, respectively, and their coalition with other nationalist parties, led to almost unmatched levels of antagonism between a member state's political leadership and the EU.[34]

The EU is hampered by the transference of domestic problems to intergovernmental forums. Individual histories, *mentalités,* and internal arrangements of nation-states, and the fact that there are twenty-seven of them, mean that finding solutions to variation in preferences is difficult. More members, especially larger states such as Turkey or Ukraine, might, as their advocates argue, invest the EU with more muscle.[35] It is also probable, however, that these states will place their interests first, increasing the chances of dissent and deadlock. Horse-trading and intergovernmental poker games are features of the EU political process and will be if the EU enlarges further still. Predictions of increased conflict appear justified, and intergovernmentalist precepts are confirmed when state executives are "able to employ a veto as a last resort."[36]

If there is tension between them, interests emerging at the national level override potential European interests, as a few examples indicate. Though the Commission is responsible for monitoring state aid, political leaderships will support industrial actors identified as important to the national economy. Robert Thomson, Jovanka Boerefijn, and Frans Stokman cite support in the UK for major art dealers and auction houses regarding resale rights for artists and of Germany moving from a position sympathetic to company takeovers to one that supported management autonomy in preventing it by not having to consult shareholders. After perceiving change in the EP's pro-autonomy stance, German industry lobbyists aiming to retain this protection shifted their focus to the Council and to German political actors. Subsequently, the German position in the Council changed to withdraw the support for shareholder consultation that Germany had initially favored.[37]

More critical is adherence to SGP rules, which curtail reflationary options and affect the scope for industrial policy. In the German case, the ironies are pervasive. The SGP and the ECB result from the Kohl government's insistence, supported by much of society, on "hard money" and concerns about *dirigiste* solutions to fiscal and social problems.[38] Although the ECB was designed to be independent to guarantee against a "political bank" favored by François Mitterrand and others in France, when the SPD-Green government got into budgetary difficulties, it shifted in that direction by ignoring the codified SGP terms. Germany exceeded the deficit target for three years (2003–2005). One measure introduced to meet SGP targets was a 3 percent rise in value-added tax to 19 percent, implemented by the succeeding government of Christian and Social Democrats.

A Constitution for Europe?

Speculation about a future European constitution has been under way for decades.[39] A related theoretical problem concerns the detaching of conceptions from previous models and understandings. One study outlined the problem this way:

> We started from the premise that a European constitution—or a Constitutional Charter, or Treaty—cannot and should not reproduce at the European level the constitutional logic of the nation-state in general, nor of any state in particular. At the same time—and this may be the fundamental tension afflicting this whole exercise—national political cultures constitute the fundamental historical and conceptual building blocks for constitutional thinking in the EU. National traditions, myth, practices, assumptions, collective likes and dislikes constrain and inspire in fundamental ways the designs of the Convention. Thus, while the EU should not become a "state writ large," in practice, the design of its institutions has been and continues to be inspired by "what we know."[40]

Can constitution building then advance European integration?[41] Whether a constitution is or is not established will be determined within and between member states rather than by nonstate actors. As a leading institutionalist notes, "In line with fusion theory, the Constitutional Treaty demonstrates that the EU is constructed by European states to serve their own objectives—in effect, not replacing but supporting them."[42] The process divulged that there was no real consistency of position by particular states, other than that they would place their own perceived interests first, regardless of (disingenuous) accusations by others that to do so undermined the greater European interest.[43]

The Convention was thought to be preceding a constitution's inevitable, if belated introduction. The discussion reached its zenith in 2002–2004. Enthusiasts of EU legal development perceived the momentum generated in support of a European constitution as confirming that (supranational) law was the propellant of integration. The CT would have provided a textual legitimacy and symbolic boost, relieving the burden of the Union's, as distinct from its member states', lack of democratic foundations. Stone Sweet's theory of European integration "focuses on specific causal relationships between three factors, or variables," which he terms "dyadic contracting, or social exchange," "triadic dispute resolution, or governance," and "normative structure, including law."[44] The CT's failure does not in itself refute this idea, but the outcome demonstrated that a normative design, "soft law," and informal networks or integrationist synergies are in certain critical instances no match for state or popular interest or anxiety politics. Even if the real targets of disapproval are domestic political actors, when the EU is not identified as a provider or sustainer, or is thought to be challenging particular or national interests, then it is unwanted.

Tony Blair's announcement that his government would hold a referendum on the CT left Chirac little room to maneuver. Chirac was immobilized by the weight of national and Gaullist tradition. Had they been in power, similar considerations would have compelled the French socialists and communists to also call a referendum. Because they were in parliamentary opposition, large sections of the left party elites and loyalist voters rejected the Chirac-supported CT. The justifications were linked to concerns about globalization and the reduced influence of France in an EU of twenty-five or more. These developments threatened the end of the French "social model" and an EU, or a Europe, constructed in the French style.[45]

The referendum discussion occurred against the background of intense presidential campaigning. Joachim Schild suggests "Chirac had a stronger focus on the 2007 election and the possibility of his renewed candidacy than on his responsibility as a European statesman in a constitutional ratification process that in any case contained more than enough risks."[46] Along with Gerhard Schröder, in domestic political terms then even more hapless, the French president tried to extract concessions from Blair on the enduring British budget rebate issue. Concomitantly, Chirac insisted that the CAP compromise reached with Schröder in October 2002 would remain. Intended to compensate French agricultural producers for rising competition, this arrangement had been linked to French support for Schröder's anti-US stand on Iraq during the German election campaign. Developments and interests from above (supra-EU) and below (domestic) converged to increase antireform pressures at the EU level.

Among other notable consequences of the French referendum was the liberal disbursement of blame. Chirac's initial responses were to sack his prime minister, Jean-Pierre Raffarin, and, joined by Schröder, to find fault with Blair. The leaders of the three most critical states for the entire EU project reverted to a standby tactic of national politicians to attribute negative outcomes in the EU context to others.[47] Desmond Dinan posits:

In whose interests were the leaders of Britain and France operating? Certainly in their own interests and those of their countries (at least as Blair and Chirac understood their countries' interests). What about the interest of the EU? That is very much a tertiary interest, although one that is bound up in the heads of state and governments' personal and national interests.[48]

According to Schild, the referendum results in France and the Netherlands represent the nadir of the "alternate penetration of European and national politics." The European crisis cannot, however, be reduced to a ratification failure of the CT. "Without a successful reconstruction of its national legitimation basis," writes Schild, "European politics can hardly be revitalized" while, conversely, the "strengthening of national legitimation resources is unthinkable without a recognizable change of political course at the European level." A factor in the French public's deliberations was EU enlargement: that which had occurred the previous year and others that may yet happen. Jacques Rupnik termed the CT referendum a delayed one on enlargement, toward which France had always been skeptical.[49] There are also high levels of opposition to Turkey's entry, a proposition that must also be put to the people. If the French, or anyone else, vote no, then Turkey cannot accede.[50] In the German case restrictions on referendums prevented a "Nein" to eastern enlargement being demonstrated there, as it would in regard to Turkey's EU membership.[51]

Schild notes that as "Euroscepticism grows in many EU member states, this type of French behavior could easily find adherents. French influence in the enlarged union was already receding before the referendum."[52] Afterward, Chirac issued a declaration in which he noted that "a period of difficulties and uncertainty" had opened "for Europe and for France."[53] The autumn 2005 riots that began in Parisian suburbs, and later spread to other parts of the country, were one indication. Those that followed in spring 2006 confirmed it again. These were further manifestations of France's socioeconomic and political malaise. The "brain of Europe" cannot hope to lead the EU forward when it is preoccupied with domestic disasters of this scale.

Conversely, the EU is being infused with more British influence, despite the alleged hostility of British governments and, even more so, publics, toward "Brussels" and most things continental. The recurring specter of a Franco-German attempt at domination of Europe is a cliché of the British media. Nonetheless, the relative success of the British economy during the Blair era, and the contemporaneous poor performance of the French and German economies, cannot be ignored. Despite traditional British suspicion of grand European designs, the Blair government supported the CT, introduced a large number of amendments to the draft, and "achieved all of its key demands," with the result that the CT "bore a strong British stamp."[54] If that was an example of British dilution of European unity, it could hardly be argued that other member states were doing much to the contrary.

Chirac's focus on Blair was also a diversion from France having "set a deep booby trap" against further enlargements by amending its constitution to ensure that they will have to be endorsed by national referendums.[55] What that represents is a "Luxembourg Compromise" by *volonté générale* (popular will). The rejection of the CT in the French referendum was an expression of "political effervescence," but not in support of the outcome favored in Brussels. Not all observers considered the endorsement of the CT a fait accompli. As the referendums drew closer, a number of scholars began to consider the options in the event of a rejection, the prospect of which became increasingly real.[56]

Table 3.1 combines the results of various surveys that give some indication of public opinion on the CT and potentially linked issues in the period leading up to the French and Dutch referendums. In these two countries, support for "the European Constitution" had fallen considerably in the year before May 2005. Negative views were also expressed on the 2004 enlargement. Ten percent of French and 15 percent of Dutch respondents were in favor of including any other countries that wished to join the EU. Forty percent of both French and Dutch respondents supported EU membership for Ukraine, compared with 48 percent and 51 percent against. Twenty-one percent of the

Table 3.1   Public Opinion on the Constitution and Related Issues (in percentage)

State	For/Against Constitution	For/Against 2004 Enlargement	Enlargement All-Some-None	For/Against Ukraine	For/Against Turkey	For/Against CT Ref. Results
Austria	41–36[a]	34–52	10–40–44	18–69	10–80	n/a
Belgium	71–20[a]	38–49	17–34–47	46–50	36–61	n/a
France	46–44	37–47	10–40–43	40–48	21–70	45–55
Germany	59–21[a]	28–56	11–44–40	30–64	21–74	n/a
Italy	Ratified	55–25	31–41–15	42–43	33–52	n/a
Luxembourg	50–28[a]	37–51	14–42–39	38–54	22–72	56–44
Netherlands	49–43	44–45	15–60–23	40–51	39–53	38–62
Sweden	38–30	54–37	35–24–27	61–28	50–40	Unsure
UK	31–30	31–40	25–34–28	45–35	45–37	Postponed
Czech Rep.	35–35	n/a	32–48–13	46–45	37–51	Postponed
Latvia	49–14[a]	n/a	30–44–16	62–23	36–44	n/a
Poland	54–20	n/a	41–45–6	76–15	54–31	Postponed
EU25	48–28	42–39[b]	23–42–25	45–41	35–52	n/a

Sources: Eurobarometer 61 (Brussels: European Commission, July 2004) and *Eurobarometer* 63 (Brussels: European Commission, September 2005).

Notes: Nineteen states of the EU25 had not ratified the CT at the time of the first survey. Spain, Italy, Hungary, Greece, Lithuania, and Slovenia had ratified it. a. Since ratified. b. EU15. By 2007 eighteen EU member states had ratified the CT. Those that had not were the Czech Republic, Denmark, France, Ireland, the Netherlands, Poland, Portugal, Sweden, and the United Kingdom.

French and 39 percent of the Dutch supported Turkey's membership. Seventy percent and 53 percent, respectively, were against. The actual referendum results were 45 to 55 percent against the CT in France and 38 to 62 percent against in the Netherlands. As all states have to ratify any constitution, the publics of France and the Netherlands will have to reverse their previous verdict, and those of the UK and others that may hold referendums will have to endorse it. There is no popular imprimatur for Turkey's, or as it appeared in 2005–2006, for Ukraine's and some others' aspirations to join the EU. In retrospect, it could be argued that the treaty rejection was an "unintended consequence" of the integration project; that when they signed the ECSC treaty and those that followed, neither member states nor institutions aimed at or even envisaged such an outcome.

If the CT referendums were a demonstration of people power, some policy fields remain the province of state executive control. Neither the EP nor even most national parliaments have any real sway over CFSP or ESDP. They can neither impel nor veto a particular direction. Intergovernmental developments in these fields will provide further evidence of how states aim to overcome obstructions. Despite the EU's legalistic features, when the governments of its most powerful member states have arrived at sufficiently common opinion and are still confronted by barriers in pushing through a consensus, such as the refusal of electorates to endorse what political elites had agreed, the governments have tried to avoid overt legal transgressions and to circumvent hurdles by delaying plans, creating an alternative route, or leaving the main task of favorable resolution up to the actor most affected. Examples might include the second Danish referendum on the Maastricht Treaty, the second Irish referendum on the Treaty of Nice, or having Turkey recognized as a candidate with which negotiations would be opened.

Overlapping legal and decisionmaking processes make the EU complicated and opaque for the ordinary citizen. The Nice Treaty enables numerous permutations of voting alliances among states. The CT would have extended majority voting but only marginally reduced these possibilities. Different levels of laws exist: primary, grounded in treaties; and secondary, based on Council decisions that allow a right of initiative for the Commission and consultation and formal acceptance by the EP. Until now there has been limited public debate on this form of legislating. In many areas, competencies that establish what level has authority are not clearly defined. Complaints about democratic legitimation and transparency proliferate. The CT proposed that the EU be given a "legal personality," as the EC possessed, which would make the EU a legally recognized international entity. European law would be superior to national law. However, this would only apply in those areas that had been agreed to by the member states and codified in a treaty. In areas where the member states had not granted the EU legal primacy, national law would retain its superior powers.

:oming Deadlock on the Constitutional Treaty

In many areas the Convention failed to do the time-consuming and detailed work required to arrive at and present coherent proposals in its draft CT. There was much speculation before the German EU presidency began in January 2007 that the German government would make a revitalization of the constitutional process one of its main aims. Several preconditions and political constellations set the framework for possible solutions. Janis Emmanouilidis proposed that a modest and pragmatic option would be to dispense with the grandiose title "Constitution" but retain the CT's core reform elements and modify the Nice Treaty accordingly. Beyond those ideas, the EU must renew itself by combining its preferences and values—at least those it can agree on—with an "ambitious yet realistic grand project." Europe's internal and external vulnerability is reason enough for this project to be in the field of security.[57]

Only two member states rejected the CT. Eighteen member states ratified the original. These eighteen states have a population of 274 million, or over 55 percent of the EU27. Those numbers suggest that opposition to the CT is outweighed by support for it. However, they are only part of the story. The absence of referendums on the CT in most states implies that a European demos remains elusive. The largest EU state, Germany, had no referendum and would not hold one. The second-largest, the UK, has neither held a referendum nor ratified the CT in Parliament. The same applies to the sixth-largest, Poland. The third-largest, France, rejected the CT. Several of those states that have ratified it did so without holding referendums. There has not been, and seemingly cannot be, a European vote by a European electorate.

Emmannouilidis listed five points of departure to be considered in any revival of a constitutional process. First, adhering to the original CT could lead to further deadlock. Under these conditions, France and the Netherlands would need to again present the draft CT to their publics in referendums. It may fail again, and there is also a possibility that it would be rejected in one or more of the other states that have not yet held referendums. Second, maintaining the situation existing after Nice would mean that the EU27 has to continue with institutions and procedures that were created for six founding members. Third, despite its deficits, the CT process has been a step forward for the enlarged EU. The EP has gained traction, and the EU has been further "profiled, personalized, and politicized." The progress that has been made should be preserved around a workable consensus. Fourth, unanimity is an unavoidable condition of any future solution. Unsound compromises may endanger the ratification process. Fifth, the origin of the constitutional crisis lies not only in the French and Dutch rejections. Broader and deeper issues of insufficient legitimacy, orientation, and trust in national and European politics are also responsible. From these bases, five possibilities for a revitalization of the constitutional process were identified:

1. *Nice plus: using existing EU law.* In principle it would be possible to change some EU procedures and regulations through intergovernmental agreements without recourse to treaties. The European Defence Agency, public meetings of the European Council, and application of the Solidarity Clause are among the examples of such changes. This method would reduce the transparency of the Union and soon reach political and legal barriers. The CT was a package deal that would be very difficult to disentangle and reassemble. This suboptimal possibility may yet be adopted, but is not considered to be a preference.

2. *Constitution minus and Constitution minus-minus.* The first variant would involve reformulating the CT, concentrating on those elements that were most disputed in an attempt to reach compromises. It could include chapters in the social and defense policy areas, some downsizing of the Commission, and areas of double majority voting. Other achievements of the original CT might be lost, and opponents could try to mobilize populations against the process and reduce the chances for ratification below those previously existing. The second variant would be to condense the CT and adjust the Nice Treaty. A less "emotion-laden" title such as "Basic Treaty" or "Basic Law" might be applied. This option would be less complex and its greater transparency might increase acceptance. Referendums in favor of the original need not be repeated. Opponents could argue that nothing fundamental had changed and that the implications of the treaty had not been reduced by fewer words. In addition, it would be difficult to achieve the compromises needed, implement them, and achieve all necessary ratifications before the next EP elections in 2009.

3. *Avant-garde or core Europe.* If the CT fails, with no resuscitation possible, a smaller group of states may attempt to take integration forward based on their own selective revision. Such a group might include the six founding members or those participating in EMU. There are problems with this scenario because potential members may find it difficult to exclude others and to build what would in practice be a breakaway neo-EU. Differentiated integration could also be discredited.

4. *Constitution plus and Constitution plus-plus.* Here the basic idea is to use appendices to the CT in order to enhance the probability of approval. These additional protocols could directly target objections, such as those related to the social dimension (or lack of it), as in France. Opponents of the CT could well interpret this as sleight of hand. It may also be counterproductive for states that have to approve any such treaty by public referendum. A more ambitious alternative, as proposed by the British member of the European Parliament, Andrew Duff, would be to leave Parts I and II of the CT unchanged but remove Part III (the Charter of Basic Rights) and deal with it as a separate document. A reorganization of Part III into economic, social, and environmental policy, enlargement, and the financial system would be undertaken, which would mean an

extension of treaty revision to include policy areas that state governments had proscribed the Convention of 2002–2003 from substantially amending for inclusion in its draft document. The problems with this approach are that it would require a major renegotiation of the original CT's content, and the member states would still be the gatekeepers. No outcome could be expected before the EP elections in 2009, the effects of substantial change are uncertain, and there is a danger of the proposed treaty being overloaded with content.

5. *Revision of Nice: Mini-treaty, core treaty, or reform.* This option aims to safeguard the substance of the CT by inserting its central elements in a "Treaty on the Reform of the Nice Treaty." It would mean reverting to more traditional patterns of EU development and building on existing treaties. Essential components and areas of possible compromises have to be identified. Such an approach could introduce basic innovations into the CT. Politically, this approach has the advantage that results could be negotiated through package deals in a foreseeable timeframe. Ratification would probably be easier because an intergovernmental revision would reduce pressure for public referendums.[58] That, however, leads back to the problem of a missing European demos and charges of an elitist EU, with governments afraid to put decisions to the people.

Before the June 2007 European Council summit it was not clear which of these options, if any, was most likely. Option five appeared a possibility as the new French president, Nicolas Sarkozy, preferred it and it was thought that the British, Poles, and Czechs would probably only agree to a minimum compromise. With the "Reform Treaty" package, the German presidency has provided a road map with suggestions for a way forward at the end of its term. After the presidential elections in France and a transfer of leadership from Tony Blair to Gordon Brown in the UK, political leadership in these major member states can give more attention to the EU.

In terms of a revived constitutional process, the outcome of the June 2007 summit is a combination of Options 1, 2, and 5 outlined above. "Reform Treaty" has become the popular descriptor for a text-in-process that will be debated during the Portuguese presidency and then has to be approved at another summit. It will then have to undergo a ratification process by national parliaments in 2008 and 2009. No further referendums are needed, although one aim is to have the Reform Treaty accepted before the EP elections in mid-2009 in order to promote public acceptance. The June 2007 compromise, which is subject to further negotiation, consists of the following main points:

- The word "constitution" has been dropped and the attempt to consolidate all existing treaties into one has been abandoned. The legal foundations of the Union will be fixed in two treaties: one on the European Union and another on the operating principles of the EU.

- Symbols such as an EU flag and an EU hymn will not be included in any legal document after the Netherlands and the UK opposed that. Symbols could, however, be used depending on the position of the member state.
- Reference to "free and undistorted competition" has been eliminated following demands by France.
- Majority voting will be extended to various areas but the principle of "double majority" (55 percent of states and 65 percent of the population) will be postponed until 2014 with a transitional period until 2017. The possibility of a simplified procedure (if there is no unanimity) for enhanced cooperation will be extended to areas of Justice and Home Affairs. The UK and Ireland will have an opt-out in this case.
- Possibilities for coordinated action on national security issues will be extended.
- Some progress has been made on resolving potential disputes in the area of social security.
- A special protocol enables action by the Commission to defend the internal market.
- A clearer definition of the relative competencies of the Union and the member states is envisaged.
- The Copenhagen criteria for enlargement are explicit in the Reform Treaty.
- Better coordination of energy policy and combating climate change are mentioned.
- A "high representative for foreign and security policy" will combine the existing positions of the EU Commissioner for External Relations and the High Representative for the CFSP. There will not be an office of "EU foreign minister."
- The European Council will be governed for two years by a president (elected with a qualified majority by the Council). Normal meetings of the Council of Ministers will still be headed by a rotating presidency.
- The Charter of Human Rights, which was passed in 2000, will become legally binding, with an exception for the UK. The charter is not part of the proposed Reform Treaty but a reference is made to it in that treaty.
- As was advocated by the Netherlands, national parliaments have been given more controlling rights concerning legal initiatives of the European Commission, which has to review its proposals if more than the half of the national parliaments demand it. It may mean the Commission has to rescind particular initiatives.[59]

As this process continues, delinking the Reform Treaty from other complicated issues would be advantageous. In 2009, EP elections will be held. A midterm review of EU policies and the financial system must occur. The UK will press for further reforms. Member states may individually recognize that it is preferable to find a solution and enable a better-functioning Union sooner rather than later. Much of the old CT will find its way into whatever the twenty-seven member states can agree on. But this will be the result of compromises that dilute what the avant-garde prefers. Most observers agree that a fundamental redefinition of the EU is necessary for it to cope with the challenges of the twenty-first century. Yet already Poland, with tacit support from some other states, has succeeded in pushing several years into the future the date when the reforms that have been preliminarily concurred on can be practically realized.

Conclusion

There may be a "Brussels consensus" of institutional officials, pro-federalist politicians, and legal and academic advocates of supranational integration. The political heart and viscera of the EU, however, is in its member states and electorates, not in the Brussels, Luxembourg, or Strasbourg institutions.

Several factors or circumstances that enabled the EU, or more so its fore-runners, to proceed with an agenda of intensifying cooperation for mutual benefit are either at least temporarily missing or have unraveled. At the forefront was the sustained absence of economic growth, most critically in core member states. Indirectly it has affected the closeness and efficacy of major dyads, particularly the Franco-German partnership. Prolonged high unemployment and anemic growth rates, coupled with and being partly responsible for political weakness, depressed the relationship's capacity for initiative and innovation. Despite the frequent media presentation of amity by Chirac and Schröder (now replaced by Sarkozy and Merkel), Franco-German relations on occasion descended to bitter antagonism. The apparent revival in response to the US-UK invasion of Saddam Hussein's Iraq should be viewed in this context. The Franco-German quarrel at Nice required external "events" to force them back together.[60]

Many commentators considered that Chirac, and the French political elite in general, approached the diplomatic clash with the Anglo-Saxons as an opportunity to assert France's independence and status globally and simultaneously to impress itself as the Franco-German tandem's senior partner in foreign policy and security issues. Anxious to avoid being isolated from all of Germany's major partners, the Schröder and Joschka Fischer government, which had exploited a possible conflict with Saddam for electoral purposes, then conceded the global stage to the UNSC permanent member, France.[61] The French pushed the German leadership's position in this forum, but only after a favorable deal for France on the CAP had been sealed. That was far from acceptable to the UK, which refused to rescind its budget rebate.

The more the EU achieves, the more is expected of it; when it does not achieve, there are expectations that it improve. Pressure has been placed on it to play the role of a "balancer" to the United States: a more civil and social actor, oriented toward human security issues and upholding the rule of law. That is the type of global player that many within and outside the EU are hoping it will be. Even if the CT had been passed, it was no panacea. The outcome confirms an unsatisfactory status quo. EU rules, having been agreed on by member states, can and do influence the national context, but their effects can be limited as states search for loopholes and deploy other tactics to avoid compliance. The EU's mass of regulation does not necessarily enable it to cope with unregulated environments, those for which there are no effective structures, institutions, offices, programs, or constitutions.

Notes

1. Cf. Robert Ladrech, "The Europeanization of Domestic Politics and Institutions: The Case of France," *Journal of Common Market Studies* 32, no. 1 (1994); Kevin Featherstone and Claudio Radaelli, eds., *The Politics of Europeanisation* (Oxford: Oxford University Press, 2003); Alec Stone Sweet, Wayne Sandholtz, and Neil Fligstein, eds., *The Institutionalization of Europe* (Oxford: Oxford University Press, 2001); Wayne Sandholtz and Alec Stone Sweet, eds., *European Integration and Supranational Governance* (Oxford: Oxford University Press, 1998); Antje Wiener and Thomas Diez, eds., *European Integration Theory* (Oxford: Oxford University Press, 2004); Frank Schimmelfennig and Ulrich Sedelmeier, eds., *The Europeanization of Central and Eastern Europe* (Ithaca: Cornell University Press, 2005); Simon Bulmer and Claudio Radaelli, "The Europeanisation of National Policy?" *Queen's Papers on Europeanisation,* no. 1 (Belfast: Queens University, 2004).

2. Cf. Robert Thomson and Madeline Holsi, "Who Has Power in the EU? The Commission, Council and Parliament in Legislative Decision-making," *Journal of Common Market Studies* 44, no. 2 (2006): 391–417.

3. Simon Bulmer, "Domestic Politics and European Community Policy-Making," *Journal of Common Market Studies* 21, no. 4 (1983): 349–363.

4. Mark Pollack, *The Engines of Integration: Delegation, Agency, and Agenda Setting in the European Union* (Oxford: Oxford University Press, 2003).

5. Bulmer and Radaelli, "The Europeanisation of National Policy?" 3; Bridget Laffan, "The European Polity: A Union of Normative, Regulatory and Cognitive Pillars," *Journal of European Public Policy* 8, no. 5 (2001): 709–727.

6. Amitai Etzioni, "The Community Deficit," *Journal of Common Market Studies* 45, no. 1 (2007): 23–42; cf. Stephen Wood, *Germany, Europe and the Persistence of Nations: Transformation, Interests and Identity, 1989–1996* (Aldershot: Ashgate, 1998).

7. Cf. Thomas Risse, "A European Identity: Europeanization and the Evolution of Nation-State Identities," in Maria Green Cowles, James Caporasa, and Thomas Risse, eds., *Transforming Europe: Europeanization and Domestic Change* (Ithaca, NY: Cornell University Press, 2001): 198–216.

8. A good examination of the EU's institutions and their functions and interactions is John Peterson and Michael Shackleton, eds. *The Institutions of the European Union* (Oxford: Oxford University Press, 2006).

9. Cf. Wolfgang Wessels, "An Ever Closer Fusion? A Dynamic Macropolitical View of the Integration Process," *Journal of Common Market Studies* 35, no. 2 (1997): 269–299; Wolfgang Wessels, "Keynote Article: The Constitutional Treaty—Three Readings from a Fusion Perspective," *Journal of Common Market Studies* 45 (Annual Review) (2005): 11–36; James March and Johan Olsen, "The Institutional Dynamics of International Political Orders," *International Organization* 52, no. 4 (1998): 943–969.

10. Johannes Lindner and Berthold Rittberger, "The Creation, Interpretation, and Contestation of Institutions: Revisiting Historical Institutionalism," *Journal of Common Market Studies* 41, no. 3 (2003): 445–473.

11. Thomas Christiansen argues interinstitutional relations are becoming more coherent, while intrainstitutional politics have led to fragmentation. "Intra-institutional Politics and Inter-Institutional Relations in the EU: Towards Coherent Governance?" *Journal of European Public Policy* 8, no. 5 (2001): 747–769.

12. George Tsebelis and Geoffrey Garrett, "The Institutional Foundations of Intergovernmentalism and Supranationalism in the European Union," *International Organization* 55, no. 2 (2001): 357–390.

13. Author interview, Directorate-General for External Affairs, European Commission, Brussels, April 2003.

14. Cf. Alec Stone Sweet, *The Judicial Construction of Europe* (Oxford: Oxford University Press, 2004), 81–82.

15. Patricia Sherrington, *The Council of Ministers: Political Authority in the European Union* (London: Pinter, 2000). Cf. Beate Kohler-Koch and Rainer Eising, eds., *The Transformation of Governance in the European Union* (London: Routledge, 1999); Liesbeth Hooghe and Gary Marks, *Multilevel Governance and European Integration* (Lanham: Rowman and Littlefield, 2001); Nick Bernard, *Multilevel Governance in the European Union* (New York: Aspen, 2004).

16. Ben Crum, "Legislative-Executive Relations in the EU," *Journal of Common Market Studies* 41, no. 3 (2003): 375–395.

17. The European Council is the term given to official gatherings of the heads of EU states and governments—the French president is head of state not of government but always attends as does the French prime minister who is head of government. The European Council meets twice per year apart from extraordinary meetings. The Council of Ministers are, across a range of policy areas, the delegated representatives of the heads of states and governments. They are in Brussels on a more permanent basis and vote there on behalf of their governments. Fuad Aleskerov, Gamze Avic, Viatcheslav Iakouba, and Z. Umut Türüm, "European Union Enlargement: Power Distribution Implications of the New Institutional Arrangements," *European Journal of Political Research* 41, no. 3 (2002): 379–394; Matti Wiberg, *New Winners and Old Losers: A Priori Voting Power in the EU25,* Discussion Paper C149 (Bonn: ZEI, 2005); Alex Moberg, "The Nice Treaty and Voting Rules in the Council," *Journal of Common Market Studies* 40, no. 2 (2002): 259–282.

18. Mikko Mattila, "Contested Decisions: Empirical Analysis of Voting in the European Council of Ministers," *European Journal of Political Research* 43, no. 1 (2004): 29–50; Simon Hix, "Dimensions and Alignments in European Union Politics: Cognitive Constraints and Partisan Responses," *European Journal of Political Research* 35, no. 1 (1999): 69–106.

19. Simon Hix and Christophe Crombez, "Extracting Ideal Point Preferences from Actors" Preferences in the EU Constitutional Negotiations," *European Union Politics* 6, no. 3 (2005): 353–376.

20. Cf. Christian Lesquesne, *Paris-Bruxelles: Comment se fait la politique européene de la France* (Paris: Presses de la Fondation nationale des Sciences Politiques, 1993).

21. Desmond Dinan, "Governance and New Institutions: A New Constitution and a New Commission," *Journal of Common Market Studies* 45 (2005): 50.

22. Andrew Moravscik, "Preferences and Power in the European Community: A Liberal Intergovernmentalist Approach," *Journal of Common Market Studies* 33, no. 4 (1993): 473–519; Moravcsik, *The Choice for Europe;* Moravscik, "Negotiating the Single European Act"; Hoffmann, *The European Sisyphus;* Milward, *The European Rescue.*

23. Stone Sweet, *The Judicial Construction of Europe,* 29, fn. 14.

24. The European Convention, also called the Convention on the Future of Europe, was a forum established by the Laeken Declaration in December 2001. The delegates comprised representatives of the then 15 member states, the then 13 candidate states, the national parliaments, the European Parliament, and the Commission. Observers were also present at the regular meetings. The chairman of the Convention, as it came to be generally known, was former French president Valéry Giscard d'Estaing. The main purpose of the Convention was to "debate the future of Europe." A Secretariat was attached to the Convention to assist it in its work. In June 2003, after months of debate and collation of submissions and other material, the Convention presented a Draft Constitution for Europe for consideration by the member states. At this stage the document had no binding legal force. After negotiation and amendments, a Constitutional Treaty was signed by the member states in Rome in October 2004. It was ratified by the parliaments of some member states and put to referendums by some member state governments. It was rejected by the French and Dutch electorates in referendums in 2005. For a lively and insightful narrative of the European Convention and Constitutional Treaty process and associated politics, see Desmond Dinan, "Governance and Institutions: The Convention and the Intergovernmental Conference," *Journal of Common Market Studies* 42 (2004): 27–42. Other interesting and useful accounts include Peter Norman, *The Accidental Constitution: The Story of the European Convention* (Brussels: EuroComment, 2003), Clive Church and David Phinnemore, *Understanding the European Constitution: An Introduction to the EU Constitutional Treaty* (London: Routledge, 2006), and Jean-Claude Piris, *The Constitution for Europe: A Legal Analysis* (Cambridge: Cambridge University Press, 2006).

25. See Bulmer and Radaelli, "The Europeanisation of National Policy?" 11–13.

26. Joschka Fischer, "Vom Staatenbund zur Föderation—Gedanken über die Finalität der europäische Integration," speech at the Humboldt University, Berlin, 12 May 2000.

27. Rosamond, *Theories of European Integration,* 112.

28. Mattila, "Contested Decisions," 30.

29. Wessels, "Keynote Article," 22.

30. David Cameron, "The Stalemate in the Constitutional IGC over the Definition of a Qualified Majority," *European Union Politics* 5, no. 3 (2004): 373–391.

31. Jonathon Rodden, "Strength in Numbers? Representation and Redistribution in the European Union," *European Union Politics* 3, no. 2 (2002): 151–175.

32. Robert Thomson, Jovanka Boerefijn, and Frans Stokman, "Actor Alignments in European Union Decision Making," *European Journal of Political Research* 43, no. 2 (2004): 237–261.

33. Cf. *Eurobarometer* 63, Brussels, CEC, September 2005.

34. Joana Radzyner, "Zurück in die Zukunft: Polens Weg in die IV. Republik," *Europäische Rundschau* 34, no. 2 (2006): 39–47.

35. Senem Aydin and E. Fuat Keyman, *European Integration and the Transformation of Turkish Democracy,* EU-Turkey WP 2 (Brussels: CEPS, 2004); Kirsty Hughes, *Turkey and the European Union: Just Another Enlargement? Exploring*

the Implications of Turkish Accession, Friends of Europe Working Paper, Brussels, 2004); "Why Europe Must Say Yes to Turkey," *Economist,* 18 September 2004, 13; M. Molkhanov, "Ukraine and the European Union: A Perennial Neighbour?" *Journal of European Integration* 26, no. 4 (2004): 451–473; Helmut Kurth and Iris Kempe, eds., *Presidential Election and Orange Revolution: Implications for Ukraine's Transition* (Kiev: Zapovit, 2005).

36. Gerald Schneider, "The Limits of Self-Reform: Institution Building in the European Union," *European Journal of International Relations* 1, no. 1 (1995): 59–86.

37. Thomson, Boerefijn, and Stokman, "Actor Alignments."

38. *Dirigiste* is a French adjective that translates as directed or guided. It is widely understood as referring to statist direction of or intervention in the economy, a French *specialité.*

39. Alec Stone Sweet, "What Is a Supranational Constitution? An Essay in International Relations Theory," *Review of Politics* 56, no. 3 (1994): 441–474; Frank Vibert, *Europe: A Constitution for the Millennium* (Aldershot: Dartmouth, 1995).

40. Kalypso Nicolaides and Stephen Weatherill, "Introduction," in Kalypso Nicolaides and Stephen Weatherill, eds., *Whose Europe? National Models and the Construction of the European Union* (Oxford: Oxford University Press, 2003): 5–27.

41. Hungdah Su, "Can Constitution-Building Advance European Integration? A Three-Pillared Institutional Analysis," *Journal of European Integration* 26, no. 4 (2004): 353–378.

42. Wessels, "Keynote Article," 13–14.

43. Cameron, "The Stalemate in the Constitutional IGC."

44. Stone Sweet, *Judicial Construction of Europe,* 50.

45. Cf. Heinz Kleger, "Erweiterung ohne Vertiefung: vom Konvent zur Ratifizierungskrise," *Welt Trends* 50 (Spring 2006): 11–26; Steven Kramer, "The End of French Europe?" *Foreign Affairs* 85, no. 4 (2006): 126–138; Ulla Holm, "The French Garden Is No Longer What It Used to Be," in Knut Erik Jørgensen, ed., *Reflective Approaches to European Governance* (London: Macmillan, 1997), 128–145.

46. Joachim Schild, "Ein Sieg der Angst: Das gescheiterte französiche Verfassungsreferendum," *Integration* 28, no. 3 (2005): 189.

47. "Europe Meltdown," *Weekend Australian,* 18–19 June 2005, 23.

48. Dinan, "Governance and New Institutions," 49.

49. Schild, "Ein Sieg der Angst."

50. Steve Wood and Wolfgang Quaisser, "Turkey's Road to the EU: Political Dynamics, Strategic Context, and Implications for Europe," *European Foreign Affairs Review* 10, no. 2 (2005): 147–173.

51. Cf. Stephen Wood, "Germany and the Eastern Enlargement of the EU: Political Elites, Public Opinion, and Democratic Processes," *Journal of European Integration* 24, no. 1 (2002): 23–38.

52. Schild, "Ein Sieg der Angst."

53. Jacques Chirac, "Déclaration aux Français sur le changement de gouvernement," speech given in Paris, 31 May 2005.

54. Dinan, "Governance and New Institutions," 46.

55. *Economist,* "The End of Enlargement?" 16–22 July 2005, 50.

56. Jürgen Bast, "The Constitutional Treaty as a Reflexive Constitution," *German Law Journal* 6, no. 11 (2005): 1433–1452; Jörg Monar, "Optionen für den Ernstfall: Auswege aus einer möglichen Ratifizierzungkrise des Verfassungsvertrags," *Integration* 28, no. 1 (2005): 16–32; Bettina Thalmaier, *Optionen für einen Plan-B im Falle des Scheiterns der Ratifikation des Verfassungsvertrags,* WP (München: CAP, 2005); Janis Emmanouilidis and Bettina Thalmaier, "2005: Non, Nee, Ne, Nie oder

Non: Konsequenzen, Optionen, und Empfehlungen im Falle einer Ablehnung der Verfassung," *EU-Reform-Spotlight* 3 (München: CAP, 2005).

57. Based on Janis Emmanouilidis, "Die Zeit der Entscheidung: Optionen, Erfolgsvoraussetzungen und Fahrplan für ein neues Primärrecht," *CAP Analyse*, no. 1 (Munich: CAP, 2007): 5–17.

58. Emmanouilidis, "Die Zeit der Entscheidung."

59. "Was kommt nun?" *Frankfurter Allegemeine Zeitung* (Sonntag) 24 June 2007, 3; Sarah Seeger and Janis Emmanouilidis, "Die Reform nimmt Gestalt an. Analyse und Bewertung des EU-Verfassungsgipfels," in *Bilanz der deutschen EU-Ratspräsidentschaft, Analyse und Bewertung des Centrums für angewandte Politikforschung, CAP Analyse* no. 6 (July 2007): 6–12.

60. Cf. Kaare Dahl Martensen, "The End of the Affair? Germany's Relationship with France," *German Politics* 14, no. 4 (2005): 401–416.

61. "Gerhard Schröder als Anhängsel Chiracs," *Neue Zürcher Zeitung,* 26 February 2003, 3.

4

Key Policy Areas: Developments, Reforms, and Resistance

The 2004, 2007, and potential further enlargements have called the EU's operational capacities into question. Partial or temporary solutions have been found, but central problems remain. Acceptance of the CT would not have led to a profound resolution and nor will the adoption of its diluted substitute treaty; the visions of individual member states are too different, and institutional reform is not enough to enable the enlarged EU to function effectively. Large-scale policy and budget changes are also required, which will affect the means and extent of interest equalization and thereby the internal balancing act of the EU club. Technical and political dimensions will either be compatible with or clash with integration concepts that are most influential in each state. Beyond traditional areas of agriculture and regionalism, internal security, the environment, and energy have risen steeply in importance. The complexity of these policy fields will exacerbate difficulties in setting or fulfilling EU priorities. A broad consensus has developed in environmental affairs as member states and societies have arrived at similar interpretations of threats and requirements. Some differences will emerge. Energy has become a strategic issue of great magnitude, though one in which preferences are less closely aligned. There is a strong case for resources to be shifted from the CAP and allocated to energy and environmental goals.

Voting Power and Funding Distribution

About 80 percent of EU funding flows into two major policy fields: agricultural and regional. The political bargaining process is focused on or otherwise linked to the concrete design of these policies, which in some ways overlap. The CAP's market intervention follows directly from EU regulations, whereas regional policy is more subject to discretionary political decisions. It is conducted through programs that specify objectives, duration, and resources. Both policy fields, and the whole EU budget, are strongly influenced by the voting power of member states. Net payers worry that the combined weight of receiver, or cohesion, countries—those in which most or all regions have incomes of 90 percent or less than the EU average—has risen significantly with enlargement. Applying the Penrose-Banzhaf Index to Council voting indicates that in only one of 2,500 permutations would Germany, with its sizable population, be in a better position as a result of the Nice Treaty.[1] There is a massive discrepancy between the funding provided by net payers and the voting power they wield. Under the Nice system, twenty-seven or more members reduce the likelihood of assembling the qualified majorities needed to make important decisions, and the threat of paralysis emerges.[2]

As Table 4.1 indicates, based on the estimates in the Commission's proposal to the Council of July 2004,[3] net payer states in the EU27 (the Netherlands, Germany, Sweden, Italy, Austria, Finland, Cyprus, Denmark, UK, Finland) would constitute an estimated 62.8 percent of the total EU population. This 62.8 percent would contribute about 77 percent of the total EU budget if we apply a measure whereby each member state's contributions to the EU correspond to each member state's GDP. Apart from some distortion caused by the British rebate, this is a fairly accurate gauge. However, in Council decisionmaking rounds, net payer states dispose of only 48.4 percent of voting power, based on what was adopted in the Nice Treaty, 46.7 percent according to the Banzhaf Index, and 55.5 percent of EP seats. The discrepancy is especially great for the largest contributors, the Netherlands, Germany, and Sweden. Although in an EU of twenty-seven members, a qualified majority of 73.9 percent of votes and a single majority of fourteen states are needed to approve a proposal, net receiver countries could conceivably exploit the system to acquire higher levels of funding. Bargaining processes imply compromises and net receivers comprise seventeen member states with 51.6 percent of votes and over 37 percent of the EU population, more than enough to block the voting preferences of the combined net payers. For the net payers, a form of safeguard clause ensures that a decision in the Council also represents a majority of the EU population.[4]

The states we term high net payers (Germany, the Netherlands, and Sweden) contribute more than 0.4 percent of their GNIs. Medium net payers (Austria, Cyprus, Denmark, France, Italy, Finland, and the UK) contribute between 0.2 percent and 0.39 percent. Medium net recipients receive up to 2.2 percent of their GNIs. This group includes Belgium, Spain, Ireland, Malta, Slovenia, Greece, and Portugal. High net recipients (the Czech Republic, Slovak Republic, Hungary, Latvia, Lithuania, Estonia, Romania, Bulgaria, and Luxembourg) receive more than 3 percent and up to 5.8 percent of their GNIs. Luxembourg's inclusion in this group is one perverse outcome of the EU system. It is the richest country per capita in the EU and is also a high net

Table 4.1   Major Indicators and Voting Power in the EU27 (in percentages)

Groups of Countries (according to their projected budgetary position in the financial period 2008–2013)	Population (2007)	EU's GDP (2007)	Nice Treaty Votes	Banzhaf Nice Treaty	European Parliament Seats	Number of States
High net payers (between 0.4% and 0.56% of their GNI)	34.1	39.6	23.5	22.5	29.2	4
Medium net payers (between 0.2% and 0.39% of their GNI)	28.7	37.5	24.9	24.2	26.3	6
Low to medium net recipients (between 0.2% and 2.2% of their GNI)	16.3	16.2	22.3	22.9	19.0	7
High net recipients (between 3% and 5.8% of their GNI)	20.9	6.7	29.3	30.4	25.5	10

Notes: The classification of different groups follows the Commission's calculation of the net position of EU member countries according to the current system of "own resources" provided in, Council of the European Union, Interinstitutional File: 2004/0170 (CNS) 2004/0171 (CNS), 11741/04 "Proposal from the Commission from 22 July 2004. Subject: Proposal for a Council Decision on the System of the European Communities' Own Resources," Brussels, 27 July 2004, available at http://register.consilium.eu.int/pdf/en/04/st11/st11741.en04.pdf. The budgetary calculations of the EU are based on Gross National Income (GNI). Economic potential is properly reflected in the Gross Domestic Product (GDP). The GDP and population shares are calculated from European Commission, Directorate-General for Economic and Financial Affairs, *European Economy,* Statistical Annex, Spring 2007, available at http://ec.europa.eu/dgs/economy_finance/index_en.htm; the shares of the Nice votes and EP seats are calculated following the *Official Journal of the European Union* "The Nice Treaty, Consolidated Version" (Document: C 321, E/136) 29 December 2006, Article 2005, available at http://eurlex.europa.eu/LexUriServ/site/en/oj/2006/ce321/ce32120061229en00010331.pdf. The Penrose-Banzhaf Index measures the power of each member in a voting system (e.g., a party in a parliament or a state in a confederation). The index accounts for not only the raw weight of each member but its capacity to participate in coalitions that can arrive at or block various outcomes. Group shares are the aggregate of voting weights for each country in the group. See Werner Kirsch, "Abstimmungsverfahren im Rat" available at http://www.ruhr-uni-bochum.de/mathphys/politik/eu/eu27.html.

recipient from the EU budget because a substantial share of the EU's bureaucracy is located there.

A major motivation behind the CT process was the desire of political and bureaucratic elites—in, above all, the original six member states, the Commission, and the EP—to avoid a political paralysis of the extended EU. The simplified voting method that the CT contained would have reduced the possibilities for building blocking minorities, especially by smaller member states. It was the reason why Poland blocked the revised and reduced treaty in Brussels in June 2007.[5] The Polish proposed alternative voting method was a square root approach, whereby voting weights would be based on the square root of each state's population.[6] This was rejected by the other member states as being too complicated. The compromise that the Polish government accepted included the CT's double majority voting system of 55 percent of the member states and 65 percent of the EU's population to pass a decision, but with a delayed date of implementation.[7] Behind a cover of some bizarre behavior and demands on the part of the Polish leadership at the June 2007 summit, other states parleyed their own particular concessions into or out of a preliminary text for a new "Reform Treaty."[8] Even if a "Reform Treaty" is adopted in 2009, which is not guaranteed, the new voting rules will not come into force until 2017, after the financial perspective for 2014 and beyond has been negotiated. Clearly financial issues are central in member states' deliberations on a revised EU voting system.

The danger of additional cost explosions, meanwhile, is mitigated by the overall limits of spending set in the multi-annual financial perspective, which has to be decided unanimously. Receiver countries cannot, therefore, overrule net payer countries. It is nonetheless a critical point that EU policies resulted from political compromise. Agricultural policy emerged as a concession to French and German farmers, so that they would support European integration in the first place. Historical, cultural, familial, and political reasons have sustained agricultural subsidization since. Regional policy was initiated by the demands of the UK and Ireland when they entered the Union. These policies were extended generously when southern countries joined in the 1980s. The EU's Carolingian core, especially West Germany, was then better equipped to fund them. Each phase of enlargement increases pressures and expenses. The design and detail of these policies became antiquated in the 1990s at the latest. In this form they hinder EU goals in and responses to the twenty-first century.[9]

The CAP

There is a fairly wide consensus among economists, political scientists, most political actors, and knowledgeable everyday consumers that the CAP is too costly and leads to an inefficient allocation of resources. A *Eurobarometer* survey in 2005 reported that 36 percent of respondents considered that ensuring "stable and adequate incomes for farmers" should be one of the CAP's three main priorities. Greece, with 61 percent, returned the highest score. Poland was second with 49 percent. Sixty-six percent supported a shift away from price subsidies and toward direct payments (income subsidies). There was no question on whether the CAP should be retained or abolished.[10] Subsidies comprise, on average, around 90 percent of pre-tax income for farmers, though large variations occur. They tend to benefit bigger producers, keep marginal farmers in production, and promote overproduction. One result is that EU surpluses are either destroyed or sold on the world market at prices below production costs. Dumping ignites frictions among EU members and between the EU and other states and trade blocs. Intensive agricultural production has also required copious amounts of fertilizers and pesticides, some of which are detrimental to flora, fauna, soil, and water systems.

Despite its excesses and deficiencies, the CAP has proven remarkably resistant to attempts at substantial reform. Although it had declined from previous heights of more than 70 percent, over 42 percent of the EU budget was still spent on funding the CAP in 2004. Agenda 2000 reduced funds for price support, while placing more emphasis on direct income support, but a tendency for market distortions persists. The Berlin summit in March 1999 did not provide expenditures for direct payments to the CEECs' farmers in its financial plan. As negotiations on accession to the EU proceeded, however, a phased integration of these farmers into the direct income scheme was initiated. It began with 25 percent of total potential financial transfers, as foreseen by existing CAP rules and relevant commitments in the budget, and will increase until 2013, when it reaches the maximum amount. As the benefits flowing to CEEC farmers increase, CAP reforms should aim at unfettered market prices for agricultural products.

One step toward real reform was made by gradually delinking direct payments from the productive capacity of farmers, which provided room for reducing subsidies in the medium and long term and, ostensibly, should assist WTO negotiations. The EU also agreed to alter the sugar market according to WTO demands. These measures assisted the incorporation of the CEECs' agriculture into the income support system. Enlargement has forced a reduction in price and export subsidies and partial replacement through the extension of financial assistance to promote structural changes in agriculture and rural development. That represents a move in the right direction. Strategies of this kind make more economic sense than sustaining marginal farmers. A more far-reaching reform would shift emphasis onto member states to decide the extent to which each supports the national farm sector, depending on collective social, economic, and ecological preferences. The CAP would be partially renationalized, but supervision of competition rules and income support schemes would remain a Commission competency. Firm resistance, before all from France, has confronted proposals for any such reform course. The French position might gradually change as its net financial position in the agricultural budget will worsen. New players, like Poland, might obstruct major alterations to the system because they are substantial net receivers.

The international context of CAP policy has changed substantially, and the General Agreement on Tariffs and Trade (GATT) Uruguay Round and WTO Doha Round intensified pressures for agricultural reforms. Carsten Daugbjerg and Alan Swinbank argue that these developments are not sufficient to explain the concrete outcomes of the MacSharry, Fischler, and Agenda 2000 reforms. The specific institutional setting is also responsible. The Council of Agricultural Ministers (CoAM) presided over the more extensive reforms (MacSharry and Fischler) despite being closely linked to farm lobbies. The European Council determined the more limited changes of Agenda 2000. The results of European Council negotiations may be explained by CAP reform being subordinated to the need for broader political agreements on a wider range of sensitive questions. There are occasionally incentives and opportunities for CoAM to pass final decisions on to the European Council in order to exculpate themselves from unpopular outcomes. If CAP reform is decided upon, as far as is possible, as a separate issue, the context, process, incentives, and results change.[11]

In the early 1990s, a bond scheme that could serve to dismantle direct payments was proposed by Danish Agriculture Minister Laurits Toernaes. According to Daugbjerg his idea was too "radical," though he suggests it may have initiated a "paradigm shift" that received further impetus with the MacSharry reform.[12] Daugbjerg and Swinbank examined the case for a bond scheme and outlined procedures for phasing out direct payments. Bonds would be issued to farmers as payments and be "completely decoupled from production." The scheme "maintains the principle of compensating farmers" but offers them and rural landowners options, including the acceptance and selling of bonds to investors. Because such financing would come from the private sector, member states could reduce the amounts of public money that they contribute to the CAP budget. This method would also break the "lock-in effect" of the CAP.[13]

There is no lack of innovative concepts for improving EU agricultural policy. What has been lacking is the political will to implement them. France is a central player in the wrangling. As Table 4.2 shows, between 1995 and 1999, France had a positive annual balance in CAP funds of about €1.9 billion (0.16 percent of GDP). By comparison, Germany had a negative balance of €5.3 billion (0.27 percent of GDP). France recognized that it would become a substantial net payer if enlargement costs, meaning the extension of full CAP funding to CEECs, were excessive. Yet if a larger portion of agricultural support is nationally co-financed, France is likely to lose relatively more, while Germany and some others gain. France might be willing to acquiesce if it is

Table 4.2 Financial Position of Selected EU States in the CAP[a]

	Net "Contribution to Own Resources"[b]		Net "Contribution to the Budget"[c]	
	In Billions of Euros	% GDP	In Billions of Euros	% GDP
France	2.502	0.20	1.971	0.16
Germany	−4.967	−0.26	−5.239	−0.27
UK	−1.272	−0.11	−0.669	−0.06
Spain	2.158	0.43	2.009	0.40

Sources: Christian Weise et al. *Die Finanzierung der Osterweiterung der EU* (Baden-Baden: Nomos, 2002); authors' calculations.

Notes: a. Annual average, 1995–1999, in € billion and percentage of member state's GDP. b. Calculation of the net position is based on each country's contribution to the EU's own resources—that is, according to its share of the EU's GDP. c. Calculation of the net position is based on each country's real contribution to the EU's budget.

offered a medium-term phase-out scheme. That could diminish political pressure from the agricultural lobby, not only in France but elsewhere. One concession in this direction was French acceptance of a review of the CAP in the mid-term of the 2007–2013 period, though that came only in conjunction with a UK concession on its rebate.

The French national context continues to present difficulties. Virtually the entire political class supports, or wants to be seen to support, the CAP, perceived as essential to the continued existence of French agriculture. Figure 4.1 indicates the gross receipts that underlie those attitudes. The spotlight on the UK rebate in 2005 tended to overlook the fact that in the British financial proposal for 2007–2013, the CAP increased its share of the EU budget to 44 percent even though it fell by 2 percent in absolute terms. As the *Economist* put it, that increase was the chief failing of the budget debate and outcomes: "Once again they fail to advance the cause of CAP reform, which remains as urgent as ever."[14]

Farm lobbies in several old member states have exercised substantial influence on national politics and thereby on EU policy. Because the CAP is closely bound with trade issues, pressure groups can influence the EU's international negotiating position.[15] The bond scheme discussed by Daugbjerg and Swinbank could have assisted the EU case in the Doha Round and further negotiations. The question of national political viability remained open. The authors did not place much emphasis on the capacity of the Commission or other community institutions to determine the course: "A reform proposal must be able to attract the support of Germany and France to be realized. If one of these two member states, or both, remains opposed to a proposal, it

Figure 4.1   CAP Receipts by Selected Member States, 2004 (in billions of euros)

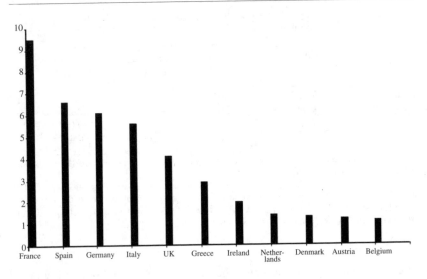

Source: "Europe's Farm Follies," *Economist,* 10 December 2005, 27.

stands a very limited chance of being adopted. Their policy positions are deter-mined by national politics."[16] Poland's accession introduced an agricultural sector that, relative to persons employed, was the largest in the EU. In 2005 it was around 17 percent. Despite the transformation that Polish agriculture underwent to meet EU entry requirements, its sustainability and profitability are largely dependent on the influx of capital into the sector and the national economy in general.[17] The budget midterm review will certainly recommend a shift of EU spending away from agriculture and toward growth and innova-tion industries. Polish politicians of all colors, and especially radical national-ist elements, have criticized the EU's treatment of Poland's farmers. Poland's phased inclusion into the full benefits of CAP support may be realized in 2013, just when the system changes—in the direction of more competition and less subsidization. (Romania has since surpassed Poland with an agricultural sec-tor of 33 percent.)

Regional Policy

Since the SEA, regional policy has been a key component in the EU's program and budget. Funding is dispersed on a regional basis, but the associated poli-tics tends to conceptualize outcomes nationally. Officially, regional policy is a demonstration of solidarity with poorer regions, building on an assumption that redistribution is needed to balance the effects of integration. It should also have an allocation function that permits poorer states to maintain higher levels of investment in physical and human capital in order to improve competitiveness and potential for sustainable development. Regional policy (sometimes termed "cohesion" or "structural policy") is a complicated affair involving several programs and instruments and administered by Directorate-General for Regional Policy.[18] In four phases of programs from 1988 until 2013, €480 billion has flowed or will flow into "less favored" regions.[19] Although the sum sounds huge, it represents less than 0.4 percent of EU GDP. Member states' public expenditures average 47 percent of their GDPs.[20] Of course those funds provide most public goods to their citizens. A standout example is the German case in which, sixteen years after reunification, transfers from West to East still amount to roughly 4 percent of West German GDP and increase the income of the Eastern *Länder* by 40 percent. As a rule, EU transfers should not exceed 3 percent of recipients' GDPs.

The main instruments of regional policy have been the Cohesion and Structural Funds. Their components are indicated in Table 4.3. These funds

Table 4.3 Regional Policy: Aims and Instruments

2000–2006		2007–2013	
Objective	Financial Instrument	Objective	Financial Instrument
Cohesion	Cohesion fund	Convergence	ERDF, ESF, Cohesion funds
Objective 1	Structural funds: ERDF, ESF, EAGGF		
Objective 2	ERDF, ESF	Regional competitiveness and employment	ERDF, ESF
Objective 3	ESF		
Inter-regional	ERDF	European territorial cooperation	ERDF, ESF
Urban	ERDF		
Equal	ESF		
RD O1[a]	ERDF—Guarantee, FIFG		

Sources: European Commission, Directorate-General Regional, *Cohesion Policy: The 2007 Watershed.*

Notes: a. Rural development outside Objective 1 regions. Structural funds comprise the European Regional Development Fund (ERDF), the European Social Funds (ESF), the European Agricultural Guidance and Guarantee Fund (EAGGF), the Financial Instrument for Fisheries Guidance (FIFG), and the Program for Interregional Cooperation (Interregional). Urban objectives promote less developed urban areas; equal objectives are part of immigration policy.

have been organized with certain objectives that have altered over time. From 2000 the formerly six objectives of the Structural Funds were reduced to three, though in substance there were only marginal changes. Between 2000 and 2006, most Structural Funds were distributed to so-called Objective 1 regions.[21] These were regarded as the regions most in need of assistance for improving their own economic and social cohesion and that of the EU as a whole. To qualify for this status, as Table 4.3 shows, the GDP per capita for a region had to be below 75 percent of the EU average in purchasing power standards (PPS). For 2007–2013, some renaming occurred, but the new "convergence" goal is practically identical with that which had applied to Objective 1. It remains the largest financial instrument with the same qualification standards. The Cohesion Fund is more oriented toward supporting convergence between member states, for example through transnational networks and infrastructure. To qualify a country must have a per capita income of no more than 90 percent of the EU average (in PPS). What were formerly termed Objective 2 regions were those deemed to be facing structural difficulties though not to the extent of that experienced by Objective 1 regions.

Like the CAP, cohesion and structural funding have been targets of mounting criticism. The Commission's second report on cohesion indicated only limited success in the convergence of regional incomes.[22] Between 1988 and 1998, incomes in the poorest areas, which included about 25 percent of the EU population, increased from 66 to 68 percent of the average. Disparities declined only marginally, whereas disparity in rates of unemployment increased substantially. In the third cohesion report, the picture was somewhat brighter but not convincing.[23] Without existing structural and cohesion funding, disparities would be greater, yet it could hardly be claimed that the policy has been an indisputable success.[24] Regional convergence is bound to national convergence and is most pronounced in countries with growth rates above the EU average. The task has now increased enormously. The 2004 enlargement reduced the EU's average per capita GDP by 9 percent. Adding Bulgaria and Romania reduced it by 13 percent.[25]

Moderate achievements are also indicated in an extensive study encompassing thirteen EU countries over seven five-year periods from 1960 to 1995.[26] The authors remark that from a neoclassical economics perspective, structural funding would be judged effective in terms of its capacity to promote growth. Some projects in which funds are invested may not focus specifically or solely on growth promotion but may have other objectives, such as the enhancement of "cultural or environmental values." Investments supported by Structural Funds have to be co-financed by recipient member states, that is, from their own tax revenues. Where there is taxation distortion, the "net growth effect may well be negative." The main point is that Structural Funds are "at best conditionally effective" and highly dependent on the "'institutional quality' of the receiving country." Employing variables related to government policy such as inflation and savings, others indicating "social cohesion" or "trust," and a third set on corruption perception, openness (to foreign competition), and governance quality (political stability, government effectiveness, rule of law), the authors found that the first two sets were of little or no significance. The third set, related to institutional quality, is significant and the basis for the study's major result: "Structural Funds as such are not effective in enhancing growth, but they are if they are seeded in fertile soil." EU policy "to promote regional growth is only conditionally effective," with openness and "direct measures" of institutional quality being of robust significance. The authors conclude: "This finding bears considerable consequences for the (re-)design of the EU cohesion policy in light of the enlargement of the EU: the funds are to be allocated towards institution building in the first instance. Once institutions are of a sufficient quality, the funds may be effective in stimulating (catching-up) growth."[27] With some caveats related to incomplete data, an extension of the analysis to the 2004 entrants, along with Bulgaria, Romania, and Turkey, suggested that "the prospects for effective use of Structural Funds in the accession countries are limited. This reflects the fact that the institutional quality and perceived corruption in most of the countries are worse than Greece, which featured the lowest values among [old] EU countries."[28] The poor performance of these countries in these areas is confirmed in Figure 4.2.

M. Beugelsdijk and S. Eijffinger present a more positive appraisal. They contend that Structural Funds have reduced regional disparities and that corruption does not appear to have a significant role in whether a state or region experiences growth. They note, however, a susceptibility to moral hazards. Funds are sometimes distributed to recipients who are not eligible but through manipulation of the system have obtained them. Thus the intent behind the policy is sabotaged and its effectiveness undermined.[29] We consider that the degree of corruption and other deficits in the institutional setting will influence absorption capacity and thereby the quality of projects (see Figure 4.3).[30]

Some progress was made before 2004 toward convergence in national income levels. Commission simulations suggest that regional policy contributed, although a solid evaluation has to consider welfare losses for net payers through higher contributions. Spain and Portugal increased their levels of per capita income toward the EU average, but the most impressive performance is that of Ireland. In 1973, when it joined the then EEC, Ireland's per capita income was 60 percent of the average. Through its years of growth, principally 1987–2000, Ireland raised its per capita GDP (in PPS) to about 20 percent above the EU average.[31] As labor demand increased to accompany this rapid growth, especially in the technology sector, qualified labor began returning to the country. In contrast, Greece's economic development is as disappointing as it was before it joined the EC in 1981.[32] In 2001 Greece entered the eurozone despite its economy being plagued by a host of problems, including an entrenched tradition of corruption.[33] Participation in EMU exerted more

Figure 4.2 Quality of Public Institutions and Degree of Corruption (correlation)

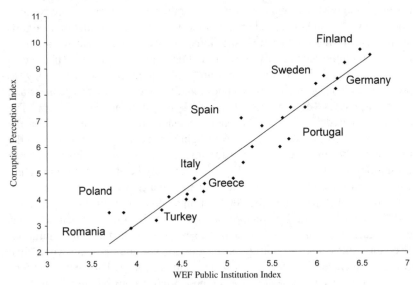

Sources: World Economic Forum, *Global Competitiveness Report, 2004–2005* (Geneva: WEF, 2004); Transparency International (www.tranparency.org/CPI/2004).

Notes: The quality of public institutions is measured by the World Economic Forum Public Institution Index. The index is based on "hard data" and "survey data" in which 1 represents the worst and 7 the best evaluation. The extent of corruption is based on the Corruption Perception Index (CPI), a composite index using data compiled between 2002 and 2004. Eighteen surveys and business assessments by country analysts from twelve independent institutions are also used. Scores, not ranking positions, are presented here. Scores range from 0 (highly corrupt) to 10 (highly clean). $R^2 = 0.9315$.

Figure 4.3 Factors Influencing Structural Funds Performance

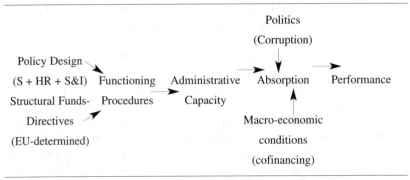

Note: S = Structures, HR = Human-Resources, S&I = Systems and Instruments

pressure for discipline in national economic policy. Yet in exchange rate terms, Greece's GDP per capita is still about 60 percent and in PPS, about 72 percent of the EU average. Greece can no longer reckon on such large shares of EU funding. This reality may exacerbate associated problems or motivate a genuine change toward better economic management.

It is contradictory and counterproductive that member states with high per capita incomes also receive sizable shares of funding. France and Germany received about 23 percent of Objective 1 and 2 funds between 1994 and 1999 and 21 percent in the period 2000–2006. During these latter years, approximately 40 percent of the EU15 lived in areas supported by these funds.[34] Ireland, which far surpassed average EU GDP, still received around €500 million from the Cohesion Fund. Once established, this type of redistribution is subject to horse-trading that persists even when its original purpose is outdated. There is a deep-seated tendency for every state to attempt to optimize and sustain its funding. Heinz-Jürgen Axt described this as a trap of interlinked interests. Bargaining that aims at harmonizing interests and dividing them proportionately determines the policymaking that results.[35] It might, euphemistically, be called a "system of concordance." Although they are ostensibly intended to promote convergence of welfare levels and EU-wide economic cohesion, Structural and Cohesion Funds are also side payments to buy political decisions. If individual veto power is emphasized, net receivers possess more power in the system, although of a "negative" character, than their apparently weak negotiating position suggests. Substantial changes are then very difficult to enforce.

Misallocations of funds could previously be borne without excessive hardship, but not after 2004. Shrill demands from Poland that it receive the same munificence as applied before it joined are futile unless it offers something desirable or necessary in return. One effect of enlargement is that EU15 regions that were previously "poor" are now statistically "richer" as average per capita GDP across the EU has fallen. Twenty-seven regions with about 49 million inhabitants face losing transfers because their GDP levels have risen above the 75 percent line. The number below the line increased from 71 million to 174 million, or 36 percent of the EU25 population. If Spain had managed to enforce its aim of maintaining the level of Structural Funds in the enlarged EU, expenditures would have inflated to a wholly unmanageable sum. Spain was able to retain about €3.2 billion that should have gone elsewhere. Three of its regions are treated with transitional arrangements, as are two in Greece and one in Ireland.[36]

As Table 4.4 outlines, €308 billion was appropriated for commitments for 2007–2013 under heading 1b. Revised to 2007 prices, this sum has risen to €347 billion.[37] Money allocated under heading 1b supports the convergence objective. At 2004 prices, the amount is €32 billion less than the original Commission proposal, though it constitutes a larger proportion (35 percent) of the total budget than in the Commission calculations (33 percent). Redirecting

Table 4.4 Cohesion for Growth and Employment Funding, 2007–2013 (heading 1b of EU budget)

Member State	€ Billion	Share of Heading 1b (%)
Germany	23.5	7.6
Greece	18.2	5.9
Spain	31.5	10.2
Portugal	19.2	6.2
France	12.7	4.1
Italy	25.7	8.3
UK	9.5	3.1
Czech Republic	23.7	7.7
Hungary	22.5	7.3
Poland	59.7	19.4
Romania	17.3	5.6
Slovak Republic	10.3	3.3
Remaining Countries	34.2	11.1
Total	308.0	100.0

Source: See also *Official Journal of the European Union,* Interinstitutional Agreement between the European Parliament, the Council, and the Commission on budgetary discipline and sound financial management (2006/C 139/01), 14 June 2006; *Financial Times,* 14 July 2004. An updated version of the distribution of Heading 1b funding that reflects 2007 prices is available at http://ec.europa.eu/budget/library/documents/multiannual_framework/2007_2013/tab_cohesion_2007-2013_en.pdf.

Note: In 2004 prices.

funds to promote growth in the CEECs is important, and the 2007–2013 perspective indicates movement in this direction. Total structural and cohesion funding will shift from a ratio of 81 percent for the EU15 and 19 percent for the ten new members in the period 2004–2006 to 49 percent for the EU15 and 51 percent for the ten 2004 entrants plus Bulgaria and Romania in 2013. The funding shift will occur in a phased manner, an issue that was central to the grueling budget negotiations. Expressed in 2004 prices, total funding for the EU15 will fall from €34 billion in 2004 to €20 billion in 2013. In the same period, the other twelve will experience a funding increase from €7 billion (2004) to €25 billion (2013).[38] Over the whole period (2007–2013), Poland will become the largest recipient, with almost €60 billion (19.4 percent), replacing Spain with almost €32 billion (10 percent).

The Commission conceives of regional policy as a key component in reaching goals of pan-EU competitiveness and convergence. More important is that allocations of funds have to be conceptualized as investments. The success or otherwise of this funding and of the Lisbon Agenda and the SM are interdependent. Some political actors have either not understood the strategic objectives of regional policy and its funding or have discounted the broader, long-term EU-wide purpose in favor of short-term national political goals.

Regional policy requires institutional capacity and a commitment to sound economic policy on the part of member states.

Budget and Financing Reform

A proper functioning of the expanding EU club depends on further reforms of its policies, which involves changes in the budget on the expenditure side to enable new solutions on the revenue side. A fundamental reorientation of spending should incorporate fiscal federalism. Iain Begg, in reference to Wallace Oats, a leading analyst of public finance, suggests that the term "fiscal federalism" might be misleading because it implies a narrow focus on budgetary matters, especially in the EU context.[39] Alternatively, it might not appear appropriate because the EU is far from a federal system. The EU is unlikely to even approximate a political form of federalism, but it may receive more public finance tasks if they can be economically justified. As Begg notes, "A lack of statehood or state building need not . . . preclude a different mix of public finance."[40] Fiscal federalism assumes an optimal assignment of competencies by considering the impacts (spillovers and externalities) of policies, voter preferences, and the legitimacy of decisionmaking.

Friedrich Heinemann has applied this approach to an integration concept.[41] Federalism is not identified here, as it often is in the British view, as a centralized state, but in diametric contrast: as a decentralized public administration in which competencies are located at different levels of the hierarchy. Decentralized decisionmaking would better reflect the preferences of citizens concerning the provision of public goods. This view is supported by the advantage of efficiency- and innovation-oriented competition between (regional) branches of public administration. Centralization would only occur if administrations at the same level profit from the same public goods (territorial externalities). From this principle of "correspondence," it follows that public goods should be the responsibility of the level at which benefits are located. In other words, public goods are financed by those who benefit from them. Goods with mostly national, regional, or local character would be left to these levels. The contribution of each state to finance these goods would be congruent with the gains of its population. A more efficient allocation can then be expected.

Fiscal federalism theory suggests three criteria that need to be met if policies are to shift to this form of administration. First, positive economics of scale should lead to a reduction of average costs to provide public goods. The aggregated sum of expenditures saved on national scales should be higher than additional expenditures on the EU level. Second, spillover effects of national policies to others might justify some centralization or coordination between states. Third, homogeneous policy preferences are a precondition for creating value-added outcomes.[42] Because preferences are not homogeneous, a social or tax policy can hardly be implemented EU-wide.[43] Some limited coordination in these fields might obviate the danger of a race to the bottom.

We cannot cover all issues and problems throughout EU policy fields but focus here on the validity or utility of some of them.[44] Current expenditures and financing do not fulfill the aforementioned criteria. EU-wide public goods and policies are not easy to precisely define, as they are bound to particular national conceptions (reflecting heterogeneous preferences), and competencies may change. Common institutions that guarantee the functioning and supervision of the SM need to be financed. Other areas are more controversial. Table 4.5 outlines a qualitative evaluation of policy areas by Heinemann. Others may estimate policies differently, but his evaluation seems plausible. Trade, basic rights, subsidy controls, and competition add value at the European level; others clearly have to be located on the national level (cultural and social policies). Some (environment) are more ambiguous. Internal and external security have transformed ever more into EU-wide public goods as border controls are removed.

Heinemann does not mean that these tasks need to be taken over by a centralized authority, but they do necessitate intensified cooperation and correspondent institutions. Agencies like Europol or an EU Operational Headquarters facility for military forces, certain EU foreign policy instruments, and diplomatic activities could make a larger contribution. More resources are being assigned to security and foreign policy but remain comparatively small. As Table 4.6 shows, commitments under relevant headings three ("Freedom, Security, and Justice") and four ("The EU as a Global Partner), not including any associated administration under heading five, will increase to €60.3 billion from 2007 to 2013. The share of the total budget is 6.9 percent. Higher absolute and relative sums will be directed to these policy areas as the essential nature and pan-EU scale of the public goods they provide become obvious.

Although shifts are visible, with agricultural and regional policy consuming 78.6 percent of expenditures, the dominating policy areas are those that do not provide genuine EU public goods. They may be justified if "solidarity" and "convergence" are privileged, but integration does not automatically lead to equally distributed welfare gains, and convergence is not always a necessary consequence. Major components of the existing system still follow a logic of political economy, with "losers" compensated to secure the project. If the system was organized efficiently and limited in size, it might be manageable. Neither of these conditions currently applies. Moreover, it is questionable whether there really are substantial losers—smaller and poorer countries benefit more from the SM, relative to GDP, than larger states.

Budget reform should be oriented to end, or at least diminish, the compensation objective in the next financial period. There should be a concentration on areas that provide real EU-wide public goods. Convergence and

Table 4.5 Qualitative Estimations in Different EU Policy Fields

Policy Field	Economies of Scale	Homogeneous Preferences	Spillovers	European Value Added
Trade policy	Yes	Rather yes (dependent on evaluation of free trade)	Yes	Yes
Basic rights	Yes	Yes	Yes	Yes
Subsidy/ competition control	Yes	Rather yes (different economic policy concepts may play a role)	Yes	Yes
Monetary policy	Yes	Some doubts due to heterogeneous economic structures	Yes	Yes (optimal size is disputed)
Tax policy	Rather no	No	No (if tax competition is positively assessed)	No
Social policy	No	No	No	No
Employment	No	Rather no (national labor markets differ widely)	Rather no	No (except some specific areas)
R&D	Rather yes	Rather no (different development levels)	Rather yes	Rather yes
Culture	No	No	No	No (except some narrow areas)
Environment	Partly	No	Yes	Rather yes (no concerning local issues)
Transportation	Rather no	Rather no	Yes	Rather yes (if related to trans-European issues)
Trans-Europe networks	Yes	Rather no	Yes	Rather yes
Agricultural policy	No	No	No	No
Cohesion policy	No	No	Low	Rather no (instrument of redistribution)
Foreign and security policy	Yes	No	Yes	Rather yes (if ESDP preferences converge)
Asylum policy	Yes	No	Yes	Rather yes
Fight against crime	Rather yes	Rather yes	Rather yes	Rather yes (for cross-border crime)

Source: Friedrich Heinemann, *EU-Finanzplanung, 2007–2013: Haushaltsoptionen, Verteilungs-wirkungen, und europäischer Mehrwert* (München: Bertelsmann, 2006), 41.

Table 4.6   Financial Framework for the Enlarged EU, 2007–2013

Commitments € Billions (2004 prices)	2007	2013	Total, 2007–2013
1. Sustainable growth	51.3	58.3	382.1
1a. Competitiveness	8.4	13.0	74.1
1b. Cohesion	42.9	45.3	308.0
2. Natural resources	55.0	51.2	371.3
Markets and payments	43.1	40.6	293.1
3. Freedom, security, and justice	1.2	2.0	10.8
3a. Security/justice	0.6	1.4	6.6
3b. Citizenship	0.6	0.6	4.1
4. The EU as a global partner	6.2	8.0	49.5
5. Administration	6.6	7.6	49.8
6. Compensation	0.4	0.0	0.8
Total commitments	120.7	127.1	864.3
As percentage of GNI	1.1	1.0	1.1
Total payments	116.7	119.0	820.8
As percentage of GNI	1.1	0.9	1.0

In percentage of total commitments	2007	2013	Total, 2007–2013
1. Sustainable growth	42.5	45.9	44.2
1a. Competitiveness	7.0	10.2	8.6
1b. Cohesion	35.5	35.7	35.6
2. Natural resources	45.6	40.3	43.0
Markets and payments	35.7	32.0	33.9
3. Freedom, security, and justice	1.0	1.6	1.2
3a. Security/justice	0.5	1.1	0.8
3b. Citizenship	0.5	0.5	0.5
4. The EU as a global player	5.1	6.3	5.7
5. Administration	5.5	6.0	5.8
6. Compensation	0.3	0.0	0.1
Total Commitments	100.0	100.0	100.0

Source: European Commission, Directorate-General for Regional Policy, "Revised Package for EU Programmes, 2007–2013: Priority for Modernisation and Economic Progress, http://europa.eu/rapid/pressReleasesAction.do?reference=IP/06/673&format=HTML&aged=0&language=EN&guiLanguage=en. Updated tables indicating the multiannual financial framework at 2007 prices and some explanation of variance in sums are in European Commission, *General Budget of the European Union for the Financial Year 2007: The Figures* (Brussels, February 2007).

solidarity should be connected to the Lisbon process in order to promote competitiveness.

In summarizing the experience so far and the outlook ahead, we suggest a three-pillar approach, represented in Table 4.7. First, member states with a per capita income above 75 percent of the EU average should organize and finance their own regional policy. Those below would receive EU funds and

Table 4.7   Proposed Objectives and Policy Instruments

Policy Orientation and Instruments	Objectives		
	Public Goods	Convergence	Solidarity
Pillar 1: Revised Structural Funds		Lower priority	High priority
Pillar 2: Revised Cohesion Funds		High priority	Lower priority
Pillar 3: Trans-European networks and Lisbon strategy	High priority	Lower priority	

have greater control over the choice of investment projects. Moves in that direction have been made, and regulations adopted in 2006 emphasize individual responsibilities. A reformed delivery system will provide for proportional and more decentralized management.[45] A higher share of co-financing would be provided by member states (more than the normal 25 percent). To prevent misuse, common standards for the allocation of funds should be designed and administered consistently. The Commission, which can be inundated by administrative details, should be freed from the selection of projects and concentrate on evaluations. Instead of excessive responsibilities for steering policy, the Commission's role should be more supervisory, including investigation of corruption and willful inefficiencies. If cases are proved, sanctions could be implemented, funds repaid, and penalties in the form of less money for the next financial period applied.

The second pillar is "national cohesion funds," an extension and modification of the existing instrument, whereby money would be distributed according to national GDP per capita (in purchasing power standards). The maximum amount would be fixed in advance and presented as an absolute sum or specified percentage of either the EU budget or total EU GDP. National cohesion funds should concentrate on the lowest-income countries. The poorer the country, the greater the adjustment costs of structural change. Transfers would not restrict the choice of projects, as long as they correspond with a macroeconomic program approved by the Commission. Pillar 2 would emphasize prudent economic policy and balanced budgets at the national level, which affect the capacity to co-finance and efficiently absorb the EU funds (up to 4 percent of GDP) available. Through their transgressions of the SGP, some old member states have set bad examples. Fiscal management problems in some new states are also unfavorable signs.

The third pillar is "trans-European networks and the Lisbon strategy," a newly designed Cohesion Fund. Here projects of "European value-added" welfare and security are financed in the fields of infrastructure, education and science, and technology and industrial policy. In the new financial framework, heading 1a funding, allocated for promoting competitiveness, will increase from €8.4 billion in 2007 to €13 billion in 2013. It still represents only 8.6 percent of the total budget over this period, which is insufficient relative to its strategic importance. A positive sign is that some reorientation did occur. Cohesion Funds expenditures should not rely only on transfers. Rather, money should be provided more in the form of preferential credits and within the framework of institutions such as the European Investment Bank (EIB).

Our recommendations are similar to those of the Sapir advisory group, appointed by former Commission President Prodi. The group's report suggested a fundamental shifting of EU expenditures away from agriculture toward three main areas: a growth fund, a convergence fund, and a restructuring fund. The eligibility of each should be based on separate, fair, and transparent criteria with an unchanged raw budget. The growth fund should be oriented toward engines identified at the EU level: R&D and innovation, education and training, and infrastructures connecting national markets. This fund corresponds to our third pillar, entailing a competitive allocation with no a priori distribution across states. The convergence fund, similar to our second pillar, will enable low-income countries to catch up through institution building and investment in physical and human capital. Money would be distributed according to relative income. The restructuring fund facilitates the reallocation of resources. They should be provided for a limited period and to sectors and social groups that most need them.[46]

As was shown in Chapter 2, EMU has economic and political implications that could justify a partly centralized fiscal policy, at least for the eurozone. Macroeconomic stabilization, policy coordination, or measures to mitigate asymmetric shocks demand some common budgetary means. Consequences could include cuts in EU expenditures in some areas and the integration of clearly defined "European and EMU value-added" areas into EU financing. If that were to occur, intergovernmental controls over the budget would have to be reduced and a greater role assigned to the EP. At the same time, appropriate safeguards against excessive spending should be put in place.[47]

A streamlining of expenditure that favored EU public goods and strategic objectives would make other solutions possible on the revenue side. A more transparent funding system could be developed, based on the relative wealth of members. It would moderate arguments over net positions, and the British rebate would become obsolete. Besides member states' "own resources" (customs duties and part of the value-added tax) and the transfers from national budgets, a special EU tax might be applied. It would be balanced by a corresponding reduction in national tax. Motivation for EU budgetary prudence would increase because citizens would have a more direct link to EU revenues and spending.[48]

Environmental Policy

Protection of the natural environment is a pressing political and existential issue of global proportions for which EU has become one of the world's chief advocates. Some member countries, prominently Denmark, Sweden, and Germany, have been leaders in applying environmentally friendly policies, technologies, and methods as well as promoting an environmental consciousness. The same cannot be said for all EU members, though things have changed and are changing. Addressing environmental degradation in the CEECs, the result of a particularly negligent political and industrial system, is an enormous and expensive task. Although there is widespread agreement in principle, the EU is faced with considerable challenges to practically implement its own ambitious goals and to convince other international actors of the credibility of its aims and means.

Roughly 500 regulations, directives, and decisions have been issued since Community environmental action began in 1972, though it was not until the TEU that the status of a policy was conferred upon it.[49] Article 3 of the amended Rome Treaty states that the "activities of the Community shall include . . . a policy in the sphere of the environment." Article 6 states, "Environmental protection requirements must be integrated into the definition and implementation of Community policies . . . in particular with a view to promoting sustainable development." Title XIX expands on related provisions.[50] The TEU moved environmental decisions almost entirely to the realm of QMV. The EP acquired co-decision powers, which were extended in 1997. Eivind Hovden says it is uncertain whether that actually encouraged more or "better" environmental legislation. However, the resort to a "legal basis game"—by states, the Commission, or EP—in order that each actor might achieve what it considers more favorable outcomes, appears to now be a less likely tactic.[51] An exception concerns "provisions of a fiscal nature and energy sources," for which the "requirement of unanimity in the Council of Ministers has severely restricted EU efforts to adopt a common carbon/energy tax."[52] Imposing an EU tax on aircraft fuel, as has been speculated, would also need unanimity.

Jon Birger Skjaerseth and Jørgen Wettestad suggest that environmental policy is the field in which the EU behaves most like an international regime. Its policymaking powers are strong, but its powers of implementation and enforcement are relatively weak. The authors argue that "since most transnational environmental problems arise as by-products of otherwise legitimate domestic activities . . . we have to focus on domestic and international institutions in order to explain differences in implementation and effectiveness."[53]

Because the Community and the member states are party to international agreements, in these instances internal decisionmaking processes can be very complicated.[54] Such international agreements include conventions on reducing water and air pollution, waste management, nature conservation, renewable energy, and other issues. Internally, a directive on environmental liability made polluters liable for repairing environmental damage. In such cases the member state in question is responsible for taking legal action against polluters in its national jurisdiction.

Forces within member state polities, that is, sympathetic public sentiment and energetic governments, or oppositions, ensured that environmental goals, formally agreed or otherwise, emerged on the political agenda and are actively pursued. A behavioral shift has occurred since the late 1980s, particularly in states and societies not noted as being especially enthusiastic supporters of EU environmental policy.[55] Many voluntary agreements for improved energy efficiency and climate change mitigation have been implemented.[56] Environmental integration, meaning that all EU policy must incorporate environmental considerations and goals, has been a requirement since the Amsterdam Treaty of 1997 and was advanced by the Cardiff process, launched in 1998.[57] Pro-environment momentum has accelerated since 2002. There is, on the surface, less tension among member states than in some other policy areas and even something of a competition in declaring the most far-reaching intentions.

The principal financial instrument for EU environmental policy is the LIFE program, with further funding coming from the EIB and national measures. LIFE is a co-financing instrument, which provides a maximum of 50 percent of eligible costs for nature conservation projects and 100 percent for accompanying measures. In exceptional cases, 75 percent of eligible costs may be funded. The third phase of the program, from 2000 to 2004, had an initial budget of €640 million. It was extended until the end of 2006, with an additional €317 million for the extra period.[58] The EU relies on the European Environment Agency (EEA), established in 1990, for much technical data and recommendations. In addition to the twenty-seven EU states, Liechtenstein, Norway, Iceland, Switzerland, and Turkey are participants. EU members are obliged to deliver material on national environmental information networks to the EEA.

In 2001 the EU adopted its sixth Environment Action Programme (EAP) for the period 2001–2010.[59] It focuses on five areas: tackling climate change; protecting nature and wildlife; addressing environment and health issues; preserving natural resources; and managing waste, of which the EU produces almost 2 billion tonnes each year, an amount predicted to rise by 40 percent by 2020. The EU orients consumers toward "environmental goods and services," the world market for which, it claims, was around €500 billion in 2003 and growing at 5 percent per year, much faster than the EU economy. Many other measures, from preserving biodiversity to requiring manufacturers to provide facilities for scrapping cars, are also being promoted.[60]

Climate change, or global warming, has become the most conspicuous of environmental issues[61] and a concern for 87 percent of the EU population.[62] The EU is a major supporter of the Kyoto Protocol and its emission control/climate change strategy is guided, technically and politically, by what was agreed in Kyoto. The strategy incorporates encouragement or education of external states, industries, and consumers to strive to minimize environmental damage and to maximize sustainability. EU political personalities and agencies have been critical of states that have not ratified Kyoto, in particular the United States and Australia, though less so of China. Former French president Chirac speculated on the imposition of a carbon tax for states that have not ratified Kyoto. Playing to national and European audiences for political purposes certainly has a role here.

The EU15 agreed to reduce greenhouse gas emissions by 8 percent over 1990 levels by 2008–2012. The 2004 and 2007 entrants have other targets. An Emissions Trading Scheme (ETS), foreseen in the sixth EAP, was introduced in 2005. It was the first such international trading system and was described by the Commission as the "cornerstone of the EU's strategy for fighting climate change."[63] The ETS was considered a cost-effective means of complying with Kyoto commitments and attempts to encourage market means as a contribution to solving pollution problems.

The ETS is backed by National Allocation Plans (NAPs), complex arrangements that determine the quantity of CO_2 emissions allocated to various sectors of the economy and society within each member state. One allowance validates the emission of one tonne of CO_2. Distribution of allowances is decided by the states. The first phase of NAPs ran from 2005 to 2007, and the second comprises 2008 to 2012. The Commission assesses the plans, which must correspond with twelve criteria specified in the Emissions Trading Directive (2003/87/EC, amended by 2004/101/EC). Any rejection by the Commission must be based on the state concerned having not fulfilled its agreement under the terms of the most recent treaty. The Commission has sole responsibility for assessing NAPs, but a Climate Change Committee of member state representatives also considers all plans. Member states may offset part of their Kyoto emission reduction commitments by investing in Joint Implementation (JI) and Clean Development Mechanism (CDM) projects in other countries. According to the Commission, the EU's Kyoto targets can be achieved at an annual cost of between €2.9 billion and €3.7 billion. Without the ETS, costs could reach €6.8 billion.[64] More than 10,000 industrial installations across the EU are covered by the ETS. In March 2007, EU states agreed to a binding cut of 20 percent of CO_2 emissions by 2020, with an endorsed objective of 30 percent.[65] The Blair government announced that the UK will aim to go further. Its Draft Climate Change Bill proposed a "statutory goal" of reducing CO_2 emissions by 60 percent by 2050 and 26–32 percent by 2020.[66]

Despite the noble aims, some evidence suggests not all initiatives have been as successful as envisaged. The March 2007 European Council invited the Commission to review the ETS. One report claimed that the EU's climate policy was "stagnating" and the ETS, "once held up as a model to be emulated, is floundering."[67] The allocation of too many emission allowance certificates meant that prices dropped. Companies then have fewer incentives to go green and are more likely to buy cheap emission certifications instead. There is some irony about the EU attempting to apply market solutions to the problem of greenhouse gas emissions and some doubt about the basis for allocations for 2013–2017 remaining as set for 2008–2012. There are no guarantees that ambitious goals will be realized in practice, and combative rhetoric on environmental concerns may start to sound a little hollow.

Energy Policy

Energy production and use is closely linked to environmental issues. Many Commission papers and EU statements refer to the incorporation of sustainable development and clean fuel goals into energy policy. In adopting a "comprehensive energy Action Plan" for 2007–2009 based on the Commission's *European Strategy for Sustainable, Competitive, and Secure Energy*, the March 2007 European Council concluded that an integrated climate and energy policy was needed.[68] However, it may not be readily or perfectly achievable. European integration began over fifty-five years ago with coal and steel. Coal is still a big industry in the EU, including in environmentally conscious Germany, which, in 2007, is constructing or planning to construct up to twenty-six new coal-fired power plants. One Green Party parliamentarian claimed that "if all of those plants end up being installed, there is no way we can reach our climate protection goals for reducing emissions."[69]

Energy use and energy policy are significant for more than strictly environmental reasons. There are employment, financial, and medium-term economic factors. Also crucial for the EU are the strategic dimensions of energy: reliability of supply and its relation to foreign and security policy or long-term economic development. In 2005, the EU was the world's second-largest consumer of energy, with 1,637,000 tonnes of oil equivalent (toe) needed to meet demand. This equated to more than 3.5 tonnes of oil per capita. In the same year (2005), 56 percent of EU energy resources were imported, a share predicted to grow to 65 percent or more by 2030.[70] Oil imports will then account for 93 percent of oil consumption and natural gas imports for 84 percent of gas consumption.[71] If a serious foreign policy crisis involving oil and gas supplies were to occur, the EU would be badly affected. Excepting Norway and to a lesser extent the UK, its principal sources of oil and gas imports are unpredictable. None are model democracies. The choice of external suppliers ranges across despotic regimes in the Middle East and North Africa, autocratic Russia, and badly governed states in sub-Saharan Africa and Central Asia.

The Commission might conceive of a "pan-European energy community" that integrated "EU energy markets and those of its neighbors" as an optimal situation for the EU. It will not be so straightforward. The "energy community" idea is a variation on the Energy Charter proposal, which has been under consideration since 1991 but needs external signatories. The EU cannot control all producers. They may perceive their own interests rather differently than the EU prefers. Some foreign and security aspects of energy are further addressed in Chapters 5 and 6. Suffice to say here that for the EU, disruptions, meteoric price increases, blackmail, and diverse crises are all possible.

In its Green Paper on sustainable, competitive, and secure energy, the Commission argued that to achieve its objectives, the EU had to address its growing dependence on energy imports, fluctuating oil and gas prices, climate change, rising demand, and barriers to competition. The EU had to achieve economies of scale and demand management power as well as invest in and promote renewable energy sources.[72] Three core objectives—sustainability, competitiveness, and security of supply—and "concrete proposals" in six priority areas were emphasized. The first priority area, "energy for growth and jobs in Europe: completing the internal European gas and energy markets," stressed a "need to complete the internal gas and electricity markets." The Commission emphasizes this because in its view, "many national energy markets are still beleaguered by protectionism and dominated by a few companies." "National reflexes" keep prices (artificially) high and infrastructure uncompetitive.[73] Some progress toward liberalization has been made and as of July 2007 consumers can purchase gas and electricity from any supplier in the EU. The Commission's hope that real EU-wide competition will play a major role in solving energy dilemmas is still confronted by protectionist barriers, especially through action by larger member states.[74]

The second priority was "security of supply: solidarity between Member States," which emphasized dependence on imports and the need for collective resolve. Implicit in this priority is a perception that interruptions, perhaps very serious, to normal supply are likely. A European Energy Supply Observatory that would function as a "mechanism for rapid solidarity" has been proposed to deal with crises following damage to infrastructure. Building robust EU strategic petroleum and strategic gas reserves is also inferred. In a recent EU-wide survey, 79 percent of respondents felt that affected member states should be able to rely on the reserves of other member states in the event of sudden oil or gas shortages.[75] In a related survey, 47 percent said that the European level was the most appropriate level to take decisions on energy, 37 percent thought the national level was best, and 8 percent were for the local level. One study, however, found that the greater the degree of import dependency of individual member states, the greater the support for national champions, with a corresponding reduction in competition.[76]

The third priority, of achieving a more sustainable, efficient, and diverse energy mix, both raises the prospect of (increased) nuclear energy use and seeks to preempt a potential intensifying of opposition by proposing a Strategic EU Energy Review that "would also serve as a basis for a transparent and objective debate on the role of nuclear energy in Europe and for formulating strategic objectives for the overall EU energy mix." States are free to determine their own energy mix.

Tackling climate change is the fourth priority, which the EU should lead as a global effort. Economic growth should be "decoupled" from energy consumption. Renewable energy sources, of which the EU has 50 percent of the world market, will be invested in and promoted. A target of a 20 percent reduction in energy use by 2020 is central to an action plan on energy efficiency.[77] Member states are asked to mobilize all political forces in combating excessive energy consumption.

Research and innovation is the fifth priority. New technologies and support for renewable energy sources are prominent here. Extensive, or better than foreseen, progress in this priority area would have considerable positive impact on the sixth priority, "a coherent external energy policy." This last is the most difficult to agree on. Although it is correct that "before looking abroad, the EU must formulate a common position with regard to . . . energy partnerships with third countries,"[78] a dialogue with energy partners does not guarantee the security of supply.

The Commission does not sketch any apocalyptic scenarios. It and the member states are, however, considering their options. The political climate and public attitudes on energy use are being closely monitored. It is quite possible that there will be a renaissance of nuclear power in the EU, even after some states have begun or declared phasing-out operations, and publics are on balance not, at present, in favor.[79] Fifteen member states have nuclear facilities. For some, nuclear power already has a high share of their overall energy mix. In France it provides about 45 percent of the primary energy supply (of all forms of fuel) and about 80 percent of electricity generation. In Belgium it is about 56 percent. Finland and Romania have recently built new reactors, and the share of nuclear power in their respective national energy mixes can be expected to rise.

Various lobbies, NGOs, politicians, and sections of EU member state populations regard a continued dependence on fossil fuels as untenable for environmental reasons. They want clean energy. Many of the same forces are also opposed to nuclear power and want to phase it out. Others regard a continued dependence on fossil fuels as untenable for different reasons, namely that the suppliers on whom the EU relies are politically unreliable and in some cases objectionable. They view the continued or increased use of nuclear energy, with extensive, state-of-the-art safeguards, as sensible and even imperative on strategic foreign and security policy grounds. Tensions between these positions, and between energy and environmental policy areas, could heighten.[80] In response to a list of alternatives that their member state government—not the EU—should focus on developing, and from which only two could be selected, 48 percent of respondents nominated solar power, 41 percent new technologies such as hydrogen and clean coal, 31 percent wind power, and 12 percent nuclear energy. Although respondents supported research and development for renewable sources, only 40 percent said they were prepared to pay more for energy from them. Only 2 percent were prepared to pay 11 to 25 percent more. Fifty-four percent were not prepared to pay any more, the same result as a similar survey several years earlier. In the new member states, 66 percent would not pay more.[81] In another survey on the use and safety of nuclear energy, 69 percent believed that it would help reduce dependence on imported oil and gas, 50 percent that it ensured lower prices (against 32 percent that disagreed), and 46 percent that it helped to limit global warming (31 percent disagreed). Thirty-eight percent perceived no risk associated with nuclear power; 53 percent said there was a risk.[82]

History and geography, along with other vested interests, have influenced and do influence the divergent preferences that exist among the member states. Jean Pisani-Ferry summarizes well the merger of internal and external contexts and its seriousness for the EU. The "big question," he argues,

> is whether the EU is part of the response to the energy challenges confronting Europe. Energy security and the environment are major concerns . . . and whether the answers to them will come from the EU or from the nation states only has become a key litmus test of the usefulness of the EU in the XXIst century . . . the more the EU agrees on the response to one of the major challenges it is confronted with, the less difficult it will be to agree on a revised treaty.[83]

Conclusion

Enlargement makes "interest-equalization" more difficult, especially when it coincides with weak growth. The EU faces substantial inequalities that will linger for some time. Because agglomeration effects are strong, the EU has changed from being a "rich man's club" to a group of countries characterized by a sizable East-West development gap. If more enlargements occur, EU policies and financial redistribution schemes will come under more pressure. Political intuition and theoretical models suggest that wrangling over EU resources will intensify.[84] It seems reasonable to use the midterm review to rethink major policies. There should be a further shift from targeting less developed regions to a stronger promotion of national convergence, especially for Lisbon objectives of growth and employment. Member states, especially the richer ones, would take on more responsibility for their own internal convergence. The criteria for funds would be reformed so that money is reallocated to poorer members.

Agricultural and regional policies were already inefficient and institutionally overloaded with fifteen members. Minor changes have occurred in the agricultural subsidy system, but more serious adjustments are needed. Even allowing for the normative criterion of solidarity, under contemporary conditions the CAP is a dubious scheme. Transfers are political side payments to ensure that the whole EU endeavor—which has produced welfare and security in other fields—is stabilized. The will to provide side payments has diminished as the objective of unifying the continent, in terms of common commitment to democracy, has on the whole been reached. Political elites in net payer states are disturbed by the prospect of heavier financial burdens. Their apprehension partly relates to forgoing domestic investments because they must deliver transfers to others. Old net receivers of structural and cohesion funds and agricultural subsidies are concerned that some of their transfers have been reallocated. Less money for poorer EU15 members, combined with increased economic and institutional competition for richer ones, undermines the willingness of taxpayers and politicians to redistribute funds.

An institutional and organizational shift toward a decentralized federation of states, with core principles of subsidiarity, competition, and solidarity, would represent a promising reorientation. Subsidiarity implies that the legislative and executive powers of the Union prevail in and are strong in those areas where only community institutions can treat major policy questions effectively. Although these proposals do not correspond totally to the theoretical approach of fiscal federalism, they share some bases. Apart from general regulations to ensure that agricultural markets function properly and that income support measures do not distort competition, agricultural and rural policy should be shifted toward national or regional administrative control. The same can be applied to cohesion, which should concentrate on producing EU-wide public goods such as trans-European networks. "European value-added" projects of this kind should be financed much more on the basis of preferential credits, extended, and through a larger role for the EP, backed by more political legitimacy.

There is also a challenge for the technical application of EU policies. Special skills are needed, and much effort was devoted to these problems during the accession process. Sustainable co-financing capacity is an issue because several countries have fiscal difficulties. It is unclear whether the CEECs can reallocate existing expenditures to new EU-funded projects. The rule of "additionality," whereby EU funds cannot replace normal budgetary spending, has to be observed. Serious absorption problems could contribute to a general frustration and provoke negative attitudes toward the EU.

Redesigned structural and cohesion funds, directing support to low-income member states with a sound economic program, would help. Redistribution should be limited and based on investment expenditures to avoid undermining competition, especially with respect to tax policy. Cohesion, meaning reduction in income disparities, is only possible and beneficial for the EU as a whole if accompanied by growth. Merely seeking to equalize incomes without sufficient attention to other factors that promote sustainable growth will result in suboptimal outcomes.

Notes

1. See Werner Kirsch at http://www.ruhr-uni-bochum.de/mathphys/politik/eu/eu27.html ; Matti Wiberg, *New Winners and Old Losers: A Priori Voting Power in the EU25*, Discussion Paper C149 (Bonn: ZEI, 2005).

2. Werner Kirsch, "Die Formeln der Macht," *Die Zeit*, 15 March 2001, 45; Richard Baldwin, Erik Berghof, Francesco Giavazzi, and Mika Widgren, *EU Reforms for Tomorrow's Europe*, Discussion Paper 2623 (London: CEPR, 2000).

3. Council of the European Union, Interinstitutional File: 2004/0170 (CNS), 2004/0171 (CNS), 11741/04, "Proposal from the Commission from 22 July 2004. Subject: Proposal for a Council Decision on the System of the European Communities' Own Resources," Brussels, 27 July 2004, available at http://register.consilium.eu.int/pdf/en/04/st11/st11741.en04.pdf.

The actual distribution of finance for 2007–2013 was dependent on further haggling and political maneuvering. Although some member states were estimated in the document cited above to be net payers, they are in fact net receivers of funds, for example, Cyprus.

4. Wolfgang Wessels, "Die Vertragsreform von Nizza—Zur institutionellen Erweiterungsreife," *Integration* 24, no. 1 (2001): 8–25; Janis A. Emmanoulidis and Thomas Fischer, "Die Machtfrage europäisch beantworten, Die Abstimmungsregeln von Nizza und im Konvent Reform," Centrum für angewandte Politikforschung, *Spotlight* No. 4 (2003).

5. Although the previous Polish government had eventually signed the Constitutional Treaty in October 2004, the succeeding government, under the prime ministership of Jaroslaw Kaczynski, determined that because the CT had been rejected in the French and Dutch referendums of 2005, all content in that now redundant document was back on the table for further negotiation, including the formula for the distribution of votes in the Council.

6. The Polish proposal recalls the formula of Lionel Penrose, "The Elementary Statistics of Majority Voting," *Journal of the Royal Statistical Society* 109, no. 1 (1946): 53–57.

7. See EurActiv, "Summit Seals Mandate for EU 'Reform Treaty,'" 24 July 2007, available at http://www.euractiv.com/en/future-eu/summit-seals-mandate-eu-reform-treaty/article-164917.

8. Stephen Mulvey, "Poles in War of Words over Voting," *BBC News*, 21 June 2007, available at http://news.bbc.co.uk/2/hi/europe/6227834.stm; George Parker, Jan Cienski, and Betrand Benoit, "Poland Cites War Dead in EU Row," *Financial Times*, 20 June 2007, available at http://www.ft.com/cms/s/fda8aac0-1f55-11dc-ac86-000b5df10621.html.

9. Cf. Sapir et al., *An Agenda for a Growing Europe.*

10. "Europeans and the Common Agricultural Policy," Special Eurobarometer 221, Brussels, CEC February 2005.

11. Carsten Daugbjerg and Alan Swinbank, "The Politics of CAP Reform: Trade Negotiations, Institutional Settings, and Blame Avoidance," *Journal of Common Market Studies* 45, no. 1 (2007): 1–22.

12. Carsten Daugbjerg, "Policy Feedback and Paradigm Shift in EU Agricultural Policy: The Effects of the MacSharry Reform on Future Reform," *Journal of European Public Policy* 10, no. 3 (2003): 421–437.

13. Carsten Daugbjerg and Alan Swinbank, "The CAP and EU Enlargement: Prospects for an Alternative Strategy to Avoid the Lock-in of CAP Support," *Journal of Common Market Studies* 42, no. 1 (2004): 99–119.

14. "Europe's Farm Follies," *Economist,* 10 December 2005, 25–27.

15. Christina Davis, "International Institutions and Issue Linkage: Building Support for International Trade Liberalization," *American Political Science Review* 98, no. 1 (2004): 153–169.

16. Daugbjerg and Swinbank, "The CAP and EU Enlargement," 112.

17. Silvia Borzutzky and Emmanuel Krandis, "A Struggle for Survival: The Polish Agricultural Sector from Communism to EU Accession," *East European Politics and Societies* 19, no. 4 (2005): 614–654.

18. See Directorate-General for Regional Policy at http://ec.europa.eu/regional_policy.

19. EuroActiv, "The New EU Cohesion Policy (2007–2013)," Agenda 200409, 5 October 2006.

20. European Commission, *A New Partnership for Cohesion: Convergence, Competitiveness, Cooperation, Third Report on Economic and Social Cohesion* (Luxembourg: European Communities, 2004).

21. For related administrative purposes, EU regions are divided into territorial units termed NUTS: *Nomenclature des unites territoriales statistiques.*

22. European Commission, *Second Report on Economic and Social Cohesion* (Brussels: CEC, 2001).

23. European Commission, *A New Partnership for Cohesion: Third Report on Economic and Social Cohesion.*

24. Michel Boldrin and Fabio Canova, "Inequality and Convergence in Europe's Regions: Reconsidering European Regional Policies," *Economic Policy* 16 (2001): 207–252.

25. Mojmir Mrak and Vasja Rant, *Challenges of EU and New Member States in Financial Perspective, 2007–2013: Convergence and Absorption of Available Cohesion Resources,* WP 2006-09 (Milan: Universita degli Studi di Milano, 2006), 5.

26. Sjef Ederveen, Henri de Groot, and Richard Nahuis, "Fertile Soil for Structural Funds? A Panel Data Analysis of the Conditional Effectiveness of European Cohesion Policy," *Kyklos* 59, no. 1 (2006): 17–42.

27. Ibid., 32.

28. Ibid., 28.

29. M. Beugelsdijk and S. Eijffinger, "The Effectiveness of Structural Policy in the European Union: An Empirical Analysis for the EU-15 in 1995–2001," *Journal of Common Market Studies* 43, no. 1 (2005): 37–51.

30. Wolfgang Quaisser and Richard Woodward, "Absorbtionsprobleme der EU-Struktur- und Regionalpolitik in den MOE-Ländern," *Beihefte zur Konjunturpolitik. Zeitschrift für angewandte Wirtschaftsforschung* 53 (2002): 115–147.

31. Paul Sweeney, *The Celtic Tiger: Ireland's Economic Miracle Explained* (Dublin: Oak Tree Press, 1998).

32. Michael Dauderstädt, "Überholen, ohne einzuholen: Irland, ein Modell für Mittel- und Osteuropa?" *Politikinformation Osteuropa* 90 (Bonn: Friedrich-Ebert-Stiftung, 2001).

33. Andrea Boltho, "What Matters for Economic Success," in Zoltan Bara and Laszlo Csaba, eds., *Small Economies' Adjustment to Global Tendencies* (Budapest: Aula, 2000), 151–169.

34. European Commission, Directorate-General Regional Policy, *Working for the Regions: Regional Policy—Inforegio,* ec.europa.eu/regional_policy/intro/working4_en.htm.

35. Heinz-Jürgen Axt, *Solidarität und Wettbewerb: Die Reform der EU-Strukturpolitik.* (Gütersloh: Bertelsmann, 2000).

36. *Official Journal of the European Union,* "Commission Decision of 4 August Drawing upon the List of Regions Eligible for Funding from the Structural Funds on a Transitional and Specific Basis Under the Regional Competitiveness and Employment Objective for the Period 2007–2013." Notified under document number C(2006) 3480, 6 September 2006.

37. See "EU support for Cohesion 2007–2013" available at http://ec.europa.eu/budget/library/documents/multiannual_framework/2007_2013/tab_cohesion_2007-2013_en.pdf.

38. Mrak and Rant, *Challenges of EU and New Member States in Financial Perspective, 2007–2013,* 13–15.

39. Iain Begg, *Funding the European Union, Making Sense of the EU Budget: What Is It For? What Should It Be For?* (London: Federal Trust for Education and Research, 2005). Cf. Wallace Oats, "An Essay on Fiscal Federalism," *Journal of Economic Literature* 37, no. 3 (1999): 1120–1149.

40. Begg, *Funding the European Union, Making Sense of the EU Budget,* 18.

41. Friedrich Heinemann, *Die Reformperspektive der EU Finanzverfassung nach den Beschlüssen zur Agenda 2000,* Discussion Paper 99-49 (Bonn: ZEW, 1999).

42. Friedrich Heinemann, *EU-Finanzplanung 2007–2013: Haushaltsoptionen, Verteilungswirkungen, und europäischer Mehrwert* (München: Bertelsmann, 2006), 37–38.

43. Fritz Scharpf, "The European Social Model: Coping with the Challenges of Diversity," in J. H. H. Weiler, Iain Begg, and John Peterson, eds., *Integration in an Expanding European Union: Reassessing the Fundamentals* (Oxford: Blackwell, 2003), 109–134.

44. Cf. Miroslav Jovanovic, *European Economic Integration: Limits and Prospects* (London: Routledge, 1997).

45. European Commission, Directorate-General for Regional Policy, *Structural Funds Regulations,* http://ec.europa.eu/regional_policy/sources/docoffic/official/regulation/newregl0713_en.htm.

46. Sapir et al., *An Agenda for a Growing Europe,* 162–163.

47. Daniel Gros and Stefano Micossi, "A Better Budget for the European Union: More Value for Money, More Money for Value," CEPS Policy Brief 66, Brussels, CEPS, February 2005.

48. Cf. Peter Becker, *Der EU-Finanzrahmen 2007–2013: Auf dem Weg zu einer europäischen Finanzverfassung oder Fortsetzung der nationalen Nettosaldenpolitik?* Study no. 36 (Berlin: SWP, November 2005).

49. This is according to the one of the EU's own information sources at http://Europa.eu/scadplus/leg/en/lvb/l28066.htm. Others cite different dates. Jon Birger Skjaerseth and Jørgen Wettestad state, "In 1998, EU environmental policy celebrated its twentieth anniversary." See Skjaerseth and Wettestad, "Understanding the Effectiveness of EU Environmental Policy: How Can Regime Analysis Contribute?" *Environmental Politics* 11, no. 3 (2002): 99.

50. *Consolidated Version of the Treaty Establishing the European Community, Official Journal* C325, 24 December 2002.

51. Eivind Hovden, "The Legal Basis of European Union Policy: The Case of Environmental Policy," *Environment and Planning C: Government and Policy* 20 (2002): 535–553.

52. Skjaerseth and Wettestad, "Understanding the Effectiveness of EU Environmental Policy," 112.

53. Ibid., 113.

54. Tom Delreux, "The European Union in International Environmental Negotiations: A Legal Perspective on the Internal Decision-Making Process," *International Environmental Agreements* 6, no. 3 (2006): 231–248.

55. See, for example, Jenny Fairbrass and Andrew Jordan, "European Union Environmental Policy and the UK Government: A Passive Observer or a Strategic Manager?" *Environmental Politics* 10, no. 2 (2001): 1–21. The authors' historical-institutionalist account suggests that from the late 1970s on, the UK was outmaneuvered in several ways and faced with unintended and unwelcome consequences. More recently, the then prime minister Tony Blair took a leading role in EU environmental affairs.

56. Paolo Bertoldi and Silvia Rezessy, "Voluntary Agreements for Energy Efficiency: Review and Results of European Experiences," *Energy and Environment* 18, no. 1 (2007): 37–73.

57. Andrew Jordan and Adriaan Schout, *The Coordination of the European Union: Exploring the Capacities of Networked Governance* (Oxford: Oxford University Press, 2006), chapter 3.

58. "LIFE: A Financial Instrument for the Environment," http://europa.eu/scad-plus/leg/en/lvb/l28021.htm

59. European Commission, *Environment 2010: Our Future, Our Choice* (Luxembourg, 2001).

60. European Commission, *A Quality Environment: How the EU Is Contributing* (Luxembourg, 2005).

61. European Commission, "Winning the Battle Against Global Climate Change," COM (2005) 35, Brussels, 9 February 2005.

62. "Attitudes on Issues Related to EU Energy Policy," *Flash Eurobarometer* 206a, Budapest: Gallup, March 2007.

63. European Commission, *Questions and Answers on Emissions Trading and National Allocation Plans for 2008 to 2012,* Memo/06/452, Brussels, 29 November 2006.

64. Ibid.

65. Council of the European Union, *Presidency Conclusions, 8–9 March 2007,* 7224/07, Brussels, 9 March 2007, 12.

66. HM Government, Presented to Parliament by the Secretary of State for Environment Food and Rural Affairs By Command of Her Majesty, *Draft Climate Change Bill* (Norwich: Stationery Office, March 2007).

67. "EU's Environmental Policy Flounders," *Deutsche Welle,* 5 April 2007, www.dw-world.de/dw/article/0,2144,2434294,00.html.

68. European Commission, *Green Paper: A European Strategy for Sustainable, Competitive, and Secure Energy,* COM(2006) 105 final, Brussels, 8 March 2006; European Commission, *An Energy Policy for Europe: Communication to the European Council and the European Parliament,* SEC (2007) 12, Brussels, 10 January 2007; Council of the European Union, *Presidency Conclusions, 8–9 March 2007,* 10–14 and Annex I.

69. "Despite Climate Concerns, Germany Plans Coal Power Plants," *Deutsche Welle,* 21 March 2007, http://www.dw-world.de/dw/article/0,2144,2396828,00.html.

70. Eurostat, "Energy in the EU: First Estimates 2005," News Release, no. 126, Luxembourg, 21 September 2006. See also European Commission, *An Energy Policy for Europe: Communication to the European Council and the European Parliament.*

71. Deutsche Bank Research, "EU Energy Policy: High Time for Action," *EU Monitor* 44, 17 April 2007.

72. European Commission, *Green Paper: A European Strategy for Sustainable, Competitive, and Secure Energy.*

73. See Scadplus (Summaries of Legislation), "Green Paper: A European Strategy for Sustainable, Competitive and Secure Energy," available at http://europa.eu/scadplus/leg/en/lvb/l27062.htm.

74. *Deutsche Welle,* "Merger Plans Reignite EU Energy Market Competition Row," 28 February 2006, http://www.dw-world.de/dw/article/0,2144,1918503,00.html.

75. "Attitudes on Issues Related to EU Energy Policy," *Special Eurobarometer* 247 (Brussels: January 2006).

76. Lars-Henrik Röller, Juan Delgado, and Hans Friederiszick *Energy: Choices for Europe* (Brussels: Bruegel, 2007)): 26–27.

77. European Commission, *Energy Efficiency—or Doing More With Less* COM(2005) 265 final, Brussels, 22 June 2005).

78. Scadplus (Summaries of Legislation), "Green Paper: A European Strategy for Sustainable, Competitive and Secure Energy," available at http://europa.eu/scadplus/leg/en/lvb/l27062.htm.

79. Dan Bilefsky, "Nuclear Power Needed, EU Told," *International Herald Tribune* (Europe), 10 January 2007 at http://www.iht.com/articles/2007/01/10/news/merkel.php; David Charter and Rory Watson, "Europe Agrees to Embrace Nuclear Option in Battle to Save the Planet," *The Times,* 10 March 2007.

80. *Deutsche Welle,* "Nuclear Energy Causes Heated Debate in Europe," 9 April 2006, http://www.dw-world.de/dw/article/0,2144,1956092,00.html.

81. "Attitudes to Energy," *Eurobarometer* special issue 247, Brussels, January 2006.

82. "Europeans and Nuclear Safety," *Eurobarometer* special issue 271, Brussels, February 2007.

83. Jean Pisani-Ferry, "Why Energy Is Key for Europe's Future," *Financial Times Deutschland,* 26 February 2007.

84. Kai Uwe Müller and Philipp Mohl, "Structural Funds in an Enlarged EU: A Politico-Economic Analysis," paper presented at the third ECPR Conference, Budapest, 8–10 September 2005 (draft version, 21 September 2005).

5

Becoming a Global Actor

Believe me, gentlemen, the way still before you is intricate, dark, and full of perplexed and treacherous mazes.

—Edmund Burke

In the Cold War years, the external presence of the European Community was primarily felt in trade and other aspects of economic policy. Since the Community became a Union, the portfolio of activities in which it projects itself has burgeoned. So have the exogenous pressures and threats to which the EU has to respond. They encompass political, diplomatic, financial, military, intelligence, and technical concerns and require an expansion and strengthening of capabilities, however they might be labeled or categorized in thematic, geographic, or budgetary terms. Some issues need internal resolution; some pertain to relations with other actors like the UN[1] and, more problematically, NATO.[2] Alongside peacemaking and peacekeeping are development and aid programs, demands for which have increased in scope. Some areas may overlap with the European Neighbourhood Policy (ENP). All these challenges underlie the EU's gradual transformation into a comprehensive global actor.

> "EU foreign policy" is probably best described as a cluster concept comprising . . . Enlargement policies, External economic policies, Developmental policies, CFSP-policies (sometimes drawing on first and third pillar instruments), ESDP-policies, Monetary policies, Grotian policies (promotion of human rights and democracy).[3]

The gamut is very broad, and Jørgensen's summary above reflects a view that includes all external involvements.[4] The EU has evolved from being a "presence" toward attaining a tangible "actorness."[5] In geographic terms it can be conceptualized as an enterprise with three main divisions: the current membership (internal or Zone One); the EU's wider neighborhood, including candidates for membership (secondary or Zone Two); and a diffuse collection of more remote states and regions (tertiary or Zone Three). These zones are in various ways interlinked (see Figure 5.1).

The EU has multifaceted influence in international politics: it is the world's largest aid donor, a leading contributor to conflict prevention and the reconstruction of disrupted states, a strong supporter of the UN, and an advocate of human rights principles. It radiates magnetism for aspiring members, and it can exert structural economic power for political ends. In other, more "classical" components of foreign policy—military deployment, sovereign and relatively rapid decisionmaking, vigorous diplomacy in pursuit of nontrade interests, and the mobilization of domestic support in a defined polity—the EU has been less certain and effective, particularly in view of its size and resources. We do not deny the achievements of its crisis management in the Balkans and Africa. Nonetheless, as Preben Bonnén, following the high representative (HR) for the CFSP, Javier Solana, maintains, if the EU does not conclusively and consistently demonstrate a capacity and will beyond external economic policy, there is a "danger of not being taken seriously." A political union is impossible or irrelevant without effective diplomacy, security, and defense.[6]

Some scholars have discerned considerable advances in the shaping and refining of interactor mechanisms (member states, Commission, EP, HR Solana, and the policy unit).[7] In contrast, two analysts have more recently termed the EU's foreign policy machinery as "ramshackle." Progress is thwarted by the lack of a cohesive institutional apparatus "even when the gov-

Figure 5.1   Zones of EU Relationships: Internal, Neighborhood, Global (2007)

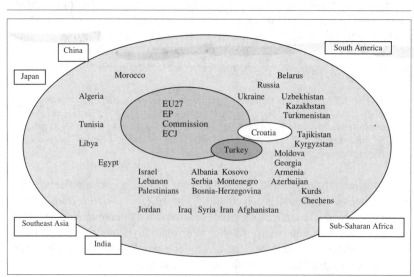

ernments do agree on what to do." It is also hindered by what the same authors regard is a "poor personal relationship" between Solana and Commissioner for External Relations Benita Ferrero-Waldner, which "makes co-operation between the two institutions difficult."[8] Others are critical not of the EU's foreign policy organization or its level of achievement but rather of an excessive focus by scholars on procedure instead of outcomes.[9] To a degree that focus reflects the introspective and legalistic tinkering engaged in by EU agencies. Committees and working groups might manifest cooperation and "act" in their own way, yet the discharging of their recommendations is dependent on (further) state agreement. If willing participants are not present internally, then little of substance can be projected externally. This situation does not seem to concern those who argue that there has been a distinct "parliamentarization" of the CFSP, principally through successive interinstitutional agreements. Still others speculate on the capacity or likelihood of the EU's channels of external action to export its model of governance, in part or in toto.[10]

Although it is frequently noted that the EU is not a (nation-)state and should not be evaluated as one, it exists in a world where these entities proliferate, though certainly not to the exclusion of other actors.[11] States include failing or failed examples that are the focus of stabilization and reconstruction efforts by organizations that incorporate supranational aspirations. Individual member state activity, including vis-à-vis each other, can be added to the corpus of EU foreign affairs involvements. A wide analytical scope demands more than positive cases where one or more states or agencies act on behalf of the Union. Disunity and contrasting goals are also expressions of EU behavior. The Iraq War that began in 2003 was a critical example where preferences diverged and conflicting interests were pursued.[12] Notwithstanding a relatively swift conciliation after that dispute, and advances made with ESDP since, there are recurring incompatibilities and rival outlooks. Moves toward community competence in foreign, security, and defense policy are often instinctively resisted, especially by some larger member states. Dissonance among them, or between them and the Commission, will not disperse completely.[13]

Alongside difficulties in reaching political agreement, achieving organizational coherence and operational efficiency, and the consequences of any deployments the EU may make are questions of how military undertakings will be paid for. They include a redirection of and increase in expenditure, for weapons and surveillance systems, R&D investment in technology, coordination and administrative units, and other outlays, some for unforeseen exigencies.[14] Although savings can be made through integrated spending, other considerations affect what the EU can achieve.

All challenges may be overshadowed, in the immediate present or longer term, by terrorism. The prospect is acknowledged in the European Security Strategy (ESS) and widely examined, including in work commissioned by member state governments.[15] Terrorism links external and internal dimensions of security. States, "rogue" or otherwise, are sometimes involved as direct supporters or havens. Terrorism will have an impact on the EU's posture and role in the world and the world's perceptions of the EU. In 2005 the British government introduced measures that some regarded as impinging on civil liberties. They pertain to entry into the UK, grants of asylum, possible deportation, and restrictions on the activities of political and religious extremists. They may even entail a withdrawal from, or altering of, EU human rights obligations. "Let no one be in any doubt that the rules of the game are changing," said Prime Minister Blair, following terrorist attacks in London.[16] A "solidarity clause," whereby the EU mobilizes all available means to assist a member state in response to such events, was adopted after the 2004 Madrid bombing. Improved intelligence, police cooperation, and a newly introduced European arrest warrant (EAW) assisted the capture and extradition in Italy of a person allegedly involved in terrorist activity in the UK. Later incidents, such as the failed attack at Glasgow airport in June 2007 and the uncovering of other plots, underlined the threat posed to EU states.

The inventory of EU contributions to the creation, sustenance, and occasional enforcement of regional and global security is growing. Like other actors, its performance has not been consistent, and its response can be slow. The EU must have internal cohesion and solidarity to function effectively, which involves defining and maintaining objectives; managing bilateral partnerships and multilateral agendas with diverse states, organizations, and other entities; acquiring a credible force projection capacity; and equipping itself for the unexpected. An essential ingredient is a critical mass of political will: manifested institutionally by sensible policy, the provision of adequate financial and human resources, and the preparedness to deploy them.

Common Foreign and Security Policy (CFSP)

The CFSP grew out of the much less ambitious European Political Cooperation (EPC), which had been operating since 1970. A Western European response to the disaster caused by the disintegration of the Soviet Union from 1989 to 1991, the CFSP was formally agreed at Maastricht and included in the 1992 TEU.[17] It aimed at better coordination of national positions and to give weight and expression in a field in which the surpassed EC had no real profile. The CFSP was to provide the institutional machinery, focused policy directorate, and symbolic core of the EU's noneconomic external personality. Its emergence into a world of vastly changed conditions resulted in a baptism by fire. The diplomatic and foreign policy traditions of member states were, notably concerning the Balkans, recast as inexperience and discord in the nascent "common" context. The EU may have had political impact, yet its shortcomings were starkly exposed.[18]

The evolving EU foreign policy system, Simon Nutall has argued, "can only be understood if the traditional bond between 'actorness' and national sovereignty is dissolved." This is a central point. In contrast to Nutall we do not believe that this "bond" has yet dissolved.[19] The Commission has a shared right to make proposals in the CFSP domain, but this policy field will not be extensively supranationalized in the foreseeable future. The treaties of Amsterdam (1997) and Nice (2000) introduced institutional innovations and extended the possibilities for QMV in determining common positions, joint actions, and common strategies. These treaties did not seriously diminish member state controls or their retention of veto rights. "Vital national interests" can be cited by one or more states in objection to a proposal agreed to by all the others. Some scholars nonetheless saw a progression toward a federalized CFSP, perceiving the outcome at Nice as indicative and positive.[20] Others were less inclined to believe it. One termed Nice an "overtrumped success."[21] A more vigorous foreign and security policy is not likely be advanced by the rejection of the CT, although that alone is unlikely to reverse cooperation either.[22] Rather, there will be a continuation of the "dialectical relationship" that "exists between the national instinct and the perceived need for solidarity." As Christopher Hill suggests, "Most states may have no intention of relinquishing their own diplomacy, but equally it would not occur to them to opt out of the CFSP."[23]

The CFSP's developing multidimensionality has enabled the EU to venture into spheres of "human security" with positive effects.[24] The mass of legal acts passed reveals a busy policy field in judicial and administrative terms.[25] If the CFSP is evaluated in terms of recognition from other actors, it falls short. The "Union," Alse Toje maintains, has "proven largely unable to coordinate member-state resources and translate this into actual influence beyond the group of countries seeking EU membership."[26] France, Germany, and the UK took it upon themselves to lead the EU's diplomatic effort in negotiating with Iran on its nuclear program. Their efforts extracted minimal response, as the United States observed from the sidelines. In contrast to "bad cop" America and its hints of a possible military strike, the EU's "good cop" role included a visit to Iran by Prince Charles, ostensibly as president of the British Red Cross.[27] Some commentators submit that the EU3's efforts resulted in a better picture of the situation inside Iran and in "important time" being won. "Money and good words" were, however, not enough to convince Iran's leadership to voluntarily end its uranium enrichment.[28] Others suggest that even if some members were critical that the EU was represented by only three states, the Iranian case and dialogue as part of the Contact Group in the former Yugoslavia are positive examples of a flexible EU diplomacy.[29] Conversely, relatively minor affairs like Morocco's occupation of an island claimed by Spain generated little EU support, not helped by a UK-Spain dispute over nearby Gibraltar.[30] Europeanization has either not taken full effect in the foreign and security policies of member states, or it has a restricted ambit when there are attempts to operationalize them.[31] A concrete day-to-day European-ization of the field would be encouraged by an EU diplomatic service. This initiative was also a victim of the CT outcome.

European Security and Defence Policy (ESDP)

Military and policing functions are among the most sensitive policy areas for any governments. A long-awaited initiative to develop a unified military and crisis management capability, which incorporated the Western European Union (WEU) into the EU, was launched in 1999.[32] Jolyon Howorth argues that:

> the decision to pool that last bastion of sovereignty—defence and security policy—with all its limitations and caveats, constitutes a sea change in the way the EU and its Member States will henceforth relate to the outside world. The reality is deeply empirical and lends itself badly, if at all, to theoretical speculation.[33]

Elsewhere the same author has expounded on the role of discourse, ideas, and epistemic communities in advancing ESDP,[34] which now entails a wide spectrum of tasks, extending well beyond the "language school" of the Eurocorps.[35] According to the research institute incorporated within its frame-work, ESDP has given legitimacy to the EU's military powers, developed "permanent and complete" structures, initiated the ESS backed by consensus among member states, and is acquiring the support of EU publics. There is also "an impression of permanent tensions and recurring political constraints," demonstrated by the schism over Iraq, and "profound differences of view on the ultimate political purpose" of integration in these fields.[36] Whether the ESS provides the guidelines to overcome difficulties and whether they will be adhered to—especially when crises occur—is unclear. As Simon Duke stress-es, "Strategies must face the test of the real world since, whatever strategies say, states and organizations often act differently."[37]

For some critics, EU states and institutions were a disparate group that would "stop identifying problems" that they "do not have the means to solve."[38] Others wrote of "Euro-paralysis" and an inability to act.[39] ESDP is a response to and, in part, a refutation of this kind of criticism—that the EU was not doing enough for its own, let alone global security—and demands that it do so. Jean-Yves Haine puts it starkly that "the tragedy of Sarajevo was the major reason behind ESDP."[40] Although that was a "problem" that could not fail to be identified, the initial treatment was ineffectual. Roy Ginsberg writes, "The only way the scarred and bruised confidence of the EU can heal so that it can act again in a zone of war is for the EU to summon the political will to improve the functioning of the CFSP and operationalize the ESDP."[41] If the EU fails to confront such problems, then ESDP will have a restricted scope. One interviewee noted that there is "always more demanded than what we will be able to do."[42] Another view rejects a common security and defense policy altogether, for a combination of reasons: the money could be better spent; political divisions and institutional shortcomings will hinder effective implementation and eventually widen fissures through the emergence of a "core" group; and if the United States is alienated before an adequate replacement defense is in place, the EU may be dangerously exposed. There are also indications of a pacifist agenda that opposes a "military power Europe" on normative grounds.[43] One example is an article by Mette Eilstrup Sangiovanni, whose arguments are well made but can be undermined by advocating more resources for, and a sharper focus on, nonmilitary conflict management, while also stating that, despite its efforts and expenditures, "Europe has little reason to be unduly proud of its soft power role" and "the EU actually acquires relatively little influence in return for its money."[44]

ESDP introduced a Political and Security Committee (PSC), Military Committee (MC), and Military Staff (MS). The PSC is a "permanent body" that "plays a major role in decision-shaping, but not decision-making proper." It is subordinate to the General Affairs and External Relations Council (GAERC) for "political/strategic decisions." The MC and MS are not treaty-based bodies. The MC comprises defense chiefs of all EU states and advises the PSC on military matters. The MS is composed of around seventy officers and provides specialized expertise in planning and crisis management operations. The entire Brussels-based staff of ESDP totals about 200 people.[45] There is a political commitment among member states to share information, but no formal legal arrangement. Intelligence sharing is "filtered," with a hierarchy of distribution. Solana "theoretically" receives the most. Some of that intelligence applies to a confidential "watch list" of unstable or potentially problem-causing states.[46] Following ESDP's introductory phase, the European Capabilities Action Plan (ECAP) was launched at Laeken in December 2001. It was to operate with four core principles: improved effectiveness and efficiency, including enhanced cooperation for smaller groups of willing states; voluntary national commitments; better coordination between EU states and with NATO; and public support. A second Capabilities Conference in May 2003 introduced "project groups" that would focus on "concrete projects" directed by designated lead nations.[47]

All this was impressive on paper. Structures and in-principle agreements are one thing; having forces available and committing them to combat situations are something else. The Helsinki Headline Goal required that the EU must be able (by 2003) to deploy up to 60,000 personnel within sixty days and sustain a mission for at least one year. The force was to be capable of conducting the full spectrum of Petersberg Tasks, a range of crisis management and conflict prevention measures first proposed by a declaration of the Western European Union at Petersberg, Germany, in June 1992. They were adopted by the EU in the Amsterdam Treaty. Some of these tasks are primarily military (peacemaking and peacekeeping) and fall within the scope of ESDP. Others are of a primarily civilian nature (humanitarian assistance, rescue). If necessary the force proposed in the Headline Goal would include air and naval elements. Burkard Schmitt cites 1.86 million total personnel from which to draw on; Julian Lindley-French and Franco Algieri suggest 1.7 million. Only about 10 percent are "usable" at any given time for combat. It is a principal "grey area for European armed forces . . . where peacekeeping meets war-fighting and lasts for a significant period." Estimates of the maximum sustainable deployment in a "hot war," from an EU population of 500 million, are about 40,000 troops: 15,000 each for the UK and France and 10,000 for Germany.[48]

The GAERC Secretariat does not use the term "rapid reaction force." Moreover, sixty days was acknowledged by an official as too long a time to wait for a force to be assembled and deployed. By 2004, when a new Headline Goal for 2010 had been adopted, the topical descriptor for combat-ready forces was "battlegroups." Seven to nine were envisaged, each comprising about 1,500 personnel plus those in training and rotation. They would be capable of a "very rapid" response. The proposal resulted from a Franco-British initiative, which Germany joined, and then became an EU undertaking. On 1 January 2007, a new Operations Centre in Brussels for commanding "missions and operations of a limited size," such as those conducted by a 2,000-troop battlegroup, came into effect. This facility gave the EU an additional option, alongside that of NATO through the Berlin Plus arrangements, or one of the member state Operational Headquarters (OHQs) located in France, the UK, Germany, Italy, and Greece. On the same date the "Battlegroup Concept" reached full operational capacity. With that, the EU is "able to fulfil its ambition of having the capacity to undertake two concurrent single battlegroup-sized rapid response operations, including the ability to launch both such operations nearly simultaneously."[49]

Some observers contend that even with adequate forces and institutions, ESDP lacks a strategic concept.[50] Far from avoiding involvement, the EU risks having to rush from one crisis to another in the role of an all-purpose firefighter, on a smaller scale but otherwise not so different from that which the United States has engaged in and often been maligned for. The EU may find itself doing so without clearly defined, overarching intention or limitations. Such a scenario represents the opposite of a restricted scope and could be construed as flexibility and a readiness to take on responsibility. The lack of discriminating rules of engagement might instigate resistance among political sectors and general populations.

Before any pretensions to being a global foreign and security policy actor can be entertained, the EU has to prove itself in a regional context. The

Balkans represented a poignant test of the EU's capacity to replace NATO and maintain regional stability, perhaps for decades.[51]

> If the EU is not ready to remain in the region and stay the course in building impartial police and judiciary institutions, then its philosophy of conflict prevention and crisis management will run into the sand. It will make a mockery of the EU's attempts to set a precedent in combining the "hard" and "soft" tools that are defence and diplomacy.[52]

In March 2003 the EU's Concordia mission relieved NATO's Allied Harmony in the Former Yugoslav Republic of Macedonia (FYROM). In December, Proxima, an EU-led police mission, replaced Concordia. After a transitional phase of several months in 2002, the EU replaced the UN force in Bosnia-Herzegovina with a police mission (EUPM) from 2003 to 2005. The EU provided 449 police and civilian personnel with another eighty coming from third states.[53] In December 2004 the EU military operation ALTHEA began in Bosnia-Herzegovina under the auspices of the General Framework Agreement for Peace (GFAP). The European Union Force (EUFOR) stationed up to 8,000 troops, to which eleven other states also contributed. The first EU "Rule of Law" mission began in Georgia in July 2004 under the appellation Themis.[54] Aiming to reform the criminal justice system, its launch was partly due to the Georgian foreign minister also being a French citizen with good contacts in the EU.[55] Far beyond the European periphery, Artemis, a bridging operation, began in the Democratic Republic of Congo (DRC) in 2003. The EU, with France as the framework nation, took on peacekeeping duties for a three-month period while UN forces were exchanged. In 2005 the EU conducted the Kinshasa mission, and in 2006 it monitored elections and the postelection period in the DRC, this time with Germany as the major provider of personnel. In late summer 2006, after intense debate within member states and in EU forums, some 7,500 primarily French and Italian troops, with German naval support, were sent to southern Lebanon to join the UN Force in Lebanon (UNIFIL) under the terms of UNSC Resolutions 1701, 425, and 426. Nineteen EU states contributed military personnel to monitor the cessation of hostilities between Hizbollah and the Israeli army.

There are no in-depth internal performance reviews on the general progression of the CFSP or ESDP. The evaluation process is one of trial and error and acting upon "lessons learned." The six-monthly European Council conclusions represent more of an overview than detailed critical assessments.[56] Since ESDP came into existence, the number of missions and operations has multiplied rapidly. Several extended beyond their original timetables. Third states often participate, and who pays how much and for what can be nebulous. ESDP missions are buttressed financially by other EU assistance packages or UN aid for which the EU has provided the largest share. In general the progress made and success achieved go beyond what could have been envisaged in 1999 when ESPD was launched (see Table 5.1).

Table 5.1 ESDP Missions

Name, Location, Dates	Personnel[a]	Cost (€ millions)
EUPM, Bosnia-Herzegovina, December 2002–2005	Member states, 418;[b] third states,[c] 90	15.7 start-up costs, plus 38.0[d]
Concordia, Former Yugoslav Republic of Macedonia (FYROM), March–December 2003	Member states, 307; third states, 50	Own costs plus 6.2[e]
Artemis, Democratic Republic of Congo (DRC), June–September 2003	Member states, 2,000	7.0
Proxima, FYROM, December 2003–December 2004	Member states, 200	7.3 start-up costs, plus 7.7
EU support to AMIS (I and II), Sudan (Darfur), January 2004 to present	Member states, 64; African Union, 2,000	242 plus 115 member states
Themis, Georgia, July 2004–July 2005 to present	Member states, 10	2.0
ALTHEA, Bosnia-Herzegovina, December 2004 to present	Member states, 5,798; third states, 858	71.0[e] plus own
Kinshasa, DRC, April 2005–June 2007	Member states, ca. 40	4.3 plus own
EUSEC DRC, DRC, June 2005–June 2007	Member states, 9	1.6 plus own
EUJUST LEX, Iraq, July 2005–December 2007	Member states, 20	21.3 (2 phases)
AMM, Aceh, September 2005–December 2006	Member states and third states,[f] ca. 200	9.3 plus own
EU BAM, Moldova/Ukraine, December 2005–December 2007	Member states, 69	8.0
EU BAM, Rafah, November 2005 to present	Member states, 70	11.47
EUPol COPPS, Palestinian Territories, January 2006 to present	Member states, 33	6.1 plus own
EUFOR DRC, DRC/Gabon, July 2006–December 2006	Germany, 780; other EU and Turkey, ca. 1,200	16.7 plus own

Sources: Antonio Missiroli,. "ESDP: How it Works," and Gustav Lindstrom, "On the Ground: EU Operations," in Nicole Gnesotto (ed.), *EU Security and Defence Policy: The First Five Years (1999–2004)* (Paris: ISS, 2004): 55–72 and 111–129; EUFOR at http://www.euforbih.org/index.html; Council of the European Union, "EU Military Operation in Bosnia and Herzegovina (EUFOR–ALTHEA)" at http://www.consilium.europa.eu/cms3_fo/showPage.asp?id=745&lang=en&mode=g; Council of the European Union "Council Joint Action 2004/523/CFSP of 28 June 2004 on the European Union Rule of Law Mission in Georgia, EUJUST Themis," *Official Journal of the European Union* L228/21, 29 June 2004; Council of the European Union, "Council Joint Action 2004/847/CFSP of 9 December 2004 on the European Union Police Mission in Kinshasa (DRC) regarding the Integrated Police Unit (EUPOL 'Kinshasa')," *Official Journal of the European Union* L367/30, 14 December 2004; Council of the European Union, "EU Police Mission in the Palestinian Territories (EUPOL COPPS) at http://www.consilium.europa.eu/cms3_fo/showPage.asp?id=974&lang=en&mode=g; "EUFOR RD Congo" at http://www.consilium.europa.eu/cms3_fo/showpage.asp?id=1091&lang=en&mode=g; Consilium at http://www.consilium.europa.eu/cms3_fo/showPage.asp?lang=EN.

Notes: a. Personnel numbers can vary. b. 395 police, 23 civil. c. Third states are neither EU members nor those in which operations are occurring, i.e., they are states assisting the EU. d. Annual costs: €20 million from the EU budget (B-7) and €18 million from member states. e. "Common costs" split 84.5%–15.5%, charged according to GDP scale (minimum 2% percent, maximum 25% percent). States also pay individual costs. f. ASEAN, Norway, Switzerland.

If ESDP confirms the EU as a military actor, there is a corollary dilution in the self-definition as, or claims of its being, a "civilian power."[57] Reinhardt Rummel has framed it as something of a dilemma for the EU, suggesting, "The Europeans may fail either way because they are destroying their image as a civilian power while remaining militarily weak, which could undermine rather than strengthen the EU's international credibility and stature."[58] The new 2010 Headline Goal "requires member states to acquire assets, such as transport planes, to increase their military prowess." The European Defence Agency (EDA) will report on progress to this end. The "beneficiaries," says Daniel Keohane, would be a "more competitive defense industry; armed forces that would get badly needed military equipment at a better price; and taxpayers who would get better value for money."

Keohane also suggests that the EDA could "name and shame" those member states that are underperforming.[59] EU publics have generally been sympathetic toward unified policy in foreign, security, and defense affairs, while governments have been hesitant about a substantial leap (a *saut qualitif*) into supranational defense. However, many citizens would condemn rather than support an increased militarization, which underlines Rummel's point above. Politicians, including those who convened the Tervuren summit in April 2003, realize that the EU will lack credibility unless it develops and if necessary deploys a military capability. Yet if it does so, it weakens the "civilian" (pacifist) cast that has differentiated it from the United States, a contrast highlighted by many academic and media commentators and played to by politicians.

Since 1998 EU security and defense cooperation has oscillated between progress, with or without complete consensus, and concrete achievement on the one hand and gridlock, even bouts of estrangement, on the other. A view forming after the CT's failure suggested that this setback was not going to unduly hinder development in the area of security policy. Instead, "institutional renewals like the introduction of a Foreign Minister of the Union, the establishing of a European Foreign Affairs Service, or a changed task profile of the External Affairs council are not necessarily dependent on the ratification of the constitutional treaty."[60] A question that then surfaces is, why include foreign policy, defense, and security in the CT at all? If a constitutional grounding is unnecessary, it indicates that interstate politics, not adherence to legal formality or community institutions, is the main determinant of the system. Several analysts have argued that if the CT is to be revived, it must be linked with a major new project in the area of security and foreign policy. Doing that would be justifiable in its own right and would also benefit from consistent public support for more common foreign policy.

One emblematic set of reform proposals urges the integration of the Council's and Commission's foreign policy sections "in a single building," better cooperation between them, and an increase in Solana's authority and resources. It could be done "if prime ministers put their political weight behind this initiative." "Bureaucratic obstacles" could then be overcome. Even if an

EU diplomatic service requires a treaty change, "in practice, staff from the two institutions should work together," and "this integration should extend to overseas delegations." If it cannot be replaced with a longer-term incumbent, the role of the rotating presidency in foreign policy should be reduced. Solana's profile should be raised with a smaller role for a "troika" of the HR, the Commissioner for External Relations, and the presidency. There should be more flexibility for officials to be alternatively the heads of Commission delegations or special representatives of Solana. The authors conclude, "None of these modest proposals would require treaty change. Taken together, however, they could boost the EU's effectiveness in global politics."[61]

Table 5.2 gives a chronological overview of developments in the CFSP/ESDP and corresponding EU and global affairs. The danger remains that an external development or "event" may impose itself on the EU. Howorth contends:

> Vulnerability—in strategic terms—is a factor, which, in the last 15 years, has risen dramatically to the top of policy-makers' agendas. It is largely exogenous and a prime example of "events." Political-institutional capacity—an endogenous ability to impose or negotiate change—has also evolved markedly in the field of the ESDP. European statesmen, even the most powerful, have been proven time and again to be inadequate to the task of driving forward a coherent European response to the external environment.[62]

National Military Forces and Defense Policies

Any EU policy field requires a minimal level of consensus, even if that means agreement that some members will proceed in a particular direction and others will opt out. ESDP is one manifestation of the EU as an intergovernmental alliance, and "enhanced cooperation" is substantially no different than what states have long engaged in, if on a selective basis. In a confined analytical domain (considering the EU alone), enhanced cooperation can appear as progress. However, the transition from EC to EU occurred in order to cope with changes in Europe *and* the world outside. Duke was critical of a "renationalization of defence" in the wake of September 11, perceiving the common European security and defense policy as the weakest component in EU counter-terrorism.[63] A credible security and defense capacity means more than autonomy from the force provision or political backing of the United States. It requires intensive support from all, especially the main players.[64] Convergence or coordination can be measured, but there is no transformation to a pan-European foreign, security, and defense policy culture, as one discourse- and identity-focused analysis suggests. Progress toward unity depends "on the will of the member states," some of which we briefly assess in the following section.[65]

Table 5.2   Evolution of CFSP/ESDP and Concurrent EU/Global Affairs

Project/Event	Date	Participants	Main Content/Evaluation
CFSP introduced	1993	EU12	Many problems; positive balance
Amsterdam IGC	1997	EU15	CFSP High Representative
St. Malo meeting	December 1998	UK, France	Impetus, breakthrough
Kosovo War	1998–1999	UK, France, Germany	US-led NATO required to resolve
Cologne Council	June 1999	EU15	Operationalize "Petersberg Tasks"
Helsinki Council	December 1999	EU15	Headline Goal: deploy force by 2003
Nice IGC	2000–2001	EU15	Introduces PSC, MC, MS
Terrorist strikes in United States	September 2001	EU15	Dramatic end to "post–Cold War era"; EU pledges solidarity
Laeken Council	December 2001	EU15	Improved capabilities drive
NATO-EU Declaration on ESDP ("Berlin Plus")	December 2002	EU15	EU access to NATO assets and planning (Turkey-EU negotiations)
EUPM (Bosnia-Herzegovina)	December 2002	France, Germany, UK, Italy	Successful (to 2005) police mission
"Letter of Eight"	January 2003	UK, CEECs	Support for US position on Iraq
Declaration on Iraq	February 2003	France/Germany	Opposition to US position on Iraq
Iraq invasion	March 2003	EU15	EU split; Chirac insults CEECs
Concordia (FYROM)	March 2003	France	First EU military operation
Tervuren summit	April 2003	France, Belgium, Germany, Luxembourg	Governments opposed to US Iraq policy discuss core defense group
Artemis	June 2003	France	Three-month military operation in DRC
IGC Brussels	December 2003	EU15 (+10)	Failure to agree on draft CT
Proxima	December 2003	Belgium	Police extension of Concordia
"Battle Group" Concept	February 2004	France, UK, Germany	Smaller-scale, more mobile shock troops deployable immediately
Madrid bombing	March 2004	Spain	Devastating confirmation of terrorist danger; Spain leaves Iraq in June
EDA	July 2004	UK, France, Germany	Movement toward consolidation of European defense procurement
ALTHEA (Bosnia-Herzegovina)	December 2004	Twenty-two EU states	EUFOR replaces NATO Stabilization Force (S-FOR)
Brussels Summit	December 2004	EU25	Turkey-EU membership negotiations
French/Dutch referendums	May–June 2005	France, Netherlands	CFSP/ESDP unaffected in substance, but proposed structures are delayed
London bombings	July 2005	UK	Reiteration of the terrorist threat
Iran	2003–2007	UK, France, Germany	Ongoing negotiations to stop Iran's uranium enrichment program
DRC deployment	July 2006	Germany	Military stabilization force
Israel-Hizbollah war	July 2006	France, Germany, Italy	Israeli invasion of southern Lebanon
Summit on a "Reform Treaty"	June 2007	EU27	UK rejects the creation of the office of EU "foreign minister"

Source: Authors' formulation.

UK

The UK is one of the EU's major military powers. The Blair government encouraged more involvement by the EU in security and defense while maintaining an intergovernmentalist-Atlanticist outlook. The St. Malo initiative surprised many, not least the Americans, and made Blair a central figure in EU defense affairs. A 2001 Ministry of Defence (MOD) paper stated that "the Government's European defense policy is about improving Europe's ability to react in times of crisis." It urged improvement in capabilities and a reduction in dependence on the United States "in dealing with crises in and around Europe." To do that, EU states must spend "more effectively and efficiently" and in some areas spend more.[66]

The MOD considered that "since St Malo, progress has been rapid," with "the basic approach" of enabling the EU to "decide on military matters while drawing on national forces and capabilities, NATO planning support and, when necessary, other NATO assets" being "widely supported." Developing the necessary structures, along with civilian crisis management capacities and the means by which non-EU states might be included in missions, did not change the fact that military capabilities were the main issue for ESDP. In order to tackle diverse missions, "nations need to address their priorities, both within defense budgets and across Government programmes more generally." Funding "must come from voluntary national contributions," which correspond with "individual circumstances" and "national decision making sovereignty." The latter point reflects the UK position that the Helsinki Headline Goal "does not mean the creation of a standing 'Rapid Reaction Force' or a "European Army." Rather, it "identifies a pool of forces or capabilities that meet exacting EU requirements, from which forces can be rapidly assembled on a case-by-case basis for particular operations, albeit with the approval of the relevant national governments."

The onus is placed squarely with the member states: "Firstly," because "it was important to set the EU nations a challenging target to encourage them to make real and effective improvements in their military capability. Secondly, it is clearly not for the EU to demand improvements in military capability from non-EU members." Additionally, the UK views ESDP as "an inclusive project designed to involve Non-EU European Allies, the candidates for accession to the EU and other states with which the EU has a political dialogue." That statement served as an encouragement for Turkey's ambitions. The MOD paper declared that ESDP:

> capitalises on the political will and momentum that the EU as a whole can generate to improve Europe's military capabilities and to give the EU an effective ability to respond to crises . . . it will strengthen European military capabilities and thereby strengthen the European contribution to NATO . . . ensure that Europe takes a fairer share of the security burden

and reinforce and sustain the relationship between Europe and North America.[67]

If that was and is the case, it is a mystery why the development of powerful, effective, common EU security and defense forces has been so difficult. A later MOD white paper stated, "The security and stability of Europe and the maintenance of the transatlantic relationship remain fundamental to our security and defense policy."

> There is currently no major conventional threat to Europe, but asymmetric forms of attack, including from international terrorism, pose a very real threat to our homelands. Such threats, along with the proliferation of WMD, are global. We must tackle them assertively at the source—wherever that might be—or in transit, using the wide range of tools available to us (political, economic and military).[68]

The Iraq War was the principal cause of political pressure on Tony Blair to depart from Downing Street. At the same time, involvements in Iraq and Afghanistan, and the provision of smaller forces in Africa and elsewhere, have put the British military under strain. Although he is seeking an exit strategy for the UK from Iraq, Blair's successor, Gordon Brown, has given no indication of a major shift in traditional British posture in the area of EU foreign, security, and defense policy.

France

France has always been the state most insistent that the EU should develop a military capacity reflective of its economic and demographic power, an aim entwined with French global political and strategic ambitions.[69] In important respects, France is the most contradictory EU state. French advocacy of the EU asserting itself as a global power is accompanied by an aversion to cede much in the way of influence over its national affairs, either to other member states or the *apatrides* (stateless persons) of the Commission.[70] French foreign and security policy activism was given extra motivation after the disasters in the Balkans.[71] Its presence in Africa included engagement in the Cote d'Ivoire and the framework nation role in Artemis in the DRC. These involvements cost France a considerable sum. French motivations were as national as they were European, and France was set to intervene with or without EU or UN support.[72]

Defense Minister Michèle Alliot-Marie's introduction to France's 2003–2008 Military Programme Bill of Law declared, "It is the government's duty to ensure the continuity of France's defence policy." The bill "reflects the determination . . . to give France a defence that matches both its requirements and its international ambitions . . . and a defence that contributes to the construction of European defence."[73] In outward appearance, much of France's global ambition is driven by an instinctive rivalry with the United States.[74] Although tensions are palpable, behind the scenes there is cooperation as well as dispute. French Foreign Ministry officials were optimistic despite all contemporary transatlantic difficulties. One concluded that both NATO and ESDP were moving in a direction that France wanted.[75]

An important development in French defense and security policy was the new nuclear deterrence doctrine announced by Chirac in January 2006.[76] It was a message to states that might assist terrorists in attacking France's vital or strategic interests that they would be subject to nuclear retaliation. It merged a realist worldview with acute awareness, confirmed in a white paper two months later, that France is internally exposed to Islamist-inspired terrorism.[77] The strategy is another instance of how policy areas from pillars two and three of the TEU overlap, in this case extending to an intersection of military and police intelligence functions with nuclear capability and potential deployment. The main targets are states where terrorist groups are resident, either while planning an attack or seeking refuge. It could be speculated that these states include Iran, Syria, Libya, and Algeria, depending on the characteristics of the regimes that are in or may come to power in these or other examples.

The new French strategy is not limited to terrorism, however. A revival of conventional threats is also considered possible. Chirac noted that France is "not shielded from an unforeseen reversal of the international system nor from a strategic surprise." According to David Yost, one rationale to acquire new long-range intercontinental ballistic missiles is "the need to be able to threaten China and other distant powers in Eurasia and the Middle East." How much Europeanization the French doctrine entails is not so clear, although its application to the securing of "strategic supplies," meaning the delivery of energy resources, could also include those for Germany and other close allies.[78] France and the UK often evade Europeanizing their special assets, preferring to exert a patrician influence. They "will not even conceive of the notion that they should relinquish their separate seats on the UN Security Council, or place their nuclear weapons in trust for the EU. They remain the only two European states capable of the projection of serious military force beyond their own theatre."[79]

Given its special interests in the region, and continuing incentives to remain at the forefront in European and global security issues, France was obliged to undertake a diplomatic effort to try to halt hostilities in southern Lebanon in 2006 and then to make a major contribution to UNIFIL. With other contingents in FYROM, Afghanistan, and the DRC, France's military capacities were, like the UK's, almost at full stretch.

Germany

Germany has moved from being, relative to its economic and demographic size, a "political dwarf" to a vital, if cautious, player in the development of EU defense and security.[80] Germany's central position in the European and transatlantic discussion on military reform and intervention is linked to a domestic debate on the relationship of the military to the broader society.[81] After reunification, conservative governments under Helmut Kohl prolonged the restriction on "out of area" involvement, partly due to SPD and Green opposition. The irony was tangible when an SPD-Green government became the first to send the FRG's military into combat—out of the NATO area and without a UN mandate.[82] It encouraged some observers to revise their views on Germany's "civilian power" status.[83] Germany then led and was the chief troop provider for the NATO operation Amber Fox in FYROM. That also influenced perceptions that Germany has resocialized into a power-political arrangement of states and motivated pleas for an alternative "offensive idealism."[84] Another set of perspectives stresses an enduring national disinclination to be involved. The post–Cold War peace dividend was eagerly accepted by Germany. From 1990 to 1999, employees in defense industries fell from 280,000 to less than 100,000.[85] In 2004 Howorth suggested that "the continuing reluctance of Germany"

> to move towards a more interventionist security policy and to increase defence spending, was putting a brake on the ESDP process and encouraging other smaller Member States, themselves more wedded to "softer" forms of power projection, to question some of the EU's military ambitions.[86]

If that view is correct, it will be difficult for Germany to push its own integrationist preferences, adequately support French Gaullist ambitions, or maintain a "silent alliance" with the UK, let alone live up to US hopes. The SPD-Green government (to November 2005) had to address pressures for military intervention as a response to maltreatment perpetrated against civilian populations. Before and after the campaign against Slobodan Milosevic in 1999, it also had to appease a constituency in which pacifist tendencies were strong. The crisis over Iraq witnessed the German government parties prioritizing the latter, this time with French support, though not without dissent in their own ranks.[87] Some suggest the Franco-German-British triangle should be rebalanced by reinforcing the London-Berlin axis.[88]

Unlike the British and French militaries, the *Bundeswehr* (German Military Forces) has a large conscript component. There is opposition to a transition to full professional status and to increasing the military budget. Spending fell over 35 percent between 1990 and 2005 as the task spectrum widened.[89] Progress in common EU defense will be affected if its largest member is hamstrung by funding and political problems. Despite the perseverance of these concerns, in October 2006 over 9,000 German personnel were deployed in operations worldwide. In the preceding summer, engagement in two theaters had, notwithstanding reservations across the political spectrum,[90] received *Bundestag* (German lower house of parliament) mandates within weeks of each other: for the DRC, where Germany agreed to lead the EUFOR deployment, and for participation in UNIFIL, for which Germany would provide a marine-based contingent off the Lebanese coast. The German defense ministry was to acclaim the tour of duty in the DRC as "one of the most successful actions of the *Bundeswehr*."[91] Concurrently, Germany provided about 2,700 personnel for combating the Taliban in northern Afghanistan as further pressures built for German participation in the more dangerous southern half of that country.

These deployments indicate that the restructuring of the *Bundeswehr* may be more advanced than some believe. A new and comprehensive defense *Weissbuch* appeared in 2006. It details perceived threats, tasks, capabilities, restructuring, and many other aspects of the German armed forces. In 2010 these forces will comprise 252,000 soldiers and another 75,000 civil personnel; 35,000 soldiers will be available for rapidly deployable intervention forces: 15,000 of them for action with the NATO Response Force and 18,000 for EU Headline Goal tasks. Another 70,000 soldiers will be available for stabilization purposes. The Eurofighter, strategic airlift planes, transport helicopters, early warning systems, and anti-ABC (atomic, biological, and chemical) weapons equipment are replacing the tank-based Cold War defense.[92] Although it is still under-funded in comparison to several EU allies, Germany's global military presence and role have undergone an extraordinary transformation. In geographic range and number of missions, it has moved a long way since 1989 or 1998 and politically even more.

Poland

The CEECs in general are much more concerned with the regional dimension of security than with the global theater. Yet this regional imperative also explains their Atlanticism, an orientation that has and will require them to manifest it through more than rhetorical or diplomatic backing for US policy. A standard characterization of Poland's posture in international relations, and especially defense and security issues, is as "America-friendly." The influence of history on the Polish population and political elite cannot be downplayed. Many consider the United States as a liberator and guarantor. These attitudes influenced Poland's participation in the 2003 Iraq War, encouraged further by the perceived arrogance of France and Germany.[93] The contretemps over Iraq, along with the dispute over the CT and tensions in other EU policies, manifest the difficulties Poland faces in successfully pursuing, or balancing, its strategic goals. It is an important component of the new NATO and in the evolving ESDP. The Polish position is similar to that of the UK: a European security and defense pillar anchored within NATO, which ensures a continued US presence in Europe, is the desired option. This orientation may need some reshaping and flexibility. Poland is a "European Atlanticist at the Crossroads" for whom "the seeming dilution of NATO"

> as a collective defense organization and effective military instrument was met by Warsaw with great disappointment. These factors point to the notion that in Iraq, Polish instinctive Atlanticism reached its apex and now needs to be rethought and adjusted. . . . If this does not occur, it is likely that Poland will fail to reconcile its two strategic objectives of being a reliable partner of the US in Europe and an influential member of the EU.[94]

Turkey

Turkey is one of the most critical actors that the EU has to deal with.[95] Its high military spending, large population, and strategic location made it an indispensable part of NATO during the Cold War and still do today. Turkey's relation to European defense is closely linked to other political issues. It previously hindered ESDP development by blocking EU access to NATO assets.[96] Ostensibly, Turkey did so because of concerns about the use of these assets without full consultation and potentially against its vital interests, above all regarding Greece and the Cyprus issue. This problem was nominally resolved with agreement on the Berlin Plus arrangements in December 2002, now acceptable to Turkey, which enabled EU use of NATO assets for crisis management.[97] The leverage Turkey exerted through its NATO membership had the ultimate goal of EU accession. It was no coincidence that also in December 2002, a "date for a date" was set, upon which the EU would decide if negotiations on Turkey's EU membership would or would not begin. In the period that followed, Turkey continued to be "extremely difficult" in security and defense issues despite the "very good conditions provided for it."[98] In 2006, EU-NATO meetings had twenty-three, not twenty-five EU state representatives, because Turkey vetoed the participation of Cyprus and Malta (the exclusion of two being more acceptable than one) on the grounds that they were not members of the Partnership for Peace (PFP).

When negotiations on EU membership were announced in December 2004, a different dynamic was introduced into EU-Turkey relations. It would change further if the prospect were fulfilled.[99] Conversely, the failure of the CT again revised outlooks. Widespread objections to an eventual EU membership will not be the last hurdle for Turkey. The first year of negotiations was not encouraging.[100] How these proceed will have ramifications for EU-Turkey security cooperation. Turkey has made major contributions to several ESDP missions. There are doubts about that continuing if the accession process were to terminally break down. With membership, Turkey would have full decision-making powers and decision-shaping privileges. It would also be expected to make available personnel, equipment, and territory for logistical purposes.[101]

Were it to join tomorrow, Turkey would have by far the largest armed forces in the EU. Its conscript army is over 400,000 strong, its navy has more than 50,000 personnel, and its air force has 60,000.[102]

Armaments and Technology

Since the end of the Cold War, national defense industries have experienced a stream of mergers, acquisitions, and restructuring.[103] Commercial as much as governmental players drove a process that could be alternatively conceived as rationalization, centralization, or Europeanization. A "Letter of Intent" signed by defense ministers of the six major arms-producing states in 1998 gave it political underpinning. And although the production of military equipment was characterized by multinational fusion, the purchasers remained state governments, if potentially for use on behalf of the EU.

In July 2004, EU governments formalized agreement on the EDA, to be headed by Solana (see Figure 5.2). The agency shall act "under the Council's

Figure 5.2   The European Defence Agency

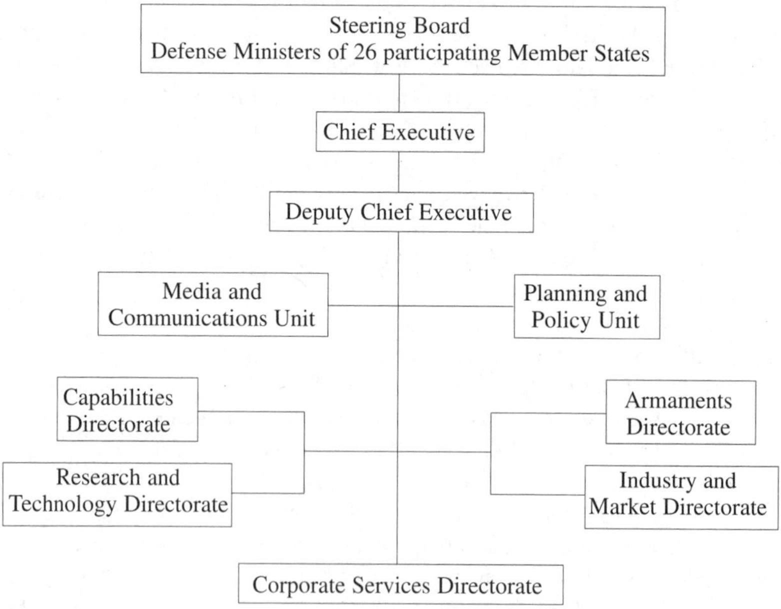

Source: EDA at http://www.eda.europa.eu/genericitem.aspx?area=Organisation&id=119.

authority" and have a legal personality. Its mission is "to support the Council and the Member States in their effort to improve the EU's defense capabilities in the field of crisis management and to sustain the ESDP as it stands now and develops in the future."[104] The agency will be financed by participating states, based on a GDP scale. There is again scope for a further burden-sharing debate if some states are prepared to support the venture as an EU good and others are content to free-ride.[105] The agency is not a purchaser of equipment but has a supervisory function, intended to ensure that member states manage their procurements in ways that promote EU-wide efficiency. Its creation provides "an opportunity to rationalize Europe's armaments institutions, transforming the existing patchwork of bodies and arrangements into a more coherent whole."[106] The EDA will coordinate with NATO—the secretary-general of which it "may decide to invite, on matters of common interest"—and work with other agencies such as the Organization for Joint Armament Cooperation (OCCAR, comprising Belgian, British, French, German, and Italian input). It may eventually incorporate some of them.

OCCAR, which, in the medium term at least, will not form part of the agency, is charged with the efficient management of multinational programs, prominently the Airbus A400M transport plane, involving seven member states with deliveries expected in 2009. Governments have allowed some cross-border commercial consolidation in the defense sector, which led to the creation of companies such as Franco-German-Spanish European Aeronautic Defence and Space (EADS).[107] This enterprise ran into problems in 2006 and faced the prospect of a publicly funded bailout. The EDA represents a move to rationalize military procurements, though if or when such an outcome will occur is uncertain.[108] The EDA's "Initial Long-term Vision for European Defence Capability and Capacity Needs" assessed the global context as "sobering" and that ESDP operations will be "directed at achieving security and stability more than 'victory.'"[109] One of the major steps toward realizing this vision is a Capability Development Plan (CDP) for which EU governments set a timetable in June 2007. According to the EDA's Steering Board, "the CDP would not be a supranational military equipment or capability plan replacing national defence plans and programmes, but would support national decision-making." The Steering Board will also commission a report "to be written by an expert known as a 'Wise Pen'—on a European Approach to Network-Enabled Capabilities."[110]

Financial Resources and Funding Mechanisms

Another set of concerns applies to funding and expenditures, which have produced considerable variation in estimations and categorizations. With the exceptions of pre-accession assistance for the 2004 enlargement (covered under heading 7 of the EU budget) and the European Development Fund

(EDF), heading 4 of the 2005 budget covered eleven policy areas.[111] Funding was concentrated in three major ones: external relations (see Table 5.3), development, and humanitarian aid, which accounted for more than 93 percent of appropriations.[112] External relations included geographically defined programs and some "thematic activities." The budget for 2004 was around €5 billion. The Commission proposed a specific CFSP budget for 2005 of €55 million, a reduction of €7.6 million below 2004. This assessment combined "expected needs, the availability of other institutionalized channels for funding and the tight situation of heading 4."[113]

The EU cannot maintain the status of an aspiring global actor with this amount of funding for its central foreign and security policy planning and administration section, along with monitoring, some crisis management costs, and other related expenses. Comparison with the foreign affairs budgets, let alone those for defense, of individual member states and others amplified the paucity of EU funding in this area. The UK Foreign and Commonwealth Office had a resource budget of £1.5 billion in 2004–2005, increasing to £1.7 billion in 2007–2008;[114] the French Ministry of Foreign Affairs budget was €4.1 billion in 2003. The US State Department estimated spending under its Discretionary Budget Authority to be $27.4 billion in 2004. Of that, $17 billion went to international assistance programs.[115] Even if these expenditures apply to an eclectic conception of "foreign affairs," roughly commensurate with the range of EU external activities, a large disparity remains. And if all member states were serious about EU defense, there would be an equalization of per capita spending in this sector.

EU members appear to have realized that if the CFSP is to sustain a substantial role, it requires more funds. After a budget increase to €99 million in

Table 5.3   External Relations Appropriations for 2005 (Community Budget)

Region or Activity	Funds appropriated (€ millions)	Increase/Decrease (%)[a]
Eastern Europe/Central Asia/Caucasus	515	+1.1
Western Balkans	554	−9.2
Mediterranean/Middle East	1,070	+6.8
Latin America	315	+0.9
Asia	648	+5.2
Human rights	45	50
Rapid Reaction Mechanism	30	0
CFSP	55	−11

Source: European Commission, *Preliminary Draft General Budget of the European Commission for the Financial Year 2005* (Brussels: 15 June 2004): 49–50, available at http://eurlex.europa.eu/budget/www/index-en.htm.

Note: a. Compared with 2004, not including consumer price index increases.

2006, the Council decided to increase annual amounts from 2007 to 2013, totaling €1.98 billion in inflation-adjusted prices over that period. To designate a more dynamic and wide-ranging actor, heading 4 of the EU budget was renamed "The EU as a Global Partner" (see Table 5.4). Sums of €11.4 billion in 2007, rising to €15.7 billion in 2013, and totaling €95.5 billion in this period, were estimated by one research institute. Another reported a 2007–2013 total of €49.4 billion, at 2004 prices, which was confirmed for 2007. A May 2006 Commission document outlined expenditures for heading 4 subfields totaling just over €56 billion at current (inflation-adjusted) prices. All included the European Neighbourhood and Partnership Instrument (ENPI), the financing mechanism for the European Neighbourhood Policy.[116]

Quantitative measures are not the sole indicator of astute or adequate spending, yet the amount of money available for some missions appears to justify Antonio Missiroli's claim that the funding provided for ESDP has been "ludicrous."[117] Despite French lobbying for a dedicated budget, ESDP operates primarily on the NATO principle of "costs lie where they fall." Individual states pay for their own "seconded" personnel, and these expenditures are differentiated from the rest of the CFSP, as determined under the TEU's Article 28.

For "operations having military or defense implications" (OMDIs), as David Scannell terms them, states are especially concerned that pecuniary contributions are paid by those who participate and at a level commensurate to their participation. Scannell argues that ESDP is "at one remove from the stan-

Table 5.4   The EU as a Global Partner: Financial Perspectives, 2007–2013

Subfield	2007–2013 Total
1. Instrument for Pre-accession aid (IPA)	11,565
2. Macroeconomic assistance	753
3. CFSP	1,980
4. Guarantees for lending	1,400
5. Emergency Aid Reserve (EAR)	1,744
6. European Neighborhood and Partnership Instrument (ENPI)	11,967
7. Development Cooperation and Economic Cooperation	17,055
8. Instrument for Stability	2,879
9. Humanitarian aid	5,614
10. Other expenditures	1,179
Total	56,136

Source: European Commission, *Communication from the Commission to the European Parliament and the Council: Technical Adjustment of the Financial Framework for 2007 in Line with Movements in GNI and Prices,* COM(2006) 327 final, Brussels, 22 June 2006; European Commission, MEMO/06/213, Brussels, 24 May 2006, Annex 1.

Notes: € million at current prices (adjusted for inflation) over 2007–2013. Subfields 1 to 5 are subject to Council decisions; 6 to 9 are co-decision programs.

dard CFSP regime, which is itself at one remove from the spheres of Member State activity regulated by the Community regime." Sensitivity about the financing of OMDIs reflects both a special "proximity to national sovereignty" and the "political and voluntary nature of Member State contributions of troops and equipment to the Union's ESDP."[118] Susan Penska and Warren Mason contend that states "opt for collective action when that course of action serves national values better than purely national action would."[119] The exception to the "costs lie where they fall" principle is funding for "common costs," for which the Athena mechanism was introduced in 2004. Common costs are charged to the member states measured against a GNP scale. These arrangements are imprecise and have been partly responsible for incoherence. Missiroli argues that "some common principles could be agreed to *measure* national contributions to ESDP: money, assets, manpower, know-how, and/or combinations thereof." That may help to "prevent the emergence of a "burden-sharing" debate inside the EU and among Europeans at large as well as to add legitimacy and transparency to the whole process."[120]

Commonality is ostensibly the whole point of the CFSP, and its component, ESDP. Although it could be interpreted as "flexible," the method of individual states paying their "own costs" has some problems. There are disproportionate responsibilities and risks for states that (1) provide personnel, with all the political costs and reduction in availability for other national tasks that this might entail, not to mention potential casualties; and (2) are required to pay the full financial costs associated with their role in ESDP actions. Those requirements could intensify burden-sharing arguments. Even if criticism directed at France for extracting generous outcomes from CAP disbursements and the UK for its budget rebate might be valid, it is those two that are expected to lead in defense issues.[121] The EU has no pretence to a credible military capacity without them. One official stated definitively, "ESDP is impossible without France and the UK."[122] Without significant changes, several others are, to varying degrees, free riders. Scannell concludes that "the provisions of Article 28 TEU suggest a difference in principle"

> between CFSP operational expenditure arising from operations having military or defence implications, on the one hand, and other CFSP operational expenditure, on the other. The manner in which those provisions have been applied by the Council to ESDP military operations suggests that the Member States of the Union are sensitive to that difference . . . a reversal of the expected operation of Article 28 TEU. Even the common costs component is run on an intergovernmental basis with all decisions "taken unanimously and without European Parliament participation."[123]

In 2000 the United States spent $335.7 billion on defense. By comparison, Germany, France, the UK, Italy, and Turkey spent $128.5 billion. The rest of the world spent $319.8 billion. In 2002, US expenditures on military equipment totaled $83 billion. Eleven European states and Turkey spent $29.8 billion. In 2003 the United States spent $94 billion, compared to these twelve states' $31 billion. The United States spent 3.5 percent of GDP on defense in 2003, Turkey 5.1 percent, and Spain 1.2 percent.[124] In 2004 the US defense budget reached $455 billion; the twenty-five EU states spent $210 billion. The UK alone had provisional expenditures of £31 billion in 2003–2004 and £30 billion in 2004–2005.[125] In 2005 the United States spent €406 billion on defense compared to the €193 billion spent by the then twenty-four EU states that participated in the EDA.[126] The total expenditure of all EU states is less than half that of the United States, but still about 80 percent more than Russia and China combined.

It is no surprise, then, that the total amount "should be enough to cover Europe's defence needs." For many commentators, however, this money is spent "ineffectively." In Keohane's view, "Europeans do not have nearly enough useful equipment or professional soldiers," and "too much European cash is wasted on conscript troops and outdated equipment." In comparison with the US inventory of "200 long-range transport planes that can carry the heaviest loads," the EU25 combined have four, all used by the UK. "Even allowing for the fact that Europeans do not have nearly so many global commitments as the US, that number is unacceptably low."[127] Others recommend that Europeans develop a "European way of war," something that does "not have to be an EU way of war."[128] That is optimistic, to say the least. It might be clear that EU states need to pool resources to undertake costly programs and acquire sophisticated equipment. But delays and funding problems have been prevalent—the Eurofighter was delivered a decade late. Exigencies will not wait for member states to organize and direct themselves as a collective.

Ulrika Mörth and Malena Britz apply a sociological-institutionalist treatment to the organization of arms production and purchase, if not their ultimate use.[129] They focus on the political tensions and functional-administrative problems inherent in this example of nascent cross-pillarization. In doing so, they follow work by Schmitt.[130] Two fields, the market and defense, are each based on combinations of regulative and constitutive rules, though they "activate different questions and actors." The "constitutive rule" for defense is intergovernmentalism because "these issues concern national sovereignty." Here "the political ambition to create a European capacity to handle military crises—and to create a European actorness on defence—is combined with an intergovernmental decision-making process." In the market field, the constitutive rule is that a "supranational decision-making process" should occur "since these issues concern Europe's economic and technological competitiveness vis-à-vis the US." Free markets are seen as the drivers of "strong European defence companies" and the necessary "ongoing industrial internationalization of technology." The Commission has attempted to combine the TEU's first and second pillars by championing open markets for armaments. A consolidation could save about €6 billion per year and was a key aim of the "Letter of Intent" in 1998. It has "not had much impact," chiefly because the governments of these signatory states, the main arms producers, are "reluctant to give regulatory power to the Commission, in order to protect their defence markets. Thus, a single defence market remains some way off."[131] Mörth and Britz note the resort to "soft law" to regulate politically sensitive issues "which cannot be decided according to the 'Community method' but need more national autonomy and flexibility." The authors claim that

> important policy areas . . . ongoing constitutionalization and other gover-
> nance processes . . . and other issues that are at the heart of state sover-
> eignty, together with the enlargement process, suggest that we are dealing
> with a would-be polity for which our traditional integration theories and
> state concepts are poorly suited.[132]

It is unclear that a "would-be polity" is a more valid analytical focus than one of states using the EU "as an arena for intergovernmental bargaining," or that a "neo-medieval empire" can better cope with the challenges of the twenty-first century, including a security regime capable of projecting itself.[133] These and related questions will be illuminated by the progress of the European Defence Equipment Market[134] initiative and how purchases are used.[135]

Transatlantic Relations and NATO

Predictions of the United States and the EU drifting apart began almost as the Berlin Wall fell (if not before) and have intensified since the early 1990s. In military-security terms, there are two main recurring and related issues: (1) whether the victorious Cold War alliance can hold together after the disappearance of the Soviet negative integration factor and (2) if the EU can and will take on more responsibility in the European neighborhood and globally.[136] Behind the dissonance over defense and security arrangements are deeper differences about economic and social models and roles in the world.[137] A simple yet not inaccurate conception posits the United States as propelling a neoliberal globalization and a continental Western Europe clinging to the model of welfare states and dirigiste economic policies. A variant outlines rival Hobbesian versus Kantian interpretations of the world.[138] There are, however, forces within the EU that covet a European leviathan, not least as a counterweight to the American goliath, and whatever the assurances or protestations to the contrary. Perceptions of political interests and feelings of prestige motivate many Europeans to reject any notion of a US-led unipolar world. There are also rivalries in the respective articulations of "soft power."[139] The EU is bifurcating between maintaining and modifying the relationship (as the UK and Poland would prefer) and developing a sustainable independence from the United States, an approach France, along with Belgium and Luxembourg, wants to pursue. Under the previous "Red-Green" government, Germany was heading in that latter direction. The "Grand Coalition" is more cautious.

A sharp criticism of the EU, or some of its member states in particular, is that it has been content to be a "consumer of security," meaning security provided by the United States. Edwina Campbell has argued that "the EU has been captive to its own conceptual definitions: 'security' was always something that one could enjoy, without having to think about defense. Linked to this concept there were 'challenges,' but no threats."[140] ESDP was instituted to address that criticism, and some US scholars have been supportive since its early days.[141] The United States backs a more active EU foreign, security, and defense agenda, but not one that inflames tensions with or within NATO. The NATO-EU "Strategic Partnership" was intended to preempt new problems or any escalation of existing ones. The UK has been the principal transatlantic bridge builder, seeking to encourage both "more Europe" and a continued solid US role: "Europe needs to improve its ability to act in circumstances where NATO is not engaged. This will in turn produce a better, more coherent and effective European contribution to NATO." However, "NATO retains sole responsibility for collective defence. . . . Nothing will change this."[142]

The "NATO-EU Declaration on ESDP" affirmed EU access to NATO assets and planning for its own military operations and emphasized political principles, including effective consultation, decisionmaking autonomy for both actors, and "coherent, transparent and mutually reinforcing development" of common military capability requirements. The details were fleshed out in the "Berlin Plus" arrangements adopted in March 2003. They provide the basis for cooperation in crisis management and enable NATO support for EU-led operations in which NATO as a whole is not engaged. Any such operations would come under the command of NATO's deputy supreme allied commander in Europe (SACEUR), "who is always a European." The provisions enable "incorporation" "within NATO's long-established defence planning system, of the military needs and capabilities that may be required for EU-led military operations, thereby ensuring the availability of well-equipped forces trained for either NATO-led or EU-led operations."[143] Although the EU has acquired a significant capability through these arrangements, NATO remains the overarching authority. It reflects US interest in a robust European defense, yet the notion of "incorporation" within a US-led military-political organization is what some Europeans find difficult to accept. Conversely, one American account—based on a reading that foresaw in the CT the planned and imminent emergence of a supranational federation with sweeping powers, including in foreign, security, and defense policy—perceived a strategic goal of "balancing rather than complementing US power." The United States must act to "save NATO from Europe," including by giving "diplomatic, financial and moral support to its closest NATO allies to counterbalance the impending EU effort to pressure them into accepting an arrangement that is strategically unacceptable."[144] The NATO Response Force project, which took far less time to be assembled and made operational than the EU version, intensified the questioning about the transatlantic defense and security relationship: Will these forces be complementary or competitors? Will the European contribution to both be constituted from largely the same personnel?

The contemporary threat of terrorism profoundly affects both the United States and EU, and they are compelled to cooperate whatever their differences.[145] Despite variance in method and language, their basic goals are perceived as similar.[146] Others argue that NATO's aims and capabilities and those of the EU are gradually moving toward alignment.[147] At the end of 2006, EU member states were contributing almost 16,000 troops, or about half the total, to NATO's International Security Assistance Force (ISAF) in Afghanistan. The UK, Germany, and Italy were the main contributors. In addition, the EC and member states had provided about €3.7 billion for reconstruction and civil projects in the period 2002–2006, with approximately €2 billion more pledged.

The EU and the United States trade and invest more with each other with than with anyone else. Their partnership accounts for over 40 percent of global trade, and they have a combined €1.5 trillion in FDI in each other's economies. They have manifold formal agreements and cooperation on consumer protection, higher education and training, space exploration, extradition arrangements, transportation security, and foreign policy matters. EU sources reiterate that, despite their differences, the United States and the EU need each other and that when they cooperate, "no challenge is too great."[148]

China

One big test of the ability of the EU and the United States to cooperate is presented by China. In October 2006, a major conference on the theme of a "global strategic triangle" of the United States, EU, and China was held in Washington, D.C., sponsored by the German Marshall Fund, the German Embassy to the United States, and the Bucerius Law School. Many US analysts see "managing the rise of China" as one of the greatest current and future challenges for the United States. One European expert defines the EU-China relationship as situated between "realpolitik and institutional dynamics."[149]

What cannot be ignored is that western business and states have engaged in a veritable stampede to secure positions in the Chinese market. EU members are in competition with each other, the United States, and others. European leaders have shown an eagerness to build a partnership with China in order to reap what they perceive will be huge economic benefits. Germany and France have been prominent in this regard. Chinese authorities may weigh access to Chinese markets and other aspects of economic relations against foreign policy or international security considerations.[150] Dealing with and in China can cause political problems, domestically and internationally. One case was the sale by Germany's former Schröder-Fischer government of a plutonium power plant to China. At the same time, Schröder pushed for a lifting of the EU's arms embargo against China. The incident inflamed existing controversy with the United States and within the German government coalition, whose Green component opposed nuclear power generation inside or outside Germany.[151] For transatlantic relations, lifting the arms embargo could have "dire consequences," warned one observer.[152]

During an EU-China summit in 2005, at which he was accompanied by the presidents of the Council and Commission, Tony Blair and José Manuel Barroso, High Representative Javier Solana noted a wide range of issues where the EU and China were enjoying productive cooperation. These included negotiations with Iran on its nuclear program, stopping the proliferation of WMDs, combating terrorism, and reforming of the UN. According to Solana, "Multilateralism and respect for international law are fundamental tenets of the EU's foreign policy. And I know the same is true for China."[153] An in-depth study by the EU-incorporated Institute for Security Studies proposed "guidelines for an EU strategy" in response to China's rise some time after Solana declared that the "EU-China strategic partnership" had been functioning well for two years. The study identifies three main areas, themselves interconnected, where China's rise has and will have global implications: the economy, energy, and global governance. It is noted that the EU should develop its own security perspective on China.[154]

Energy Security

One dimension of foreign and security policy not noted in Jørgensen's taxonomy cited at the beginning of this chapter, though it is in the ESS, is energy supply. The EU is one of the largest energy consumers and importers. It requires investments of €1 trillion in the sector over the next twenty years. The Commission stresses market freedoms as the solution to EU needs.[155] Pressing and latent problems of international politics, such as the Iraq War, tensions with a volatile Iran, or dealing with North African despots, are underplayed. The EU is very dependent on external suppliers. The shock of the Russia-Ukraine gas dispute reverberated through EU capitals and institutions. Similar incidents involving Russia only intensified the concerns about dependence on it.

Robert Miller suggests that the weight of gas and oil in EU-Russia relations influenced a common opposition to some US foreign policy undertakings.[156] Frank Umbach argues that as Gazprom's share of the EU energy mar-

ket grows, so does dependence on the Russian state, and that this, like dependence on Middle Eastern and Maghreb states, is untenable.[157] Apart from
Russia, the other main candidates are emergent producers in chaotic sub-
Saharan Africa, or Central Asia, where democracy and reliability are also not
widespread. Gawdat Bahgat underlines EU vulnerability.[158] The energy debate
encompasses arguments for a reversal of planned exits from nuclear power.[159]
Energy policy is disputed among EU members, and there is no definitive united position, despite efforts to reach one.[160] There is recurring acute friction
between Poland and Baltic states on the one hand and Russia on the other. A
plan to circumvent Poland and Baltic states with a marine gas pipeline from
Russia to Germany remains controversial. Poland advocates an "energy
NATO," specifically excluding Russia.

What can be detected in Commission and Council documentation, and in
statements by various leaders in the member states, is a growing concern about
the EU's increasing import dependency, the critical factor being *on whom* the
EU is dependent. Despite the contemporaneous focus on combating global
warming and pursuing environmentally conscious energy policies, in several
European capitals the need to ensure reliable supplies of oil and gas is considered more critical.

Internal Security and Terrorism

It might not seem appropriate to situate internal security within a discussion of
the EU as a global actor. If it is to become one, however, its home front must
be protected. Physical boundaries between exogenous and endogenous security are eroding, as are analytical distinctions between them. The CFSP and
ESDP are more closely linked to internal security than they first appear. Most
security threats originate outside the EU and, as such, are located in the external policy sphere. But many EU states are very concerned about their internal
situations: they influenced the French and German positions regarding an
attack on Saddam Hussein's Iraq. Both states have large Muslim populations
and have witnessed the results of the instrumentalizing of religion for terrorist
purposes in the UK and Spain.[161] These concerns are intensified by the possibility that terrorist groups might acquire weapons of mass destruction
(WMDs), the "most frightening scenario," according to the ESS. The emergence of "home-grown" terrorists complicates the labeling of threats. Many of
these are citizens of one or another member state of the EU. Combating them
is a form of "defense," even if undertaken by police and paramilitary forces
that normally operate within national borders. Operations in Afghanistan are a
"forward defense" whose aims include preventing or lessening the probability
of terrorist activity within the EU as much as furthering its interests externally. How successful these efforts are or will be is another matter.

Although clearly not in all specific cases or subfields, the TEU pillars of justice and home affairs on the one hand, and the CFSP, with its offspring the ESDP on the other, are converging. This is partly a result of decisions taken by the EU—or most of it—like Schengen's removal of internal border controls and eastern enlargement's extension of the external border—and partly the result of "events." Illegal immigration; the smuggling of people, drugs, weapons, and atomic material; and the permeation of organized crime from outside to inside the EU require the strengthening of agencies like Europol or the border troop, Frontex, and increased resources. Threats to critical infrastructure or the supply of strategic resources also entail an overlapping of policy and legal domains.[162] Although some states and national societies may be more directly affected or at risk than others, security is a EU-wide public good that necessitates a concerted political, policy, and financial response. Close and extensive cooperation among EU states, or globally for that matter, is not a transgression or reduction of state sovereignty. Infiltration by terrorists is.

Conclusion

In the enlarging policy area of security, common EU interests will not be prioritized over national or party political preferences in all instances. To arrive at and implement the necessary will requires congruence among twenty-seven states, which may mean resisting or overriding popular preferences by governments. Doing so would indicate that, rather than only being possible with or as a reflection of public opinion, the political will of governments may only count if it is enforced against public wishes. Should that occur, it would reemphasize elite dominance and criticism of deficiencies in democratic legitimacy. As long as the EU delivered economic success and moderated rivalries, such actions by governments were acceptable. In the current phase, it is harder, and governments are constrained to respond to the diverse preferences of national electorates. The funding available for CFSP is small compared to the expectations of it and in relation to other spending. Security and defense is susceptible to horse-trading, side payments, and other forms of bargaining across policy fields. On the EU foreign minister post, Howorth opined that "the bottom line is clear": "The requirements of coordination in the broad field of the CFSP and in the more critical field of the ESDP are now so urgent that the creation of this post literally imposed itself. Almost all think-tank papers on the issue in the years prior to the Convention proposed its creation. Now it is (almost) here."[163] After 31 May and 4 June 2005, the word "almost" acquired greater significance. It meant that some key reforms of CFSP, including a European foreign minister, had to be held in abeyance or reformulated and prepared for introduction in another manner. Continuing implementation of ESDP flexibility arrangements, "permanent structured cooperation," and the EDA may also be affected, as the CT would have embedded CFSP and ESDP in a "unified formal framework" and strengthened the "profile and credibility of the EU *vis-à-vis* other international actors."[164] A common defense is not farther away because of the referenda results per se. Although some less contentious aspects may not be subject to unanimity, CFSP and ESDP will remain primarily intergovernmental arrangements. Reforms in both will be returned to, if perhaps approached differently.

Hill has noted the EU's quiet yet important progress and ability to overcome disputes in a more or less civil manner, as well as its "failure to live up to some dramatic challenges along the road." The "new situation" after September 11 and Iraq shows "that the Member States are neither regrouping around a common position, however cautious, nor renationalizing. . . . Instead, we have witnessed an EU disunity of a dramatic but possibly only temporary kind, and among governments more than peoples."[165] Hill also declares, "All states, whether EU members or not, are subject to the structural forces that inhibit the CFSP from playing a serious role in a crisis."[166] That opinion is interesting because it seems to (unintentionally) render any achievements of the EU in the foreign and security policy field secondary at best. Any actor can—or should be able to—operate more or less competently outside the pressures of a crisis situation; if it cannot do so, then its status as an "actor" is called into question.

The importance of internal coherence is clear. A recent Commission paper, which also denoted that institution's interest in having more say in the Council-dominated CFSP and ESDP, stressed three factors for success "in the world": (1) "political agreement among the Member States on the goals to be achieved through the EU"; (2) appropriate policy instruments and resources; and (3) "the role and responsibility of the EU institutions and the legal environment."[167] For the EU, convincing diplomacy, ensuring a credible security zone for itself and its immediate surroundings, building on force projection and peacekeeping beyond that, and possessing the capacity to react in crises are imperatives in themselves and will demonstrate a global actor at work.

Notes

1. Council of the European Union, *EU-UN Co-operation in Military Crisis Management Operations: Elements of Implementation of the EU-UN Joint Declaration,* adopted by the EU Council, Brussels, 17–18 June 2004.

2. Council of the European Union, *EU-NATO: The Framework for Permanent Relations and Berlin Plus,* Brussels, 2003, http://ue.eu.int/uedocs/cmsUpload/03-11-11%20Berlin%20Plus%20press%20note%20BL.pdf. See also Johannes Varwick, ed., *Die Beziehungen zwischen NATO und EU: Partnerschaft, Konkurrenz, Rivalität?* (Opladen: Budrich, 2005); and Jolyon Howorth and John Keeler, eds., *The EU, NATO, and the Quest for European Autonomy* (New York: Palgrave, 2003).

3. Knud Erik Jørgensen, "Three Doctrines on European Foreign Policy," *Welt Trends* 42, no. 1 (2004): 27–36.

4. Cf. Hazel Smith, *European Union Foreign Policy: What It Is and What It Does* (London: Pluto, 2002); Charlotte Bretherton and John Vogler, *The European Union as a Global Actor* (London: Routledge, 1999); Karen Smith, *European Foreign Policy in a Changing World* (London: Polity, 2003); Christopher Hill and Michael Smith, eds., *International Relations and the European Union* (Oxford: Oxford University Press, 2005).

5. Ben Rosamond, "Conceptualising the EU Model of Governance in World Politics," *European Foreign Affairs Review* 10, no. 4 (2005): 465–466.

6. Preben Bonnén, *Towards a Common European Security and Defence Policy: The Ways and Means of Making It a Reality* (Münster: LIT, 2003), 131.

7. Michael Smith, "Toward a Theory of EU Foreign Policy-making: Multi-level Governance, Domestic Politics, and National Adaptation to Europe's Common Foreign and Security Policy," *Journal of European Public Policy* 11, no. 4 (2004): 740–758.

8. Charles Grant and Mark Leonard, "How to Build a Better EU Foreign Policy," *Bulletin* 47 (Brussels: Centre for European Reform, 2006).

9. Hazel Smith, *European Union Foreign Policy.*

10. Mary Farrell, "EU External Relations: Exporting the EU Model of Governance?" *European Foreign Affairs Review* 10, no. 4 (2005): 451–462.

11. James Caporaso, "The European Union and Forms of State: Westphalian, Regulatory or Post-modern?" *Journal of Common Market Studies* 34, no. 1 (1996): 29–52.

12. Brian Crowe, "A Common European Foreign Policy After Iraq?" *International Affairs* 79, no. 3 (2003): 533–546.

13. Siegfried Schwartz, "Zur Geschichte einer gemeinsamen europäischen Außenpolitik," *Welt Trends* 42, no. 1 (2004): 51–63.

14. Reinhard C. Meier-Walser, ed., *Gemeinsam sicher? Vision und Realität europäischer Sicherheitspolitik* (München: Hanns-Seidel-Stiftung, 2004).

15. *A Secure Europe in a Better World:* European Security Strategy, Brussels, 2003; Michael Tarnby, *Recruitment of Islamic Terrorists in Europe: Trends and Perspectives* (Aarhus: Centre for Cultural Research, 2005); Daniel Keohane, *The EU and Counter-Terrorism* (London: CER, 2005); Jean-Luc Marret, "The Long Threat: Terrorism and International Jihadism," in Hans-Georg Ehrhart and Burkard Schmitt, eds., *Die Sicherheitspolitik der EU im Werden: Bedrohungen, Aktivitäten, Fähigkeiten* (Baden-Baden: Nomos, 2004): 21–31.

16. Simon Jeffery, "The Rules of the Game Are Changing," *Guardian,* 5 August 2005.

17. Elfriede Regelsberger, ed., *Die Gemeinsame Aussen- und Sicherheitspolitik der Europäischen Union: Profilsuche mit Hindernissen* (Bonn: Europa Union Verlag, 1993).

18. Cf. Roy Ginsberg, *The European Union in International Politics: Baptism by Fire* (Lanham, MD: Rowman and Littlefield, 2001), 57–104.

19. Simon Nuttall, "The Commission: The Struggle for Legitimacy," in Christopher Hill, ed., *The Actors in Europe's Foreign Policy* (London: Routledge, 1996), 131–146.

20. Cf. Wolfgang Wessels, "Nice Results: The Millennium IGC in the EU's Evolution," *Journal of Common Market Studies* 39, no. 2 (2001): 197–219.

21. Simon Duke, "Nice: ESDP's Overtrumped Success," *European Foreign Affairs Review* 6, no. 2 (2001): 155–175.

22. Cf. Nadia Klein and Wolfgang Wessels, "Eine Stimme, zwei Hüte—viele Pioniere?" *Welt Trends* 42, no. 1 (2004): 11–26.

23. Christopher Hill, "Renationalizing or Regrouping? EU Foreign Policy Since 11 September 2001," *Journal of Common Market Studies* 42, no. 1 (2004): 143–163.

24. Cf. Study Group on European Security, *A Human Security Doctrine for Europe: Barcelona Report of the Study Group on European Security* (London: LSE, 2004).

25. Council of the European Union, *Actes Juridiques PESC* (Brussels: Council of the EU, 2003).

26. Asle Toje, "The 2003 European Security Strategy: A Critical Appraisal," *European Foreign Affairs Review* 10, no. 1 (2005): 117–133.

27. For an interpretation extolling the EU's performance in this case, see Eileen Denza, "Non-proliferation of Nuclear Weapons: The European Union and Iran," *European Foreign Affairs Review* 10, no. 3 (2005): 289–312.

28. Michael Brzoska and Götz Neunenk, "Verhandlungen und andere Optionen im Atomstreit mit dem Iran," *Internationale Politk und Gesellschaft* 4 (2006): 11–27.

29. Christoph Schwegmann, "Kontaktgruppen und EU-3-Verhandlungen," SWP-Aktuell 62 (Berlin: SWP, 2005). For an extensive coverage of EU-Iranian relations and Iran more broadly, see Walter Posch, ed., *Iranian Challenges,* Chaillot Paper 89 (Paris: ISS, 2006).

30. Bonnén, *Towards a Common European Security and Defence Policy,* 135.

31. Cf. Reuben Wong, "The Europeanization of Foreign Policy," in Christopher Hill and Michael Smith, eds., *International Relations and the European Union,* (Oxford: Oxford University Press, 2005), 134–153.

32. Nicole Gnesotto, ed., *EU Security and Defence: The First Five Years (1999–2004)* (Paris: Institute for Security Studies, 2004), 195–201; Ehrhart and Schmitt, eds., *Die Sicherheitspolitik der EU.*

33. Jolyon Howorth, "The European Draft Constitutional Treaty and the Future of the European Defence Initiative: A Question of Flexibility," *European Foreign Affairs Review* 9, no. 4 (2004): 483–508.

34. Jolyon Howorth, "Discourse, Ideas and Epistemic Communities in European Security and Defence Policy," *West European Politics* 27, no. 2 (2004): 29–52.

35. David Buchan, *Europe: The Strange Superpower* (Aldershot: Dartmouth 1993).

36. Nicole Gnesotto, "Introduction: ESDP: Results and Prospects," in Nicole Gnesotto, ed., *EU Security and Defence Policy: The First Five Years (1999–2004)* (Paris: Institute for Security Studies, 2004), 11–31.

37. Simon Duke, "The European Security Strategy in a Comparative Framework: Does It Make for Secure Alliances in a Better World?" *European Foreign Affairs Review* 9, no. 4 (2004): 479.

38. Susan Penska and Warren Mason, "EU Security Cooperation and the Transatlantic Relationship," *Cooperation and Conflict* 38, no. 3 (2003): 256.

39. Jan Zielonka, *Explaining Euro-Paralysis: Why Europe Is Unable to Act in International Politics* (New York: St. Martin's Press, 1998).

40. Jean-Yves Haine, "An Historical Perspective," in Nicole Gnesotto, ed., *EU Security and Defence Policy: The First Five Years (1999–2004)* (Paris: Institute for Security Studies, 2004), 53.

41. Ginsberg, *The European Union in International Politics,* 85.

42. Author interview, GAERC Secretariat, Brussels, November 2004.

43. Mette Eilstrup Sangiovanni, "Why a Common Security and Defence Policy Is Bad for Europe," *Survival* 45, no. 3 (2003): 196–203.

44. Sangiovanni, "Why a Common Security and Defence Policy Is Bad," 200.

45. Antonio Missiroli, "ESDP—How It Works," in Nicole Gnesotto, ed., *EU*

Security and Defence Policy: The First Five Years (1999–2004). Paris: Institute for Security Studies, 2004, 55–72.

46. Author Interview, GAERC Secretariat, Brussels, November 2004.

47. Burkard Schmitt, "European Capabilities—How Many Divisions?" in Nicole Gnesotto, ed., *EU Security and Defence Policy: The First Five Years (1999–2004)* (Paris: Institute for Security Studies, 2004), 89–110.

48. Cf. Schmitt, "European Capabilities," 100; Julian Lindley-French and Franco Algieri, *A European Defence Strategy* (Gütersloh: Bertelsmann, 2004), 32.

49. GAERC, *ESDP Newsletter* 3 (Brussels: GAERC, January 2007).

50. Sven Biscop, "In Search of a Strategic Concept for the ESDP," *European Foreign Affairs Review* 7, no. 4 (2002): 473–490.

51. Christoph Schwegmann, *Kann die EU die NATO auf dem Balkan ersetzen?* S43 (Berlin: SWP, 2002).

52. Judy Dempsey, quoted in Nicole Gnesotto, ed., *EU Security and Defence Policy: The First Five Years (1999–2004)* (Paris: Institute for Security Studies, 2004), 201.

53. Gustav Lindstrom, "On the Ground: ESDP Operations," in Nicole Gnesotto, ed., *EU Security and Defence Policy: The First Five Years (1999–2004)* (Paris: Institute for Security Studies, 2004), 111–129.

54. *ESDP Presidency Report,* Brussels, 17 December 2004.

55. Author Interview, GAERC Secretariat, Brussels, November 2004. Cf. Salomé Zourabichvili, *Une femme pour deux pays* (Paris: Grasset, 2006).

56. Author interview, GAERC Secretariat, Brussels, November 2004.

57. François Duchêne, "Europe's Role in World Peace," in Richard Mayne, ed., *Europe Tomorrow: Sixteen Europeans Look Ahead* (London: Fontana, 1972): 32–47; Richard Whitman, "The Fall, and Rise, of Civilian Power Europe?" WP15 (Canberra: National Europe Centre, 2002); Hanns Maull, "Germany and Japan: The New Civilian Powers," *Foreign Affairs* 69, no. 5 (1990): 91–106; Adrian Treacher, "From Civilian Power to Military Actor: The EU's Resistable Transformation," *European Foreign Affairs Review* 9, no. 1 (2004): 49–66; Steve Wood, "The Iraq War: Five European Roles," WP112 (Canberra: National Europe Centre, 2003).

58. Reinhardt Rummel, "From Weakness to Power with ESDP?" *European Foreign Affairs Review* 7, no. 4 (2002): 454.

59. Daniel Keohane, "EU on the Offensive About Defence," *European Voice,* 22–28 July 2004, www.cer.org.uk.

60. Franco Algieri, Thomas Bauer, and Klaus Brummer, *Entwicklungspotenzial auch ohne Verfassungsvertrag: Optionen für GASP und ESVP* (München: CAP, 2005), 4. Cf. Ulrich Petersohn and Sibylle Lang, *Die Zukunft der ESVP nach den gescheiterten Referenden,* SWP-Aktuell 34 (Berlin: SWP, August 2005).

61. Grant and Leonard, "How to Build a Better EU Foreign Policy."

62. Howorth, "European Draft Constitutional Treaty," 504.

63. Simon Duke, "CESDP and the EU Response to 11 September: Identifying the Weakest Link," *European Foreign Affairs Review* 7, no. 2 (2002): 169.

64. Jolyon Howorth, "Britain, France and the European Defence Initiative," *Survival* 42, no. 2 (2000): 33–55.

65. Britta Joerißen and Bernhard Stahl, eds., *Europäische Außenpolitik und Nationale Identität* (Münster: LIT, 2003).

66. United Kingdom, Ministry of Defence, *European Defence,* Policy Paper No. 3 (London: MOD, 2001): 1–2.

67. Ministry of Defence, *European Defence,* Policy Paper No. 3.

68. Ministry of Defence, *Delivering Security in a Changing World* (London:

MOD, 2003), 5. This paper was released within a few days of the ESS. Many of the same observations and recommendations are found in both.

69. Jolyon Howorth, "France," in Jolyon Howorth and Anand Menon, eds., *The European Union and National Defence Policy* (London: Routledge 1997): 23–48.

70. Stephen Wood, *Germany, Europe, and the Persistence of Nations: Transformation, Interests, and Identity, 1989–1996* (Aldershot: Ashgate, 1998).

71. William Pfaff, *The Wrath of Nations: Civilization and the Furies of Nationalism* (New York: Simon and Schuster, 1993), 218.

72. Author Iinterview, GAERC Secretariat, Brussels, November 2004.

73. Republique Française, *2003–2008 Military Programme Bill of Law* (Paris: Ministère de la Défense, 2002).

74. Charles Cogan, *French Negotiating Behavior: Dealing with La Grande Nation* (Washington, DC: Institute of Peace Press, 2003).

75. Author interviews, Ministère de l'Etrangere, Paris, September 2004; "La France s'engage dans l'Alliance," *Le Figaro,* 26 June 2004.

76. Jacques Chirac, speech in Brest, 19 January 2006.

77. Secrétariat Général de la Défense, *Nationale La France face au terrorisme: Livre Blanc du Gouvernement sur la sécurite intérieure face au terrorisme* (Paris: La Documentation Française, March 2006).

78. David Yost, "France's New Nuclear Doctrine," *International Affairs* 82, no. 4 (2006): 701–721.

79. Hill, "Renationalizing or Regrouping?" 160.

80. For a comprehensive introduction to German foreign and security policy, see Wilfried von Bredow, *Die Außenpolitik der Bundesrepublik Deutschland: Eine Einführung* (Wiesbaden: Verlag für Sozialwissenschaften, 2006).

81. Wilfried von Bredow, "Defense Reforms and Current Problems of Civil-Military Relations in Western Societies," (Marburg: Institut fur Politikwissenschaft, no date).

82. Steve Wood, "German Foreign and Security Policy After Kohl and Kosovo," *Government and Opposition* 37, no. 2 (2002): 250–270.

83. Hanns Maull, "Germany and the Use of Force: Still a Civilian Power?" *Survival* 42, no. 2 (2000): 56–80; cf. Henning Tewes, *Germany, Civilian Power, and the New Europe: Enlarging NATO and the European Union* (Houndmills: Palgrave, 2002).

84. Gunther Hellmann, "Wider der machtpolitische Resozialisierung der deutschen Außenpolitik: Plädoyer für offensiven Idealismus," *Welt Trends* 42, no. 1 (2004): 79–88.

85. Burkard Schmitt, *From Cooperation to Integration: Defence and Aerospace Industries in Europe,* Chaillot Paper 40 (Paris: ISS, 2000), 13.

86. Howorth, "The European Draft Constitutional Treaty."

87. Anja Dalgaard-Nielsen, "Gulf War: The German Resistance," *Survival* 45, no. 1 (2003): 99–116; Sebastian Harnisch, "German Non-Proliferation Policy and the Iraq Conflict," *German Politics* 13, no. 1 (2004): 1–34.

88. Christian Schweiger, "British-German Relations in the European Union After the War on Iraq," *German Politics* 13, no. 1 (2004): 35–55.

89. "Die Schattenkrieger," *Der Spiegel,* 4 September 2006, 24–30.

90. "Das große Zaudern," *Der Spiegel,* 7 August 2006, 30–32; "Abenteuer Nahost," *Der Spiegel,* 21 August 2006, 24–27.

91. Jens Wiegmann, "Einer der erfolgreichsten Einsätze der Bundeswehr," *Die Welt,* 4 December 2006.

92. Bundesministerium der Verteidigung, *Weissbuch 2006: Zur Sicherheitspolitik Deutschlands und zur Zukunft der Bundeswehr* (Berlin: October 2006).

93. Marcin Zaborowski, "Between Power and Weakness: Poland—A New Actor in Transatlantic Security," *Reports and Analyses* 14/03 (Warsaw: Center for International Relations, 2003); Wood, *Germany and East-Central Europe*, 197–204.

94. Olaf Osica, "Poland: A New European Atlanticist at the Crossroads?" *European Security* 13, no. 4 (2004): 300–322.

95. Wood and Quaisser, "Turkey's Road to the EU."

96. Antonio Missiroli, "EU-NATO Cooperation in Crisis Management: No Turkish Delight for ESDP," *Security Dialogue* 33, no. 1 (2002): 9–26.

97. *NATO-EU Declaration on ESDP,* 16 December 2002, www.nato.int/docu/pr/2002/p02-142e.htm.

98. Author interview, General Affairs Council Secretariat, Brussels, November 2004.

99. Quaisser and Wood, *EU Member Turkey?*

100. "Rehn ermahnt die Türkei," *Frankfurter Allgemeine Zeitung,* 5 October 2006, 1–2.

101. Patrick Fitscher and Seda Serdar, "Die ESVP und die Türkei—Auf der Suche nach einer strategischen Partnerschaft," in Erhart and Schmitt eds., *Die Sicherheitspolitik der EU,* 118–129.

102. International Institute of Strategic Studies, *The Military Balance, 2004–2005* (Oxford: Oxford University Press, 2004).

103. Schmitt, *From Cooperation to Integration.*

104. Council of the European Union, "Council Joint Action 2004/551/CFSP of 12 July 2004 on the Establishment of the European Defence Agency," *Official Journal* L 245/17, 17 July 2004.

105. The general "free rider" problem is examined in a slightly different context by Anders Ahnlid, "Free or Forced Riders?" *Cooperation and Conflict* 27, no. 3 (1992): 241–276. Another example involving European states is Avery Goldstein, "Discounting the Free Ride: Alliances and Security in the Postwar World," *International Organization* 49, no. 1 (1995): 39–71.

106. Schmitt, "European Capabilities," 100–101.

107. Keohane, "EU on the Offensive."

108. "Council Joint Action 2004/551/CFSP of 12 July 2004," 1.

109. European Defence Agency, *An Initial Long-Term Vision for European Defence Capability and Capacity Needs,* LTV—3 October 2006—SB MoDs Levi (Ixelles, Belgium: EDA, 2006), 2, http://www.eda.europa.eu/genericitem.aspx?area=Organisation&id=146.

110. European Defence Agency, "EU Governments Set Timetable for Initial Plan to Strengthen Defence Capabilities" Press Release, Brussels, 28 June 2007, http://www.eda.europa.eu.

111. The EDF is an intergovernmental arrangement with no fixed contributions from individual members. France has usually contributed the largest amount, consistent with its special interests in Africa. A total of €13.8 billion was made available for 2000–2005.

112. European Commission, *Preliminary Draft General Budget of the European Commission for the Financial Year 2005* (Brussels: CEC, 2004), Part 6.3. Economic and financial affairs and fisheries receive 6 percent, and the remaining 1 percent is distributed over six smaller fields.

113. European Commission, *Preliminary Draft General Budget of the European Commission for the Financial Year 2005.*

114. United Kingdom, HM *Treasury Spending Review 2004* (London: Her Majesty's Treasury, 2004).

115. United States, Office of Management and Budget, *Budget of the United*

States Government: Fiscal Year 2004 (Washington, DC: Executive Office of the President, 2003), 223.

116. Cf. Roman Maruhn and Janis Emmanouilidis, *Agenda 2007: Der Konflikt um den Finanzrahmen, 2007–2013,* Reform Spotlight 1 2005 (München: CAP, 2005); Annegret Bendiek and Hannah Whitney-Steele, *Wein predigen and Wasser ausschenken: Die Finanzierung der EU-Außenpolitik,* SWP-Aktuell 31 (Berlin: SWP, July 2006); European Commission, *Communication from the Commission to the European Parliament and the Council: Technical Adjustment of the Financial Framework for 2007 in Line with Movements in GNI and Prices* COM(2006) 327 final (Brussels: 22 June 2006); European Commission, MEMO/06/213, (Brussels: 24 May 2006), Annex 1.

117. Antonio Missiroli, *Euros for ESDP: Financing EU Operations,* Occasional Paper 45 (Paris: ISS, 2003), 3, 8.

118. David Scannell, "Financing ESDP Military Operations," *European Foreign Affairs Review* 9, no. 4 (2004): 532–533.

119. Penska and Mason, "EU Security Cooperation," 260.

120. Antonio Missiroli, "Defence Spending in Europe: Is Europe Prepared to Pay for Improved Capabilities?" Paper presented at the Cicero Foundation Conference on ESDP, Paris, 13–15 December 2001.

121. Much of this criticism has derived from and been directed at each other.

122. Author interview, GAERC Secretariat, Brussels, November 2004.

123. Scannell, "Financing ESDP Military Operations," 549.

124. Elmar Wassenberg, "Europäische und amerikanische Rüstunganstrengungen im Vergleich," in Reinhard C. Meier-Walser, ed., *Gemeinsam sicher? Vision und Realität europäischer Sicherheitspolitik* (München: Hanns-Seidel-Stiftung, 2004), 383–403.

125. United Kingdom, Ministry of Defence, *UK Defence Statistics* (London: MOD, 2004); International Institute of Strategic Studies, *The Military Balance, 2004–2005.*

126. European Defence Agency, "European–United States Defence Expenditure in 2005," Brussels, 19 December 2006, http://www.eda.europa.eu.

127. Keohane, "EU on the Offensive"; Julian Lindley-French, "Plugging the Expanded Petersberg Tasks Gap? Europe's Capabilities and the European Capabilities Action Plan (ECAP)," in Hans-Georg Ehrhart and Burkard Schmitt, eds., *Die Sicherheitspolitik der EU im Werden: Bedrohungen, Aktivitäten, Fähigkeiten* (Baden-Baden: Nomos, 2004), 201–213.

128. Steven Everts et al., *A European Way of War* (London: Centre for European Reform, 2004).

129. Ulrika Mörth and Malena Britz, "European Integration as Organizing: The Case of Armaments," *Journal of Common Market Studies* 42, no. 5 (2004): 957–973.

130. Cf. Schmitt, *From Cooperation to Integration.*

131. Keohane, "EU on the Offensive about Defence."

132. Mörth and Britz, "European Integration as Organizing."

133. Sven Biscop, "Able and Willing? Assessing the EU's Capacity for Military Action," *European Foreign Affairs Review* 9, no. 4 (2004): 509–527.

134. European Commission, *Green Paper on Defence Procurement,* COM (2004) 608 (Brussels: CEC, 2004).

135. Burkhard Schmitt (Rapporteur), *Defence Procurement in the European Union: The Current Debate* (Paris: ISS, May 2005).

136. Reinhard Wolf, "Was hält siegreich Verbündete zusammen? Machtpolitische, institutionelle und innenpolitische Faktoren in Vergleich," *Zeitschrift für Internationale Beziehungen* 7, no. 1 (2000): 33–78.

137. Max Kaase and Andrew Kohut, *Estranged Friends: The Transatlantic Consequences of Societal Change* (Gütersloh: Bertelsmann 1996); Werner Weidenfeld, *Kulturbruch mit Amerika?* (Gütersloh: Bertelsmann, 1996); John Palmer et al., *Repairing the Damage: European Disunity and Global Crisis,* Challenge Europe 9 (Brussels: EPC, 2003).

138. Robert Kagan, *Of Paradise and Power: America and Europe in the New World Order* (New York: Knopf, 2003).

139. Stanley Sloan and Heiko Borchert, "Transatlantic Power Gaps and the Future of EU-US Relations," in Hans-Georg Ehrhart and Burkard Schmitt, eds., *Die Sicherheitspolitik der EU im Werden: Bedrohungen, Aktivitäten, Fähigkeiten* (Baden-Baden: Nomos, 2004), 133–145.

140. Edwina Campbell, "Vorstellung und Realität der europäischen Sicherheitspolitik aus der Sicht der USA," in Reinhard C. Meier-Walser, ed., *Gemeinsam Sicher? Vision und Realität europäischer Sicherheitspolitik* (München: Hanns-Seidel-Stiftung, 2004), 311–323.

141. Charles Kupchan, "In Defence of European Defence: An American Perspective," *Survival* 42, no. 2 (2000): 16–32.

142. United Kingdom, Ministry of Defence, *European Defence,* Policy Paper No. 3, 1. See also Jolyon Howorth, "Britain, NATO and CESDP: Fixed Strategy, Changing Tactics," *European Foreign Affairs Review* 5, no. 3 (2000): 377–396.

143. Council of the European Union, *EU-NATO: The Framework for Permanent Relations and Berlin Plus,* Brussels, 2003.

144. Jeffrey Cimbalo, "Saving NATO from Europe," *Foreign Affairs* 83, no. 6 (2004): 111–117.

145. Cf. United States, The White House, *National Security Strategy of the United States of America* (Washington, DC: 2002); Council of the European Union, *A Secure Europe in a Better World: European Security Strategy* (Brussels, 2003).

146. Volker Heise, *ESVP in transatlantischer Perspektive: Mehr Unterschiede als Gemeinsamkeiten?* Diskussionspapier 2006/1 (Berlin: SWP, 2006).

147. Natalia Touzovskaja, "EU-NATO Relations: How Close to a Strategic Partnership?" *European Security* 15, no. 3 (2006): 235–258.

148. European Commission, *The European Union and the United States: Global Partners, Global Responsibilities* (Brussels: Delegation of the European Commission to the United States, 2006).

149. Franco Algieri, "Die Europäische Union und China: Zwischen Realpolitik und institutionelle Dynamik," in Susanne Luther and Peter Optiz, eds., *China's Rolle in der Weltpolitik* (München: Hanns Seidel Stiftung, 2000), 191–198.

150. Cf. Margaret Pearson, "The Business of Governing Business in China," *World Politics* 57, no. 3 (2005): 296–322.

151. Robin Mishra, "Diplomatisches Desaster," *Rheinischer Merkur,* 11 December 2003.

152. Robin Niblett, "The United States, the European Union, and Lifting the Arms Embargo on China," *Euro-Focus* 10, no. 3 (2004) (Washington, DC: CSIS).

153. Javier Solana, "Driving the EU-China Partnership Forward," *Hampton Roads International Security Quarterly* 4 (2005): 37–39.

154. Marcin Zaborowski, ed., *Facing China's Rise: Guidelines for an EU Strategy,* Chaillot Paper 94 (Paris: ISS, December 2006).

155. European Commission, *Green Paper: A European Strategy for Sustainable, Competitive, and Secure Energy,* COM(2006) 105 final. Brussels, 8 March 2006.

156. Robert Miller, *Russia and Europe: National Identity, National Interest, Pragmatism, or Delusions of Empire?* Working Paper 2006/1 (Canberra: ANU, 2006).

157. Frank Umbach, 2004, "Sichere Energieversorgung auch in Zukunft: Die notwendigkeit einer europäischen Strategie," *Internationale Politik* 59, no. 8 (2004): 17–28; Frank Umbach, "Europas nächster Kalter Krieg," *Internationale Politik* 61, no. 2 (2006): 6–14.

158. Gawdat Bahgat, "Europe's Energy Security: Challenges and Opportunities," *International Affairs* 82, no. 5 (2006): 961–975.

159. Claude Mandil, "Atomkraft, ja bitte!," *Internationale Politik* 61, no. 2 (2006).

160. European Commission, *An Energy Policy for Europe*.

161. Jeremy Shapiro and Bénédicte Suzan, "The French Experience of Counter-Terrorism," *Survival* 45, no. 1 (2003): 67–98; Tarnby, *Recruitment of Islamic Terrorists in Europe;* Thérese Delpech, *International Terrorism and Europe*, Chaillot Paper 56 (Paris: ISS, 2002).

162. European Commission, *Protecting Europe: Ensuring the Security of Energy and Transport Services Across the European Union* (Brussels: 2005).

163. Howorth, "The European Draft Constitutional Treaty," 501.

164. Algieri, Bauer, and Brummer, *Entwicklungspotenzial,* 4.

165. Hill, "Renationalizing or Regrouping?" 154.

166. Hill, "Renationalizing or Regrouping?" 153. Elsewhere, Hill has argued that agency in world politics has not received the recognition it deserves, and the possibilities for its practical application have been underplayed. Cf. Christopher Hill, *The Changing Politics of Foreign Policy* (Houndmills: Palgrave, 2003); Christopher Hill, "What Is to Be Done? Foreign Policy as a Site for Political Action," *International Affairs* 79, no. 2 (2003): 233–255.

167. European Commission, *Europe in the World—Some Practical Proposals for Greater Coherence, Effectiveness and Visibility,* Communication from the Commission to the European Council of June 2006, COM(2006) 278 final, Brussels, 8 June 2006.

6

Dealing with the Neighbors

In 2004 the EU completed an orderly integration of the CEECs into its institutional structures, an objective that engendered new strategic implications.[1] The EU now faces an extended challenge to build durable partnerships with a panoply of other states and peoples while functioning as a credible promoter of reform. It has strong incentives to implement a comprehensive strategy for a disparate, unpredictable, and expanding "neighborhood," which is larger and contains more constituents than as defined by the European Neighbourhood Policy (ENP). Geographically, it comprises an arc from Morocco through the Maghreb, the eastern Mediterranean, the Balkans, Turkey, Iraq, Iran, and north through Transcaucasia, Moldova, Ukraine, Belarus, and Russia. The area for ENP alone is vast in scope, as is the gamut of tasks. ENP does not include the Balkans, Turkey, Iraq, or Iran, though they are included in the present analysis as part of the EU's broader surroundings. The Balkan countries have a membership perspective. Their Stabilisation and Association Process (SAP) is likely to be a prelude, if a very long one, to accession. Turkey has begun negotiations to join the EU, although the outcome is uncertain.

The potential for instability among this diverse assemblage is considerable. Some will use weakness as leverage to extract (more) aid, to pressure the EU for recognition as candidates, or to begin negotiations. The EU has to accept major responsibility for regions with many real and latent flashpoints. Its approach combines rationalist and constructivist components whereby incentives and conditionality are used to promote reform and socialization into western norms. The palette of cooperative arrangements involves political dialogue, technical and financial assistance, partial economic integration, and selective diplomatic support, which will have varying prominence across states and at different times. There is also a significant ad hoc element. Much of the expansive neighborhood is an area of political and strategic competition between the EU, Russia, and the United States.[2]

The Limits of Ambiguity

The macro-incentive of full membership has enabled the EU to exert considerable control over transformation processes and would-be entrants generally. Its shaping and steering capacity is less robust when based on quixotic formulations that depict a "ring of friends" who will "share everything but institutions."[3] In 2003 Michael Emerson noted that what was then "Wider Europe" comprised 360 million people, or 80 percent of the EU25 population, and produced 10 percent of the EU25's $10 trillion GDP, "despite containing the great natural resources of Russia." The "Greater Middle East" would add "392 million people, but again only 10 percent more income, despite the fabulous oil wealth of the Middle East." Emerson argued that "these disproportions speak trouble" and that the EU's "initiatives are not credibly articulated so far."[4]

The conception that became the ENP took shape in 2003–2004. Through tailor-made "action plans" (APs), ENP aims to build on, give impulse to, and perhaps supersede partnership and cooperation agreements (PCAs) with states that were part of the Soviet Union, and association agreements (AAs) for those in the Euro-Mediterranean Partnership (EMP)/Barcelona Process.[5] Action plans have been devised for Ukraine, Moldova, Morocco, Israel, the Palestinian Authority, Jordan, and Tunisia.[6] Others are in process for Azerbaijan, Egypt, Georgia, Armenia, and Lebanon. Algeria will follow. Syria, Libya, and Belarus are the main problem cases.

With these hoped-for confidence-building measures, the EU targets two main objectives: to improve its own security through sponsorship of reliable partners on its periphery and to deal with overstretch and meltdown that could result from the admission of too many new members. Aspirants will be offered "attractive alternatives to accession." Emerson was also skeptical about the substance of this scheme.[7] The EU is imprecise about these "alternatives" and whether exclusion from membership is permanent. The APs tacitly indicate that those for whom they have been drawn up will never be full EU members. The Commission, the EP, and most member states have pursued a "conscious ambiguity." Because "they neither can nor want to resolve the lack of clarity, a tacit distinction between accession and other forms of privileged partnership" must be assumed.[8] That will encourage a form of realpolitik whereby actors with governance and economic problems try to exploit concerns in the EU. If claims to candidature or negotiations remain unfulfilled, some may strive for other concessions. Turkey is a relevant case. An extended associate membership (EAM) could be an option.[9]

Before the EU can support reliable partners, it has to transform unreliable regimes. Because concrete goals and how they will be achieved are unclear, the EU gives the impression that it is playing for time until, hopefully assisted by economic revival, it can put something more long-term and convincing in place.[10] The rest of the world, including the EU's neighborhood (see Table 6.1), may not wait. Scholars and politicians now argue that "ambiguity is not

Table 6.1 Evolution of EU Policy Toward Neighboring States

States	Relationship	Instruments	Problems
Turkey	1963 association status; 2005 accession negotiation	Customs Union realized 1996; pre-accession aid	Full membership disputed
Croatia	Accession candidate June 2004	SAP, Pologne-Hongrie: Assistance à la restructuration des economies (PHARE), Instrument for Structural Policies for Pre-Accession (ISPA), and Special Accession Programme for Agriculture and Rural Development (SAPARD)	War criminals to be delivered
Serbia-Montenegro	Feasibility Study says negotiate SAA	Enhanced Permanent Dialogue (EPD)	War criminals; legal, economic, administrative problems
Kosovo	"Anchored" in SAP; no "contractual relations"	Community Assistance Reconstruction, Development, and Stabilisation (CARDS); UNSC Resolution	Ethnic conflict; status unclear
FYR Macedonia	April 2004 SAA; EUPM	CARDS, European Community Humanitarian Aid Office (ECHO), SAP	Corruption, organized crime
Bosnia-Herzegovina	Feasibility Study SAA accepted in November 2004	SAP, ECHO, PHARE, Obnova	Instability, ethnic conflicts
Albania	Negotiations opened for an SAA in 2003	CARDS, SAP	Crime, corruption; weak economy
Ukraine	PCA, ENP "priority country"	"Market economy status"; ENPI, AP	Economic and political fragility
Moldova	Generalized System of Preferences (GSP), PCA 1998, ENP 2004	Technical Assistance for the Commonwealth of Independent States (TACIS), ECHO, Food Security Program (FSP)	Criminality widespread; poverty; Transnistria
Russia	PCA 1997; Permanent Partnership Council; "Common Spaces"	TACIS, European Instrument for Democracy and Human Rights (EIDHR), ECHO; Joint Action for disarmament and nonproliferation	Authoritarianism; Kaliningrad; Chechnya; Georgia; energy supply
Georgia	PCA 1999; ESDP Rule of Law mission; GSP	TACIS, FSP, ECHO, EIDHR, exceptional financial assistance (EFA)	Regional conflicts; economic failure; Russian interference
Armenia	PCA in force 1999; EU-Armenia Council	TACIS, FSP, ECHO, EFA	Poverty; relations with Turkey

(continues)

Table 6.1   Continued

States	Relationship	Instruments	Problems
Israel	AA 2003; EMP; ENP	Mésures d'accompagnement financiers et techniques (MEDA), Scientific and Technical Coop., AP	Palestinian question
Morocco	Accession refused 1987; AA, EMP, ENP	MEDA, EIB loans, AP	Institutions, market economy

Sources: Directorate-General for Enlargement at http://ec.europa.eu/dgs/enlargement /index_en.htm; Eurostat http://epp.eurostat.ec.europa.eu/portal/page?_pageid=1090,30070682, 1090_33076576&_dad=portal&_schema=PORTAL; European Neighbourhood Policy at http://ec .europa.eu/world/enp/index_en.htm; Directorate General for External Affairs at http://ec.europa .eu/dgs/external_relations/index_en.htm; Europe Aid Cooperation Office at http://ec.europa.eu/ europeaid/index_en.htm; authors' formulation.

working." Instead, the EU's final borders must be defined and a "clearer incentive structure" provided. That would mean clarity about potential members and definitive nonmembers.[11] Table 6.1 presents an overview of the evolution of EU policy toward neighboring states.

Concurrently, in the extant member states, attitudes toward further enlargements are unenthusiastic. Emphasis on democratic procedures, and the growing sensitivity of political actors to public opinion on European issues, suggests publics will have more influence on the shaping of neighborhood policy and whether it transforms into accessions more than usual. Popular influence was demonstrated in the debate on Turkey's membership and in referendums on the proposed CT in France and the Netherlands. Discontent with aspects of national and EU politics underpinned its rejection in both countries. The prospect of more members was a pertinent issue.

These circumstances confront the EU with a dilemma. The Commission and EP have generally supported both more integration and enlargements. At critical junctures, the interests of national governments have sufficiently corresponded with these institutions and enabled "deepening" or "widening" initiatives. The context and estimations have altered. The EU is in a tension field between the disinclination of populations and much of the political elite in key member states toward membership increases and a perceived need to enhance EU security, mainly through the promotion of democracy, civil society, and reform in the neighborhood. Economic lethargy and unemployment in several polities, preferences for a deeper rather than wider EU, misgivings about the cultural suitability of some applicants, and concern about the institutional and financial capacity to absorb more countries influence aversions toward further enlargements. The last item is a criterion for accession that was previously not so important but is now strongly emphasized. Another argument has it that security through democratic reform can only be successfully pursued with the inducement of membership. The alternatives will be instability and dysfunctional or authoritarian regimes on the EU's borders.[12] The EU is thus faced with a predicament whereby "realising the promise of openness to all 'European' states that demonstratively uphold principal EU values may overburden the EU to the point of paralysis or collapse."[13]

Democratization, Stabilization, and Security

The "neighborhood" is primarily a security issue, or a cluster of them. The EU is stimulated more by potential negative developments than by a profusion of opportunities. ENP is part of an emergent geopolitical design linked to the European Security Strategy.[14] Unlike in 2004, accession is not the means by which the EU aims to strengthen regional security—at least not by preference.[15] Academic and media commentators have conjectured on a division between EU "insiders" and "outsiders" or the construction of a "Paper Curtain" across Europe.[16] Neighborhood policy as a substitution for membership was predicted by Judy Batt and her colleagues.[17] Most analysts conceptualize the situation as one in which the EU, as a core, strives to stabilize, democratize, or "Europeanize" the components of a periphery.[18] Bruno Coppieters and his colleagues define Europeanization as "a process that is activated and encouraged by European institutions—primarily the European Union—by linking the final outcome of a conflict to some degree of integration into European structures for the opposing sides."[19]

Although the EU's rhetoric has multilateral and regional tones, the practical orientation is to bilateralism. The motif is case-by-case stabilization rather than complex integration, though there are intentions and funding for cross-border programs. A favorable "Country Report" must be received before an AP is implemented. In political economy terms, the EU hopes to implement a process similar to that which worked quite successfully for the CEECs: financial assistance and phased market access granted in return for extensive reform, technical help for implementing legal structures that will inspire investor confidence, and the attraction of private investment to propel expansion. In the period 2007–2013, a consolidated European Neighbourhood and Partnership Instrument (ENPI) will distribute funding to countries "without a current accession perspective."[20]

The Commission had proposed a sum of almost €15 billion at 2004 prices; the sum agreed to by the Council was €10.59 billion at 2004 prices (almost €12 billion at inflation-adjusted prices), as is shown in Table 6.2. When a regulation of the Council and the European Parliament on ENPI was announced in October 2006, this sum had been adjusted to €11.18 billion over the 2007–2013 period.[21] Countries with "accession prospects" receive pre-accession funding. Though their entry is not certain, they are among the "insiders" and not officially "neighbors," who are tacitly the "outsiders."

**Table 6.2   European Neighbourhood and Partnership Instrument
(in millions of € at 2004 prices)**

Year	2007	2008	2009	2010	2011	2012	2013	2007–2013
Proposed Amount	1,433	1,569	1,877	2,083	2,322	2,642	3,003	14,929
Actual Amount	1,390	1,400	1,437	1,470	1,530	1,640	1,720	10,587

Source: European Commission, *Proposal for a Regulation of the European Parliament and of the Council Laying Down General Provisions for a European Neighbourhood and Partnership Instrument,* COM (2004) 628 final, Brussels, CEC, 29 September 2004.

To bind all in discursive commonality, the Commission states that the "objective" of ENP is "to share the EU's stability, security and prosperity with neighboring countries in a way that is distinct from EU membership."[22] This optimistic vision awaits effective long-term realization apropos a 5,000-kilometer, mainly land-based eastern frontier and a largely maritime southern border of similar length. The nexus of the EU's two "open flanks" lies in the vicinity of eastern Anatolia and the Black Sea.[23] This expanse includes peoples without states—Palestinians, Kurds, Chechens, Kosovars—whose situations also pose fundamental political, security, and humanitarian questions for the EU.

Democratization is foreseen as the principal generator of security. By applying "soft power," of which ENPI or pre-accession funding are elements, the EU endeavors to acquire influence over states poorly credentialed in democratic governance, independent judiciaries, and civil rights.[24] Turkey experienced two constitutional reforms, eight legislative packages, and practical progress in the period 2002–2005 but still had not sufficiently met the EU's democracy criteria. Freedom House rankings in Table 6.3 indicate that Turkey is a partly free country. The Western Balkan countries are similarly evaluated; Ukraine is improving; Belarus and Russia are worsening; the Caucasus countries are stable. In the southern Mediterranean, only Israel qualified as a free country.

Ostensibly the neighborhood strategy does not anticipate the deployment of hard power. Nonetheless, the geopolitical element and military factors cannot be ignored.[25] The emergence of an EU "strategic culture" indicates that goals and methods associated with a "civilian power" require the insurance of military capability.[26] Even with progress in this field, for the foreseeable future the EU will rely on the presumed readiness of NATO, which cannot be disregarded in considerations of the total context. Scholars of varying theoretical inclination include NATO, and the United States more broadly, as an equally important actor in the project of exporting stability and promoting democratization.[27] NATO's indirect involvement fashions a very different scenario from one in which the EU was to attempt democratization in the region without the background presence of the US-led military-political alliance. The EU's achievements are at least partly dependent on NATO's reserve or operational-

Table 6.3   Evaluation of Political Rights and Civil Freedoms, 2005

	Political Rights	Civil Freedoms	Together	Trend	Classification
EU15	1.0	1.0	1.0	Stable	Free
CEE Round 1	1.1	1.1	1.1	Positive	Free
CEE Round 2	1.5	2.5	2.0	Negative	Free
Western Balkans	3.3	2.7	3.0	Positive	Partly Free
Turkey	3.0	3.0	3.0	Positive	Partly Free
Russia	6.0	5.0	5.5	Negative	Not Free
Ukraine	4.0	3.5	3.75	Positive	Partly Free
Belarus	7.0	6.0	6.5	Negative	Not Free
Moldova	3.0	4.0	3.5	Stable	Partly Free
Caucasus	4.6	4.3	4.5	Stable	Partly Free
Israel	1.0	3.0	2.0	Stable	Free
South-Med-3 (Tunisia, Egypt, Morocco)	5.6	4.6	5.1	Positive	Partly Free

Source: Freedom House, *Freedom in the World* (Washington, DC: Freedom House, 2005).
   Note: 1 represents the best and 7 the worst evaluation. Countries ranked from 1 to 3 are classified as "free," from 3 to 5.5 as "partly free," and over 5.5 as "not free." Ratings reflect global events from December 2003 to November 2004.

ized power. The "peace" reached in the former Yugoslavia is one example.[28] An implicit realism can be added to rationalist and constructivist elements in and appraisals of the EU method.

   Even with the availability of substantial soft and hard power resources, there are no guarantees of success. Democratization is primarily a homegrown process. It can be encouraged but not imposed by the EU.[29] Nor, as Iraq shows, can US hyperpower compel it: at least not without enormous cost. Western attempts to promote civil society as an internal generator of democratization sometimes overlook the diversity of interpretations and participants that it might engender. Not all will correspond with liberal ideals, which has implications for political objectives and the specificities of program implementation.[30] Differing conceptions of "democracy" are at issue: Does it mean the institutionalization and operation of pluralist politics, the rule of law and civil liberties, or does it mean the "people rule"? The success of Hamas in the Palestinian election of January 2006 was an example that underlined a basic question: "How are we to build a democracy with people we don't consider democrats?"[31] One analyst has suggested that the EU's promotion of democratization may be a "disingenuous strategy."[32]

   Michael Emerson and his colleagues critique EU policy toward neighboring states and peoples as neither generous nor resolute enough. Some have displayed a "superficial Europeanisation," enough to extract benefits from Brussels, before falling into inadequacy.[33] Are the only alternatives, then, to admit states to the EU in order to fully democratize them, or to exclude them and have them remain, to some degree, authoritarian or dysfunctional? Ratings of democracy and market economy in Table 6.4 indicate that few neighbors will reach standards comparable to those of the EU at any time soon. Ironically, success in encouraging democracy (even if the EU is not primarily responsible) will increase accession pressures, perhaps from several aspirants simultaneously, an undesirable scenario for the EU. Democratization and Europeanization are not the same thing. Although democratic practices are part of Europeanization, not all neighbors are regarded as European.

In contrast to the focus on positive enticement, "negative incentives" are rarely applied by the EU. When they are, it is usually in alignment with the United States. Sanctions against Belarus were a case in point.[34] Countries that receive EU munificence can be assured that the socioeconomic conditions they experience will not, as a result of EU measures, worsen beyond what they were before assistance was provided, if they do not do what the EU prefers. It may take decades before fulfillment of conditionality attached to financial aid is manifested. If it is not, there is little chance of the EU recovering what has been distributed. The Commission's 2004 proposal to the Council and EP for a funding instrument for ENP notes that a "Peace Group" formed to identify priorities and instruments had underlined that "performance-based allocations do not mean conditionality in the traditional sense and the issue of political conditionality should be approached cautiously, on the basis of lessons drawn from experience."[35]

Interests, Values, and Power

What are the motivations for the EU's neighborhood strategy, and what does it hope to achieve? Is the EU first of all an inculcator of values, a "norm entrepreneur" with missionary zeal for which material self-interest is far down the scale of considerations; or is it more accurately a group of states seeking gains in security, political leverage, and prosperity, or at least stability, and minimizing the costs required to achieve them?

In early 2004, Herbert Brücker, Philipp Schröder, and Christian Weise analyzed the imminent enlargement as a game-theoretic "war of attrition" bargaining and waiting scenario. The authors presumed that an economic win-win outcome awaited old and new member states, with the proviso that reforms and other measures requisite to meeting the *acquis* were adequately implemented. They noted that even if models and estimations of "economic cost-benefit calculations may suggest a win-win situation, the political cost-benefit balance may look different."[36] Bargaining and waiting also apply to post-2004 circumstances. Evaluation of the political cost-benefit stimulated the EU to indicate that membership is not a guaranteed terminus.

Frank Schimmelfennig argues that liberal values, rules, and norms were

Table 6.4 Levels of Development in Democracy and the Market Economy, 2005

State	Democracy	Market Economy	EU Relations
Afghanistan	3.0	3.1	Reconstruction assistance
Albania	7.3	6.0	SAP/Accession perspective
Algeria[a]	4.2	4.6	AA/Country Report in prep.
Armenia[a]	6.1	6.4	PCA/Action Plan negotiations
Azerbaijan[a]	3.8	5.2	PCA/Action Plan negotiations
Belarus[a]	4.0	5.0	ENP not activated
Bosnia-Herzegovina	6.8	6.4	SAP/Accession perspective
Bulgaria	8.5	7.5	Accession 2007–2008
Croatia	9.1	8.3	Accession negotiations
Egypt[a]	4.1	4.5	AA/Action Plan negotiations
Georgia[a]	6.1	5.4	PCA/Action Plan negotiations
Iran	3.8	4.2	Nuclear disarmament negotiations
Iraq	2.7	2.9	Reconstruction assistance
Israel[a, b]			AA/Action Plan
Jordan[a]	4.1	6.1	AA/Action Plan
Kazakhstan	4.2	6.8	PCA/TACIS program
Kyrgyzstan	4.1	5.4	PCA/TACIS program
Lebanon[a]	5.6	5.8	AA/Action Plan negotiations
Libya[a]	3.0	5.0	ENP not activated
Macedonia (FYR)	7.6	6.6	SAP/Accession perspective
Moldova[a]	5.4	4.7	Action Plan/ENP
Morocco[a]	4.5	4.8	Action Plan/ENP
Palestinian Authority[a, b]			Action Plan/ENP
Romania	8.2	7.6	Accession 2007–2008
Russia	5.7	6.6	"Strategic Partner"
Serbia-Montenegro	7.4	6.5	SAP/Accession perspective
Syria[a]	3.0	4.3	AA pending
Tajikistan	3.6	3.4	TCA/TACIS program
Tunisia[a]	3.8	6.5	AA/Action Plan
Turkey	7.1	6.8	Accession negotiations
Turkmenistan	2.6	3.8	PCA/TACIS program
Ukraine[a]	7.1	6.8	PCA/Action Plan
Uzbekistan	3.1	3.8	PCA/TACIS/ECHO

Source: Bertelsmann Transformation Index 2006; author's formulation.
Notes: a. ENP. b. Not evaluated. Worst rating is 1 up to a possible 10 for a fully functioning democracy.

the basis for the EU's (and NATO's) enlargement policy in regard to the CEECs and that the technique used by accession candidates to gain entry was one of "rhetorical action." That means the instrumentalizing of values and moral appeals to achieve material aims. Schimmelfennig's deft methodological resolution of coexistent rationalist and constructivist presumptions is a "sequencing" or "two-step" process whereby each alternatively provides the underlying explanation. Along with transatlantic perceptions of security enhancement, it was the CEECs' manipulation of rules and values in pursuit of "egoistic interests," rather than a normative adherence, that facilitated their entry to the EU.[37] Or, as one reviewer phrased it, "they talked their way in."[38] If, from the converse perspective of the EU as gatekeeper, norms and values are the principal impetus for enlargements, then a consistent logic suggests that the EU should include any actors that manifest these norms and values and want to join. Yet after 2004 the EU is cautious about more admissions, in particular of large and poor states and/or those whose geographic or cultural credentials are disputed. Questions of who or what is "European" have resurfaced. While values, rules, and norms are reiterated in official pronouncements, the likelihood of other aspirants deploying rhetorical action to the extent of "talking their way in" is less than for the CEECs that entered in 2004 or 2007. Their proximity to the EU15 made their stabilization a more pressing concern, while their economic standards and educational levels were, in an entire neighborhood context, relatively high. There was also little dispute about the CEECs as "belonging to Europe."

Wider Europe's fortunes are contingent on the stance of major international actors and on internal EU efficiency. As Nicole Gnesotto notes, "The development, security and stability of the wider Europe's partners are indeed inseparable from the success of the institutional functioning of the Union itself." With twenty-seven member states, there is "greater differentiation, even divergence over individual countries' national priorities regarding neighboring zones or CFSP instruments."[39] Individual EU member states have concerns about negative developments on or close to their own frontiers (geopolitical, economic, environmental, crime-related, or demographic, involving large-scale population movements). Differing proximity influences national positions on ENP or specific regions and states within it: France, Spain, and Italy toward North Africa; Austria, Hungary, and Slovenia in regard to the Balkans; Greece regarding Macedonia or Turkey. Poland is eager to mobilize EU resources in the service of an eastern policy that is unambiguously oriented toward Polish interests.[40] That the EU may not entirely concur with it is influenced by tensions over the Iraq War and other Atlanticist-Gaullist differences.

In preparation for the German EU presidency that began in January 2007, the German foreign ministry worked on an initiative for a "modernization partnership" with the states of the former Soviet Union. The line of reasoning behind this was that "European neighbors must be more strongly linked [to the EU] than the neighbors of Europe." The former, it was proposed, would be the focus of a "neighborhood policy plus." It would differentiate the broadly defined eastern and southern ENP regions into European and non-European and, in effect, introduce another category, or subzone, between EU membership and the southern ENP partners. Ukraine represented the most pressing case for why ENP needed a "new direction" and why Ukraine must be offered conditions that confirm it as more special than others, as a consolation for having to forgo membership candidacy indefinitely.[41] The German plan, perceived as a rival to the Commission's, was developed in response to discontent among the European former Soviet states, prominently with their having, in the ENP conception, the same status as African and Middle Eastern countries. Connected to this new plan was the German recognition of a need to develop and deepen a more "constructive engagement" with Russia.[42]

German foreign minister Frank-Walter Steinmeier toured the Central Asian republics in 2006, which proved to be judicious preparation for what was to come in the first half of the following year. Although it was well known that during its six-month presidency of the EU, Germany would strive to resuscitate the CT, if under a new name, it also invested considerable effort in promoting cooperation with Central Asia. Germany's endeavors as EU president were in the service of common EU interests but were also of particular importance to Germany itself, which feels particularly exposed to potential crises in the field of energy security. The EU's relatively recent discovery of Central Asia as a region of strategic partners is partly based on geopolitical reasoning, reflecting concern about Russian, Iranian, and Chinese involvement there, as well as that of diverse terrorist groups. Central Asia's real significance is founded on its reserves of raw materials. The EU's principal interest in this part of the world is in securing durable partnerships with alternative suppliers of oil and gas.[43] As the German presidency's carefully worded strategy document implies, the EU wants to do this without stimulating aspirations from the states of Central Asia to join the ENP, perhaps as a prelude to eventually launching their own campaigns for membership of the EU.

As these developments in the worlds of European diplomacy and strategic planning unfolded, a corpus of scholarly literature, media discussion, and political statements continued to speculate on a much more "differentiated EU."[44] Such an implicitly de-integrating, if not disintegrating, entity would find it even more difficult to pursue a credible, cohesive foreign and security policy, especially for its "neighborhood." The difficulty would be further complicated by great variation among the neighbors. The EU as a whole wants to instill reliability, order, and a political culture that encourages civic and commercial exchange and enables economy and society to prosper. Consequently, EU states and populations should be more secure vis-à-vis neighboring countries in which these conditions prevail and attain opportunities for economic benefit. These are rational goals as much as they represent the propagation of norms and values. To achieve them, the EU deploys a form of checkbook diplomacy, in a different context to but reminiscent of that specialized in by the former West Germany and in evidence during Germany's reunification phase. It was financial realism, with money used as a soft weapon. It could be suspended, increased, or extended depending on the conduct of the recipient "partner."[45] The EU *may* make a future offer of deeper integration if reforms are realized. In the interim there is money, technical help, and partial market access for those displaying satisfactory internal and international behavior. According to the responsible Commissioner for External Relations and ENP:

> Our neighbours are not just citizens of "third countries," they are our close partners and friends. We share practical interests, ideals, and aspirations, and we face common challenges to our security ... we offered this "ring of friends" a new, *special* relationship. ... In return for concrete steps being taken towards economic reform, and our shared values—good governance, human rights, democracy, and the rule of law—it offers our partners deeper political and economic integration with the EU.[46]

If the values in question are already shared, then why are "concrete steps" toward them required by anyone? And if "practical interests, ideals and aspirations" are also shared while "security challenges" are "common," why should any state or nation need to be reminded of that? Skepticism about reference to values in the context of EU policy extends to philosophers. For Hermann Lübbe, the term *values* (*Werte*) belongs to economics, not morality or politics. In political discussions the concept is superfluous and hypocritical, verbally deployed in an instrumental fashion, as "rhetorical action" might suggest. Talk of disseminating "the EU's values," in some cases by extending the EU itself, is "irritating."[47] The EU has never activated the human rights clause of its association agreements with states that are now ENP partners, despite the countless or, in some cases, permanent grounds for it to do so.[48] If the EU cannot impose upon its interlocutors, many of them relatively weak and usually in receipt of some form of assistance, what its foundational treaties and regular external policy statements assert is its defining raison d'être, then this discourse is unconvincing. Lübbe also dismisses related claims that the EU and its predecessors are responsible for peace in Europe. In his view it was NATO that secured the peace.[49]

How far, then, does the EU's capacity extend, or, what has and can it do without the assistance of others? Some initiatives have only been possible because of the presence of NATO. The "Concerted Approach for the Western Balkans" was one example. In regard to the "Northern Dimension," many "contentious issues in the region ... have been beyond the competencies of the EU as such" and "to the extent that they have been confronted, this has occurred without the direct involvement of the EU."[50] As a broker in secessionist conflicts, the EU has been far from achieving optimal outcomes and has repeatedly found itself facing the still imposing presence of Russia.[51]

EU Public Opinion and the Shift from Future Members to "Friends"

In pursuing such an extensive neighborhood strategy, the EU will have to contend with internal complications. Table 6.5 shows that surveys confirm lukewarm support for more members. Enlargement fatigue is palpable. Given the stress on democratic procedures, inclusion, and transparency, the EU's publics are likely to affect the shaping and implementation of neighborhood policy. Open debate and popular voting rights on issues of central importance must apply in a political union "of states and citizens." The prospect of outcomes that do not concur with those preferred by technocrats or government leaders can no longer limit public influence. Credibility loss is otherwise unavoidable.[52] An expression of popular will on proposed increases in membership is a formal requirement in several states. Especially in the EU15, large sections of national publics and political elites want accessions strictly limited or halted for the foreseeable future. It is in the (former) motor of integration, France and Germany, that opposition is strongest.

Politicians in EU member states realize it is unlikely that ENP will put an end to membership aspirations. Bavarian Minister-President Edmund Stoiber, whose Christian Social Union (CSU) party shares incumbency in Germany's "grand coalition" government, is among the most stringent critics of "automatic entry." Traditionally pro-enlargement sources are also questioning accession for any that want it. In March 2006 the EP asked the Commission to define the nature of the EU, including its borders.[53] A press release stated:

> The European Union should keep its promises to candidate countries and possible candidate countries but also take the EU's absorption capacity fully into account. . . . If necessary, the Commission should propose a close multilateral relationship to all European countries which currently have no recognised "membership perspective." Countries which do have such a perspective should be free to join this multilateral framework as an intermediate step towards full membership. . . . Parliament asks the Commission to submit a report by the end of this year setting out the principles defining the EU's absorption capacity. In order to do so *"the nature of the EU, including its geographical borders,"* should be defined. It also asks the Commission to draw up a communication strategy *"so as to meet the legitimate concerns of the European public regarding European enlargement and integration."*

Members of the European Parliament noted that "the stalemate in the ratification of a constitutional treaty is preventing the EU from increasing its absorption capacity and that no new Member States should be allowed in before the necessary budgetary resources are available."[54]

In response to institutional inertia and widespread aversions, the director-general of the Commission's External Relations directorate, Eneko Landaburu, floated an evaluation of why there cannot be unlimited enlargements. He stated that "it is a reality that the EU cannot expand ad infinitum." Other options were presented as just as worthy and beneficial as full membership. The question of whether this or that state would or would not accede to the EU was depicted as the wrong one.[55] It is the question that members, candidates, possible applicants, and states with which negotiations have begun, want answered.

Table 6.5 Support for Enlargements in EU Member States (in percentage)

	For	Against	Change[g]
February 2004:			
To include ten states in May 2004[a]			
EU15	42	39	−5
Germany	28	56	−10
France	37	47	+3
UK	31	40	−7
Austria	34	52	−7
October–November 2004: To accept more			
states in following years[b]			
EU25	53	35	
EU15	49	n.a.	
New member states (2004 entrants)	72	n.a.	
Germany	36	57	
France	39	51	
UK	50	n.a.	
Austria	28	62	
May–June 2005: To include all states			
wishing to join[c]			
EU25	50	38	−3
EU15	45	42	−4
New member states (2004 entrants)	72	15	0
Germany	33	61	−3
France	32	58	−7
UK	48	39	−2
Austria	31	58	+3
October–November 2005: To include other			
states in future years[d]			
EU25	49	39	−1
EU15	44	44	−1
New member states (2004 entrants)	69	17	−3
Germany	36	59	+3
France	31	60	−1
UK	43	43	−5
Austria	29	60	−3
April–May 2006: To include other states			
in future years[e]			
EU25	45	42	−7
EU15	41	46	−3
New member states (2004 entrants)	66	21	−3
Germany	28	66	−8
France	31	62	0
UK	44	42	+1
Austria	27	61	−2
September–October 2006: To include other			
countries in future years[f]			
EU25	46	42	+1
EU15	41	47	0
New member states (2004 entrants)	72	18	+6
Germany	30	64	+2
France	34	58	+3
UK	36	51	−8
Austria	31	57	+4

Sources: Eurobarometer, various issues: a. 61; b. 62; c. 63; d. 64; e. 65; f. 66.
Note: g. Change in percentage "for" since previous survey.

Table 6.6 EU Relations with Neighbors, October 2006

Promised accession: Romania, Bulgaria. Doubts publicly expressed, with extensive corruption and poor public administration cited. A Commission report in May 2006 was inconclusive; September 2006 report recommended entry by January 2007 with stronger conditionality (negative incentives).

Candidates: Croatia, Turkey. Enlargement was possible in principle and for Croatia almost inevitable. In the case of Turkey, there were internal and international uncertainties. Several EU members harbored strong opposition to Turkey's accession.

"European Perspective": Serbia-Montenegro (including Kosovo), Bosnia-Herzegovina, Albania, Macedonia. Regarded as "European," with eventual if distant membership foreseen.

ENP with Action Plan: Ukraine, Moldova, Morocco, Israel, Palestinian Authority, Jordan, Tunisia. Considered not to have a "European perspective"; nominally excluded from membership.

ENP Without Action Plan: Libya, Armenia, Azerbaijan, Egypt, Georgia, Algeria. Considered not to have a "European perspective." Nominally excluded from membership. Action plans possible, especially in the short term. Belarus could be included after major political change occurred. Syria's status is vague.

Strategic Partnership: Russia has a special partnership with the EU comprising four "common spaces." The Russian political elite has shown little interest in Russia becoming an EU member, but Russia strives to retain influence on the EU's relations with other states in its vicinity.

Some figures, such as Nicholas Sarkozy during his campaign for the French presidency, are against further enlargements on tactical grounds. Like the rest of the *classe politique*, Sarkozy was and is aware of popular opposition to more accessions.[56] EP member Elmar Brok, of Germany's Christian Democratic Union (CDU) party, again proposed an interim status between full membership and association.[57] Table 6.6 indicates categories of relationships with neighbors in 2006.

The Eastern Flank

In the 1990s Russia, Ukraine, Moldova, Armenia, Azerbaijan, and Georgia were linked to the EU by individual PCAs and the Technical Assistance for the Commonwealth of Independent States (TACIS) program. A PCA did not come into force with Belarus. Trade was liberalized according to most-favored-nation standards, and quantitative restrictions were eliminated, but the PCAs did not imply preferential treatment in trade or a timetable for regulatory approximation.[58] They involved cooperation in science and technology, justice and home affairs (especially concerning crime), and political dialogue on international issues and human rights. Transition obligations fell on the partner countries. The PCAs did not offer the possibility of accession. ENP suggested possibilities for moving beyond their "static" quality, though it is not clear to where.

Concurrent to these processes, Lucan Way observes a "pluralism by default" in Russia, Belarus, Ukraine, and Moldova. They are unconsolidated autocracies that lack iron rule, not from a shortage of intent but from a lack of competence and the strength of national identity, which sustains skepticism toward political rulers. In the early to mid-1990s, all "exhibited dynamic and competitive politics." The "absence of consistent Western pressure via the European Union or other institutions" is the first reason listed by Way as facilitating autocracy.[59] In 2003–2004 incomplete "revolutions" occurred in Georgia and Ukraine. The Community of Democratic Choice, a forum started in these countries, announced itself as a nonauthoritarian presence.[60] Durable democratic politics, market economies, and emancipated civil societies are far from secured. There are doubts about the depth of the EU's normative agenda, and a problem of "faith" intensifies. Dov Lynch argues that the EU presents itself to its eastern neighbors as an agnostic God, but they perceive it as an atheist God. Beyond participation in a "dimension" or "process," these states and peoples must be the focus of "political engagement, the acceptance of security responsibility," and "concrete commitment to propagating stability" on the part of the EU.[61]

Russia

Dialogue on political and security matters, energy, and other issues[62] has not resolved the centuries of ambivalence that characterizes the relationship between Europe and Russia.[63] Following an EU "Common Strategy on Russia" in 1999, a "strategic partnership" with four "common spaces" was proposed in 2003. "Road maps" for those spaces (the economy; freedom, security, and justice; external security; and research, education, and culture) were agreed to in 2005. Russia rejected participation in the ENP, perceiving a reduction in status equivalent to less important states. It is included in ENPI.

Some analysts interpreted a pragmatic turn in Russian foreign policy under Vladimir Putin, whereby reincorporation of its near abroad and outright opposition to western activity in the post-Soviet space is receding.[64] Alongside a range of old and new tensions, EU-Russia relations also involve cooperation and recognition of respective interests. The EU had some success in environmental policy but deferred on more difficult issues like Kaliningrad and Russian minorities.[65] For other observers, "recent developments in the EU-Russia relationship are worrying," and "effective strategic partnership seems elusive."[66] Differing conceptions of EU "foreign policy" or of bilateral relations held by Russian participants and those from EU member states at a forum of political, academic, cultural-industry, and businesspeople seemed to confirm that view.[67] If some positives in relations can be detected, they are paralleled by increasingly autocratic governance in Russia. According to former US deputy secretary of state Strobe Talbott, "Russia's internal regime determines its external behaviour. A Russia that rules its own people by force and edict rather than consent and enfranchisement is virtually certain, sooner or later, to intimidate its neighbours and to make itself one of the world's problems rather than a contributor to their solution."[68] Putin practices a "controlled tension"[69] and, Talbott argues, wants to reestablish a "highly centralized, vertical state with power concentrated in the Kremlin." "Russia's self-designation as a federal state" and the "fate of pluralistic democracy" is threatened. The direct election of regional governors has been abolished in favor of personal appointment. The media are constrained, and there is no independent television station. Putin disguises neo-authoritarianism as a proactive stance on terrorism and crime, even as the system enables terrorists and others to bribe public officials. Talbott claimed that "despite muted criticism from Washington, the policy of the Bush administration is more 'understanding' than that of the European Union."[70] However, the EU's "transformational agenda" is compelled to recognize Russia's geopolitical and military presence and the energy needs of member states.[71]

Although some contend that Russian foreign policy prioritizes economic criteria, Moscow remains influenced by geostrategic thinking. Dependent neighbors could be favored or extorted on political as much as financial grounds.[72] In Alexander Rahr's estimation, "Today's significant community-oriented EU partnership with Russia will concede to a pragmatic partnership of interests. The EU will not succeed in democratising Russia or transferring its western liberal model there. Despite this, in issues of energy security and supply the EU will be chiefly dependent on its partnership with Russia."[73] If the EU fails to democratize Russia, its efforts in other Soviet successor states are likely to be confronted with some form of resistance. Russian coercion was demonstrated by the withholding of gas supplies for Ukraine. Russia was also accused of blowing up pipes near Georgia.[74] Such incidents stimulated anxieties in the EU about the extent of its exposure to brinkmanship or blackmail.[75]

Contemporaneously, Germany was prominent in developing a new pipeline from Russia through the Baltic Sea to Western Europe, which did not please some Central European and Baltic nations. Besides recalling historical anxieties, they are concerned that the EU has permanently adopted a German preference of "Russia first." These were intensified by former Chancellor Schröder's candidly enthusiastic friendship with Putin.[76] A corollary of their personal relations was the virtual exclusion of other figures in Russian politics from contact with the highest level of Germany's political leadership.[77] Schröder defended Putin's governance as a necessary "reconstruction of statehood."[78] One Russian reporter described Schröder as "Putin's mole in the EU."[79] The relationship of German and Russian leaders has changed since Schröder's departure, with new chancellor Merkel less Russia-friendly and more publicly supportive of the interests of CEECs.

Former UK ambassador to Moscow Roderick Lyne presents an optimistic perspective on EU-Russia relations in which Russia is considered a possible future EU member.[80] Others alternatively suggest restrained diplomacy or a more forceful approach, with support for countries in what Russia regards as its sphere of influence.[81] The EU recognizes that Russia has legitimate security interests. Although both face "soft security threats stemming from the 'shared neighbourhood,'" they have a "surprisingly modest record of cooperation."[82] Perhaps the most spectacular instance of degeneration in relations between Russia and an EU member state was that of the alleged poisoning in London in November 2006 of former Russian Federal Security Bureau agent Alexander Litvinenko by Andrei Lugovoi, who much of the world's media speculated was acting on orders of the Kremlin.[83] Mutual expulsions of Russian and British diplomats followed in July 2007. These events occurred as the atmosphere of Russian relations with the West in general was deteriorating badly. The Portuguese presidency of the EU expressed "disappointment at Russia's failure to cooperate constructively with the UK authorities." It added that "the EU hopes for a satisfactory solution to this matter, which raises important questions of common interest to EU member states."[84]

Anne de Tinguy posits that Russia views the EU as more of a competitor than partner in their common neighborhood, though simultaneously it does not take the EU completely seriously, preferring to focus its diplomacy on leading member states. Contrasting views on how terrorism and independence movements should be dealt with, above all regarding the Chechens, are central to Russia-EU differences. So too are values. In this area the EU is revealed as more or less impotent. "As long as the Kremlin is convinced that democratisation processes are incompatible with its interests," de Tinguy asserts, and "that Ukraine or any other CIS country cannot have a privileged partnership with Russia and the EU at the same time, and as long as its analysis is based on a zero-sum idea, the relationship between Russia and the EU will remain very difficult."[85]

The EU is a large donor with much assistance directed to democratization ventures.[86] Aid to Russia continues, even though it has overcome a reliance on loans from international financial institutions, generated trade and budget surpluses, accumulated foreign currency reserves, and reestablished itself in world politics. All that is contemporaneous to what many see as increasingly autocratic internal governance. As renewal of the EU-Russia Partnership Agreement approaches, the Russian leadership is in a stronger position to exert preferences than when the first such agreement was signed. Putin, as will his successor, holds the energy resources card. Without the rapid development or discovery of alternative forms of energy, the EU's dependency on Russia will continue to grow. As this occurs, competing Russian conceptions may complicate plans that the EU has to implement its own agenda in the former Soviet geopolitical and geoeconomic space. The way that the EU partnership with

Russia is currently evolving indicates that the promotion of democratic values and institutions will not take precedence over other considerations.[87]

Ukraine

There has been a gradual shift in Ukraine away from viewing relations with Russia as foreign policy priority number one and toward the EU and NATO.[88] This orientation is accompanied by steadily growing trade and other economic relations.[89] Politically, the pro-West dynamic reached its zenith with the "Orange Revolution" led by Viktor Yushchenko in December 2004. On the one hand it represented an optimistic development for the EU; on the other the EU's responsibilities to assist in maintaining such a trajectory mean that an offer of membership will be hard to avoid. Such an offer is not viewed as desirable in most old member states. CEECs, led by Poland, are in favor.

Ukraine's size and relative level of economic development would add huge integrative challenges to those already facing the EU. Those factors and Ukraine's geopolitical importance make it a leading motivation for and key state in the neighborhood strategy.[90] The EU will attempt to promote and sustain a reform-oriented, EU-friendly Ukraine while excluding it from membership for the foreseeable future. The Orange Revolution increased the difficulty of this balancing act.[91] As it gathered momentum, commentators wrote of the country's division into two halves: pro-West and pro-Russia.[92] Ukraine may be the object of a struggle between external forces,[93] and the presidential election was characterized by geographic polarization, but the land is not about to split.[94] Yushchenko is not the only promoter of EU accession. Desires for closer relations were expressed during the more Russia-friendly Kuchma presidency, and Viktor Yanukovych indicated that this goal would be maintained if he were to become president. Lynch writes that "the contest in Ukraine was never as simple as it was portrayed—Victor Yanukovych was never Russia's man, nor is Victor Yushchenko anti-Russian. However, Yushchenko's election on a platform to undertake EU-orientated reform will resound throughout the former Soviet Union."[95]

An action plan is the point at which, for the present, Ukraine's integration with the EU ends. Many arguments supporting a membership perspective are based on the country's European cultural and historical identity. Advocates contend that Ukraine cannot be equated with African and Middle Eastern states. Some construed the EU's opening negotiations with Turkey as an affront. Winfried Schneider-Deters argues that in late 2004, "Ukrainian society proved that it has more democratic maturity than the populations of the two candidate states Romania and Bulgaria, whose entry in the year 2007 is a concluded issue. Turkey is being reformed from above, while, in contrast, democracy in Ukraine is an achievement of the people."[96] The hesitant EU, Schneider-Deters contends, is partly responsible for the delayed democratization of Ukraine. Its policy is an acknowledgment of Russian claims to primacy in the region. EU relations with Russia, a state with no clear ambition to join the EU itself, were affected by developments in Ukraine. The German position remained the same, even as the Schröder-Putin friendship was put under pressure by the events in late 2004.[97] In its first year of incumbency, the succeeding grand coalition government made no decisive changes.

After meeting in Kazakhstan in early 2006, Presidents Putin and Yushchenko said that Russian-Ukrainian relations were good, despite the only just resolved gas dispute being, for Yushchenko, "one of the most difficult times of our relationship."[98] Not all observers interpreted Russian actions as solely negative. Eugene Rumer argues that they will compel an overdue modernization of Ukrainian industry and weaken Russian leverage. In the interim, Ukraine would require additional western assistance.[99] Euphoria was soon replaced by divergence between Yushchenko and former allies, including short-term prime minister Julia Timoshenko. Corruption and blackmail persist in the security service, public administration, and other sections of the state apparatus, which cannot be reformed overnight.[100] For liberals the March 2006 election resulted in a formally democratic but politically retrograde outcome.[101] By August the inability of Yushchenko and Timoshenko to form a stable government led to Yushchenko proposing Yanukovych as prime minister, the man he and thousands of Ukrainians had protested against in 2004.[102] Despite the latter's assurances that he would pursue closer relations with the EU and NATO, the Orange Revolution turned a shade red. For proponents of Ukraine's EU aspirations, the old system, and Russia, will retain influence if no membership perspective is conferred. Reversal to a more Russia-friendly government was met by the Kremlin with price reductions and a resumption of reliable energy supplies.

Belarus

In the 1990s the EU and several member states provided financial and technical assistance to Belarus, which contributed to economic conditions that were relatively good compared to other post-Soviet republics.[103] The assistance did not prevent a slide into authoritarianism under Alexander Lukashenko. Belarus does not participate in ENP, although the EU leaves the opportunity open. In December 2004 the European Council declared it would inform the Belarusian population about the benefits of the policy.[104] Lukashenko deemed that aggressive. There has also been recurring dissension with Russia, and Putin has no liking for Lukashenko. However, if Lukashenko is "Europe's last dictator," but dependent on a supportive Russia, then what does that make Putin? Russia's desire to retain influence over its near abroad involves a toleration of Lukashenko. Russian gas supplies to Belarus have been heavily subsidized, with costs two to three times less than for Ukraine or Moldova.[105] A price increase in 2006 was interpreted as pressure for a merger with Russia,[106] an objective for which Putin has apparently never shared the enthusiasm of his predecessor, Boris Yeltsin.

In Belarus, the EU's soft powers of persuasion face a critical test. Lukashenko seems unfazed by international isolation.[107] He has played off Russia and the West while suppressing alternatives by centralizing power, revising the constitution to enable himself to rule longer, and other coercive actions. The prospects for EU or other external influence effecting an imminent democratization are not bright.[108] An OECD report on the 2006 election documented a wholly undemocratic process featuring media monopolization, vote falsification, and oppression of Lukashenko's rivals and peaceful protestors.[109]

Moldova

Since Moldova gained independence in 1991, it has been in conflict over the separatist region of Transnistria, whose indeterminate status outside the international legal system facilitates criminal activity, human rights transgressions, and soft security threats for the EU. The conflict is not grounded in sectarian antagonism but driven by lucrative financial and political advantages attained under lawless circumstances. Transnistria is dependent on Russian support, including the provision of cheap raw materials. Nicu Popescu argues that the EU should apply "targeted sanctions" to sections of the Transnistrian economy, which, incongruously, has a high degree of trade with the EU and the United States.[110] In a March 2006 resolution, the EP declared that it "recognises Moldova's European aspirations and the importance of Moldova as a country with deep historical, cultural and economic links to the Member States." Among the resolution's points was a demand for an end to Russian backing for Transnistria and the withdrawal of its troops. The resolution stressed that "under the decision taken at the 1999 OSCE Summit in Istanbul, the troops should have been withdrawn by the end of 2002" and that the EP "calls on the Council to include this item on the agenda of the next EU-Russia summit."[111] Apart from solving the conflict, the EU-Moldova action plan aims to "significantly advance the approximation of Moldovan legislation, norms and standards to those of the European Union." The plan also "acknowledges Moldova's European aspirations and its "concept for the integration of the republic of Moldova into the EU." There is no mention of a membership perspective.[112]

The Caucasus

The Caucasus countries are among the poorest in the EU's neighborhood. They are also beleaguered by separatist ethnic conflict. Georgia, the largest, was once among the richest of the Soviet republics. Now there are many reasons, Lynch suggests, for the EU to avoid getting too involved in Georgia. It is "the setting for a unique combination of security risks and threats—and it lies on the EU's border." But it is also a "democracy in the making."[113] Georgia has been wracked by conflict, and Russia sided with separatists in the breakaway regions of Abkhazia and South Ossetia. In 2003 Georgia attracted attention through its "Rose Revolution," a protest against electoral fraud and corruption. The incumbent president, former Soviet foreign minister Eduard Shevardnadze, was ousted and replaced by the pro-Western Mikhail Saakashvili. The new Georgian foreign minister, also a French citizen, was able to bring the first EU "Rule of Law" mission (Themis) to Georgia in July 2004.[114] In the same month, the government established a Commission on Georgia's Integration into the EU to seek to build on the 1996 PCA. Oil (Baku-Ceyhan) and gas (Baku-Ezrum) pipelines became operational in 2005–2006. An EU-Georgia action plan was under development. The Rose Revolution, however, is fragile, and Russian behavior provokes rather than solves problems. The presence of Chechen rebels on Georgian territory adds complications. In Georgia the EU "faces the challenge of developing genuine foreign policy—without the luxurious conditions offered by the policy of enlargement."[115]

A serious deterioration of the Georgia-Russia relationship in October 2006 exemplified the complex challenge confronting the EU's attempt to stabilize its periphery. Against a background of striving to reintegrate Abkhazia and South Ossetia under Tbilisi's control, and aspirations to join NATO, the Georgian government accused Russian military officers of espionage and held several in custody. Moscow responded with counter-accusations of Georgian warmongering and reprisal measures that included closing some Georgian businesses in Russia and expelling Georgians. The Russian-Georgian border was closed. The president of the Russian Duma threatened Georgia with further revenge, possibly extending to military action.[116]

Azerbaijan has emerged as an oil producer with a rapidly growing economy.[117] The development and global integration of its oil industry is likely to be affected by Russian influence on its political system and foreign affairs orientation. Azerbaijan has been in conflict with Armenia over Nagorno-Karabakh for many years. The EU is one of several mediators. In March 2005 the Commission recommended a "significant intensification" of relations with these countries. Both were expected to progress in strengthening the rule of law, conflict resolution, and regional cooperation. For each it was noted that elections "fell short of international standards" and that "prudent macroeconomic policies need to be maintained to support effective implementation" of proposed action plans. Armenia was required to decommission a nuclear power plant.[118]

Several of the states noted above are salient as transit routes for energy supplies to the EU. Eighty percent of Russian gas exports to Europe travel through Ukraine, which has the world's highest volume of gas transit. The Baku-Ceyhan pipeline highlighted Azerbaijan's emergence and reemphasized the critical role of Turkey. Transportation is a matter of great expense and is vulnerable to disruption from political disputes or terrorist activity. Russia inherited pipelines totaling 46,000 kilometers for crude oil, 15,000 kilometers for petroleum products, and 152,000 kilometers for natural gas from the Soviet Union. All are under state control, as are those originating in or crossing other former Soviet republics. The United States has four times more oil pipelines and double the gas pipelines, almost of none of which are under state control.[119]

The Southern Flank

The predominantly Islamic North Africa and Middle East represent the southern dimension of the EU's neighborhood strategy. The Barcelona Process achieved limited results in its first five years from 1995 to 2000 when the global context was more favorable.[120] Indeed, the EU's attempts to generate peace and stability, let alone prosperous democratic polities, depend on conditions prevailing in the larger geopolitical context. Stephen Jones and Michael Emerson argue: "Discussion on EU policies in this area cannot be divorced from the wider context: first, consideration of the role that the US plays and the extent to which it will in practice enforce the strong political conditionality that appears to be emerging as its dominant form of engagement."[121] Since 2001 the global environment has become more intimidating. The southern and eastern Mediterranean has intensified as a "zone of instability and conflict on a scale no longer found in Europe."[122] The EU has sought a negotiated two-state solution to the central Israeli-Palestinian conflict, based on a "land for peace" policy supported by promotion of economic development, provision of aid, and the establishment of durable dialogue forums. The Mésures d'accompagnement financiers et techniques (MEDA) I and II financial instruments provided €8.75 billion over the period 1995–2006, with another €12.2 billion coming in loans from the European Investment Bank.[123] Despite the EU's funding and commitment for the Middle East, some scholars perceive few positive results in terms of democratization or regional security.[124]

Maghreb

In 1987 Morocco applied for membership in the then EC and was rejected. Almost twenty years later, its ENP Action Plan states that "rapproachment with the Union represents a fundamental foreign policy choice" and "will allow Morocco to progress towards advanced status." The opportunity for deeper economic integration and a "stake in the internal market" is outlined.

There are also many qualifications. Depending on fulfillment of the plan's objectives and the "overall evolution of EU-Morocco relations, consideration will be given to the possibility of a new contractual relationship," a "European Neighbourhood Agreement."[125] One analysis suggests hesitancy by both parties: by the Moroccan authorities to implement measures that will introduce genuine change in accordance with the EU's liberal orientation, and by the EU to seriously enforce such change.[126]

Although it points to many shortcomings, if Tunisia's action plan is a guide, the Commission is pleased with progress there and optimistic about future relations. A role for Tunisia in promoting links among Maghreb countries is foreseen. Cooperation in integrating African and EU energy markets and "effective management of migration flows" are also noted.[127]

Algeria has stabilized since a 2002 report criticized its evolution after joining the Barcelona Process.[128] An association agreement was ratified in March 2005, and Commissioner Benita Ferrero-Waldner visited in June "to give increased visibility to the relaunch of EU relations with Algeria" and work toward an action plan "when considered appropriate by the EU's Algerian partners."[129] A country report is in preparation. Even without its own action plan, Algeria is one of, if not the most successful, attractor of FDI among all the EU's ENP partners.

As was the case for EMP, Libya is eligible for ENP but does not participate. It would probably have to join the former arrangement, where it had observer status, before it could join ENP. A rapproachement of sorts with the West has occurred since Libya was bombed by the United States, most pertinently a deal to discontinue any intentions to produce or acquire WMDs. Internally, Muammar Qaddafi's "grossly authoritarian regime" may have been strengthened.[130] In May 2005 Commissioner Ferrero-Waldner visited Libya as part of an attempt to advance relations. She made representations on behalf of one Palestinian and five Bulgarian medical workers imprisoned since the late 1990s. This case is related to an outbreak of HIV/AIDs in Benghazi, for which the EU has developed a special action plan. A Commission head of delegation in Libya has also been appointed.[131] In July 2005 Commission President Barroso followed with a visit to the African Union Assembly, hosted by Libya in Sirte, where he spoke at the opening session.[132]

Mashreq

Bernard Lewis maintains that the fear that democracy cannot be established in the Middle East is "expressed by many in the United States" and is "almost a dogma in Europe."[133] Official French sources confirmed that profound doubt about implanting democracy in Iraq was why France opposed the 2003 military action.[134] This pessimism, or cautious realism, is less obvious in the official discourse accompanying ENP and other EU initiatives.

Egypt links the Mashreq and Maghreb countries and is considered of high political importance by western actors. The Mubarak regime has been supported, especially by the United States, as a relatively predictable if undemocratic alternative to a radical Islamic government. The EU's country report was not very favorable, although the findings did not prevent an action plan from being developed. Egypt is one of the largest receivers of EU aid and will benefit further from ENPI. It has serious shortcomings in freedom of expression, judicial processes, and the unhindered activity and chances of opposition political parties.[135]

From most Western perspectives, Jordan has one of the more moderate and accommodating regimes in the Arab world. The ENP action plan is conceived as supporting the Jordanian National Plan for Political Development and National Social and Economic Action Plan. ENPI finance will be "better targeted" to support the "modernisation agenda of the Jordanian government." Within this framework, the EU's priorities are to further a "national dialogue on democracy and political life," "develop an independent and impartial judiciary," improve "freedom of the media and freedom of expression," "promote equal treatment of women," and "strengthen political dialogue." A range of trade and business promotion measures is also prioritized. Greater detail is given in sixty-eight specific points. In conclusion, the action plan states that it "can be amended and/or updated to reflect progress in addressing the priorities."[136] A more critically engaged study details the shortcomings of both Jordan and the EU. Much of the analysis alludes to the problem of encouraging more democracy as a positive, even absolute value, only for it to result in a radical Islamic republicanism, which would very likely pose a greater challenge for the EU than the relatively predictable soft-authoritarianism that currently prevails.[137]

Excepting Norway, Iceland, and Switzerland, Israel is the only established democracy in the EU's neighborhood. In economic terms Israel is also much closer to the EU, with a per capita GDP slightly under the EU average and higher than many member states. The EU is Israel's most important trade partner. Some scholars have criticized Israel for its lack of a "grand strategy towards the EU." Though it enjoys a special status, "Israel behaves as if it were an island in the Atlantic Ocean rather than a nation neighboring the enlarged EU." The EU has also had strategic shortcomings in regard to Israel.[138] The EU-Israel action plan attempts to correct these problems. Along with expanded economic relations, CFSP/ESDP cooperation is stressed. Under this heading, "concrete measures" are listed, including legislative ones, against anti-Semitism, Islamophobia, and terrorism and weapons proliferation. A European Neighbourhood Agreement is anticipated as the next step after the action plan.[139]

Largely due to French pressure, the EU has sought to balance US backing for Israel with political and economic aid for the Palestinian territories. Since its Venice Declaration of 1980, the EU (then the EC) has been the largest donor to the Palestinians and a leading supporter of a settlement to the Israeli-Palestinian conflict. A "permanent two-state solution" is proposed in the EU-Israel action plan and "the establishment of an independent, viable, sovereign and contiguous Palestinian state" in the EU–Palestinian Authority action plan, the only such plan with a nonstate entity. In it the EU builds on its participation in the Quartet group, in which it is joined by the United States, UN, and Russia in endeavoring to reach a durable peace acceptable to all parties. More "targeted financial support" will be available for developing the economy, fighting terrorism, alleviating humanitarian crises, consolidating democratic, accountable institutions, and advancing the "approximation of Palestinian legislation, norms and standards to those of the European Union."[140] Anne Le More is skeptical. She argues that despite declaratory intent and large-scale international financial assistance, neither a Palestinian state nor a presumed consequential end to the Middle Eastern conflict is in sight.[141]

France was prominent in EU policy toward the Levant and cooperated successfully with the United States in coercing a withdrawal of Syrian forces from Lebanon.[142] Building on a 1978 Cooperation Agreement, an association agreement between Lebanon and the EU came into effect in 2005. ENPI financing will continue the MEDA concentration on reforming the judicial and public administration systems and macroeconomic stabilization. Counter-terrorism was the subject of a separate exchange of letters. A reduction in Syrian influence enabled Lebanon's political structures to operate more freely, which seemed to offer an opportunity for the EU to raise its profile in Lebanon.[143] The dramatic escalation of the Israeli-Hizbollah war, the resulting invasion and destruction of much of southern Lebanon, and the continued involvement of Syria and Iran as supporters of Hizbollah set back all bilateral relations and plans.

In a 2002 Commission document, Syria was declared a "full participant in the Barcelona Process" at the same time as its "policy agenda in the area of political system, human rights and civil society remains modest."[144] The EMP National Indicative Programme that followed in 2005–2006 presented an uncritical appraisal.[145] Negotiations on an association agreement have been stalled since 2003 and little progress in the aforementioned and other areas has been achieved although Syria is formally eligible for ENP. More critically, since ENP was launched, the EU has not been able to compel Syria to desist from destabilizing activity, in particular support for Hizbollah's terrorism. Along with Libya and Belarus, Syria is most clearly in conflict with the normative agenda asserted by the EU.

Iraq and Iran

The intra-EU and transatlantic rifts opened up by the war against Saddam Hussein have not prevented an EU role in the reconstruction of Iraq, though its involvement remains very secondary to that of the United States. Compared with around US$20 billion from the United States, the EC provided €518 million between 2003 and 2005 and €200 million in 2006, €10 million of it for "human rights and democracy."[146] Individual member states have given additional aid, and France, Germany, the UK, and Italy each canceled Iraqi debts worth several billion euros or pounds. British, Polish, Danish, Romanian, Czech, and Bulgarian military and other personnel remain present. As of July 2007 Poland had about 900 troops in Iraq. A complete US withdrawal from Iraq would ameliorate some domestic political problems for these US-loyalist EU states, as it would mean they could also leave without slighting their principal global security ally.

Iran represents another not-so-distant danger. It demonstrated to the EU that approaching foreign policy as empathetic management does not always work.[147] The EU3 of France, Germany, and the UK reached agreement in November 2004 on the ending of Iran's nuclear program. After this accord was broken for the second time, it seemed that Iran was outmaneuvering the West.[148] Ayatollah Jalal Ganjei, an opponent of fundamentalist Islam, described the EU as "naïve." He advised it to "avoid the failures of the past decade and no longer pursue a policy of appeasement with the regime." The EU's negotiations, he claimed in January 2006, had "failed."[149] The EU3 and EU High Representative Javier Solana sought to "clarify" whether there were further grounds to continue negotiations with Iran.[150] In April the Iranian leadership declared that Iran was a nuclear power and had a right to be. By May 2006, more overt US involvement and increasingly generous incentives for Iran had superseded previous EU diplomacy. A Declaration on Iran in December 2006 by the then Finnish presidency of the EU, expressing concern "about the negative effects of Iranian policies on stability and security in the Middle East" and other aspects of Iran's international and internal behavior, had little effect on the Iranian leadership.[151]

For many observers, the balance sheet indicates that the EU has lacked influence in altering the nature of regimes in the Maghreb and Middle East despite the years of aid, strategy papers, and agreements. An effective regionalism has never been realized.[152] Regardless of how frequently the EU emphasizes them—more so, it sometimes appears, to Western audiences than those whose states and societies it is attempting to transform—there has been little progress in the development of democratic institutions, market economics, and civil freedoms. Nor have conflict and violence been brought under control. The appearance of ENP does not infer impending and remarkable change.

The Balkans

The EU's failures in the Balkans, much closer to its core member states, are well known. This crisis region has required US intervention to enforce peace and establish a foundation for stability. Only then has the EU been able to progress with reconstruction efforts. Croatia received the status of a candidate country in June 2004. It has experienced problems since, notably regarding the capture and delivery of alleged war criminals to the International Court of Justice. Bosnia-Herzegovina, Macedonia, Albania, and Serbia are also not included in ENP. Montenegro's vote for independence in May 2006 adds another state likely to obtain a membership perspective. It might well be asked, however, when did Balkan countries share "European values," as the EU defines them, as normal political practice internally and in relation to each other? The Kosovo problem will occupy the EU for many years. Serbian officials have said they will enable a "decentralization" but want Kosovo to remain part of Serbia, according to UN Security Council Resolution 1244. Albanian Muslims want an independent state. Presently the "contact group" excludes a division of Kosovo.[153] Franz-Lothar Altmann argues persuasively that the Western Balkans have "earned" an EU membership perspective, not because they have progressed more rapidly than other neighbors but because they present a very proximate threat to the EU's stability. If evaluated by the Copenhagen criteria and the fulfilling of EU conditionality, "all five countries of the Western Balkans" "have large deficits in practically all areas ... an EU membership in the foreseeable future appears illusory. Even Croatia ... received a recommendation from the Commission to start entry negotiations partly as a political advance gift, although most observers do not considered this objectively justifiable."[154]

Turkey

Turkey, a strategic partner of the West during the Cold War, has had an association agreement with the EEC/EU since 1963. Several attempts to begin membership negotiations failed, mainly because Turkey defaulted on the preconditions. Military coups and other forms of undemocratic politics were customary. When the Erdogan government came to power, it concentrated its energy on implementing the necessary reforms. These efforts contributed to the Council decision of December 2004 to start accession negotiations with Turkey the following year. That was a turning point in EU enlargement processes.[155] Turkey's potential membership remains hotly debated. The beginning of membership negotiations does not indicate that the EU is united in its position vis-à-vis Turkey. This issue has and will remain a political football of contested interests.[156] It is questionable whether Ankara has realistic prospects of full membership or, alternatively, will have to settle for some kind of special relationship. Whatever the case, the negotiation process for Turkey will be more conditional than for previous enlargement rounds.[157]

As Turkish authorities struggled with the task of implementing the mountain of required reforms, the first year of formal negotiations was not especially encouraging for supporters of Turkey's membership. Deterioration in the relationship with the EU could be observed, and there were few signs that opponents in both the EU and Turkey would fade from the scene. Whether Turkey accedes or not may ultimately be decided not by states or the EU but by one or more of the EU15's electorates. Current indications are that Turkey's membership will be rejected in a referendum. Even if granted a special status, it would (still) be one of the EU's neighbors and move from being a temporary quasi-insider back to being an "outsider." Domestic unrest over the presidential candidacy of Abdullah Gül in the spring of 2007 and the persisting crisis over Cyprus have done nothing to improve Turkey's accession chances.[158] European politicians and foreign affairs analysts are well aware, however, that an alienation of Turkey could be costly in various security areas, including energy supply and the battle against terrorism.

Conclusion

How much further might the "neighborhood" then extend? Beyond the "immediate" frontiers, a "tulip" revolution occurred in Kyrgyzstan in 2005. Other former Soviet republics in Central Asia may press for inclusion in ENP. Then there is Afghanistan, for which a "multi-annual pledge" of €1 billion is to be continued without its being to the "detriment of the aid to other beneficiaries in the region."[159] Most EU citizens, and much of its political elite, have not comprehended the size and complexity of the task that the EU faces to stabilize and reform its enlarging neighborhood. The principal impetus behind the attempt to deal with this multifaceted challenge is not the promotion of values. It is a response to disagreeable or even threatening circumstances, intended to contribute to the security and welfare of EU states and publics while avoiding an overloading of institutional, financial, and societal absorption capacities. Normative features are balanced by material needs and the limits of international maneuverability. Energy dependence, for example, could influence the EU's "resolve in promoting its agenda of political and economic reforms."[160]

Along with reforms and good behavior, the EU wants alignment of national legislation with its own *acquis* before access to the Single Market ensues. Such a step might be interpreted as logical and necessary for a process that will culminate in EU membership. States that have no intention of joining the EU, or those that see no prospect of invitation, however, may question the requirement to adopt EU legislation. Each ENP participant will ask why it should implement EU rules, with all the difficulties and possible political fallout that may entail, yet forgo the full benefits of membership. On the one hand, the EU's offer of gradual market integration is presumed to encourage FDI and a galvanizing of partner economies. On the other, the action plans place an onus on the partners to ensure a "climate conducive to foreign investment, growth and sustainable development." Action plans are complicated, sometimes running to hundreds of points. They stress democratization, good governance, and the ending of conflicts and are also very technical. All emphasize cooperation in combating terrorism. In November 2005 the Commission outlined a "Year of Progress" in ENP. There was not much concrete to list under the heading "main achievements to date," only mentions of "progress" and "preparations" being "well underway."[161]

It is possible that, as happened during the accession process ending in 2004, aspirants will compete for recognition based on their relative progress with reforms, thereby qualifying earlier for benefits and moving forward in a nominal EU entry queue. The EU may encourage this by rewarding its best pupils, but it does not mean they will enter. The EU has a legal "exit strategy" in the form of the criterion specifying that it must be capable of incorporating new members and delivering transfers to them. An EP report indicated how the neighborhood strategy might be or was being interpreted. It called on the EU "to take firm measures, accompanied by an information campaign, to explain the Barcelona Process and the new neighbourhood policy, so as to erase the image of a fearful Europe, more concerned with its own security and combating immigration than with the sustainable development that is both expected and necessary."[162] In Fabrizio Tassinari's analysis, the neighborhood is where the EU's idealism and a more widely applicable realism meet, "where the quest for compatibility between 'inside' and 'outside,' between 'widening' and 'deepening,' and, ultimately between 'security' and 'integration' becomes a more daunting project."[163] The political and normative clash is not so much between integration and security but between whether hard and "societal security" within the EU is better served by integrating more states and peoples on the periphery into the Union or by keeping them out.[164] It is not only populists who argue that the second option, at least for the present, is the one to pursue.

The EU's neighborhood strategy is a development of potentially great import—either through its success or lack of it. There are diverse considerations and questions that cannot be fully addressed here. Is the EU in a position of strength vis-à-vis its neighborhood? It may be true in bilateral instances, but not so when the entire disparate collection of actors is considered together. How many "neighbors" are there, and how many are "friends"? Why are they friends, and how long will they remain so? EU responsibility could be interpreted as condescension: Should the EU act as if it is determining the agenda? There are also internal pressures. How much will the neighborhood cost, and can the cost be justified to EU publics? A contradiction between promoting democratic values externally and upholding them internally will sharpen if popular views are ignored. The dilemma of being open to all European states as a security-enhancing political undertaking on one hand and opposition from current member state populations and significant sections of political elites to more members on the other is revealing. When individual, popular, party-political, or member state interests, and even the existence of the EU itself, are perceived as under threat, the means and will to enforce ideals are limited. Grandiose themes of unity based on shared and observed values are subordinated and more pragmatic alternatives sought.

Notes

1. Iris Kempe, *Direct Neighbourhood: Relations Between the Enlarged EU and the Russian Federation, Ukraine, Belarus, and Moldova* (Gütersloh: Bertelsmann, 1998); Esther Brimmer and Stefan Fröhlich, eds., *The Strategic Implications of European Union Enlargement* (Washington, DC: Center for Transatlantic Relations, Johns Hopkins University, 2005).

2. Roberto Aliboni, "The Geopolitical Implications of the European Neighbourhood Policy," *European Foreign Affairs Review* 10, no. 1 (2005): 1–16; Andreas Marchetti, "The European Neighbourhood Policy: Foreign Policy at the Periphery," C158 (Bonn: ZEI, 2006).

3. Horst Bacia, "Ein ring von Freunden," *Frankfurter Allgemeine Zeitung,* 12 January 2006; Elisabeth Johansson-Nogues, "'A Ring of Friends'? The Implications of the European Neighbourhood Policy for the Mediterranean," *Mediterranean Politics* 2 (2004): 240–247.

4. Michael Emerson, *The Wider Europe Matrix* (Brussels: CEPS, 2003).

5. Martin Ortega, "A New EU Policy on the Mediterranean?" in Judy Batt et al., *Partners and Neighbours: A CFSP for a Wider Europe,* Chaillot Paper 64 (Paris: ISS, 2003), 86–98; Michael Emerson and Gergana Noutcheva, *From Barcelona Process to Neighbourhood Policy: Assessments and Open Issues,* Working Document 220 (Brussels: CEPS, March 2005).

6. European Commission, *Communication to the Council on the Commission Proposals for Action Plans Under the European Neighbourhood Policy,* (ENP) (COM) 795, Brussels, 9 December 2004.

7. Michael Emerson, *European Neighbourhood Policy: Strategy or Placebo?* Working Document 215 (Brussels: CEPS, 2004).

8. Waldemar Hummer, "Die Union und ihre Nachbarn—Nachbarschaftspolitik vor und nach dem Verfassungsvertrag," *Integration* 28, no. 3 (2005): 233–245.

9. Steve Wood and Wolfgang Quaisser, "Turkey's Road to the EU: Political Dynamics, Strategic Context and Implications for Europe." *European Foreign Affairs Review* 10, no. 2 (2005): 147–173.

10. Martin Koopman and Christian Lequesne, eds., *Partner oder Beitrittskandidaten? Die Nachbarschaftspolitik der Europäischen Union auf dem Prüfstand* (Baden-Baden: Nomos, 2006).

11. Karen Smith, "The Outsiders: The European Neighbourhood Policy," *International Affairs* 81, no. 4 (2005): 757–773.

12. Cf. Kirsty Hughes, *Turkey and the European Union: Just Another Enlargement? Exploring the Implications of Turkish Accession,* Working Paper (Brussels: Friends of Europe, 2004); Michael Emerson and Nathalie Tocci, *Turkey as a Bridgehead and Spearhead: Integrating EU and Turkish Foreign Policy,* EU-Turkey Working Paper 1 (Brussels: CEPS, 2004); Senem Aydin and E. Fuat Keyman, *European Integration and the Transformation of Turkish Democracy,* EU-Turkey Working Paper 2 (Brussels: CEPS, 2004); Helmut Kurth and Iris Kempe, eds.,

Presidential Election and Orange Revolution: Implications for Ukraine's Transition (Kiev: Zapovit, 2005); Ulrich Beck and Edgar Grande, *Kosmopolitisches Europa* (Frankfurt: Suhrkamp, 2004).

13. Emerson, *European Neighbourhood Policy: Strategy or Placebo?*

14. Council of the European Union, *A Secure Europe in a Better World: European Security Strategy.* Brussels, 2003.

15. European Commission, *European Neighbourhood Policy Strategy Paper*, COM (2004) 373 Final, Brussels, 12 May 2004.

16. Julie Smith and Charles Jenkins, eds., *Through the Paper Curtain: Insiders and Outsiders in the New Europe* (London: RIIA/Blackwell, 2003).

17. Judy Batt et al., *Partners and Neighbours: A CFSP for a Wider Europe*, Chaillot Paper 64 (Paris: ISS, 2003).

18. Paul Kubicek, ed., *The European Union and Democratization* (London: Routledge, 2003); Michael Emerson and Gergana Noutcheva, *Europeanisation as a Gravity Model of Democratisation*, Working Document, 214 (Brussels: CEPS, November 2004).

19. Bruno Coppieters et al., *Europeanization and Ethnic Conflict: Case Studies from the European Periphery* (Ghent: Academic Press, 2004), 1.

20. European Commission, *Proposal for a Regulation of the European Parliament and of the Council Laying Down General Provisions for a European Neighbourhood and Partnership Instrument*, COM (2004) 628 final, Brussels, CEC, 29 September 2004.

21. "Regulation (EC) No 1638/2006 of the European Parliament and of the Council of 24 October 2006, laying down general provisions establishing a European Neighbourhood and Partnership Instrument," *Official Journal of the European Union* L 310, Article 29, 9 November 2006.

22. European Commission, "European Neighbourhood Policy: The Next Steps," IP/05/236 Press Release, Brussels, 2 March 2005.

23. Ernst Piehl, Peter Schulze, and Heinz Timmermann, *Die offene Flanke der Europäischen Union: Russische Föderation, Belarus, Ukraine und Moldau* (Berlin: Berliner Wissenschafts Verlag, 2005).

24. Joseph Nye, *Bound to Lead: The Changing Nature of American Power* (New York: Basic Books, 1990); Joseph Nye, *Soft Power: The Means to Success in World Politics* (New York: Public Affairs, 2004).

25. Aliboni, "The Geopolitical Implications of the European Neighbourhood Policy."

26. Paul Cornish and Geoffrey Edwards, "The Strategic Culture of the European Union: A Progress Report," *International Affairs* 81, no. 4 (2005): 801–820.

27. Cf. Ronald Asmus and F. Stephen Larrabee, "NATO and the Have-Nots: Reassurance After Enlargement," *Foreign Affairs* 75, no. 1 (1998): 13–20; Frank Schimmelfennig, *The EU, NATO, and the Integration of Europe: Rules and Rhetoric* (Cambridge: Cambridge University Press, 2003); Karin Fierke and Antje Wiener, "Constructing Institutional Interests: EU and NATO Enlargement," *Journal of European Public Policy* 6, no. 5 (1999): 721–742; Gregory Flynn and Henry Farrell, "Piecing Together the Democratic Peace: The CSCE, Norms and the 'Construction' of Security in Post–Cold War Europe," *International Organization* 53, no. 3 (1999): 505–536.

28. Cf. Jean-Yves Haine, "An Historical Perspective," in Nicole Gnesotto, ed., *EU Security and Defence Policy: The First Five Years* (Paris: ISS, 2004): 40–42.

29. Michael Emerson, "Introduction," in Michael Emerson, ed., *Democratisation in the European Neighbourhood* (Brussels: CEPS, 2005): 1–12.

30. Beatrice Pouligny, "Civil Society and Post-Conflict Peacebuilding:

Ambiguities of International Programmes Aimed at Building 'New' Societies," *Security Dialogue* 36, no. 4 (2005): 495–510.

31. Oliver Roy, "The Predicament of 'Civil Society' in Central Asia and the 'Greater Middle East,' *International Affairs* 81, no. 5 (2005): 1001–1012.

32. Richard Youngs, "The European Union and Democracy Promotion in the Mediterranean: A New or Disingenuous Strategy?" *Democratization* 9, no. 1 (2002): 40–62.

33. Emerson, "Introduction," in Emerson, *Democratisation in the European Neighbourhood,* 2.

34. "EU and USA wollen Lukaschenko bestrafen," *Süddeutsche Zeitung,* 25–26 March 2006, 1. More generally, on positive and negative incentives, see James Davis, *Threats and Promises* (Baltimore: Johns Hopkins University Press, 2000).

35. European Commission, *Proposal for a Regulation ... for a European Neighbourhood and Partnership Instrument,* 40.

36. Herbert Brücker, Philipp Schröder, and Christian Weise, "Doorkeepers and Gatecrashers: EU Enlargement and Negotiation Strategies," *Journal of European Integration,* 26, no. 1 (2004): 3–23.

37. Schimmelfennig, *The EU, NATO and the Integration of Europe,* cf. 4–5, 284–285.

38. Adrian Hyde-Price, book review in *European Foreign Affairs Review* 10, no. 3 (2005): 446–448.

39. Nicole Gnesotto, "Preface," in Batt et al., *Partners and Neighbours,* 5–6.

40. Pawel Kowal, ed., *The EU's Eastern Dimension: Opportunity for or Idée Fixe of Poland's Policy?* trans. Bohdan Ambroziewicz (Warsaw: Centre for International Relations, 2002); Olaf Osica, "Poland: A New European Atlanticist at a Crossroads?" *European Security* 13, no. 4 (2004): 301–322.

41. Author interview, German Foreign Ministry, Berlin, September 2006.

42. "Berlin entwickelte neue Nachbarschaftspolitik für die EU," *Frankfurter Allgemeine Zeitung,* 3 July 2006, 1.

43. See German Foreign Ministry, "The EU and Central Asia: Strategy for a New Partnership" (Berlin: May 2007), available in English at http://www.auswaertiges-amt.de/diplo/en/Europa/Aussenpolitik/Regionalabkommen/Zentralasien.html.

44. Werner Weidenfeld, "Die Europäische Union neu ausrichten," *Welt Trends* 50 (Spring 2006): 55–65.

45. Patricia Davis, *The Art of Persuasion: Positive Incentives and German Economic Diplomacy* (Ann Arbor: University of Michigan Press, 1999).

46. "Europe's Neighbours—Towards Closer Integration," speech by Commissioner Benita Ferrero-Waldner, Brussels Economic Forum, Brussels, 22 April, 2005. Emphasis in original.

47. Hermann Lübbe, "Wert und Interesse," *Frankfurter Allgemeine Zeitung,* 11 January 2006, 6.

48. Stephen Jones and Michael Emerson, *European Neighbourhood Policy in the Mashreq Countries: Enhancing Prospects for Reform,* Working Document 229 (Brussels: CEPS September, 2005), iv, 20.

49. Lübbe, "Wert und Interesse."

50. Marius Vahl, *Models for the European Neighbourhood Policy: The European Economic Area and the Northern Dimension,* Working Document 218 (Brussels: CEPS, 2005), 2.

51. Coppieters et al., *Europeanisation and Ethnic Conflict.*

52. Rolf Gustavsson and Richard Swartz, "Die Unvollendete," *Süddeutsche Zeitung,* 12 January 2006, 11.

53. European Parliament, *European Parliament Resolution on the Commission's*

2005 Enlargement Strategy Paper, P6_TA-PROV (2006) 0096, Strasbourg, 16 March 2006.

54. European Parliament Press Release, "Enlargement: EU Must Keep Its Promises but Take Account of Absorption Capacity," Strasbourg, 16 March 2006. Emphases in original.

55. Eneko Landaburu, "From Neighbourhood to Integration Policy: Are There Concrete Alternatives to Enlargement?" Speech at the CEPS conference "Revitalising Europe," Brussels, 23 January 2006. Later published under the same title as Policy Brief 95, Brussels, CEPS, March 2006.

56. "Desperately Seeking a Policy," *Economist,* 21 January 2006, 49–50.

57. European Parliament, Plenary Session Debate, Strasbourg, 15 March 2006.

58. European Commission, *Wider Europe—Neighbourhood: A Framework for Relations with Our Eastern and Southern Neighbours,* Brussels, March 2003.

59. Lucan Way, "Authoritarian State Building and the Sources of Regime Competitiveness in the Fourth Wave: The Cases of Belarus, Moldova, Russia, and Ukraine," *World Politics* 57, no. 2 (2005): 231–261. Cf. Kempe, *Direct Neighbourhood.*

60. Michael Emerson, "What Should the Community of Democratic Choice Do?" Policy Brief 98/2006 (Brussels: CEPS, 2006).

61. Dov Lynch, "The New Eastern Dimension of the Enlarged EU," in Judy Batt et al., *Partners and Neighbours: A CFSP for a Wider Europe.* Chaillot Paper 64 (Paris: ISS, 2003), 34–59.

62. European Commission, *The EU's Relation with Russia,* http://europa.eu.int/comm/external_relations/russia/intro/.

63. Vladimir Baranovsky, "Russia: A Part of Europe or Apart from Europe?" *International Affairs* 76, no. 3 (2000): 443–458.

64. Cf. Oksana Antonenko and Kathryn Pinnick, eds., *Russia and the European Union* (London: Routledge, 2004); Roland Dannreuther, ed., *European Foreign and Security Policy: Towards a Neighbourhood Strategy* (London: Routledge, 2004); Dov Lynch, ed., *What Russia Sees,* Chaillot Paper 74 (Paris: ISS, 2005).

65. Vahl, *Models for the European Neighbourhood Policy.*

66. Emerson, *The Wider Europe Matrix.*

67. Bergedorfer Gesprächskreis, *Russland und der Westen: Chance für eine neue Partnerschaft* (Hamburg: Körber Stiftung, 2005).

68. Strobe Talbott, "The Strains of Putin's Clampdown," *Financial Times,* 27 September 2004.

69. "A Colder Coming We Have of It," *Economist,* 21 January 2006, 48–49; Cf. Bobo Lo, *Vladimir Putin and the Evolution of Russian Foreign Policy* (London: RIIA/Blackwell, 2003).

70. Talbott, "The Strains of Putin's Clampdown."

71. Roland Dannreuther, "Developing the Alternative to Enlargement: The European Neighbourhood Policy," *European Foreign Affairs Review* 11, no. 2 (2006): 183–201.

72. Cf. Sabine Fischer, "Rußland und die Ukraine: Fehlkalkulation oder neoimperialer Impuls?" *Osteuropa* 55, no. 1 (2006): 64–76.

73. Alexander Rahr, "Schröders Russlandpolitik," *Welt Trends* 50 (Spring 2006): 93–94. Author's translation.

74. *Deutsche Welle* (Television News), 20 January 2006.

75. "Das ist ein Weckruf," *Der Spiegel,* 9 January 2006, 34–38.

76. Ilya Prizel, "Putin's Russia, the Berlin Republic, and East-Central Europe: A New Symbiosis?" *Orbis* (Fall 2002): 678–693.

77. Jochen Franzke, "Netzwerke für Demokratie statt Achsen mit Autokraten," *Welt Trends* 49 (Winter 2005–2006): 125–133.

78. Reinhard Veser, "Schröder und Putin," *Frankfurter Allgemeine Zeitung,* 1 December 2004, 1.

79. "Er bringt uns gute alte Mär," *Frankfurter Allgemeine Zeitung,* 22 December 2005, 31.

80. Roderick Lyne, "Russia in the EU? We Should Never Say Never," *Europe's World* (Spring 2006): 38–41.

81. Cf. Igor Zevelev and Kirill Glebov, "If You Want Democracy, Don't Push Putin," and Mark Brzezinski, "Speak Up, for the Neighbors' Sake," *International Herald Tribune,* 13 March 2006, 6.

82. Andrei Zagorski, "Russia and the Shared Neighbourhood," in Dov Lynch, ed., *What Russia Sees,* Chaillot Paper 74 (Paris: ISS, 2005), 61–77.

83. Anne Penketh, "Obituary: Alexander Litvinenko," *The Independent,* 25 November 2006; Mary Jordan and Peter Finn, "Radioactive Poison Killed Ex-Spy," *Washington Post Foreign Service,* 25 November 2006, http://www.washingtonpost.com/wp-dyn/content/article/2006/11/24/AR2006112400410_pf.html; David Leppard and Mark Franchetti, "Litvinenko: Clues Point to Kremlin," *Sunday Times,* 22 July 2007.

84. Council of the European Union, *Declaration by the Presidency on Behalf of the European Union on the Litvinenko Case,"* 11976/07 (Presse 174), Brussels, 18 July 2007.

85. Anne de Tinguy, "Konkurrenten statt Partner: Die russische Sicht auf die EU und die Nachbarschaftspolitik," in Martin Koopman and Christian Lesquesne, eds., *Partner oder Beitrittskandidaten? Die Nachbarschaftspolitik der Europäischen Union auf dem Prüfstand* (Baden-Baden: Nomos, 2006), 85–108.

86. Tomila Lankina, "Explaining European Union Aid to Russia," *Post-Soviet Affairs* 21, no. 4 (2005): 309–334.

87. Rolf Schuette, *EU-Russia Relations: Interests and Values—A European Perspective,* Paper 54 (Washington, DC: CEIP, 2004).

88. Ann Lewis, ed., *The EU and Ukraine: Neighbours, Friends, Partners?* (London: Federal Trust, 2002).

89. Volodymyr Tereschenko, *Evolution der politischen Beziehungen zwischen der Ukraine und der EU, 1991–2004* (Frankfurt: Peter Lang, 2005).

90. The Council of the EU stressed strategic importance in a "Declaration on Ukraine," in its revised *Presidency Conclusions 16–17 December 2004,* 16238/1/04 REV 1, Brussels, 1 February 2005.

91. Cf. Adrian Karatnycky, "Ukraine's Orange Revolution," *Foreign Affairs* 84, no. 2 (2005): 35–52.

92. "Where Does Europe End and Asia Begin?" *International Herald Tribune,* 1 December 2004, 1; Stefan Wagstyl, "Kiev's Voice of Protest," *Financial Times,* 27–28 November 2004, 7.

93. Jochen Hoenig and Markus Ziener, "Kiew spaltet die EU und Russland," *Handelsblatt,* 26–28 November 2004, 2.

94. Gerhard Simon, "Neubeginn in der Ukraine," *Osteuropa* 55, no. 1 (2005): 16–33.

95. Dov Lynch, "Misperceptions and Divergences," in Lynch, ed., *What Russia Sees,* Chaillot Paper 74 (Paris: ISS, 2005), 13–14.

96. Winfried Schneider-Deters, "Die Palliative Ukrainepolitik der EU," *Osteuropa* 55, no. 1 (2005): 50–63; Anthony Browne, "Yushchenko Snubbed as EU Insists There's No Room for Ukraine," *Australian,* 11–12 December 2004, 13.

97. Andreas Rinke, "Balanceakt für den Bundeskanzler," *Handelsblatt*, 26–28 November 2004, 2.

98. "Putin und Juschtchenko nähern sich an," *Frankfurter Allgemeine Zeitung*, 12 January 2006, 5.

99. Eugene Rumer, "Russia's Strong Arm Tactics May Do Ukraine a Favour," *Financial Times*, 3 January 2006.

100. Mykola Rjabcuk, "Die Ukraine am Scheideweg: Ist ein Erpresserstaat reformierbar?" *Osteuropa* 55, no. 1 (2005): 4–14.

101. Frank Nienhuysen, "Wehmut nach der Revolution: Ukraine, Georgien, Kirigisien," *Süddeutsche Zeitung*, 25–26 March 2006, 2.

102. "Parlament wählt Janukowitsch zum Ministerpräsident," *Süddeutsche Zeitung*, 5–6 August 2006, 8.

103. Axel Sell and Tobias Schauf, eds., *Bilanz und Perspektiven der Transformation in Osteuropa* (Münster: LIT, 2003).

104. Council of the European Union, *Presidency Conclusions, 16–17 December 2004*.

105. Way, "Authoritarian State Building," 252.

106. Daniel Brössler, "Russland droht Weißrussland," *Suddeutsche Zeitung*, 13–14 May 2006, 8.

107. Astrid Sahm, "Nach der Wahl ist vor der Wahl: Belarus weiter auf Isolationkurs?" *Osteuropa* 55, no. 1 (2005): 77–90.

108. Joerg Forbrig, David Marples, and Pavol Demes, eds., *Prospects for Democracy in Belarus* (Washington, DC: German Marshall Fund, 2006); Rainer Lindner, *Präsidentschaftswahl in Belarus: Autoritäres Regime, abhängige Staatswirtschaft, internationale Isolation*, S6 (Berlin: Stiftung Wissenschaft und Politik, 2006).

109. OSCE/ODIHR, *Election Observation Mission Report, Republic of Belarus: Presidential Election, 19 March 2006*, Warsaw, June 2006.

110. Nicu Popescu, *The EU in Moldova: Settling Conflicts in the Neighbourhood*, Occasional Paper 60 (Paris: ISS, October 2005).

111. European Defence Agency, *Resolution on Human Rights in Moldova, and in Transnistria in Particular*, P6 TA-PROV2006 0099, Strasbourg, 16 March 2006.

112. European Commission, *EU-Moldova Action Plan* (Brussels: December 2004).

113. Dov Lynch, *Why Georgia Matters*, Chaillot Paper 86 (Paris: ISS, February 2006), 9.

114. Author interview, EU General Affairs Council, Brussels, November, 2004.

115. Lynch, *Why Georgia Matters*, 12.

116. Steven Myers and Michael Schwirtz, "Russian Officials Pledge More Sanctions to Cut Off Cash to Georgia," *New York Times*, 4 October, 2006; Steven Myers, "Russia Deports Georgians and Increases Pressures on Businesses and Students," *New York Times*, 7 October 2006; "Russlands Präsident wirft Georgien Kriegstreiberei vor," *Frankfurter Allgemeine Zeitung*, 5 October 2006, 8; "Moskau setzt Georgien mit Razzien zu," *Handelsblatt* 5 October 2006, 9.

117. E. Majidow, "Is Azerbaijan Going to Continue to Get Massive Inward Foreign Investments?" *Caucasian Journal of European Affairs* 1 (Winter 2006).

118. European Commission, *Staff Working Paper*, SEC(2005), 286/3 "Annex to 'European Neighbourhood Policy': Country Report Azerbaijan," COM (2005) 72 Final, Brussels, 2 March 2005); European Commission *Staff Working Paper*, SEC(2005), 285/3, "Annex to 'European Neighbourhood Policy': Country Report Armenia," COM (2005) 72 Final, Brussels, 2 March 2005; European Commission, "European Neighbourhood Policy: Armenia," IP/05/237, and "European Neighbourhood Policy: Azerbaijan," IP/05/238, Brussels, 2 March 2005.

119. Edward Chow, "Russian Pipelines: Back to the Future?" *Georgetown Journal of International Affairs* (Winter–Spring 2004): 27–33.

120. Raffaella Del Sarto and Tobias Schumacher, "From EMP to ENP: What's at Stake with the European Neighbourhood Policy Towards the Southern Mediterranean?" *European Foreign Affairs Review* 10, no. 1 (2005): 17–28.

121. Jones and Emerson, *European Neighbourhood Policy in the Mashreq Countries*, 21.

122. Ortega, "A New EU Policy on the Mediterranean?"

123. Ortega, "A New EU Policy on the Mediterranean?" 91.

124. Cf. Richard Youngs, *Europe and the Middle East in the Shadow of September 11* (Boulder: Lynne Rienner, 2006).

125. European Commission, *EU-Morocco Action Plan,* Brussels, December 2004.

126. Elena Baracani, "From EMP to ENP: A New European Pressure for Democratisation? The Case of Morocco," Working Paper (CSEPS: Beer Sheva, 2005).

127. European Commission, *EU-Tunisia Action Plan,* Brussels, December 2004.

128. European Commission, *Partenariat Euro-Med Algerie: Document de Strategie 2002–2006 and Programme Indicatif National, 2002–2004,* Brussels, no date.

129. European Commission, "Commissioner Benita Ferrero-Waldner in Algiers," IP/05/790, Brussels, 24 June 2005.

130. Aliboni, "Geopolitical Implications of ENP," 8–9.

131. European Commission, "Commissioner Ferrero-Waldner's Trip to Libya," IP/05/605, Brussels: CEC, 25 May 2005.

132. José Manuel Barroso, "From Schuman to Sirte: A Tale of Two Unions," Speech/05/413, Sirte, 4 July 2005.

133. Bernard Lewis, "Freedom and Justice in the Modern Middle East," *Foreign Affairs* 84, no. 3 (2005): 36–51.

134. Author interview, French Embassy, Canberra, June 2004.

135. European Commission, *Commission Staff Working Paper,* "Annex to 'European Neighbourhood Policy': Country Report Egypt," SEC(2005) 287/3, Brussels, 2 March 2005.

136. European Commission, *EU-Jordan Action Plan,* Brussels, CEC, 2004.

137. Jones and Emerson, *European Neighbourhood Policy in the Mashreq Countries.*

138. Yehezkel Dror and Sharon Pardo, "Approaches and Principles for an Israeli Grand Strategy Towards the European Union," *European Foreign Affairs Review* 11, no. 1 (2006): 17–44.

139. European Commission, *Proposed EU-Israel Action Plan,* Brussels, December 2004.

140. European Commission, *EU-Palestinian Authority Action Plan*, Brussels, December 2004.

141. Anne Le More, "Killing with Kindness: Funding the Demise of a Palestinian State," *International Affairs* 81, no. 5 (2005): 981–999.

142. Fouad Ajami, "The Autumn of the Autocrats," *Foreign Affairs* 84, no. 3 (2005): 20–35.

143. European Commission, *Commission Staff Working Paper,* "Annex to 'European Neighbourhood Policy': Country Report Lebanon," SEC(2005) 289/3, Brussels, 2 March 2005.

144. European Commission, *Euro-Med Partnership Syria: Country Strategy Paper 2002–2006 and National Indicative Programme, 2002–2004,* Brussels, CEC, 2002.

145. European Commission, *Euro-Med Partnership Syria: National Indicative Programme, 2005–2006*, Brussels, CEC, no date.

146. European Commission, *Reconstructing Iraq: State of Play and Implementation to Date*, Brussels, November 2005; European Commission, *European Community Iraqi Assistance Programme, 2006*, E/2006/470–C(2006)864, Brussels, 28 March 2006; European Commission, *Preliminary Draft General Budget of the European Commission for the Financial Year 2005*, Brussels, 2004.

147. Michael Costello, "Diplomacy Has Failed and the Choice Is Clear," *Australian*, 20 January 2006, 12.

148. Christiane Hoffmann, "Vom Westen unbeeindruckt," *Frankfurter Allgmeine Zeitung*, 12 January 2006, 3; Nikolaus Blome, "Endstation Hoffnung," *Die Welt*, 12 January 2006, 3.

149. "Die Europäische Union war naiv," *Die Welt*, 12 January 2006, 3.

150. "Die EU in Sorge um den Weltfrieden: Teheran—Klamauk des Westens," *Frankfurter Allgemeine Zeitung*, 12 January 2006, 1.

151. Council of the European Union, "Declaration on Iran," in *Brussels European Council December 14–15 2006, Presidency Conclusions*, 16879/1/06 REV 1, CONCL 3, Brussels 12 February 2007, Annex 3, pp. 24–25.

152. Dorothée Schmid, "Die Europäische Nachbarschaftspolitik und die euromediterrane Partnerschaft: Das Ende einer regionalen Ambition?" in Martin Koopman and Christian Lesquesne, eds., *Partner oder Beitrittskandidaten? Die Nachbarschaftspolitik der Europäischen Union auf dem Prüfstand* (Baden-Baden: Nomos, 2006), 111–128; Del Sarto and Schumacher, "From EMP to ENP."

153. Bernhard Küppers, "Komplizierter Kosovo," *Süddeutscher Zeitung*, 12 January 2006, 4.

154. Franz-Lothar Altmann, *EU und westlicher Balkan: Von Dayton nach Brüssel—ein allzu langer Weg?* S1 (Berlin: SWP, 2005), 24.

155. Barbara Lippert, "Die Türkei als Sonderfall und Wendepunkt der klassischen EU-Erweiterungspolitik," *Integration*, 28, no. 2 (2005): 119–135.

156. Heinz Kramer, *Türkei-Verhandlungen als Spielball der Interessen*, SWP-Aktuell 42 (Berlin: SWP, 2005).

157. Quaisser and Wood, *EU Member Turkey?*; Wood and Quaisser, "Turkey's Road to the EU."

158. Doga Ulas Eralp and Nimet Beriker, "Assessing the Conflict Resolution Potential of the EU: The Cyprus Conflict and Accession Negotiations," *Security Dialogue* 36, no. 2 (2005): 175–192.

159. European Commission, *Preliminary Draft General Budget of the European Commission for the Financial Year 2005*, Brussels, 2004.

160. Dannreuther, "Developing the Alternative to Enlargement."

161. European Commission, "European Neighbourhood Policy: A Year of Progress," IP/05/1467, Brussels, 24 November 2005.

162. European Parliament, *Report on the European Neighbourhood Policy*, rapporteur Charles Tannock, FINAL 06-0399/2005, Strasbourg, 7 December, 2005, 17, point 47.

163. Fabrizio Tassinari, *Security and Integration in the EU Neighbourhood: The Case for Regionalism*, Working Document 226, Brussels, CEPS, July 2005.

164. Ole Waever et al., *Identity, Migration, and the New Security Agenda in Europe* (London: Pinter, 1993).

7

Considering Europe's Future

Motivated by fears related to globalization and EU enlargements, as well as discontent with their own governments, voters in France and the Netherlands rejected the proposed Constitutional Treaty in May and June 2005. The cumbersome document, featuring 465 articles, five protocols, and three declarations, could not be considered a genuine "European Constitution" but rather a response to circumstances in which EU decisionmaking had become increasingly unwieldy. It may have improved the functioning of the extended EU, but much would have remained vague, or controversial, such as social regulations.[1] A change to double majority voting would not have occurred until 2009 and the restructuring of the Commission not until 2014. The symbolic significance of the CT's rejection may be as important as practical considerations.

The EU in Crisis

During the British presidency that followed the CT referenda, negotiations on the financial perspective for 2007–2013 were accompanied by disputes more petulant than usual. Wrangling of this order gave some insight into the nature of the contemporary EU. As it grows in size, the preparedness of statespeople and publics to willingly provide for a common cause—or determine one—is decreasing. The conflict between deepening and widening has triggered many questions: Have the limits of both been reached? Have elites themselves lost faith in the EU project and begun searching for alternatives? Is it mainly due to marketing problems?[2] "Crisis" is a recurring condition, even a specialty, for the EU.[3] The current phase precipitated proposals that the EU undertake a "period of reflection."

Although some prominent figures, including new German chancellor Angela Merkel, endorsed a refloating of the idea, presenting a constitution again to an enlightened public after a little time, as occurred with a second referendum on the Nice Treaty in Ireland, was an illusion in the political climate persisting into 2007.[4] Reviving single elements for ratification by national parliaments is also problematic. The CT was a package solution based on complicated compromises, and selecting only certain parts will encounter resistance.[5] There is no reason to believe that member states, with quite different integration concepts, would all accept proposals outside the arrangements already offered. Although a thoroughgoing reform and reinvigoration action is the optimal course, the only realistic alternative seems a pragmatic, lowest-common-denominator approach. It would attempt to deal with existing, especially economic, problems in an unspectacular way. It might transpire that this path is dangerous, however, as it involves the possibility of states being detached from particular initiatives.

The Luxembourg premier, Jean-Claude Juncker, identified four main mistakes or causes of the EU's malaise:

1. The Union's own heads of state and government—among which he presumably included himself—disparaged the EU and its institutions.

2. The deeper meaning and imperative of eastern enlargement was never clarified to publics.

3. Following the "miserable" outcome at Nice, with insufficient reform of the EU's institutions, the "Constitution" was inappropriately named and badly promoted. EU elites wanted to impress the rest of the world but frightened their own citizens. Some perceived it as an assault on the nation-states that would replace their own constitutions. Terming the CT a "Europe Treaty" and presenting a streamlined version would have been a better option.

4. The impression was given that the EU was predominantly a "money affair." Consequently, many people viewed it through this prism, if from opposite ends: some states and publics believed that they paid too much and others that they received too little. Juncker observed that:

> A crisis does not fall from the sky; political crises are not unforeseeable natural catastrophes, which one stands helpless in the face of. They build gradually, accumulating explosive power piece by piece, and then after years of negligence, they are detonated. The heads of state and government behaved nonchalantly as the crisis mounted; they made no attempt to comprehend the dark clouds that gathered over the European pathways.[6]

Juncker's pessimism may be tempered after the June 2007 summit. Some hopes were revived with the Reform Treaty, which, though it will not solve everything, can assist in lessening the probability of crises and serious divisions in the EU and improve its functionality. Nevertheless, a trend of differentiation, or clubs within the EU club, will continue. Differentiation is almost inevitable either in an orderly form, or through dispute and opt-outs. If no consensus can be reached, for example if the Reform Treaty fails even without rejection in a referendum, then another of the crises that all parties wish to avoid will emerge. In the meantime, it appears that any more enlargements, with the probable exception of Croatia, have been deferred until well into the future as a long phase of attempted consolidation begins.

The EU's successes—the single market, EMU, eastern enlargement—do not obscure that it missed an opportunity to restructure and equip itself in order to better cope with pressures confronting it now and more tests that lie ahead. Summits ostensibly dealing with institutional reforms (Amsterdam, Nice, Brussels) did not result in substantial, positive renovation. Reforms in agricultural and structural policy were inadequate. These events contributed to the disappointment of populations, yet large sections of them were also against change. They wanted solutions and improvement without costs. Contemporaneously, the basic arguments of how to widen and deepen simultaneously were reversed: internal reforms were not considered necessary to enlargement, but rather enlargement should stimulate reforms. This strategy, some lamented, failed because of public "stubbornness."

The EU has an optimistic motto: *unity in diversity*. If only it were so simple in practice. The basic integration concepts that are most influential within individual member states are so varied that fundamental consensus on the EU's goals, direction, organization, and methods of operation is unattainable. German approaches favor a federal Europe with defined institutions and competencies; French proposals center on a "core Europe" and imply French leadership; the predominant British view favors a looser association of states; CEECs are more ambivalent. Political elites want to avoid dominance by more powerful members while being sufficiently integrated to benefit from communal policies.

Where the UK and Scandinavian states prefer enlargement to deepening, France and Germany tried to combine both paths, in theory and political practice. They could do that in previous decades. However, neither country is sufficiently prepared in national and European policy to cope with deepening and widening in the present era. France has had a particularly hard time dealing with changed constellations within the enlarged EU. The support of its political elite for enlargement was not enthusiastic but was rather the outcome of grand-scale issue-linkage with EMU and CAP funding, and a realization that France's options for opposing the accession of CEECs were narrow. Germany's close links to France mean it is also affected. Fears in Mediterranean states of being among the losers after enlargement incited further reform blockades and assisted Blair's defense of the UK rebate.

Haggling over agricultural and structural policies and financial transfers is central to EU politics. Side payments and compensation for relative losers secured the EU in the past. The political economy is now much more difficult. The EU has become very heterogeneous, and the available resources of net contributors like Germany have declined. Notwithstanding the rhetoric, symbolism, and expectations, in institutional and financial terms the 2004 enlargement to include ten states, with two more projected for 2007, was premature. A differentiated approach based on individual readiness would have been more appropriate but was overruled by the perceived special interests of various EU15 members in including particular states in the first wave of entrants. An assortment of package deals resulted. The immediate attempt to push negotiations on Turkey's accession aggravated skeptical popular sentiment. This situation demands a slowdown of the enlargement drive.

The EU as Lame Duck? The Limits of the "European Economic and Social Model"

These problems would not be so serious if core EU members could produce the oft-mentioned growth and welfare benefits of enlargement and globalization. Although exports from some grew significantly, jobs failed to materialize. Despite an upturn in mid-2006, which may be based on the short-lived stimuli of the football World Cup[7] and the then impending 3 percent value-added tax increase of January 2007, the crucially important German economy has suffered from weak growth and high unemployment for many years. France and Italy are in some ways worse. They, like much of the EU, have become dependent on a German locomotive effect. Initiatives for employment creation and innovation have been ineffectual and even officially conceded as failures. In part, this situation explains the reluctance of net payers to provide fresh money for such policies.

Globalization and enlargement have placed the economic and social models of several member states under extreme pressure. Among wide sections of CEEC populations—not so different from much of the EU15—the illusion of a pan-EU social welfare model persists. Attempts to export such a model will fail. Elites and publics have not fully understood the magnitudes of disparity that now characterize the EU club. That is true for incomes and structural differences as well as for economic growth. The consequences for labor markets—wage pressure and differentiation—are only slowly and grudgingly acknowledged. In some cases, pressure to reverse even modest reforms has intensified. States with more liberal economies, like the UK and Ireland, have fewer problems of this nature.

The creation of a single economic and social model is ever more evanescent. Enlargement promoted an extension of rules and regulations, with transitional periods, but it has hampered deepening. The EU failed to streamline the *acquis* and apply better coordination in public spending, labor markets, decreased tax wedges (tax and social security contributions paid by employers in addition to wages), and deregulation. In areas such as taxation, social security systems, and environmental legislation, harmonization will be limited to minimum standards. Tight economic and social policy coordination by twenty-seven or more member states looks unachievable. Rules that all members can support, as the Stability and Growth Pact case demonstrates (see Chapter 2), are sometimes hard to sustain in practice. The "self-binding" arrangements envisaged proved ineffective or too rigid. The main actors, or resisters, are national governments, and they, in the Council, ultimately decide what should be done regarding transgressions. Community sanctions have only limited effect.

The EU's diversity is more compatible with the British or Scandinavian integration approach. In the framework of an advanced customs union aligned with democratic values, system competition in economic and social policy will emerge. Europe à la carte, learning from best practices and failures, will be a defining feature of this model.[8] The present SM concept allows for wide borders as long as functioning market economies exist and common rules are followed. In this regard, deepening, understood as the steadily increasing integration of markets, is a liberalization project because it sets in motion the full power of economic force and laws, especially factor-price equalization. However, a large proportion of Europeans reject an unlimited EU. Supporters of widening are confronted by the problem of harmonization being reduced through further enlargements.

The Consequences of EMU

The British orientation would be more persuasive if the EU had no political dimension or aspiration and if EMU, which is not a major priority for the UK, did not exist. Here the earlier continental debate should be noted. Initially, many argued that a currency union should follow a political union. This "crown theory" was especially strong in Germany, at least among those not demanding a complete rejection of the euro. The timing and the causality were later reversed, and it was argued that EMU would promote a political union. The linkage between these two has since eroded. EMU worked partly because officials, most of all in the Commission, treated it as a technical project.

Others interpreted it as consummately political, including the many Germans who did not want to sacrifice the deutsche mark, and the British, Danes, and Swedes who did not join EMU. It is debatable whether the ECB's interest rates are too high, even if disappointing growth performance cannot be explained solely by reference to this. The political implications of the euro are more extensive than those of the SM. It engendered lower transaction costs and currency stability. Yet without flexible exchange rates, every alteration in competitiveness has to be borne by the real economy, which primarily means wages. That leads to a situation, leaving aside smaller economies, in which the French cannot ignore low growth in the German economy. Germans and French worry whether Italy can really jettison an inflation mentality and if its economy is losing competitiveness.[9] A greater concern would emerge among eurozone members if a general strike were to paralyze the public sector in Paris or if a government with a radical social program, like that of Mitterrand in the early 1980s, were to induce an economic disaster.

Despite the euro's solid performance, it remains open whether EMU will survive if progress toward a political union is not made. It need not culminate in a European superstate but would entail rigorous policy coordination. Creating a common space of peace and freedom backed by law is not enough for the EU to ensure that European values and preferences, varied as they are, can prevail in a world of intensifying competition.

British Europe or Core Europe?

"British Europe," with its emphasis on widening, is realizable through competition-based integration. For it to work, extensive changes in the side-payments system would be necessary. In this respect Blair's demands were rational, even if domestic considerations played an important role. The EU could then operate with much more efficient agricultural and regional policies, which would help to promote cohesion. Traditional binding forces provided by the existing interest equalization mechanism would, however, be weakened, which might erode the integration idea and the accord to implement it. Liberalization of the service sector and free movement of labor could lose support as states shifted toward mitigating unemployment. Such tendencies are already apparent.

A possible remedy would be to reanimate the idea of "Core Europe" or to strengthen bilateral or trilateral cooperation. Such a configuration could be organized around large EMU states, especially France and Germany. Variable geometries in other policy areas would be possible, but it would be essential that the EMU participants cooperate much more closely in economic and social affairs. Doing so would involve firmer connections to the ECB, removing all barriers to competition, and vigorously promoting commercial and industrial innovation. It must go beyond the Economic and Financial Affairs Council (ECOFIN) since that entity is often politically compromised. Political leaders bear the chief responsibility. The contravention of rules and the blockade of reforms because of supposed national interests are serious violations of common objectives.

Individually and through their triangular relations, France, the UK, and Germany are decisive to the EU's direction and prospects. The outcome of Germany's 2005 federal election motivated Commission President Barroso to appeal to rival party leaderships to instill stability in the EU's largest economy and most populous member state. The message was that investors had to be reassured and the EU reinvigorated. If anything, the torpor in France was more deeply entrenched. Both engines of Europe's erstwhile "motor" displayed inertia reflective of a profound fear of change. When these two critical polities could not demonstrate much dynamism or capacity for reform, others asked why they should do so and incapacitated the EU as a whole.

Forming another axis in the triangle, France and the UK recognize each other, according to a Foreign Office source, as equals above other member states.[10] Enduring rivalry and mutual respect can coexist as the pomp of the entente cordiale anniversary and clashes over referendums and the budget displayed. Notwithstanding ongoing tensions, the French elite realize that cooperation with the British is essential. So do the Germans. Soon after her investiture, Merkel visited Chirac, Barroso, and Blair in quick succession. In London she emphasized that Germany's partnership with the UK would be intensified, though not at the expense of relations with France.[11] Merkel's introduction to the highest level of EU politics placed her in a delicate position. She was in general agreement with Blair on economic reform yet also hoped to convince him to reduce the UK rebate. The British saw Merkel as a potential ally in the battle to reform the CAP, meaning a reduction in Anglo-German payments and French receipts. Convincing Chirac to give up France's privileges in this area was the other principal test for Merkel in the context of financial politics among the big three, especially when she had to ensure her own political survival. Sarkozy has given the impression that he will be more amenable to CAP reform. Net receivers looked on, hoping for a compromise that would maintain their levels of funding.

Defense, Security, and the Fight Against Terrorism

Domestic preoccupations have distracted member states from a more intensive engagement with tasks in foreign, security, defense, and neighborhood policy. If a serious external crisis that demands a concerted response were to coincide with protracted internal strains, it could make or break the EU. Conversely, a negative integration factor may provide the imperative for resolute action. The EU must be able to protect itself, though the precise means by which it will do so is not yet clear.[12] A focus on security resonates of realism in a context of institutionalized and partly supranational politics; it also reinforces a link between identity and interests in global affairs.[13] Strategic imperatives, known and unknown threats, and international rivalries compel the EU to devise and instigate a credible security system. It would entail a distinctive fusion of soft and hard power with ramifications beyond Europe.

One essential is that the EU must spend more, despite counter-pressures from domestic politics and budgetary constraints. In 1985 the UK spent about 5.3 percent of GDP on defense, (West) Germany slightly over 3 percent, and France a little over 4 percent. In 1999 these states spent about 2.5, 1.5, and 2.8

percent, respectively.[14] The peace dividend after the Cold War is welcome, but other possible threats have multiplied. In geostrategic terms the scope of the security zone has extended well beyond the former EC. The CEECs now both contribute to and are beneficiaries of a common security space. Some scholars accent national strategic cultures and the need for a fuller representation of the CEECs in analyses of European security.[15] Their preferences for a substantial US role in Europe means that these nation-states are important actors in the difficult process of refiguring compatible and convincing Euro-Atlantic defense and security arrangements.

Felix Berenskoetter argues that the EU's understanding of its "responsibility for global security" "is that it is something taken on by default rather than by calling." This is in sharp contrast to the US national security strategy. If the European Security Strategy is an accurate reflection, Berenskoetter contends, then the EU's principal responsibility is continued integration and "promoting political order" in its immediate neighborhood. There is "an unresolved tension between global outlook" and the continued importance of a narrower geography, or geopolitics, on the EU's "strategic horizon."[16] Nonetheless, the ESS states that "the future will depend partly on our actions." The document does not rate aggression in conventional military terms as likely. Terrorism is listed as the first "key threat" to the states and populations of the EU, followed by the proliferation of WMDs, regional conflicts, state failure, and organized crime.[17] The EU's fight against terrorism is a cross-pillar activity involving the Common Foreign and Security Policy and Justice and Home Affairs. Beyond that, it requires intensive cooperation with other actors. Combating organized crime may also involve the combined deployment of instruments nominally situated in one or the other TEU pillar. An official at the General Affairs and External Relations Council suggested that the ESS would provide the basis for EU security for the foreseeable future, with no plans to update it.[18]

In the summer of 2006, cooperation among EU states contributed to, among other antiterror successes, the foiling of a plan to blow up planes departing London's Heathrow airport for the United States, and the capture of train terrorists in Germany. Alternatively, doubts about the EU as a force in global politics reemerged when its member states reacted with initial assurances and then irresolution regarding the provision of troops to a UN-sponsored peacekeeping contingent for southern Lebanon. Chirac presented France as prepared to lead a mission and provide 5,000 troops before reducing the proposed troop contingent to 200 and trying to goad others, including Germany, into making a substantial offer. No one in German politics wanted to be part of this militarily, for several reasons quite apart from the usual pacifist resistance. One was that the *Bundeswehr*, having taken on peacekeeping tasks in Congo and with multiple deployments elsewhere, risked overstretch if it was to send personnel to patrol the Lebanese-Israeli border. Another reason was historical sensitivity. Some raised the hypothetical situation of a German soldier accidentally killing an Israeli and determined that they were grounds to categorically exclude any German military involvement. Others argued that a special German responsibility for Israel was the foundation for a necessary participation by the *Bundeswehr* in a UN force. In September the Bundestag voted to send a maximum of 2,400 German personnel and eight marine craft. Its main purpose was to prevent the smuggling of arms for Hizbollah.[19] An initial one-year tour of duty was confirmed. The French contribution was meanwhile raised to 2,000 personnel. Italy offered to take over operational command from France in February 2007.

The Lebanon deployment was a test for the EU. If it was not credible in this instance, how could it hope to control Iran, a case in which the EU has invested considerable diplomatic effort? Iran has ambitious goals: to achieve nuclear capability and a resulting defense and energy self-sufficiency. It may also have more nefarious intentions. Whatever it does, Iran has few rules that restrict its endeavors. The EU, however, has many rules and, sometimes it seems, no clear goal or method of achieving one. The EU's rules are the legacy of a post–World War II peace project. Vis-à-vis a nuclear-armed Iran, the EU's mass of rules and regulations could make it inflexible and limited in response.

Wider Europe, Wider Responsibility, Wider Risk

The 2004 enlargement did not imply closure on where the frontiers of the EU lay or how to deal with actors that remained beyond them. On the contrary, there are a host of current and prospective applicants for accession and other actors with whom partnerships need to be developed. Against this background, the nature, ambitions, and capacities of the entity evolving under the designation "European Union" is unclear. With many countries aspiring to enter the EU, each bid for accession raises the question anew: Who or what is European and who or what is not?[20] Ulrike Guérot and Andrea Witt pronounce that "no-one knows these days what Europe actually is, where its borders lie, and which domains demand European steering."[21] Manifold issues of solidarity and integrative capacity, which influence the EU's efficiency and the perceived value of membership for individual states, are involved. Along with our own speculations, we have drawn on studies of the EU's future general development and a more specific security-related perspective, to outline hypothetical scenarios that the EU might evolve toward or confront.[22]

Future Scenario A: Reforms Fail. In this scenario the world is relatively benign, at least as far as EU member states and societies are concerned (see Figure 7.1). They cannot reach agreement on critical issues, and it becomes apparent that they prefer independence to integration. Economic policy coordination weakens; community policies are renationalized; vetoes, opt-outs, and national interests prevail over "permanent structured cooperation" in foreign,

Figure 7.1   Future Scenario A: Reforms Fail

Reforms fail and pressures from within and outside lead to the EU's dissolution before many more members join. A post-EU Europe and world results.

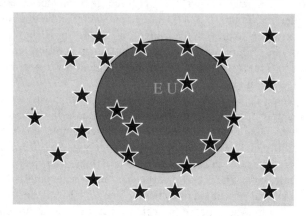

security, and defense affairs. The Lisbon Agenda evaporates after failing to stimulate an innovative, dynamic, economic space. High unemployment persists in several polities. The voting system continues to hinder decisionmaking focused on pan-EU issues; the twenty-eight member states concentrate their political energies more on making deals to secure national or party-political interests. While a core group of states attempts to preserve the EU and direct it according to its own preferences, a common will to revive the integration proj-

Figure 7.2   Future Scenario B: Clubs Within the Club

Clubs within the club form. New permutations in policy, institutional, and alliance participation emerge. Variable geometry is complex but certain coalitions consolidate.

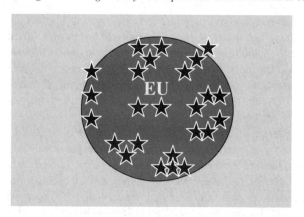

ect has terminally diminished. Europe is not seriously threatened existentially, although the economic and technological performance of the former EU member states is erratic, and most decline in political authority. Some, following the Norwegian and Swiss examples, are more successful outside the now nonexistent EU than they were in it.

Future Scenario B: Clubs Within the Club. This scenario probably most approximates the tendencies in 2006 (see Figure 7.2). There have always been special partnerships within the EU and its forerunners, but in times when the external environment and internal circumstances were very different. In the scenario's optimistic variant, the formation of coalitions does not lead to a splintering of the EU but generates a stability of its own. A division of labor and a broad-based prosperity ensues. Some institutional and legal changes occur, but all EU members remain formally equal. Leadership by example is a critical factor and motivates more hesitant members to enthusiastically support initiatives of informal "group leaders." Vigorous competition contributes to a durable pan-European economic vitality. In the pessimistic variant, some coalitions strengthen, and large projects are pursued without a majority. Solidarity weakens to the extent that the coalitions or alliances see no imperative to assist others, including, or even especially, when these others face security threats. Intergroup competition becomes dangerous rather than mutually galvanizing.

Future Scenario C: A Pan-European Identity. This represents the ideal development for advocates of supranational institutionalism and an authentic global power EU (see Figure 7.3). Intergovernmentalists and, more so, nationalists, are initially less enthused yet accept the EU's growing power as enhanc-

Figure 7.3   Future Scenario C: A Pan-European Identity

A pan-European identity based on solidarity and cooperation prevails, extensive reforms are implemented, and a powerful EU exerts unified interests on a global scale.

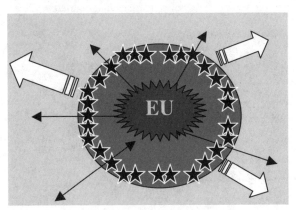

ing the interests of their own nation-states in a global context. The EU maximizes its potential: technological innovation proceeds, economic growth and prosperity return, unemployment and social conflict decrease, new members are smoothly integrated, regional disparities diminish, waste and inefficiency disappear, and internal and external security is improved. The EU exerts itself as a promoter of democratic stability worldwide, where necessary by deployment of its powerful, ultramodern military forces. The European institutions gain the trust and support of citizens who now widely identify themselves foremost as Europeans rather than belonging to diverse nations. The authority that the EU acquires in reaching this level of solidarity and influence decreases the possibilities for any so inclined member states or individuals to sabotage the communal venture. The vision of a united Europe is realized.

Future Scenario D: Vulnerability to External Forces. This is similar to Scenario A, but with externalities both more negative and more pressing (see Figure 7.4). A pessimistic interpretation might find similarities with the present situation. Formally, the EU remains intact but has no verve. Innovation and support to drive forward common projects are lacking. Gridlock or unsatisfactory compromises are the normal outcomes of Council forums and intergovernmental conferences. The EU experiences a steady weakening of influence among member states and populations. External actors are also aware of this process. The EU's credibility loss is most serious in the foreign, security, and defense policy areas. Several minor and medium-level tests of the EU's resolve indicate serious shortcomings in political and technical response. In economic matters, other states and trade blocs exploit similar deficiencies. In the formal context of international organizations, the EU is regularly outmaneuvered. In an increasingly dangerous world of unpredictable states and other volatile actors, the EU is open to blackmail and other forms of coercion.

Figure 7.4   Future Scenario D: Vulnerability to External Forces

The EU endures, but incoherence makes it susceptible to external forces.

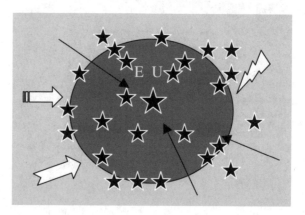

Figure 7.5 Future Scenario E: The Demise of the EU

A major international crisis occurs. Though the EU's vital interests are threatened, it does not have the military or political capability to repel the threat.

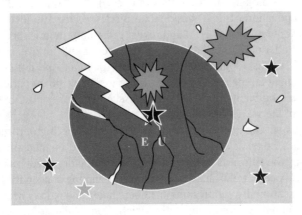

Future Scenario E: The Demise of the EU. The crisis in this scenario could be propelled by one of the many forms or sources of terrorism; a capricious regime or fanatical group with WMDs; "soft security" hazards such as crime, disease, or illegal immigration leading to a proliferation of social problems; or a more conventional threat from the "Westphalian universe" of states (see Figure 7.5). It could occur through the EU being drawn into an escalating conflict that envelops many actors: great, medium-sized, and smaller powers, national and subnational groups, religious zealots. The ESS infers that any of these developments are possible. Historians later contend that failures to invest in R&D or to organize military structures to repel threats were critical factors behind the EU's demise. Possessing these capabilities, combined with an assertive diplomacy that unambiguously articulated the EU's resolve and preparedness to protect itself and its values, would have precluded intimidation, the primarily non-European historians argued.

Conclusion

As key features of the vision and circumstances that sustained its progress come under challenge, the EU is heading into uncharted territory. A status quo of incremental progress under relatively benign conditions cannot be maintained. The EU will move toward becoming a global superpower and engender increased prosperity and security or gradually become dysfunctional, which will have negative consequences for its members and the world.

One optimistic emerging school of thought conceptualizes Europe as an empire. Not a traditional or "imperial" empire, argue Ulrich Beck and Edgar

Grande, but an empire of "consensus and law."[23] Or as Jan Zielonka contends, a "neo-mediaeval empire."[24] This idea has similarities to earlier interpretations of contemporary (postmodern) Europe as a neo-medieval construction or patchwork.[25] Although Zielonka does not see it as "postmodern," he argues against a replication of the "Westphalian model" at the EU level. Beck and Grande attribute much power to and reveal great faith in law, specifically EU law. We consider politics to be decisive. As noted in the preface, since ancient Rome no power has dominated the continent for long. And not even the EU has yet "brought all the rude and wild people to that excellent perfection in all good fashions, humanity, and civil gentleness, wherein they now go beyond all the people of the world."[26]

There is an alignment between the views of some high-profile political figures and a body of literature that argues that the method of integration employed by the EU or its forerunners, as well as the organization and financing of central policy fields, have to change.[27] Prevailing conceptions of the EU held in its institutions, within some member states, and among sections of the academic community are in need of revision. Some hitherto influential interpretations, political designs, and philosophical preferences for the EU's roles in the world and its evolution or end-state are unlikely to be realized.[28] Mere optimism, belief in a "community of destiny," or reliance on someone else are insufficient and will worsen a legitimacy crisis already threatening the EU. The future financing of projects is hardly guaranteed as clashes over the financial perspective for 2007–2013 showed. The funding and redistribution of all budgets will be fiercely contested.

Contemporaneously, a continuance of the EU's self-defined role as a supporter of international law and an exporter of democracy is becoming more dependent on the possession of cogent security capabilities, among them the deployment of military power. Some analysts argue it is time for an extroverted "European geopolitics."[29] An increase in relevant capacities could extend and deepen the EU's global influence but is likely to be accompanied by political conflicts within member states and internationally. The transatlantic dimension is vital. The level of cooperation or dispute between the EU and the United States will have a great impact on the evolving global order.[30]

For member state leaders and foreign policy elites, the EU is a blessing and a curse. Membership places these actors under pressure to reach common directions and solutions. They can follow this route and present a constructive, consensus-oriented image to their own and other populations. Alternatively, if the circumstances are evaluated as necessitating it, they can take a unilateral position or one in alliance with a smaller group of states. They can then depict themselves to domestic audiences as an avant-garde or devoted to the "national cause." A "classical example" of EU horse-trading across policy fields in pursuit of self-centered interests involved a vote on sanctions against Belarus, which the UK, France, and Scandinavian states wanted to impose. Poland,

Latvia, and Lithuania were opposed. In return for the votes of Poland and Lithuania to apply a customs duty on leather shoes from China, Italy abstained from voting to apply sanctions against Belarus and so enabled a blocking majority on that issue.[31]

In all important policy areas, the ingredient of unified political will recurs as critical and is highlighted as such in scholarly literature and the media. When this element is active, progress is made; when it is missing, there is inertia or regression. It may be that political will exists in Europe, but principally it seems to exist as a collection of disparate national wills, frequently pitted against one or more fellow member states. Political will reflects interests, values, and histories, but they are not communal enough to realize what twenty-seven or thirty or thirty-two states and their populations could achieve. For the EU to cope with current conditions and what looms before it, a resolute political will must emerge in Europeanized form. Only then can the "self-assertion of Europe" be manifested and sustained.[32]

A strategically important effect of the 2004 and 2007 enlargements is that the EU directly borders or is much closer to a host of unstable regions: "frozen conflicts" in the Caucasus and Moldova, a resurgent Russia fighting a vicious war with Chechen rebels, a Turkey preoccupied by aggressive Kurdish separatism while engaged in EU membership negotiations, boundless violence in Iraq, and an Iran of some 70 million people with a leadership striving to acquire nuclear weapons. Besides these problems, several traumatic events demonstrated to the EU that it is part of a world under siege from terrorism inspired by radical Islam. If the EU had no such seriously threatening concerns, it could take time to solve internal troubles or even tolerate them indefinitely. The EU is not hermetically sealed; the sometimes malevolent outside world is not only uncomfortably close but intruding. ENP is an attempt to deal with this, though it will not be enough. Could, for example, the SM and the Schengen rules really be extended to either eastern or southern ENP partner countries? Movements of labor and services are still restricted by some EU15 states. And in the present climate it is unlikely that the UK and Ireland will alter their policy to fully align with the Schengen arrangement. An intensification of border controls is more probable. Instead of "no dividing lines," the EU's relations with its neighbors will be distinguished by boundaries of one form or other, as through opt-outs, participation and nonparticipation, and informal alliances, it is internally. The "community of destiny" proclaimed by François Mitterrand and Helmut Kohl may exist somewhere, but it has slipped out of sight.

A united Europe cannot be built following an idealistic blueprint, and no single EU summit can be expected to bring a decisive breakthrough to resolving the Union's final form. European integration has been path-dependent since it was initiated. Institutional evolution has paralleled an incremental engagement with problems, or attempts to, including those arising from eastern enlargement. Discouraging aspects of the EU's condition can only be overcome by attacking economic weakness and addressing institutional and policy shortcomings. Further enlargement must be deferred and a serious debate conducted on the objectives, operational procedures, and borders of the EU. The centerpiece should be: What are EU-level tasks and in which areas are nation-states or regions doing better? Instead of a fixation on its possible end-state, the EU's first aim should be to ensure functionality. If it is not attained, centrifugal forces could cause the EU to spin apart or suffer paralysis. A ten-year goal and a twenty-year goal should then be defined. In pursuing them the EU must give itself options, so that it can act flexibly when one or another of a range of possible developments, or a completely unexpected event, ensues. During the first years of this consolidation phase, the SM must be completed and the Lisbon Agenda revitalized. The period could also be used to prepare more radical changes, which would make the EU fit for the years beyond.

All this does not mean an end to community-level policies, with their links to ideals of integration, solidarity, and so on. Rather, the predominating features of community policies should shift from subsidization of a more or less status quo condition and redistribution as a contribution toward financial equalization to the promotion of growth, competitiveness, and innovation-based activity. There are more options than the extremes of leaving everything unchanged or building a centralized "federal European state." Pragmatism and resolve could be applied to organize the EU more efficiently. This still unavoidably requires political will on the part of governments (and opposition parties) and an ability to adapt. *Die Tat ist alles, nichts der Ruhm:* The deed is everything, fame nothing.

Notes

1. The proposed draft Constitutional Treaty is available at europa.eu/constitution/index_en.htm. Jacek Saryusz-Wolski argues that EU citizens are not especially concerned about institutional reform, that enlargement was falsely associated with the CT's rejection, and that despite the Nice system's faults, it had not (yet) caused a total paralysis in Council voting. See Jacek Saryusz-Wolski, "Institutional Reform: A Pragmatic Point of View," *The International Spectator* 41, no. 1 (2006).

2. "Europa? Nein danke!" *Der Spiegel* Jahres-Chronik 2005, 136–139.

3. Ulrich Sedelmeier and Alisdair Young, "Crisis, What Crisis? Continuity and Normality in the European Union in 2005," *Journal of Common Market Studies* 44 (Supplement) (2006): 1–5.

4. Merkel's idea would not include an opportunity for the German public to approve or reject the proposition. Toby Helm and Colin Randall, "Merkel Alarms Blair over EU Constitution," *Telegraph,* 25 November 2005.

5. For example, Irish Prime Minister Bertie Ahern's stated opposition to a "mini-constitution" of selected components. "Irland stützt EU-Verfasssung," *Süddeutsche Zeitung,* 30 September–1 October 2006, 10.

6. Jean-Claude Juncker, "Wir waren furchtbar naiv," *Der Spiegel* Jahres-Chronik 2005, 260–262.

7. Steffen Rätzel and Joachim Weimann, "Der Maradona Effekt: Wie viel Wohlfahrt schafft die deutsche Nationalmannschaft?" *Perspektiven der Wirtschaftpolitik* 7, no. 2 (2006): 257–270.

8. Hans-Werner Sinn, *The New Systems Competition* (Oxford: Blackwell, 2003).

9. Fabrizio Saccomanni, "Italy and Europe: Key Challenges Again, Ten Years Later," *International Spectator* 41, no. 1 (2006).

10. Author interview, Foreign and Commonwealth Office, London, April 2003.

11. Andrew Grice, Philip Thornton, and Stephen Castle, "Merkel Hints at Support for Blair over Economic Reform of Europe," *Independent,* 25 November 2005.

12. Cf. Simon Duke, "CESDP and the EU Response to 11 September: Identifying the Weakest Link," *European Foreign Affairs Review* 7, no. 2 (2002): 153–169; Duke, "The European Security Strategy in a Comparative Framework: Does It Make for Secure Alliances in a Better World?" *European Foreign Affairs Review* 9, no. 4 (2004): 459–481; Brian Crowe, "A Common European Foreign Policy After Iraq?" *International Affairs* 79, no. 3 (2003): 533–546; Julian Lindley-French and Franco Algieri, *A European Defence Strategy* (Gütersloh: Bertelsmann, 2004); Reinhard C. Meier-Walser, ed., *Gemeinsam Sicher? Vision und Realität europäischer Sicherheitspolitik* (München: Hanns-Seidel-Stiftung, 2004).

13. Ole Waever, "Identity, Integration, and Security: Solving the Sovereignty Puzzle in E.U. Studies," *Journal of International Affairs* 48, no. 2 (1995): 389–431; Friedrich Kratochwil and Yosef Lapid, eds., *The Return of Culture and Identity in IR Theory* (Boulder, CO: Lynne Rienner, 1996); Bill McSweeney, *Security, Identity, and Interests: A Sociology of International Relations* (Cambridge: Cambridge University Press, 1999); Franz Mayer and Jan Palmowski, "European Identities and the EU: The Ties That Bind the Peoples of Europe," *Journal of Common Market Studies* 42, no. 3 (2004): 573–598.

14. John Lis and Zachary Selden, *NATO Burdensharing After Enlargement* (Washington, DC: Congressional Budget Office, 2001), 4.

15. Kerry Longhurst and Marcin Zaborowski, "The Future of European Security," *European Security* 13, no. 4 (2004): 381–391.

16. Felix Berenskoetter, "Mapping the Mind Cap: A Comparison of US and European Security Strategies," *Security Dialogue* 36, no. 1 (2005): 77.

17. Council of the European Union, *A Secure Europe in a Better World: European Security Strategy,* Brussels, 2003.

18. Author interview, GAERC Secretariat, Brussels, November 2004.

19. Peter Blechschmidt, "Bundestag stimmt Libanon-Einsatz zu," *Süddeutsche Zeitung,* 21 September 2006, 6.

20. Julie Smith and Charles Jenkins, eds., *Through the Paper Curtain: Insiders and Outsiders in the New Europe* (London: RIIA/Blackwell, 2003).

21. Ulrike Guérot and Andrea Witt, "Europas neue Geostrategie," *Aus Politik und Geschichte* B17, 19 April 2004, 5–12.

22. Franco Algieri, Janis Emmanouilidis, and Roman Maruhn, *Europas Zukunft: 5 EU-Szenarien* (München: Centrum für Angewandte Politikforschung 2003); Jean-Yves Haine et al., *European Defence: A Proposal for a White Paper* (Paris: Institute for Security Studies, 2004), 67–98; Gilles Bertrand, Anna Michalski, and Lucio Pench, *Scenarios Europe 2010,* Working Paper (Brussels: CEC Forward Studies Unit, 1999).

23. Ulrich Beck and Edgar Grande, "Empire Europe: Politische Herrschaft jenseits von Bundesstaat und Staatenbund," *Zeitschrift für Politik* 52, no. 4 (2005): 397–420.

24. Jan Zielonka, *Europe as Empire: The Nature of the Enlarged European Union* (Oxford: Oxford University Press, 2006).

25. Alain Minc, *Le Nouveau Moyen Age* (Paris: Editions Gallimard, 1993).

26. Thomas More, *Utopia* [1516]. Abridged edition (London: Phoenix, 1996), 2.

27. Lars-Erik Cedermann, ed., *Constructing Europe's Identity: The External Dimension* (Boulder, CO: Lynne Rienner, 2001); Fraser Cameron, ed., *The Future of Europe: Integration and Enlargement* (London: Routledge, 2004); Carsten Daugbjerg and Alan Swinbank, "The CAP and EU Enlargement: Prospects for an Alternative Strategy to Avoid the Lock-in of CAP Support." *Journal of Common Market Studies* 42, no. 1 (2004): 99–119.

28. Cf. François Heisbourg, "Europe's Strategic Ambitions: The Limits of Ambiguity," *Survival* 42, no. 2 (2000): 5–15; Philippe de Schoutheete, *The Case for Europe: Unity, Diversity, and Democracy in the European Union,* trans. Andrew Butler (Boulder, CO: Lynne Rienner, 2000); Craig Calhoun, "The Virtues of Inconsistency: Identity and Plurality in the Conceptualization of Europe," in Lars-Erik Cederman, ed., *Constructing Europe's Identity: The External Dimension* (Boulder, CO: Lynne Rienner, 2001), 35–56; Loukas Tsoukalis, *What Kind of Europe?* (Oxford: Oxford University Press, 2003); Kjell Torbiörn, *Destination Europe: The Political and Economic Growth of a Continent* (Manchester: Manchester University Press, 2003); J. H. H. Weiler, Iain Begg, and John Peterson, eds., *Integration in an Expanding European Union: Reassessing the Fundamentals* (Oxford: Blackwell, 2003); Dietrich von Kyaw, "The EU After the Agreement on a Constitutional Treaty," *European Foreign Affairs Review* 9, no. 4 (2004): 455–458.

29. Guérot and Witt, "Europas neue Geostrategie."

30. Howard Hensel, ed., *The United States and Europe: Policy Imperatives in a Globalizing World* (Aldershot: Ashgate, 2002); Robert Kagan, *Of Paradise and Power: America and Europe in the New World Order* (New York: Knopf, 2003).

31. "EU schont Weißrussland," *Süddeutsche Zeitung,* 7–8 October 2006, 8.

32. Helmut Schmidt, *Die Selbstbehauptung Europas* (Stuttgart: DVA, 2000).

Acronyms

AA	association agreement
ABC	atomic, biological, and chemical (weapons)
AP	action plan
CAP	Common Agricultural Policy
CARDS	Community Assistance Reconstruction, Development, and Stabilisation
CDM	Clean Development Mechanism
CDP	Capability Development Plan
CDU	Christliche Demokratische Union (Christian Democratic Union)
CEE	Central and Eastern Europe
CEECs	Central and Eastern European countries
CESDP	Common European Security and Defence Policy (also called ESDP)
CFSP	Common Foreign and Security Policy
COAM	Council of Agriculture Ministers
COMECON	Council of Mutual Economic Assistance
COREPER	Committee of Permanent Representatives
CPI	Corruption Perception Index
CSU	Christliche Soziale Union (Christian Social Union)
CT	Constitutional Treaty
D-G	Directorate-General
DRC	Democratic Republic of Congo
EADS	European Aeronautic Defence and Space
EAGGF	European Agricultural Guidance and Guarantee Fund
EAM	extended associate membership
EAW	European arrest warrant
EC	European Community
ECAP	European Capabilities Action Plan

ECB	European Central Bank
ECJ	European Court of Justice
ECSC	European Coal and Steel Community
EDA	European Defence Agency
EDC	European Defence Community
EDF	European Development Fund
EEA	European Economic Area
EEA	European Environment Agency
EAP	Environment Action Programme
ECHO	European Community Humanitarian Office
EEC	European Economic Community
EFA	exceptional financial assistance
EFM	European Foreign Minister (proposed)
EIB	European Investment Bank
EIDHR	European Instrument for Democracy and Human Rights
EMP	Euro-Mediterranean Partnership
EMU	Economic and Monetary Union
ENP	European Neighbourhood Policy
ENPI	European Neighbourhood and Partnership Instrument
EP	European Parliament
EPC	European Political Cooperation
ERDF	European Regional Development Fund
ERM	exchange rate mechanism
ESD	European security and defense
ESDP	European Security and Defence Policy
ESF	European Social Funds
ESS	European Security Strategy
ETS	Emissions Trading Scheme
EU	European Union
EUFOR	European Union Force
EUPM	European Union Police Mission (in Bosnia and Herzegovina)
EU3	European Union Three (France, Germany, and the United Kingdom)
FDI	foreign direct investment
FRG	Federal Republic of Germany
FIFG	Financial Instrument for Fisheries Guidance
FSP	Food Security Program
FYROM	Former Yugoslav Republic of Macedonia
GAERC	General Affairs and External Relations Council
GDP	gross domestic product
GFAP	General Framework for Peace (in Bosnia and Herzegovina)
GNI	gross national income
GSP	Generalized System of Preferences
HDI	Human Development Index

HR	High Representative (for CFSP)
IMF	International Monetary Fund
Interreg	Program for Interregional Cooperation
IPA	Instrument for Pre-accession Aid
ISAF	International Security Assistance Force
JHA	Justice and Home Affairs
JI	Joint Implementation
LIFE	Financial Instrument for the Environment
MC	Military Committee (of ESDP)
MEPs	members of the European Parliament
MOD	Ministry of Defence (UK)
MS	Military Staff (of ESDP)
NAPs	National Allocation Plans
NATO	North Atlantic Treaty Organization
NGOs	nongovernmental organizations
OCCAR	Organisation Conjointe de Coopération en matièere d'Armaments (Organization for Joint Armament Cooperation)
OECD	Organization for Economic Cooperation and Development
OHQ	Operational Headquarters
OMC	Open Method of Coordination
OMDI	operations having military or defense implications
PCA	partnership and cooperation agreement
PFP	Partnership for Peace
PHARE	Poland-Hongrie Assistance à la Restructuration des Economies
PPP	Purchasing Power Parity
PPS	purchasing power standards (official EU measure)
PSC	Political and Security Committee (of ESDP)
QMV	qualified majority voting
R&D	research and development
SAA	Stabilisation and Association Agreements
SACEUR	Supreme Allied Commander in Europe
SAP	Stabilisation and Association Process
SAPARD	Special Assistance Programme for Agriculture and Rural Development
SEA	Single European Act
SGP	Stability and Growth Pact
SM	Single Market
SMEs	small and medium-sized enterprises
SPD	Sozialdemokratische Partei Deutschlands
TACIS	Technical Assistance for the Commonwealth of Independent States
TEU	Treaty on European Union

toe	tonnes of oil equivalent
UK	United Kingdom
UN	United Nations
UNIFIL	United Nations Force in Lebanon
UNSC	United Nations Security Council
WEF	World Economic Forum
WEU	Western European Union
WMDs	weapons of mass destruction
WTO	World Trade Organization

Bibliography

Adam, Ruth. "Ein Wirtschafts- und Socialmodell für Europa? Untersuchung eines instrumentellen Begriffs." *CAP aktuell,* München, 25 October 2005.

Ahnlid, Anders. "Free or Forced Riders?" *Cooperation and Conflict* 27, no. 3 (1992): 241–276.

Ahrens, Joachim, Herman Hoen, and Renate Ohr. "Deepening Integration in an Enlarged EU: A Club-Theoretical Perspective." *Journal of European Integration* 27, no. 4 (2005): 417–439.

Ajami, Fouad. "The Autumn of the Autocrats." *Foreign Affairs* 84, no. 3 (2005): 20–35.

Alesina, Alberto, and Francesco Giavazzi. *The Future of Europe: Reform or Decline.* Cambridge, MA: MIT Press, 2006.

Aleskerov, Fuad, Gamze Avic, Viatcheslav Iakouba, and Z. Umut Türum. "European Union Enlargement: Power Distribution Implications of the New Institutional Arrangements." *European Journal of Political Research* 41, no. 3 (2002): 379–394.

Algieri, Franco. "Die Europäische Union und China: Zwischen Realpolitik und institutionelle Dynamik." In Susanne Luther and Peter Optiz, eds., *China's Rolle in der Weltpolitik.* München: Hanns Seidel Stiftung, 2000, 191–198.

Algieri, Franco, Thomas Bauer, and Klaus Brummer. *Entwicklungspotenzial auch ohne Verfassungsvertrag: Optionen für GASP und ESVP.* München: CAP, 2005.

Algieri, Franco, Janis Emmanouilidis, and Roman Maruhn. *Europas Zukunft: 5 EU-Szenarien.* München: CAP, 2003.

Aliboni, Roberto. "The Geopolitical Implications of the European Neighbourhood Policy." *European Foreign Affairs Review* 10, no. 1 (2005): 1–16.

Altmann, Franz-Lothar. *EU und westlicher Balkan, Von Dayton nach Brüssel: Ein allzu langer Weg?* S1. Berlin: SWP, 2005.

Alvarez-Plata, Patricia, Herbert Brücker, and Boriss Siliverstovs. *Potential Migration from Central and Eastern Europe into the EU-15: An Update. Report for the Commission.* Brussels: CEC, 2003.

Antonenko, Oksana, and Kathryn Pinnick, eds. *Russia and the European Union.* London: Routledge, 2004.

Archibugi, Daniele, and Alberto Coco. "Is Europe Becoming the Most Dynamic Knowledge Economy in the World?" *Journal of Common Market Studies* 43, no. 3 (2005): 433–459.

Asmus, Ronald, and F. Stephen Larrabee. "NATO and the Have-Nots: Reassurance After Enlargement." *Foreign Affairs* 75, no. 1 (1998): 13–20.

Axt, Heinz-Jürgen. *Solidarität und Wettbewerb: Die Reform der EU-Strukturpolitik.* Gütersloh: Bertelsmann, 2000.

Aydin, Senem, and E. Fuat Keyman. *European Integration and the Transformation of Turkish Democracy.* EU-Turkey WP 2. Brussels: CEPS, 2004.

Baas, Timo, Herbert Brücker, and Elmar Hönekopp. "EU-Osterweiterung: Beachtliche Gewinne für die deutsche Volkswirtschaft." *IAB Kurzbericht* 6/2007. Nürnberg: IAB/Bundesanstalt für Arbeit, March 2007.

Bahgat, Gawdat. "Europe's Energy Security: Challenges and Opportunities." *International Affairs* 82, no. 5 (2006): 961–975.

Baldwin, Richard, Erik Berghof, Francesco Giavazzi, and Mika Widgren. "EU Reforms for Tomorrow's Europe." Discussion Paper 2623. London: CEPS, 2000.

Baldwin, Richard, Joseph Francois, and Richard Portes. "The Costs and Benefits of Eastern Enlargement: The Impact on the EU and Central Europe." *Economic Policy* 24 (1997): 127–176.

Bara, Zoltan, and Laszlo Csaba, eds. *Small Economies' Adjustment to Global Tendencies.* Budapest: Aula, 2000.

Baracani, Elena. "From EMP to ENP: A New European Pressure for Democratisation? The Case of Morocco." Working Paper. CSEPS: Beer Sheva, 2005.

Baranovsky, Vladimir. "Russia: A Part of Europe or Apart from Europe?" *International Affairs* 76, no. 3 (2000): 443–458.

Barroso, José Manuel. "From Schuman to Sirte: A Tale of Two Unions." Speech/05/413, Sirte, 4 July 2005.

Bast, Jürgen. "The Constitutional Treaty as a Reflexive Constitution." *German Law Journal* 6, no. 11 (2005): 1433–1452.

Batt, Judy, et al. *Partners and Neighbours: A CFSP for a Wider Europe.* Chaillot Paper 64. Paris: ISS, 2003.

Bauer, Thomas, Barbara Dietz, Klaus Zimmermann, and Eric Zwintz. "German Migration: Development, Assimilation, and Labour Market Effects." In Klaus Zimmermann, ed., *European Migration: What Do We Know?* Oxford: Oxford University Press, 2005, 197–261.

Bauer, Thomas, and Klaus Zimmermann. *Assessment of Possible Migration Pressure and Its Labour Market Impact Following EU Enlargement to Central and Eastern Europe.* Bonn: IZA, 1999.

Beck, Ulrich, and Edgar Grande. "Empire Europe: Politische Herrschaft jenseits von Bundestaat und Staatenbund." *Zeitschrift für Politik* 52, no. 4 (2005): 397–420.

———. *Kosmopolitisches Europa.* Frankfurt: Suhrkamp, 2004.

Becker, Peter. *Der EU-Finanzrahmen 2007–2013: Auf dem Weg zu einer europäischen Finanzverfassung oder Fortsetzung der nationalen Nettosaldenpolitik?* Study no. 36. Berlin: SWP, November 2005.

Begg, Iain. *Funding the European Union, Making Sense of the EU Budget: What Is It For? What Should It Be For?* London: Federal Trust for Education and Research, 2005.

Begg, Iain, et al. "Reforming Fiscal Policy Coordination Under EMU: What Should Become of the Stability and Growth Pact?" *Journal of Common Market Studies* 42, no. 5 (2004): 1023–1059.

Bendiek, Annegret, and Hannah Whitney-Steele. *Wein predigen and Wasser ausschenken: Die Finanzierung der EU-Außenpolitik.* Stiftung Wissenschaft und Politik (SWP) Aktuell 31. Berlin: SWP, July 2006.

Berenskoetter, Felix. "Mapping the Mind Cap: A Comparison of US and European Security Strategies." *Security Dialogue* 36, no. 1 (2005): 71–92.

Berger, Helge. "Unfinished Business? The ECB Reform Ahead of the Euro Area Enlargement." *CESifo Forum* 7, no. 4 (2006): 39–40.

Bernard, Nick. *Multilevel Governance in the European Union.* New York: Aspen, 2004.

Bertrand, Gilles, Anna Michalski, and Lucio Pench. *Scenarios Europe 2010.* Brussels: European Commission Forward Studies Unit, 1999.

Bertoldi, Paolo, and Silvia Rezessy. "Voluntary Agreements for Energy Efficiency: Review and Results of European Experiences." *Energy and Environment* 18, no. 1 (2007): 37–73.

Beugelsdijk, M., and S. Eijffinger. "The Effectiveness of Structural Policy in the European Union: An Empirical Analysis for the EU-15 in 1995–2001." *Journal of Common Market Studies* 43, no. 1 (2005): 37–51.

Biscop, Sven. "Able and Willing? Assessing the EU's Capacity for Military Action." *European Foreign Affairs Review* 9, no. 4 (2004): 509–527.

———. "In Search of a Strategic Concept for the ESDP." *European Foreign Affairs Review* 7, no. 4 (2002): 473–490.

Boeckhout, Sjaak, Luc Boot, Menno Hollanders, Klass-Jan Reinike, and Jan de Vet. *Key Indicators for Candidate Countries to Effectively Manage the Structural Funds.* Final Report, NEI Regional and Urban Development. Rotterdam: ECO-RYS, 2002.

Boer, Pim den. "Europe to 1914: The Making of an Idea." In Kevin Wilson and Jan van der Dussen, eds., *The History of the Idea of Europe.* London: Open University/Routledge, 1995, 13–82.

Boeri, Tito, and Herbert Brücker. *The Impact of Eastern Enlargement on Employment and Labour Markets in the EU Member States.* Brussels: CEC, 2001.

———. *Migration, Coordination Failures, and EU Enlargement.* Discussion Paper 1600. Bonn: IZA, May 2005.

Bofinger, Peter. *Wir sind besser als wir glauben: Wohlstand für alle.* München: Rowohlt, 2005.

Boldrin, Michel, and Fabio Canova. "Inequality and Convergence in Europe's Regions: Reconsidering European Regional Policies." *Economic Policy* 16 (2001): 207–252.

Bolle, Michael, and Oliver Pamp. "It's Politics, Stupid: EMU Enlargement Between an Economic Rock and a Political Hard Place." *CESifo Forum* 7, no. 4 (2006): 26–28.

Boltho, Andrea. "What Matters for Economic Success." In Zoltan Bara and Laszlo Csaba, eds., *Small Economies' Adjustment to Global Tendencies.* Budapest: Aula, 2000, 151–169.

Bonnén, Preben. *Towards a Common European Security and Defence Policy: The Ways and Means of Making It a Reality.* Münster: LIT, 2003.

Borzutzky, Silvia, and Emmanuel Krandis. "A Struggle for Survival: The Polish Agricultural Sector from Communism to EU Accession." *East European Politics and Societies* 19, no. 4 (2005): 614–654.

Bredow, Wilfried von. "Defense Reforms and Current Problems of Civil-Military Relations in Western Societies." Marburg: Institut fur Politikwissenschaft, no date.

———. *Die Außenpolitik der Bundesrepublik Deutschland: Eine Einführung.* Wiesbaden: Verlag für Sozialwissenschaften, 2006.

Bretherton, Charlotte, and John Vogler. *The European Union as a Global Actor.* London: Routledge, 1999.

Breuss, Fritz. *Austria, Finland and Sweden After 10 Years in the EU: Expected and Achieved Integration Effects.* Working Paper 65. Vienna: WIFO, 2005.

————. *Macroeconomic Effects of EU Enlargement for Old and New Members*. WP 142. Vienna: WIFO, 2001.

Brimmer, Esther, and Stefan Fröhlich, eds. *The Strategic Implications of European Union Enlargement*. Washington, DC: Center for Transatlantic Relations, Johns Hopkins University, 2005.

Brooks, Stephen, and William Wohlforth. "Hard Times for Soft Balancing." *International Security* 30, no. 1 (2005): 72–108.

Brown, Drusilla, Alan Deardoff, Simeon Djankov, and Robert Stern. "An Economic Assessment of the Integration of Czechoslovkia, Hungary, and Poland into the European Union." In Stanley Black, ed., *Europe's Economy Looks East. Implications for Germany and the European Union*. Cambridge: Cambridge University Press, 1997, 23–60.

Brücker, Herbert. "EU-Osterweiterung Effekte der Migration." *DIW-Wochenbericht*, 17 April 2004.

————. "EU-Osterweiterung: Übergangsfristenführen zu Umlenkung der Migration nach Großbritannien und Irland." *DIW-Wochenbericht*, 22 June 2005.

Brücker, Herbert, Philipp Schröder, and Christian Weise. "Doorkeepers and Gatecrashers: EU Enlargement and Negotiation Strategies." *Journal of European Integration* 26, no. 1 (2004): 3–23.

Brzoska, Michael, and Götz Neunenk. "Verhandlungen und andere Optionen im Atomstreit mit dem Iran." *Internationale Politik und Gesellschaft* 4 (2006): 11–27.

Buch, Claudia. *Capital Mobility and EU Enlargement*. Working Paper 908. Kiel: IWE, 1998.

Buchan, David. *Europe: The Strange Superpower*. Aldershot: Dartmouth, 1993.

Buchanan, James. "An Economic Theory of Clubs." *Econometrica* 32, no. 1 (1965): 1–14.

Bull, Hedley. "Civilian Power Europe: A Contradiction in Terms?" *Journal of Common Market Studies* 21, no. 1 (1982): 149–164.

Bulmer, Simon. "Domestic Politics and European Community Policy-Making." *Journal of Common Market Studies* 21, no. 4 (1983): 349–363.

Bulmer, Simon, and Claudio Radaelli. "The Europeanisation of National Policy?" *Queen's Papers on Europeanisation* 1/2004. Belfast: Queens University, 2004.

Bundesministerium der Verteidigung. *Weissbuch 2006: Zur Sicherheitspolitik Deutschlands und zur Zukunft der Bundeswehr*. Berlin: October 2006.

Busemeyer, Marius, Christian Kellermann, Alexander Petring, and Andrej Stuchlik. "Politische Positionen zum Europäischen Wirtschafts- und Sozialmodell: Eine Landkarte der Interessen." Bonn: Friedrich Ebert Stiftung, August 2006.

Calhoun, Craig. "The Virtues of Inconsistency: Identity and Plurality in the Conceptualization of Europe." In Lars-Erik Cederman, ed., *Constructing Europe's Identity: The External Dimension*. Boulder, CO: Lynne Rienner, 2001, 35–56.

Cameron, David. "The Stalemate in the Constitutional IGC over the Definition of a Qualified Majority." *European Union Politics* 5, no. 3 (2004): 373–391.

Cameron, Fraser, ed. *The Future of Europe: Integration and Enlargement*. London: Routledge, 2004.

Campbell, Edwina. "Vorstellung und Realität der europäischen Sicherheitspolitik aus der Sicht der USA." In Reinhard C. Meier-Walser, ed., *Gemeinsam Sicher? Vision und Realität europäischer Sicherheitspolitik*. München: Hanns-Seidel-Stiftung, 2004, 311–323.

Caporaso, James. "The European Union and Forms of State: Westphalian, Regulatory or Post-modern?" *Journal of Common Market Studies* 34, no. 1 (1996): 29–52.

Cecchini, Paolo. *The European Challenge 1992: The Benefits of a Single Market.* Aldershot: Wildwood House, 1988.

Cederman, Lars-Erik. "Political Boundaries and Identity Trade-Offs." In Lars-Erik Cederman, ed., *Constructing Europe's Identity: The External Dimension.* Boulder, CO: Lynne Rienner, 2001, 1–32.

———, ed. *Constructing Europe's Identity: The External Dimension.* Boulder, CO: Lynne Rienner, 2001.

Center for Economic Studies/Institute for Economic Research (CES/ifo). *The EEAG Report on the European Economy 2007.* Munich: CES/ifo, 2007.

CES/ifo. *Report on the European Economy 2004.* Munich: CES/ifo, 2004.

Chirac, Jacques. "Déclaration aux Français sur le changement de gouvernement." Speech given in Paris, 31 May 2005.

Chow, Edward. "Russian Pipelines: Back to the Future?" *Georgetown Journal of International Affairs* (Winter–Spring 2004): 27–33.

Christiansen, Thomas. "Intra-institutional Politics and Inter-institutional Relations in the EU: Towards Coherent Governance?" *Journal of European Public Policy* 8, no. 5 (2001): 747–769.

Christiansen, Thomas, and Simona Piattoni, eds. *Informal Governance in the European Union.* Cheltenham: Edward Elgar, 2003.

Chryssochoou, Dimitris, Michael Tsinisizelis, Stelios Stavridis, and Kostas Ifantis. *Theory and Reform in the European Union.* Manchester: Manchester University Press, 1999.

Church, Clive, and David Phinnemore. *Understanding the European Constitution: An Introduction to the EU Constitutional Treaty.* London: Routledge, 2006.

Cimbalo, Jeffrey. "Saving NATO from Europe." *Foreign Affairs* 83, no. 6 (2004): 111–117.

Clement, Hermann, et al. *Ostmitteleuropa vor der Konsolidierung? Wirtschaftliche Lage in Mittel- und Südosteuropa sowie der Ukraine.* Working Paper 227. München: Osteuropa-Institut, 2000.

Cogan, Charles. *French Negotiating Behavior: Dealing with La Grande Nation.* Washington, DC: Institute of Peace Press, 2003.

Coppieters, Bruno, et al. *Europeanization and Ethnic Conflict: Case Studies from the European Periphery.* Ghent: Academic Press, 2004.

Cornish, Paul, and Geoffrey Edwards. "The Strategic Culture of the European Union: A Progress Report." *International Affairs* 81, no. 4 (2005): 801–820.

Council of the European Union. *Actes Juridiques PESC.* Brussels, 2003.

———. "Council Joint Action 2004/523/CFSP of 28 June 2004 on the European Union Rule of Law Mission in Georgia, EUJUST Themis." *Official Journal of the European Union* L228/21, 29 June 2004.

———. "Council Joint Action 2004/551/CFSP of 12 July 2004 on the Establishment of the European Defence Agency." *Official Journal,* L 245/17, 17 July 2004.

———. "Council Joint Action 2004/847/CFSP of 9 December 2004 on the European Union Police Mission in Kinshasa (DRC) Regarding the Integrated Police Unit (EUPOL 'Kinshasa')." *Official Journal of the European Union* L367/30, 14 December 2004.

———. *ESDP Presidency Report.* Brussels, 17 December 2004.

———. "EU Police Mission in the Palestinian Territories (EUPOL COPPS)." http://www.consilium.europa.eu/cms3_fo/showPage.asp?id=974&lang=en&mode=g.

———. "EU Military Operation in Bosnia and Herzegovina (EUFOR – ALTHEA)." http://www.consilium.europa.eu/cms3_fo/showPage.asp?id=745&lang=en&mode=g.

———. *EU-NATO: The Framework for Permanent Relations and Berlin Plus.* Brussels, 2003.

————. *EU-UN Co-operation in Military Crisis Management Operations: Elements of Implementation of the EU-UN Joint Declaration Adopted by the EU Council.* Brussels, 17–18 June 2004.

————. *Presidency Conclusions, 8–9 March 2007.* 7224/07. Brussels, 9 March 2007.

————. *Presidency Conclusions, 16–17 December 2004.* 16238/1/04 REV 1. Brussels, 1 February 2005.

————. *A Secure Europe in a Better World: European Security Strategy.* Brussels, 2003.

Crespo-Guaresma, Jesus, Maria Antoinette Dimitz, and Doris Ritzberger-Grünwand. "The Impact of European Integration on Growth: What Can We Learn for EU Accession?" In Gertrude Tumpel-Gugerell and Peter Mooslechner, eds., *Economic Convergence and Divergence in Europe: Growth and Regional Development in an Enlarged European Union.* Cheltenham: Edward Elgar, 2003, 55–71.

Crowe, Brian. "A Common European Foreign Policy After Iraq?" *International Affairs* 79, no. 3 (2003): 533–546.

Crum, Ben. "Legislative-Executive Relations in the EU." *Journal of Common Market Studies* 41, no. 3 (2003): 375–395.

Dalgaard-Nielsen, Anja. "Gulf War: The German Resistance." *Survival* 45, no. 1 (2003): 99–116.

Dannreuther, Roland. "Developing the Alternative to Enlargement: The European Neighbourhood Policy." *European Foreign Affairs Review* 11, no. 2 (2006): 183–201.

————, ed. *European Foreign and Security Policy: Towards a Neighbourhood Strategy.* London: Routledge, 2004.

Dauderstädt, Michael. "Cohesive Growth in the Enlarging Euroland: Patterns, Problems and Politics." In Michael Dauderstädt and Lothar Witte, eds., *Cohesive Growth in the Enlarging Euroland.* Bonn: Friedrich-Ebert-Stiftung, 2001.

————. "Überholen, ohne einzuholen: Irland, ein Modell für Mittel- und Osteuropa?" *Politikinformation Osteuropa* 90. Bonn: Friedrich-Ebert-Stiftung, 2001.

Daugbjerg, Carsten. "Policy Feedback and Paradigm Shift in EU Agricultural Policy: The Effects of the MacSharry Reform on Future Reform." *Journal of European Public Policy* 10, no. 3 (2003): 421–437.

Daugbjerg, Carsten, and Alan Swinbank. "The CAP and EU Enlargement: Prospects for an Alternative Strategy to Avoid the Lock-in of CAP Support." *Journal of Common Market Studies* 42, no. 1 (2004): 99–119.

————. "The Politics of CAP Reform: Trade Negotiations, Institutional Settings and Blame Avoidance." *Journal of Common Market Studies* 45, no. 1 (2007): 1–22.

Davies, Norman. *Europe: A History.* Oxford: Oxford University Press, 1996.

Davis, Christina. "International Institutions and Issue Linkage: Building Support for International Trade Liberalization." *American Political Science Review* 98, no. 1 (2004): 153–169.

Davis, James. *Threats and Promises.* Baltimore: Johns Hopkins University Press, 2000.

Davis, Patricia. *The Art of Persuasion: Positive Incentives and German Economic Diplomacy.* Ann Arbor: University of Michigan Press, 1999.

"Declaration on the Fiftieth Anniversary of the Signature of the Treaties of Rome." Berlin, 25 March 2007, www.eu2007.de/en/About_the_EU/Constitutional_Treaty/BerlinerErklaerung.html.

Delpech, Thérese. *International Terrorism and Europe.* Chaillot Paper 56. Paris: ISS, 2002.

Delreux, Tom. "The European Union in International Environmental Negotiations: A

Legal Perspective on the Internal Decision-Making Process." *International Environmental Agreements* 6, no. 3 (2006): 231–248.

Del Sarto, Raffaella, and Tobias Schumacher. "From EMP to ENP: What's at Stake with the European Neighbourhood Policy Towards the Southern Mediterranean?" *European Foreign Affairs Review* 10, no. 1 (2005): 17–28.

De Melo, Martha, Cevdet Denizer, Alan Gelb, and Stoyan Tenev. "Circumstance and Choice: The Role of Initial Conditions and Policies in Transition Economies." *World Bank Economic Review* 15 (2001): 1–31.

Dempsey, Judy. "13," in "Actors and Witnesses." In Nicole Gnesotto, ed., *EU Security and Defence Policy: The First Five Years (1999–2004)*. Paris: Institute for Security Studies, 2004, 195–201.

Denza, Eileen. "Non-proliferation of Nuclear Weapons: The European Union and Iran." *European Foreign Affairs Review* 10, no. 3 (2005): 289–312.

Deutsch, Karl. *The Analysis of International Relations*. Englewood Cliffs, NJ: Prentice Hall, 1968.

Deutsche Bank Research. "EU Energy Policy: High Time for Action." *EU Monitor* 44, 17 April 2007.

Dicke, Hugo, and Federico Foders. *Wirtschaftliche Auswirkungen einer EU-Erweiterung auf die Mitgliedstaaten*. Kieler Studie 309. Tübingen: Mohr Siebeck, 2000.

Dieppe, Alistair, Keith Küster, and Peter McAdam. "Optimal Monetary Rules for the Euro Area: An Analysis Using the Area-Wide Model." *Journal of Common Market Studies* 43, no. 3 (2005): 507–537.

Dietz, Barbara. "Ost-West-Migration nach Deutschland im Kontext der EU-Erweiterung." *Aus Politik und Zeitgeschichte* B 5–6, 4 February 2004.

Dinan, Desmond. *Europe Recast: A History of the European Union*. Boulder, CO: Lynne Rienner, 2004.

———. "Governance and Institutions: The Convention and the Intergovernmental Conference," *Journal of Common Market Studies* 42 (2004): 27–42.

———. "Governance and New Institutions: A New Constitution and a New Commission." *Journal of Common Market Studies* 45 (Annual Review) (2005): 37–54.

Dror, Yehezkel, and Sharon Pardo. "Approaches and Principles for an Israeli Grand Strategy Towards the European Union." *European Foreign Affairs Review* 11, no. 1 (2006): 17–44.

Duchêne, François. "Europe's Role in World Peace." In Richard Mayne, ed., *Europe Tomorrow: Sixteen Europeans Look Ahead*. London: Fontana, 1972, 32–47.

Duke, Simon. "CESDP and the EU Response to 11 September: Identifying the Weakest Link." *European Foreign Affairs Review* 7, no. 2 (2002): 153–169.

———. "The European Security Strategy in a Comparative Framework: Does It Make for Secure Alliances in a Better World?" *European Foreign Affairs Review* 9, no. 4 (2004): 459–481.

———. "Nice: ESDP's Overtrumped Success." *European Foreign Affairs Review* 6, no. 2 (2001): 155–175.

Dustman, Christian, and Albrecht Glitz. *Immigration, Jobs and Wages: Theory, Evidence and Opinion*. London: Centre for Comparative European Policy Evaluation, 2005.

Economist. "Special Report on the European Union." 17 March 2007.

Ederveen, Sjef, Henri de Groot, and Richard Nahuis. "Fertile Soil for Structural Funds? A Panel Data Analysis of the Conditional Effectiveness of European Cohesion Policy." *Kyklos* 59, no. 1 (2006): 17–42.

Ehrhart, Hans-Georg, and Burkard Schmitt, eds. *Die Sicherheitspolitik der EU im Werden: Bedrohungen, Aktivitäten, Fähigkeiten.* Baden-Baden: Nomos, 2004.

El-Chekeh, Tanja, Max Steinhardt, and Thomas Straubhaar. "Did the European Free Movement of Persons and Residence Directive Change Migration Patterns Within the EU? A First Glance." *CESifo Dice Report* 4, no. 4 (2006): 14–20.

Emerson, Michael. "Introduction." In Michael Emerson, ed., *Democratisation in the European Neighbourhood.* Brussels: CEPS, 2005, 1–12.

———. *European Neighbourhood Policy: Strategy or Placebo?* Working Document 215. Brussels: CEPS, 2004.

———. "What Should the Community of Democratic Choice Do?" Policy Brief 98. Brussels: CEPS, 2006.

———. *The Wider Europe Matrix.* Brussels: CEPS, 2003.

———, ed. *Democratisation in the European Neighbourhood.* Brussels: CEPS, 2005.

Emerson, Michael, and Gergana Noutcheva. *From Barcelona Process to Neighbourhood Policy: Assessments and Open Issues.* Working Document 220. Brussels: CEPS, March 2005.

———. *Europeanisation as a Gravity Model of Democratisation.* Working Document 214. Brussels: CEPS, November 2004.

Emerson, Michael, and Nathalie Tocci. *Turkey as a Bridgehead and Spearhead: Integrating EU and Turkish Foreign Policy.* EU-Turkey Working Paper 1. Brussels: CEPS, 2004.

Emerson, Michael, et al. *The Economics of 1992: The EC's Commission Assessment of the Economic Effects of Completing the Internal Market.* Oxford: Oxford University Press, 1988.

Emmanouilidis, Janis. "Die Zeit der Entscheidung: Optionen, Erfolgsvoraussetzungen und Fahrplan für ein neues Primärrecht." *CAP Analyse* 1/2007. Munich: CAP, 2007, 5–17.

Emmanouilidis, Janis, and Bettina Thalmaier. "2005: Non, Nee, Ne, Nie oder Non. Konsequenzen, Optionen, und Empfehlungen im Falle einer Ablehnung der Verfassung." *EU-Reform-Spotlight* 3. München: CAP, 2005.

Eralp, Doga Ulas, and Nimet Beriker. "Assessing the Conflict Resolution Potential of the EU: The Cyprus Conflict and Accession Negotiations." *Security Dialogue* 36, no. 2 (2005): 175–192.

Etzioni, Amitai. "The Community Deficit." *Journal of Common Market Studies* 45, no. 1 (2007): 23–42.

EurActiv. "The New EU Cohesion Policy (2007–2013)." http://www.euractiv.com/en/future-eu/new-eu-cohesion-policy-2007-2013/article-131988. Accessed 5 October 2006.

European Commission. "Commissioner Benita Ferrero-Waldner in Algiers." IP/05/790. Brussels, 24 June 2005.

———. "Commissioner Ferrero-Waldner's Trip to Libya." IP/05/605. Brussels, 25 May 2005.

———. *Communication from the Commission to the European Parliament and the Council: Technical Adjustment of the Financial Framework for 2007 in Line with Movements in GNI and Prices.* COM(2006) 327 final. Brussels, 22 June 2006.

———. *Communication to the Council on the Commission Proposals for Action Plans Under the European Neighbourhood Policy.* (ENP) (COM) 795. Brussels, 9 December 2004.

———. *Employment in Europe, 2006.* Brussels, 2007.

———. *Energy Efficiency—or Doing More with Less.* COM(2005) 265 final. Brussels, 22 June 2005.

————. *An Energy Policy for Europe: Communication to the European Council and the European Parliament.* SEC (2007) 12. Brussels, 10 January 2007.

————. *Environment 2010: Our Future, Our Choice.* Luxembourg, 2001.

————. *EU-Jordan Action Plan.* Brussels, December 2004.

————. *EU-Moldova Action Plan.* Brussels, December 2004.

————. *EU-Morocco Action Plan.* Brussels, December 2004.

————. *EU-Palestinian Authority Action Plan.* Brussels, December 2004.

————. *Eurobarometer.* Brussels, various issues.

————. *Eurobarometer* special issue: "Europeans and the Common Agricultural Policy," no. 221. Brussels, CEC, February 2005.

————. *Euro-Med Partnership Syria: Country Strategy Paper 2002–2006 and National Indicative Programme, 2002–2004.* Brussels, 2002.

————. *Euro-Med Partnership Syria: National Indicative Programme 2005–2006.* Brussels, no date.

————. *European Community Iraqi Assistance Programme 2006.* E/2006/470–C(2006)864. Brussels, 28 March 2006.

————. "European Neighbourhood Policy: Armenia." IP/05/237. Brussels, 2 March 2005.

————. "European Neighbourhood Policy: Azerbaijan." IP/05/238. Brussels, 2 March 2005.

————. "European Neighbourhood Policy: A Year of Progress." IP/05/1467. Brussels, 24 November 2005.

————. *European Neighbourhood Policy Strategy Paper.* COM (2004) 373 Final. Brussels, 12 May 2004.

————. "European Neighbourhood Policy: The Next Steps." IP/05/236 Press Release. Brussels, 2 March 2005.

————. *The European Union and the United States: Global Partners, Global Responsibilities.* Brussels, Delegation of the European Commission to the United States, 2006.

————. *Europe in the World: Some Practical Proposals for Greater Coherence, Effectiveness, and Visibility.* Communication from the Commission to the European Council of June 2006. COM(2006) 278 final. Brussels, 8 June 2006.

————. *The EU's Relation with Russia,* http://europa.eu.int/comm/external_relations/russia/intro/.

————. *EU-Tunisia Action Plan.* Brussels, December 2004.

————. "Financial Markets: Inter-institutional Monitoring Group Publishes First Report on 'Lamfalussy Process.'" Press Release IP/06/361, 22 March 2006, www.europa.eu/rapid/pressReleasesAction.do?reference=IP/06/361&format=HTML&aged=0&language=DE&guiLanguage=en.

————. *General Budget of the European Union for the Financial Year 2007: The Figures.* Brussels, February 2007.

————. *General Report on the Pre-Accession Assistance (PHARE-ISPA-SAPARD) in 2003.* Brussels, CEC, May 2005.

————. *Green Paper: A European Strategy for Sustainable, Competitive, and Secure Energy.* COM(2006) 105 final. Brussels, 8 March 2006.

————. *Green Paper on Defence Procurement.* COM (2004) 608. Brussels, 2004.

————. *A New Partnership for Cohesion: Convergence, Competitiveness, Cooperation: Third Report on Economic and Social Cohesion.* Luxembourg: European Communities, 2004.

————. *Partenariat Euro-Med Algerie: Document de Strategie 2002–2006 and Programme Indicatif National 2002–2004.* Brussels: no date.

————. *PHARE,* europa.eu.int/comm/enlargement/pas/phare/index.htm.

————. *Preliminary Draft General Budget of the European Commission for the Financial Year 2005.* Brussels, 2004.

————. *Proposal for a Regulation of the European Parliament and of the Council Laying Down General Provisions for a European Neighbourhood and Partnership Instrument.* COM (2004) 628 final. Brussels, CEC, 29 September 2004.

————. *Proposed EU-Israel Action Plan.* Brussels, December 2004.

————. *Protecting Europe: Ensuring the Security of Energy and Transport Services Across the European Union.* Brussels, 2005.

————. "Q&A on the Legislative Package of EU Programmes for the Financial Programming Period 2007–2013." MEMO 06/213. Brussels, 24 May 2006. http://europa.eu/rapid/pressReleasesAction.do?reference=MEMO/06/213&format=HTML&aged=0&language=EN&guiLanguage=fr.

————. *A Quality Environment: How the EU Is Contributing.* Luxembourg, 2005.

————. *Questions and Answers on Emissions Trading and National Allocation Plans for 2008 to 2012.* Memo 06/452. Brussels, 29 November 2006.

————. *Reconstructing Iraq: State of Play and Implementation to Date.* Brussels, November 2005.

————. *Second Report on Economic and Social Cohesion.* Brussels, CEC, 2001.

————. *Staff Working Paper.* SEC(2005) 285/3. "Annex to 'European Neighbourhood Policy': Country Report Armenia." COM (2005) 72 final. Brussels, 2 March 2005.

————. *Staff Working Paper.* SEC(2005) 286/3. "Annex to 'European Neighbourhood Policy': Country Report Azerbaijan." COM (2005) 72 final. Brussels, 2 March 2005.

————. *Staff Working Paper.* "Annex to 'European Neighbourhood Policy': Country Report Egypt." SEC(2005) 287/3. Brussels, 2 March 2005.

————. *Staff Working Paper.* "Annex to 'European Neighbourhood Policy': Country Report Lebanon." SEC(2005) 289/3. Brussels, 2 March 2005.

————. *Wider Europe—Neighbourhood: A Framework for Relations with Our Eastern and Southern Neighbours.* Brussels, March 2003.

————, Directorate General for Economic and Financial Affairs. *The Economic Impact of Enlargement.* Brussels, 2001.

————, Directorate General for Economic and Financial Affairs. *European Economy Enlargement, Two Years After: An Economic Evaluation.* Occasional Paper 24. Brussels, CEC, May 2006.

————, Directorate-General for Economic and Financial Affairs. *European Economy: Statistical Annex.* Brussels, Spring 2006.

————, Directorate-General for Regional Policy. *Structural Funds Regulations,* ec.europa.eu/regional_policy/sources/docoffic/official/regulation/newregl0713_en.htm.

————, Directorate-General for Regional Policy. *Working for the Regions: Regional Policy—Inforegio,* ec.europa.eu/regional_policy/intro/working4_en.htm.

European Community. *Consolidated Version of the Treaty Establishing the European Community. Official Journal* C325, 24 December 2002.

European Defence Agency. *An Initial Long-Term Vision for European Defence Capability and Capacity Needs.* LTV—3 October 2006—SB MoDs Levi (Ixelles, Belgium: EDA, 2006), http://www.eda.europa.eu/genericitem.aspx?area=Organisation&id=146.

————. "EU Governments Set Timetable for Initial Plan to Strengthen Defence Capabilities." Press release, Brussels, 28 June 2007. http://www.eda.europa.eu.

————. "European–United States Defence Expenditure in 2005." Brussels, 19 December 2006. http://www.eda.europa.eu.

European Parliament. "Enlargement: EU Must Keep Its Promises but Take Account of Absorption Capacity." Press Release. Strasbourg, 16 March 2006.

————. *European Parliament Resolution on the Commission's 2005 Enlargement Strategy Paper.* P6_TA-PROV (2006) 0096. Strasbourg, 16 March 2006.

————. *Plenary Session Debate.* (comments of Elmar Brok) Strasbourg, 15 March 2006.

————. *Report on the European Neighbourhood Policy* (rapporteur Charles Tannock). FINAL A6-0399/2005. Strasbourg, 7 December 2005.

————. *Resolution on Human Rights in Moldova, and in Transnistria in Particular.* P6 TA-PROV2006 0099. Strasbourg, 16 March 2006.

European Union. *Draft Constitutional Treaty,* europa.eu/constitution/index_en.htm.

Everts, Steven, et al. *A European Way of War.* London: Centre for European Reform, 2004.

Fairbrass, Jenny, and Andrew Jordan. "European Union Environmental Policy and the UK Government: A Passive Observer or a Strategic Manager?" *Environmental Politics* 10, no. 2 (2001): 1–21.

Farrell, Mary. "EU External Relations: Exporting the EU Model of Governance?" *European Foreign Affairs Review* 10, no. 4 (2005): 451–462.

Featherstone, Kevin, and Claudio Radaelli, eds. *The Politics of Europeanisation.* Oxford: Oxford University Press, 2003.

Ferré, Montserrat. "Should Fiscal Authorities Co-operate in a Monetary Union with Public Deficit Targets?" *Journal of Common Market Studies* 43, no. 3 (2005): 539–550.

Ferrero-Waldner, Benita. "Europe's Neighbours—Towards Closer Integration." Speech given at the Brussels Economic Forum, Brussels, 22 April 2005.

Fertig, Michael. "The Economic Impact of EU Enlargement: Assessing the Migration Potential." *Empirical Economics* 26, no. 4 (2001): 707–720.

Fierke, Karin, and Antje Wiener. "Constructing Institutional Interests: EU and NATO Enlargement." *Journal of European Public Policy* 6, no. 5 (1999): 721–742.

Fischer, Joschka. "Vom Staatenbund zur Föderation: Gedanken über die Finalität der europäische Integration." Speech given at Humboldt University, Berlin, 12 May 2000.

Fischer, Sabine. "Rußland und die Ukraine: Fehlkalkulation oder neoimperialer Impuls?" *Osteuropa* 55, no. 1 (2006): 64–76.

Fitscher, Patrick, and Seda Serdar. "Die ESVP und die Türkei: Auf der Suche nach einer strategischen Partnerschaft." In Hans-Georg Ehrhart, and Burkard Schmitt, eds., *Die Sicherheitspolitik der EU im Werden: Bedrohungen, Aktivitäten, Fähigkeiten.* Baden-Baden: Nomos, 2004, 118–129.

Flynn, Gregory, and Henry Farrell. "Piecing Together the Democratic Peace: The CSCE, Norms, and the 'Construction' of Security in Post–Cold War Europe." *International Organization* 53, no. 3 (1999): 505–536.

Forbrig, Joerg, David Marples, and Pavol Demes, eds. *Prospects for Democracy in Belarus.* Washington, DC: German Marshall Fund, 2006.

Franzke, Jochen. "Netzwerke für Demokratie statt Achsen mit Autokraten." *Welt Trends* 49 (Winter) 2005–2006: 125–133.

Frenkel, Michael, and Christiane Nickel. "How Symmetric Are the Shocks and the Shock Adjustment Dynamics Between the Euro Area and Central and Eastern European Countries?" *Journal of Common Market Studies* 43, no. 1 (2005): 53–74.

German Foreign Ministry., "The EU and Central Asia: Strategy for a New Partnership." Berlin: May 2007. http://www.auswaertiges-amt.de/diplo/en/Europa/Aussenpolitik/Regionalabkommen/Zentralasien.html.

Gesprächskreis, Bergedorfer. *Russland und der Westen: Chance für eine neue Partnerschaft.* Hamburg: Körber Stiftung, 2005.

Ginsberg, Roy. *The European Union in International Politics: Baptism by Fire.* Lanham: Rowman and Littlefield, 2001.

Gnesotto, Nicole. "Introduction: ESDP: Results and Prospects." In Nicole Gnesotto, ed., *EU Security and Defence Policy: The First Five Years (1999–2004).* Paris: Institute for Security Studies, 2004, 11–31.

———, ed. *EU Security and Defence Policy: The First Five Years (1999–2004).* Paris: Institute for Security Studies, 2004.

Goldstein, Avery. "Discounting the Free Ride: Alliances and Security in the Postwar World." *International Organization* 49, no. 1 (1995): 39–71.

Gow, James. "EU Enlargement and Security: Turning the Inside Out." In Julie Smith and Charles Jenkins, eds., *Through the Paper Curtain: Insiders and Outsiders in the New Europe.* London: RIIA/Blackwell, 2003, 61–76.

Grant, Charles, and Mark Leonard. "How to Build a Better EU Foreign Policy." *Bulletin* 47. Brussels: Centre for European Reform, 2006.

Grassini, M. "Eastern Enlargement of the EU. Economic Costs and Benefits for EU Present Member States? The Case of Italy." Study BUDG/B1/0001. Brussels, CEC, 2001.

Grauwe, Paul de. "Enlargement of the Euro Area: On Monetary and Political Union." *CESifo Forum* 7, no. 4 (2006): 3–10.

Green Cowles, Maria, James Caporaso, and Thomas Risse, eds. *Transforming Europe: Europeanization and Domestic Change.* Ithaca: Cornell University Press, 2001.

Gros, Daniel, and Stefano Micossi. "A Better Budget for the European Union: More Value for Money, More Money for Value." CEPS Policy Brief 66. Brussels, CEPS, February 2005.

Gros, Daniel, and Alfred Steinherr. *Economic Transition in Central and Eastern Europe.* Cambridge: Cambridge University Press, 2004.

Guardia, N. Diez, and K. Pichelmann. *Labour Migration Patterns in Europe: Recent Trends, Future Challenges.* Economic Papers 256. Brussels: ECFIN, September 2006.

Guérot, Ulrike, and Andrea Witt. "Europas neue Geostrategie." *Aus Politik und Geschichte* B17, 19 April 2004, 5–12.

Haas, Ernst. *The Obsolescence of Regional Integration Theory.* Berkeley: Institute of International Studies, 1975.

———. *The Uniting of Europe: Political, Social and Economical Forces, 1950–57.* London: Stevens and Sons, 1958.

Habermas, Jürgen, and Jacques Derrida. "What Binds Europeans Together." In Daniel Levy, Max Pensky, and John Torpey, eds., *Old Europe, New Europe, Core Europe: Transatlantic Relations After the Iraq War.* London: Verso, 2005. Originally published as "Nach Dem Krieg: Die Wiedergeburt Europas." *Frankfurter Allgemeine Zeitung,* 31 May 2003.

Haine, Jean-Yves. "An Historical Perspective." In Nicole Gnesotto, ed., *EU Security and Defence Policy: The First Five Years (1999–2004).* Paris: Institute for Security Studies, 2004, 35–53.

Haine, Jean-Yves, et al. *European Defence: A Proposal for a White Paper.* Paris: Institute for Security Studies, 2004.

Harnisch, Sebastian. "German Non-Proliferation Policy and the Iraq Conflict." *German Politics* 13, no. 1 (2004): 1–34.

Havrylyshyn, Oleg, and Thomas Wolf. "Determinants of Growth in Transition Countries." *Finance and Development* (June 1999): 12–15.

Hefeker, Carsten. *Ressourcenverteilung in der EU: Eine polit-ökonomische Perspektive*. Discussion Paper 252. Hamburg: HWWA, November 2003.

Heinemann, Friedrich. *Die Reformperspektive der EU Finanzverfassung nach den Beschlüssen zur Agenda 2000*. Discussion Paper 99-49. Bonn: ZEW, 1999.

———. *EU-Finanzplanung 2007–2013: Haushaltsoptionen, Verteilungswirkungen, und europäischer Mehrwert*. München: Bertelsmann, 2006.

Heinemann, Friedrich, Sebastian Hauptmeister, Michael Knogler, Dan Stegarescu, and Volkhart Vincentz. *Analyse ausgewählter Aspekte der Haushaltseinnahmen und – ausgaben sowie von außerbudgetären Fonds und Eventualverbindlichkeiten in den neuen Mitgliedsstaaten*. Bonn/München: ZEW/Osteuropa Institut München, February 2006.

———. *Transparenz und Nachhaltigkeit der Haushaltspolitik in den neuen EU-Staaten*. Baden-Baden: Nomos, 2006.

Heisbourg, François. "Europe's Strategic Ambitions: The Limits of Ambiguity." *Survival* 42, no. 2 (2000): 5–15.

Heise, Volker. *ESVP in transatlantischer Perspective: Mehr Unterschiede als Gemeinsamkeiten?* Diskussionspapier 2006/1. Berlin: SWP, 2006.

Hellmann, Gunther. "Wider der machtpolitische Resozialisierung der deutschen Außenpolitik: Plädoyer für offensiven Idealismus." *Welt Trends* 42, no. 1 (2004): 79–88.

Hensel, Howard, ed. *The United States and Europe: Policy Imperatives in a Globalizing World*. Aldershot: Ashgate, 2002.

Herd, Graeme. "Russia and the European Union." In Julie Smith and Charles Jenkins, eds., *Through the Paper Curtain: Insiders and Outsiders in the New Europe*. London: RIIA/Blackwell, 2003, 123–146.

Hill, Christopher. "The Capability-Expectations Gap, or Conceptualising Europe's Foreign Policy." *Journal of Common Market Studies* 31, no. 3 (1993): 305–328.

———. *The Changing Politics of Foreign Policy*. Houndmills: Palgrave, 2003.

———. "Renationalizing or Regrouping? EU Foreign Policy Since 11 September 2001." *Journal of Common Market Studies* 42, no. 1 (2004): 143–163.

———. "What Is to Be Done? Foreign Policy as a Site for Political Action." *International Affairs* 79, no. 2 (2003): 233–255.

Hill, Christopher, ed. *The Actors in Europe's Foreign Policy*. London: Routledge 1996.

Hill, Christopher, and Michael Smith, eds. *International Relations and the European Union*. Oxford: Oxford University Press, 2005.

Hishow, Ognian. "Das Wirtschafts- und Sozialmodell der nordischen EU-Mitglieder." SWP Aktuell 47. Berlin: SWP, November 2005.

Hitris, Theo. *European Union Economics*. 5th ed. Harlow: Pearson Education, 2003.

Hix, Simon. "Dimensions and Alignments in European Union Politics: Cognitive Constraints and Partisan Responses." *European Journal of Political Research* 35, no. 1 (1999): 69–106.

Hix, Simon, and Christophe Crombez. "Extracting Ideal Point Preferences from Actors' Preferences in the EU Constitutional Negotiations." *European Union Politics* 6, no. 3 (2005): 353–376.

HM Government, Presented to Parliament by the Secretary of State for Environment Food and Rural Affairs By Command of Her Majesty. *Draft Climate Change Bill*. Norwich: Stationery Office, 2007.

Hoffmann, Stanley. *The European Sisyphus: Essays on Europe, 1964–1994*. Boulder, CO: Westview, 1995.

Holm, Ulla. "The French Garden Is No Longer What It Used to Be." In Knut Jørgensen, ed., *Reflective Approaches to European Governance.* London: Macmillan, 1997, 128–145.

Hooghe, Liesbeth, and Gary Marks. *Multilevel Governance and European Integration.* Lanham: Rowman and Littlefield, 2001.

Horvat, Andrej, and Gunther Maier. "Regional Development, Absorption Problems and the EU Structural Funds." Paper presented at the European Regional Science Association Conference, August 2004.

Hovden, Eivind. "The Legal Basis of European Union Policy: The Case of Environmental Policy." *Environment and Planning C: Government and Policy* 20 (2002): 535–553.

Howorth, Jolyon. "Britain, France and the European Defence Initiative." *Survival* 42, no. 2 (2000): 33–55.

———. "Britain, NATO and CESDP: Fixed Strategy, Changing Tactics." *European Foreign Affairs Review* 5, no. 3 (2000): 377–396.

———. "Discourse, Ideas and Epistemic Communities in European Security and Defence Policy." *West European Politics* 27, no. 2 (2004): 29–52.

———. "The European Draft Constitutional Treaty and the Future of the European Defence Initiative: A Question of Flexibility." *European Foreign Affairs Review* 9, no. 4 (2004): 483–508.

———. "France." In Jolyon Howorth and Anand Menon, eds., *The European Union and National Defence Policy.* London: Routledge, 1997, 23–48.

———. "France, Britain and the Euro-Atlantic Crisis." *Survival* 45, no. 4 (2003–2004): 173–192.

Howorth, Jolyon, and John Keeler, eds. *The EU, NATO, and the Quest for European Autonomy.* New York: Palgrave, 2003.

Howorth, Jolyon, and Anand Menon, eds. *The European Union and National Defence Policy.* London: Routledge, 1997.

Hüfner, Martin. *Europa: Die Macht von morgen.* München: Hanser, 2006.

Hughes, Kirsty. *Turkey and the European Union: Just Another Enlargement? Exploring the Implications of Turkish Accession.* Working Paper. Brussels: Friends of Europe, 2004.

Hummer, Waldemar. "Die Union und ihre Nachbarn: Nachbarschaftspolitik vor und nach dem Verfassungsvertrag." *Integration* 28, no. 3 (2005): 233–245.

Hyde-Price, Adrian. "Book review of Frank Schimmelfennig, *The EU, NATO and the Integration of Europe: Rules and Rhetoric.* Cambridge: Cambridge University Press, 2003." In *European Foreign Affairs Review* 10, no. 3 (2005): 446–448.

Ilzkovitz, Fabienne, Adriaan Dierx, Viktoria Kovacs, and Nuno Sousa. *Steps Towards a Deeper Economic Integration: The Internal Market in the Twenty-First Century.* European Economy Economic Papers 271. Brussels: European Commission, January 2007.

Informationsdienst des Institut der deutschen Wirtschaft Köln 31, no. 8 (September 2005).

International Institute of Strategic Studies. *The Military Balance, 2004–2005.* London: IISS, 2005.

Jean Monnet–Robert Schumann: Correspondence 1947–1953. Lausanne: Fondation Jean Monnet, 1986.

Joerißen, Britta, and Bernhard Stahl, eds. *Europäische Außenpolitik und Nationale Identität.* Münster: LIT, 2003.

Johansson-Nogues, Elisabeth. "'A Ring of Friends'? The Implications of the European Neighbourhood Policy for the Mediterranean." *Mediterranean Politics* 2 (2004): 240–247.

Jones, Stephen, and Michael Emerson. *European Neighbourhood Policy in the Mashreq Countries: Enhancing Prospects for Reform.* Working Document 229. Brussels: CEPS, September 2005.

Jordan, Andrew, and Adriaan Schout. *The Coordination of the European Union: Exploring the Capacities of Networked Governance.* Oxford: Oxford University Press, 2006.

Jørgensen, Knud Erik. "Three Doctrines on European Foreign Policy." *Welt Trends* 42, no. 1 (2004): 27–36.

——, ed. *Reflective Approaches to European Governance.* London: Macmillan, 1997.

Jovanovic, Miroslav. *European Economic Integration: Limits and Prospects.* London: Routledge, 1997.

Judt, Tony. "Nineteen Eighty-Nine: The End of *Which* European Era?" *Dædelus* 123, no. 2 (1994): 1–19.

Kaase, Max, and Andrew Kohut. *Estranged Friends: The Transatlantic Consequences of Societal Change.* Gütersloh: Bertelsmann, 1996.

Kagan, Robert. *Of Paradise and Power: America and Europe in the New World Order.* New York: Knopf, 2003.

Karatnycky, Adrian. "Ukraine's Orange Revolution." *Foreign Affairs* 84, no. 2 (2005): 35–52.

Keeler, John. "Mapping EU Studies: The Evolution from Boutique to Boom Field, 1960–2001." *Journal of Common Market Studies* 43, no. 3 (2005): 551–582.

Kempe, Iris. *Direct Neighbourhood: Relations Between the Enlarged EU and the Russian Federation, Ukraine, Belarus and Moldova.* Gütersloh: Bertelsmann, 1998.

Keohane, Daniel. *The EU and Counter-Terrorism.* London: CER, 2005.

——. "EU on the Offensive About Defence." *European Voice,* 22–28 July 2004.

Keuschnigg, Christian, and Wilhelm Kohler. *Eastern Enlargement to the EU: Economic Costs and Benefits for the EU Present Member States.* Study XIX/B1/9801. Brussels: CEC, 1999.

——. *Eastern Enlargement to the EU: Economic Costs and Benefits for the EU Present Member States Final Report on Study XIX/B1/9801.* Brussels: CEC, 1999.

Kleger, Heinz. "Erweiterung ohne Vertiefung: vom Konvent zur Ratifizierungskrise." *Welt Trends* 50 (Spring 2006): 11–26.

Klein, Nadia, and Wolfgang Wessels. "Eine Stimme, zwei Hüte—viele Pioniere?" *Welt Trends* 42, no. 1 (2004): 11–26.

Kluge, Jürgen, and Heino Fassbender. *Wirtschaftsmacht Europa.* Wien: Ueberreuter, 2003.

Kohler-Koch, Beate, and Rainer Eising, eds. *The Transformation of Governance in the European Union.* London: Routledge, 1999.

High-Level Group, chaired by Wim Kok (Kok Report). *Facing the Challenge: The Lisbon Strategy for Growth and Employment.* Luxembourg: European Communities, 2004.

Koopman, Martin, and Christian Lequesne, eds. *Partner oder Beitrittskandidaten? Die Nachbarschaftspolitik der Europäischen Union auf dem Prüfstand.* Baden-Baden: Nomos, 2006.

Kowal, Pawel, ed. *The EU's Eastern Dimension: Opportunity for or Idée Fixe of Poland's Policy?* Trans. Bohdan Ambroziewicz. Warsaw: Centre for International Relations, 2002.

Kramer, Heinz. *Türkei-Verhandlungen als Spielball der Interessen.* SWP-Aktuell 42. Berlin: SWP, 2005.

Kramer, Steven. "The End of French Europe?" *Foreign Affairs* 85, no. 4 (2006): 126–138.

Kratochwil, Friedrich, and Yosef Lapid, eds. *The Return of Culture and Identity in IR Theory.* Boulder, CO: Lynne Rienner, 1996.

Kristensen, Tony, and Peter Jensen. "The Case of Denmark." In *Eastern Enlargement of the EU: Economic Costs and Benefits for EU Present Member States.* Study BUDG/B1/0001. Brussels: CEC, 2001.

Krugman, Paul. "Competitiveness: A Dangerous Obsession." *Foreign Affairs* 73, no. 2 (1994): 28–45.

———. *Geography and Trade.* Cambridge, MA: MIT, 1991.

Krugman, Paul, and Maurice Obstfeld. *International Economics: Theory and Policy.* 2nd ed. New York: Harper Collins, 1991.

Kubicek, Paul, ed. *The European Union and Democratization.* London: Routledge, 2003.

Kupchan, Charles. "In Defence of European Defence: An American Perspective." *Survival* 42, no. 2 (2000): 16–32.

Kurth, Helmut, and Iris Kempe, eds. *Presidential Election and Orange Revolution: Implications for Ukraine's Transition.* Kiev: Zapovit, 2005.

Kyaw, Dietrich von. "The EU After the Agreement on a Constitutional Treaty." *European Foreign Affairs Review* 9, no. 4 (2004): 455–458.

Ladrech, Robert. "The Europeanization of Domestic Politics and Institutions: The Case of France." *Journal of Common Market Studies* 32, no. 1 (1994).

Laffan, Bridget. "The European Polity: A Union of Normative, Regulatory and Cognitive Pillars." *Journal of European Public Policy* 8, no. 5 (2001): 709–727.

Landaburu, Eneko. "From Neighbourhood to Integration Policy: Are There Concrete Alternatives to Enlargement?" Speech at the CEPS conference "Revitalising Europe." Brussels, 23 January 2006. Also published as *Policy Brief* 95. Brussels: CEPS, March 2006.

Lankina, Tomila. "Explaining European Union Aid to Russia." *Post-Soviet Affairs* 21, no. 4 (2005).

Le More, Anne. "Killing with Kindness: Funding the Demise of a Palestinian State." *International Affairs* 81, no. 5 (2005): 981–999.

Lesquesne, Christian. *Paris-Bruxelles: Comment se fait la politique européene de la France.* Paris: Presses de la Fondation nationale des Sciences Politiques, 1993.

Levy, Daniel, Max Pensky, and John Torpey, eds. *Old Europe, New Europe, Core Europe: Transatlantic Relations After the Iraq War.* London: Verso, 2005.

Lewis, Ann, ed. *The EU and Ukraine: Neighbours, Friends, Partners?* London: Federal Trust, 2002.

Lewis, Bernard. "Freedom and Justice in the Modern Middle East." *Foreign Affairs* 84, no. 3 (2005): 36–51.

Libscher, Klaus, et al., eds. *The Economic Potential of a Larger Europe.* Cheltenham: Edward Elgar, 2004.

Lindberg, Leon. *The Political Dynamics of European Economic Integration.* Stanford: Stanford University Press, 1963.

Lindley-French, Julian. "Plugging the Expanded Petersberg Tasks Gap? Europe's Capabilities and the European Capabilities Action Plan (ECAP)." In Hans-Georg Ehrhart and Burkard Schmitt, eds., *Die Sicherheitspolitik der EU im Werden: Bedrohungen, Aktivitäten, Fähigkeiten.* Baden-Baden: Nomos, 2004, 201–213.

Lindley-French, Julian, and Franco Algieri. *A European Defence Strategy.* Gütersloh: Bertelsmann, 2004.

Lindner, Johannes, and Berthold Rittberger. "The Creation, Interpretation and

Contestation of Institutions: Revisiting Historical Institutionalism." *Journal of Common Market Studies* 41, no. 3 (2003): 445–473.

Lindner, Rainer. *Präsidentschaftswahl in Belarus: Autoritäres Regime, abhängige Staatswirtschaft, internationale Isolation.* S6. Berlin: Stiftung Wissenschaft und Politik, 2006.

Lindstrom, Gustav. "On the Ground: ESDP Operations." In Nicole Gnesotto, ed., *EU Security and Defence Policy: The First Five Years (1999–2004).* Paris: Institute for Security Studies, 2004, 111–129.

Lippert, Barbara. "Die Türkei als Sonderfall und Wendepunkt der klassischen EU-Erweiterungspolitik." *Integration* 28, no. 2 (2005): 119–135.

Lis, John, and Zachary Selden. *NATO Burdensharing After Enlargement.* Washington, DC: Congressional Budget Office, 2001.

Lo, Bobo. *Vladimir Putin and the Evolution of Russian Foreign Policy.* London: RIIA/Blackwell, 2003.

Longhurst, Kerry, and Marcin Zaborowski. "The Future of European Security." *European Security* 13, no. 4 (2004): 381–391.

Lynch, Dov. "Misperceptions and Divergences." in Lynch, ed. *What Russia Sees.* Chaillot Paper 74. Paris: ISS, 2005, 7–22.

———. "The New Eastern Dimension of the Enlarged EU." in Judy Batt et al., *Partners and Neighbours: A CFSP for a Wider Europe.* Chaillot Paper 64. Paris: ISS, 2003, 34–59.

———. *Why Georgia Matters.* Chaillot Paper 86. Paris: ISS, February 2006.

———, ed. *What Russia Sees.* Chaillot Paper 74. Paris: ISS, 2005.

Lyne, Roderick. "Russia in the EU? We Should Never Say Never." *Europe's World* (Spring 2006): 38–41.

Majidow, E. "Is Azerbaijan Going to Continue to Get Massive Inward Foreign Investments?" *Caucasian Journal of European Affairs* 1 (Winter) 2006.

Mallossesk, Jörg. *Die Erweiterung der Europäischen Union um die mittel- und osteuropäischen Länder, Wirtschaftspolitischer Reformbedarf bei gegebenen Budgetrestriktionen.* Köln: Institut für Wirtschaftspolitik, 1999.

Mandil, Claude. "Atomkraft, ja bitte!" *Internationale Politik* 61, no. 2 (2006).

March, James, and Johan Olsen. "The Institutional Dynamics of International Political Orders." *International Organization* 52, no. 4 (1998): 943–969.

Marchetti, Andreas. "The European Neighbourhood Policy: Foreign Policy at the Periphery." C158. Bonn: ZEI, 2006.

Marret, Jean-Luc. "The Long Threat: Terrorism and International Jihadism." In Hans-Georg Ehrhart, and Burkard Schmitt, eds., *Die Sicherheitspolitik der EU im Werden: Bedrohungen, Aktivitäten, Fähigkeiten.* Baden-Baden: Nomos, 2004, 21–31.

Martensen, Kaare Dahl. "The End of the Affair? Germany's Relationship with France." *German Politics* 14, no. 4 (2005): 401–416.

Maruhn, Roman, and Janis Emmanouilidis. *Agenda 2007: Der Konflikt um den Finanzrahmen, 2007–2013.* Reform Spotlight 1 2005. München: CAP, 2005.

Mattila, Mikko. "Contested Decisions: Empirical Analysis of Voting in the European Council of Ministers." *European Journal of Political Research* 43, no. 1 (2004): 29–50.

Maull, Hanns. "Germany and Japan: The New Civilian Powers." *Foreign Affairs* 69, no. 5 (1990): 91–106.

———. "Germany and the Use of Force: Still a Civilian Power?" *Survival* 42, no. 2 (2000): 56–80.

Mayer, Franz, and Jan Palmowski. "European Identities and the EU: The Ties That

Bind the Peoples of Europe." *Journal of Common Market Studies* 42, no. 3 (2004): 573–598.

Mayhew, Alan. *Re-creating Europe: The European Union's Policy Towards Central and Eastern Europe.* Cambridge: Cambridge University Press, 1998.

Mayne, Richard, ed. *Europe Tomorrow: Sixteen Europeans Look Ahead.* London: Fontana, 1972.

McSweeney, Bill. *Security, Identity and Interests: A Sociology of International Relations.* Cambridge: Cambridge University Press, 1999.

Meier-Walser, Reinhard C., ed. *Gemeinsam sicher? Vision und Realität europäischer Sicherheitspolitik.* München: Hanns-Seidel-Stiftung, 2004.

Meyer, Thomas, and Hanns Jacobsen. "Ever Closer Monetary Union? Euro Goes Central Europe." *Welt Trends* 51 (Summer 2006): 137–146.

Miller, Robert. *Russia and Europe: National Identity, National Interest, Pragmatism, or Delusions of Empire?* Working Paper 2006/1. Canberra: ANU, 2006.

Milward, Alan. *The European Rescue of the Nation-State.* 2nd ed. London: Routledge, 2000.

Minc, Alain. *Le Nouveau Moyen Age.* Paris: Editions Gallimard, 1993.

Missiroli, Antonio. "Defence Spending in Europe: Is Europe Prepared to Pay for Improved Capabilities?" Paper presented at the Cicero Foundation Conference on ESDP, Paris, 13–15 December 2001.

———. "ESDP: How It Works." In Nicole Gnesotto, ed., *EU Security and Defence Policy: The First Five Years (1999–2004).* Paris: Institute for Security Studies, 2004, 55–72.

———. "EU-NATO Cooperation in Crisis Management: No Turkish Delight for ESDP." *Security Dialogue* 33, no. 1 (2002): 9–26.

———. *Euros for ESDP: Financing EU Operations.* Occasional Paper 45. Paris: ISS, 2003.

Moberg, Alex. "The Nice Treaty and Voting Rules in the Council." *Journal of Common Market Studies* 40, no. 2 (2002): 259–282.

Molkhanov, M. "Ukraine and the European Union: A Perennial Neighbour?" *Journal of European Integration* 26, no. 4 (2004): 451–473.

Monar, Jörg. "Optionen für den Ernstfall: Auswege aus einer möglichen Ratifizierzungskrise des Verfassungsvertrags." *Integration* 28, no. 1 (2005): 16–32.

Moravcsik, Andrew. *The Choice for Europe: Social Purpose and State Power from Messina to Maastricht.* London: UCL Press, 1998.

———. "Negotiating the Single European Act: National Interests and Conventional Statecraft in the European Community." *International Organization* 45, no. 1 (1991): 19–56.

———. "Preferences and Power in the European Community: A Liberal Intergovernmentalist Approach." *Journal of Common Market Studies* 33, no. 4 (1993): 473–519.

More, Thomas. *Utopia* [1516]. Abridged edition. London: Phoenix, 1996.

Mörth, Ulrika, and Malena Britz. "European Integration as Organizing: The Case of Armaments." *Journal of Common Market Studies* 42, no. 5 (2004): 957–973.

Mrak, Mojmir, and Vasja Rant. *Challenges of EU and New Member States in Financial Perspective, 2007–2013: Convergence and Absorption of Available Cohesion Resources.* WP 2006-09. Milan: Universita degli Studi di Milano, 2006.

Müller, Kai Uwe, and Philipp Mohl. "Structural Funds in an Enlarged EU: A Politico-Economic Analysis." Paper presented at the third ECPR Conference, Budapest, 8–10 September 2005 (draft version, 21 September 2005).

Munchau, Wolfgang. *Das Ende der Sozialen Marktwirtschaft.* München: Hanser, 2006.

Mundell, Robert. "A Theory of Optimum Currency Areas." *American Economic Review* 51, no. 4 (1961): 657–665.

NATO-EU Declaration on ESDP. 16 December 2002, www.nato.int/docu/pr/2002/p02-142e.htm.

Niblett, Robin. "The United States, the European Union, and Lifting the Arms Embargo on China." *Euro-Focus* 10, no. 3 (2004).

Nicolaides, Kalypso, and Stephen Weatherill. "Introduction." In Kalypso Nicolaides and Stephen Weatherill, eds., *Whose Europe? National Models and the Construction of the European Union.* Oxford: Oxford University Press, 2003, 5–27.

———, eds. *Whose Europe? National Models and the Construction of the European Union.* Oxford: Oxford University Press, 2003.

Norman, Peter, *The Accidental Constitution: The Story of the European Convention.* Brussels: EuroComment, 2003.

Nuttall, Simon. "The Commission: The Struggle for Legitimacy." In Christopher Hill, ed., *The Actors in Europe's Foreign Policy.* London: Routledge, 1996, 131–146.

Nye, Joseph. *Bound to Lead: The Changing Nature of American Power.* New York: Basic Books, 1990.

———. *Soft Power: The Means to Success in World Politics.* New York: Public Affairs, 2004.

Oats, Wallace. "An Essay on Fiscal Federalism." *Journal of Economic Literature* 37, no. 3 (1999): 1120–1149.

Ochel, Wolfgang. "The EU Directive on Free Movement: A Challenge for the European Welfare State?" *CES/ifo Dice Report* 4, no. 4 (2006): 21–32.

Official Journal of the European Union. "Commission Decision of 4 August Drawing upon the List of Regions Eligible for Funding from the Structural Funds on a Transitional and Specific Basis Under the Regional Competitiveness and Employment Objective for the Period 2007–2013." Notified under document number C(2006) 3480, 6 September 2006.

Ortega, Martin. "A New EU Policy on the Mediterranean?" In Judy Batt et al., *Partners and Neighbours: A CFSP for a Wider Europe.* Chaillot Paper 64. Paris: ISS, 2003, 86–99.

OSCE/ODIHR. *Election Observation Mission Report, Republic of Belarus: Presidential Election, 19 March 2006.* Warsaw: June 2006.

Osica, Olaf. "Poland: A New European Atlanticist at the Crossroads?" *European Security* 13, no. 4 (2004): 300–322.

Palmer, John, et al. *Repairing the Damage: European Disunity and Global Crisis.* Challenge Europe Issue 9. Brussels: EPC, 2003.

Paolo, Francesco. "What Is European Economic and Monetary Union Telling Us About the Properties of Optimum Currency Areas?" *Journal of Common Market Studies* 43, no. 3 (2005): 607–635.

Pearson, Margaret. "The Business of Governing Business in China." *World Politics* 57, no. 3 (2005): 296–322.

Penrose, Lionel. "The Elementary Statistics of Majority Voting." *Journal of the Royal Statistical Society* 109, no.1 (1946): 53–57.

Penska, Susan, and Warren Mason. "EU Security Cooperation and the Transatlantic Relationship." *Cooperation and Conflict* 38, no. 3 (2003): 255–280.

Petersohn, Ulrich, and Sibylle Lang. *Die Zukunft der ESVP nach den gescheiterten Referenden.* SWP-Aktuell 34. Berlin: SWP, August 2005.

Pfaff, William. *The Wrath of Nations: Civilization and the Furies of Nationalism.* New York: Simon and Schuster, 1993.

Piehl, Ernst, Peter Schulze, and Heinz Timmermann. *Die offene Flanke der Europäischen Union: Russische Föderation, Belarus, Ukraine, und Moldau.* Berlin: Berliner Wissenschafts Verlag, 2005.

Piris, Jean-Claude. *The Constitution for Europe: A Legal Analysis.* Cambridge: Cambridge University Press, 2006.

Pisani-Ferry, Jean. "The Accidental Player: The EU and the Global Economy." Paper presented to the Indian Council for Research on International Economic Relations, New Delhi, 25 November 2005.

———. "Speeding Up European Reform: A Master Plan for the Lisbon Agenda." *CESifo Forum* 6, no. 2 (2005): 21–30.

Pollack, Mark. *The Engines of Integration: Delegation, Agency, and Agenda Setting in the European Union.* Oxford: Oxford University Press, 2003.

Popescu, Nicu. *The EU in Moldova: Settling Conflicts in the Neighbourhood.* Occasional Paper 60. Paris: ISS, October 2005.

Posch, Walter, ed. *Iranian Challenges.* Chaillot Paper 89. Paris: ISS, 2006.

Pouligny, Beatrice. "Civil Society and Post-Conflict Peacebuilding: Ambiguities of International Programmes Aimed at Building 'New' Societies." *Security Dialogue* 36, no. 4 (2005): 495–510.

Preston, Christopher. "Russia in the EU or the EU in Russia? Approaches to Kaliningrad." In Julie Smith and Charles Jenkins, eds., *Through the Paper Curtain: Insiders and Outsiders in the New Europe.* London: RIIA/Blackwell, 2003, 147–167.

Pridham, Geoffrey. *Designing Democracy: EU Enlargement and Regime Change in Post-Communist Europe.* Basingstoke: Palgrave, 2005.

Prizel, Ilya. "Putin's Russia, the Berlin Republic, and East-Central Europe: A New Symbiosis?" *Orbis* (Fall 2002): 678–693.

Prodi, Romano. "A Wider Europe: A Proximity Policy as the Key to Stability." Speech at the conference "Peace, Security and Stability: International Dialogue and the Role of the EU," Brussels, December 2002.

Quaisser, Wolfgang, and John Hall. *Towards Agenda 2007: Preparing the EU for Eastern Enlargement.* WP240. München: Osteuropa Institut, 2002.

Quaisser, Wolfgang, Monika Hartmann, Elmar Hönekopp, and Michael Brandmeier. *Die Osterweiterung der Europäischen Union: Konsequenzen für Wohlstand und Beschäftigung in Europa.* Bonn: Friedrich-Ebert-Stiftung, 2000.

Quaisser, Wolfgang, and Volkhart Vincentz. "Wachstumsfaktoren in Osteuropa." *ifo-Schnelldienst* 30 (October 1999): 16–24.

Quaisser, Wolfgang, and Steve Wood. *EU Member Turkey? Preconditions, Consequences and Integration Alternatives.* München: Forost, 2004.

Quaisser, Wolfgang, and Richard Woodward. "Absorptionsprobleme der EU-Struktur- und Regionalpolitik in den MOE-Ländern." *Beihefte der Konjunkturpolitik, Zeitschrift für angewandte Wirtschaftsforschung* 53 (2002): 115–147.

Radzyner, Joana. "Zurück in die Zukunft: Polens Weg in die IV. Republik." *Europäische Rundschau* 34, no. 2 (2006): 39–47.

Rahr, Alexander. "Schröders Russlandpolitik." *Welt Trends* 50 (Spring 2006): 93–94.

Rätzel, Steffen, and Joachim Weimann. "Der Maradona Effekt: Wie viel Wohlfahrt schafft die deutsche Nationalmannschaft?" *Perspektiven der Wirtschaftpolitik* 7, no. 2 (2006): 257–270.

Raveaud, Gilles. "The European Employment Strategy: Towards More and Better Jobs?" *Journal of Common Market Studies* 45, no. 2 (2007): 411–434.

Regelsberger, Elfriede, ed. *Die Gemeinsame Aussen- und Sicherheitspolitik der Europäischen Union: Profilsuche mit Hindernissen.* Bonn: Europa Union Verlag, 1993.

Remsperger, Hermann. "Comments on the Enlargement of the EU and EMU." Speech given at Johannes Gutenberg University, Mainz, 6 July 2005, www.bundesbank.de/download/presse/reden/2005/20050606remsperger.en.php.

Republique Française. *2003–2008 Military Programme Bill of Law.* Paris: Ministère de la Défense, 2002.

Risse, Thomas. "A European Identity: Europeanization and the Evolution of Nation-State Identities." In Maria Green Cowles, James Caporasa, and Thomas Risse, eds., *Transforming Europe: Europeanization and Domestic Change.* Ithaca, NY: Cornell University Press, 2001, 198–216.

Rjabcuk, Mykola. "Die Ukraine am Scheideweg: Ist ein Erpresserstaat reformierbar?" *Osturopa* 55, no. 1 (2005): 4–14.

Rodden, Jonathon. "Strength in Numbers? Representation and Redistribution in the European Union." *European Union Politics* 3, no. 2 (2002): 151–175.

Röller, Lars-Henrik, Juan Delgado, and Hans Friederiszick. *Energy: Choices for Europe.* Brussels: Bruegel, 2007.

Rosamond, Ben. "Conceptualising the EU Model of Governance in World Politics." *European Foreign Affairs Review* 10, no. 4 (2005): 463–478.

———. *Theories of European Integration.* Houndmills: Macmillan, 2000.

Rosati, Dariusz. *Economic Disparities in Central and Eastern Europe and the Impact of EU Enlargement.* München: Osteuropa Institut, 1999.

Rotte, Ralph, and Sascha Derichs. *Krise und Ende des Europäischen Stabilitäts- und Wachstumspakt.* Aktuelle analysen 39. München: Hanns-Seidel-Stiftung, 2005.

Roy, Oliver. "The Predicament of 'Civil Society' in Central Asia and the 'Greater Middle East.'" *International Affairs* 81, no. 5 (2005): 1001–1012.

Rummel, Reinhardt. "From Weakness to Power with ESDP?" *European Foreign Affairs Review* 7, no. 4 (2002): 453–471.

Saccomanni, Fabrizio. "Italy and Europe: Key Challenges Again, Ten Years Later." *The International Spectator* 41, no. 1 (2006).

Sahm, Astrid. "Nach der Wahl ist vor der Wahl: Belarus weiter auf Isolationkurs?" *Osteuropa* 55, no. 1 (2005): 77–90.

Sandholtz, Wayne, and Alec Stone Sweet, eds. *European Integration and Supranational Governance.* Oxford: Oxford University Press, 1998.

Sangiovanni, Mette Eilstrup. "Why a Common Security and Defence Policy Is Bad for Europe." *Survival* 45, no. 3 (2003): 196–203.

Sapir, André. "Globalisation and the Reform of European Social Models." *Policy Brief,* January 2005, 6, www.bruegel.org.

———. "Globalization and the Reform of European Social Models." *Journal of Common Market Studies* 44, no. 2 (2006): 369–390.

Sapir, André, et al. *An Agenda for a Growing Europe: Making the EU Economic System Deliver.* Brussels: CEC, 2003.

Saryusz-Wolski, Jacek. "Institutional Reform: A Pragmatic Point of View." *International Spectator* 41, no. 1 (2006).

Scannell, David. "Financing ESDP Military Operations." *European Foreign Affairs Review* 9, no. 4 (2004): 529–549.

Scharpf, Fritz. "The European Social Model: Coping with the Challenges of Diversity." In J. H. H. Weiler, Iain Begg, and John Peterson, eds., *Integration in an Expanding European Union: Reassessing the Fundamentals.* Oxford: Blackwell, 2003, 109–134.

Schild, Joachim. "Ein Sieg der Angst: Das gescheiterte französiche Verfassungsreferendum." *Integration* 28, no. 3 (2005): 187–200.

Schimmelfennig, Frank. *The EU, NATO, and the Integration of Europe: Rules and Rhetoric.* Cambridge: Cambridge University Press, 2003.

Schimmelfennig, Frank, and Ulrich Sedelmeier, eds. *The Europeanization of Central and Eastern Europe.* Ithaca: Cornell University Press, 2005.

Schmid, Dorothée. "Die Europäische Nachbarschaftspolitik und die euromediterrane Partnerschaft: das Ende einer regionalen Ambition?" In Martin Koopman and Christian Lequesne, eds., *Partner oder Beitrittskandidaten? Die Nachbarschaftspolitik der Europäischen Union auf dem Prüfstand.* Baden-Baden: Nomos, 2006, 111–128.

Schmidt, Helmut. *Die Selbstbehauptung Europas.* Stuttgart: DVA, 2000.

Schmitt, Burkard (rapporteur). *Defence Procurement in the European Union: The Current Debate.* Paris: ISS, May 2005.

———. "European Capabilities—How Many Divisions?" in Nicole Gnesotto, ed., *EU Security and Defence Policy: The First Five Years (1999–2004).* Paris: Institute for Security Studies, 2004, 89–110.

———. *From Cooperation to Integration: Defence and Aerospace Industries in Europe,* Chaillot Paper 40. Paris: ISS, 2000.

Schneider, Gerald. "The Limits of Self-Reform: Institution Building in the European Union." *European Journal of International Relations* 1, no. 1 (1995): 59–86.

Schneider-Deters, Winfried. "Die Palliative Ukrainepolitik der EU." *Osteuropa* 55, no. 1 (2005): 50–63.

Schoutheete, Philippe de. *The Case for Europe: Unity, Diversity and Democracy in the European Union.* Trans. Andrew Butler. Boulder, CO: Lynne Rienner, 2000.

Schröder, Wolfgang. "Arbeitsbeziehungen in Mittel- und Osteuropa: Weder wilder Osten noch europäisches Sozialmodell." *Politikinformationen Osteuropa* 119. Bonn: Friedrich Ebert Stiftung, June 2004.

Schuette, Rolf. *EU-Russia Relations: Interests and Values—A European Perspective.* Paper 54. Washington, DC: Carnegie Endowment for International Peace, 2004.

Schwartz, Siegfried. "Zur Geschichte einer gemeinsamen europäischen Außenpolitik." *Welt Trends* 42, no. 1 (2004): 51–63.

Schwegmann, Christoph. *Kann die EU die NATO auf dem Balkan ersetzen?* S43. Berlin: SWP, 2002.

———. "Kontaktgruppen und EU-3-Verhandlungen." SWP-Aktuell 62. Berlin: SWP, 2005.

Schweiger, Christian. "British-German Relations in the European Union After the War on Iraq." *German Politics* 13, no. 1 (2004): 35–55.

Sedelmeier, Ulrich, and Alisdair Young. "Crisis, What Crisis? Continuity and Normality in the European Union in 2005." *Journal of Common Market Studies* 44 (Supplement) (2006): 1–5.

Seeger, Sarah, and Janis Emmanouilidis. "Die Reform nimmt Gestalt an. Analyse und Bewertung des EU-Verfassungsgipfels." In *Bilanz der deutschen EU-Ratspräsidentschaft, Analyse und Bewertung des Centrums für angewandte Politikforschung, CAP Analyse* no. 6, July 2007: 6–12.

Sell, Axel, and Tobias Schauf, eds. *Bilanz und Perspektiven der Transformation in Osteuropa.* Münster: LIT, 2003.

Sevjnar, Jan. "Structural Reforms and Competitiveness: Will Europe Overtake America?" In Gertrude Tumpel-Gugerell and Peter Mooslechner, eds., *Structural Challenges for Europe.* Cheltenham: Edward Elgar, 2004, 35–59.

Shapiro, Jeremy, and Bénédicte Suzan. "The French Experience of Counter-Terrorism." *Survival* 45, no. 1 (2003): 67–98.

Sherrington, Patricia. *The Council of Ministers: Political Authority in the European Union.* London: Pinter, 2000.

Siebert, Horst. *Germany in the European Union: Economic Policy Under Ceded Sovereignty.* WP 1217. Institute for World Economics: Kiel, 2004.

———. *The World Economy,* 2nd ed. London: Routledge, 2002.

Simon, Gerhard. "Neubeginn in the Ukraine." *Osteuropa* 55, no. 1 (2005): 16–33.

Sinn, Hans-Werner. "Basar-Ökonomie Deutschland, Exportweltmeister oder Schlußlicht?" *ifo Schnelldienst* 6 (Sonderausgabe) March 2005.

———. *Ist Deutschland noch zu retten?* Berlin: Ullstein, 2005.

———. *The New Systems Competition.* Oxford: Blackwell, 2003.

Sinn, Hans-Werner, Gerhard Flaig, Martin Werding, S. Münz, N. Düll, and H. Hoffmann. *EU Erweiterung und Arbeitskräftemigration: Wege zu einer schrittweisen Annäherung der Arbeitsmärkt.* München: ifo, 2001.

Skach, Cindy. "We, the Peoples? Constitutionalizing the European Union." *Journal of Common Market Studies* 43, no. 1 (2005): 149–170.

Skjaerseth, Jon Birger, and Jørgen Wettestad. "Understanding the Effectiveness of EU Environmental Policy: How Can Regime Analysis Contribute?" *Environmental Politics* 11, no. 3 (2002): 99–120.

Sloan, Stanley, and Heiko Borchert. "Transatlantic Power Gaps and the Future of EU-US Relations." In Hans-Georg Ehrhart, and Burkard Schmitt, eds., *Die Sicherheitspolitik der EU im Werden: Bedrohungen, Aktivitäten, Fähigkeiten.* Baden-Baden: Nomos, 2004, 133–145.

Smith, Hazel. *European Union Foreign Policy: What It Is and What It Does.* London: Pluto, 2002.

Smith, Julie, and Charles Jenkins, eds. *Through the Paper Curtain: Insiders and Outsiders in the New Europe.* London: RIIA/Blackwell, 2003.

Smith, Karen. "The End of Civilian Power EU: A Welcome Demise or Cause for Concern?" *The International Spectator* 35, no. 2 (2002): 11–28.

———. *European Foreign Policy in a Changing World.* London: Polity, 2003.

———. "The Outsiders: The European Neighbourhood Policy." *International Affairs* 81, no. 4 (2005): 757–773.

Smith, Michael. "Toward a Theory of EU Foreign Policy-making: Multi-level Governance, Domestic Politics and National Adaptation to Europe's Common Foreign and Security Policy." *Journal of European Public Policy* 11, no. 4 (2004): 740–758.

Solana, Javier. "Driving the EU-China Partnership Forward." *Hampton Roads International Security Quarterly* 4 (2005): 37–39.

Statistisches Bundesamt. *Volkswirtschaftliche Gesamtrechnung. Input-Output-Rechnung. Importabhängigkeit der deutschen Exporte 1991, 1995, 2000 und 2002.* Wiesbaden: SBA, 2004.

Steunenberg, Bernard, ed. *Widening the European Union: The Politics of Institutional Change and Reform.* London: Routledge, 2002.

Stiglitz, Joseph, and Shahid Yusuf. *Rethinking the East Asian Miracle.* Washington, DC: Oxford University Press, 2001.

Stone Sweet, Alec. *The Judicial Construction of Europe.* Oxford: Oxford University Press, 2004.

———. "What Is a Supranational Constitution? An Essay in International Relations Theory." *Review of Politics* 56, no. 3 (1994): 441–474.

Stone Sweet, Alec, Wayne Sandholtz, and Neil Fligstein, eds. *The Institutionalization of Europe.* Oxford: Oxford University Press, 2001.

Study Group on European Security. *A Human Security Doctrine for Europe: Barcelona Report of the Study Group on European Security.* London: LSE, 2004.

Su, Hungdah. "Can Constitution-Building Advance European Integration? A Three-Pillared Institutional Analysis." *Journal of European Integration* 26, no. 4 (2004): 353–378.

Sweeney, Paul. *The Celtic Tiger: Ireland's Economic Miracle Explained.* Dublin: Oak Tree Press, 1998.

Tarnby, Michael. *Recruitment of Islamic Terrorists in Europe: Trends and Perspectives.* Aarhus: Centre for Cultural Research, 2005.

Tassinari, Fabrizio. *Security and Integration in the EU Neighbourhood: The Case for Regionalism.* Working Document 226. Brussels: CEPS, July 2005.

Tereschenko, Volodymyr. *Evolution der politischen Beziehungen zwischen der Ukraine und der EU, 1991–2004.* Frankfurt: Peter Lang, 2005.

Tewes, Henning. *Germany, Civilian Power, and the New Europe: Enlarging NATO and the European Union.* Houndmills: Palgrave, 2002.

Thalacker, Patrick. "Ein Sozialmodell für Europa? Die EU-Sozialpolitik nach der Erweiterung." *Gesellschaft-Wirtschaft-Politik* (February 2002): 165–181.

Thalmaier, Bettina. *Optionen für einen Plan-B im Falle des Scheiterns der Ratifikation des Verfassungsvertrags.* Working Paper. München: CAP, 2005.

Thomson, Robert, Jovanka Boerefijn, and Frans Stokman. "Actor Alignments in European Union Decision Making." *European Journal of Political Research* 43, no. 2 (2004): 237–261.

Thomson, Robert, and Madeline Holsi. "Who Has Power in the EU? The Commission, Council and Parliament in Legislative Decision-making." *Journal of Common Market Studies* 44, no. 2 (2006): 391–417.

Tinguy, Anne de. "Konkurrenten statt Partner: Die russische Sicht auf die EU und die Nachbarschaftspolitik." In Martin Koopman and Christian Lequesne, eds., *Partner oder Beitrittskandidaten? Die Nachbarschaftspolitik der Europäischen Union auf dem Prüfstand.* Baden-Baden: Nomos, 2006, 85–108.

Toje, Asle. "The 2003 European Security Strategy: A Critical Appraisal." *European Foreign Affairs Review* 10, no. 1 (2005): 117–133.

Torbiörn, Kjell. *Destination Europe: The Political and Economic Growth of a Continent.* Manchester: Manchester University Press, 2003.

Touzovskaja, Natalia. "EU-NATO Relations: How Close to a Strategic Partnership?" *European Security* 15, no. 3 (2006): 235–258.

Treacher, Adrian. "From Civilian Power to Military Actor: The EU's Resistable Transformation." *European Foreign Affairs Review* 9, no. 1 (2004): 49–66.

Tsakatika, Myrto. "Claims to Legitimacy: The European Commission Between Continuity and Change." *Journal of Common Market Studies* 43, no. 1 (2005): 193–220.

Tsebelis, George, and Geoffrey Garrett. "The Institutional Foundations of Intergovernmentalism and Supranationalism in the European Union." *International Organization* 55, no. 2 (2001): 357–390.

Tsoukalis, Loukas. *What Kind of Europe?* Oxford: Oxford University Press, 2003.

Tumpel-Gugerell, Gertrude, and Peter Mooslechner, eds. *Economic Convergence and Divergence in Europe: Growth and Regional Development in an Enlarged European Union.* Cheltenham: Edward Elgar, 2003.

———. *Structural Challenges for Europe.* Cheltenham: Edward Elgar, 2004.

Umbach, Frank. "Europas nächster Kalter Krieg." *Internationale Politik* 61, no. 2 (2006): 6–14.

———. "Sichere Energieversorgung auch in Zukunft: Die notwendigkeit einer europäischen Strategie." *Internationale Politik* 59, no. 8 (2004): 17–28.

United Kingdom, Ministry of Defence. *Delivering Security in a Changing World.* London: MOD, 2003.

———. *European Defence.* Policy Paper No. 3. London: MOD, 2001.

———. *UK Defence Statistics.* London: MOD, 2004.

United Kingdom, Treasury. *Spending Review 2004.* London: Her Majesty's Treasury, 2004.

United Nations Economic Commission for Europe. "Towards a New European Model of a Reformed Welfare State: An Alternative to the United States Model." In *Economic Survey of Europe* 1/2005. New York: United Nations, 2005, 105–114.

United States, Office of Management and Budget. *Budget of the United States Government: Fiscal Year 2004.* Washington, DC: Executive Office of the President, 2003.

United States, White House. *National Security Strategy of the United States of America.* Washington, DC: 2002.

Vahl, Marius. *Models for the European Neighbourhood Policy: The European Economic Area and the Northern Dimension.* Working Document 218. Brussels: CEPS, 2005.

Varwick, Johannes, ed. *Die Beziehungen zwischen NATO und EU: Partnerschaft, Konkurrenz, Rivalität?* Opladen: Budrich, 2005.

Vibert, Frank. *Europe: A Constitution for the Millennium.* Aldershot: Dartmouth, 1995.

Vincentz, Volkhart. "Deutsche Direktinvestitionen in Osteuropa weiter rückläufig: Arbeitsplatzeffekte geringer als befürchtet." *Kurzinformationen und Analysen* 3. München: Osteuropa Institut, April 2002.

Vincentz, Volkhart, and Michael Knogler. *Szenarien der mittelfristigen Konvergenz der EU Beitrittsländer Polen, Slowakische Republik und Ungarn.* WP 244. München: Osteuropa Institut, 2003.

Vogt, Line. *The EU's Single Market: At Your Service?* WP449. Paris: OECD, October 2005.

Waever, Ole. "Identity, Integration and Security: Solving the Sovereignty Puzzle in E.U. Studies." *Journal of International Affairs* 48, no. 2 (1995): 389–431.

Waever, Ole, et al. *Identity, Migration and the New Security Agenda in Europe.* London: Pinter, 1993.

Wagener, Hans Jürgen, Thomas Eger, and Heiko Fritz. *Europäische Integration: Recht und Ökonomie, Geschichte und Politik.* München: Franz Vahlen, 2006.

Waltz, Kenneth. *Theory of International Politics.* Reading, MA: Addison Wesley, 1979.

Wanlin, Aurore. *The Lisbon Scorecard VI: Will Europe's Economy Rise Again?* London: Centre for European Reform, 2006.

Wassenberg, Elmar. "Europäische und amerikanische Rüstunganstrengungen im Vergleich." In Reinhard C. Meier-Walser, ed., *Gemeinsam sicher? Vision und Realität europäischer Sicherheitspolitik.* München: Hanns-Seidel-Stiftung, 2004, 383–403.

Way, Lucan. "Authoritarian State Building and the Sources of Regime Competitiveness in the Fourth Wave: The Cases of Belarus, Moldova, Russia, and Ukraine." *World Politics* 57, no. 2 (2005): 231–261.

Weidenfeld, Werner. "Die Europäische Union neu ausrichten." *Welt Trends* 50 (Spring 2006): 55–65.

———. *Kulturbruch mit Amerika?* Gütersloh: Bertelsman, 1996.

Weiler, J. H. H., Iain Begg, and John Peterson, eds. *Integration in an Expanding European Union: Reassessing the Fundamentals.* Oxford: Blackwell, 2003.

Weise, Christian, et al. *Die Finanzierung der Osterweiterung der EU.* Baden-Baden: Nomos, 2002.

Wessels, Wolfgang. "Die Vertragsreform von Nizza: Zur institutionellen Erweiterungsreife." *Integration* 24, no. 1 (2001): 8–24.

———. "An Ever Closer Fusion? A Dynamic Macropolitical View of the Integration Process." *Journal of Common Market Studies* 35, no. 2 (1997): 269–299.

———. "Keynote Article: The Constitutional Treaty—Three Readings from a Fusion Perspective." *Journal of Common Market Studies* 45 (Annual Review) (2005): 11–36.

———. "Nice Results: The Millennium IGC in the EU's Evolution." *Journal of Common Market Studies* 39, no. 2 (2001): 197–219.

Whitman, Richard. "The Fall, and Rise, of Civilian Power Europe?" WP15. Canberra: National Europe Centre, 2002.

Wiberg, Matti. *New Winners and Old Losers: A Priori Voting Power in the EU25.* Discussion Paper C149. Bonn: ZEI, 2005.

Wiener, Antje, and Thomas Diez, eds. *European Integration Theory.* Oxford: Oxford University Press, 2004.

Wilson, Kevin, and Jan van der Dussen, eds. *The History of the Idea of Europe.* London: Open University/Routledge, 1995.

Wolf, Reinhard. "Was hält siegreich Verbündete zusammen? Machtpolitische, institutionelle und innenpolitische Faktoren in Vergleich." *Zeitschrift für Internationale Beziehungen* 7, no. 1 (2000): 33–78.

Wong, Reuben. "The Europeanization of Foreign Policy." in Christopher Hill and Michael Smith, eds., *International Relations and the European Union.* Oxford: Oxford University Press, 2005, 134–153.

Wood, Stephen. "Germany and the Eastern Enlargement of the EU: Political Elites, Public Opinion, and Democratic Processes." *Journal of European Integration* 24, no. 1 (2002): 23–38.

———. *Germany, Europe, and the Persistence of Nations: Transformation, Interests, and Identity, 1989–1996.* Aldershot: Ashgate, 1998.

Wood, Steve. "A Common European Space? National Identity, Foreign Land Ownership and EU Enlargement: The Polish and Czech Cases." *Geopolitics* 9, no. 3 (2004): 588–607.

———. "German Foreign and Security Policy After Kohl and Kosovo." *Government and Opposition* 37, no. 2 (2002): 250–270.

———. *Germany and East-Central Europe: Political, Economic and Socio-Cultural Relations in the Era of EU Enlargement.* Aldershot: Ashgate, 2004.

———. "The Iraq War: Five European Roles." WP112. Canberra: National Europe Centre, 2003.

Wood, Steve, and Wolfgang Quaisser. "Turkey's Road to the EU: Political Dynamics, Strategic Context and Implications for Europe." *European Foreign Affairs Review* 10, no. 2 (2005): 147–173.

World Bank. *World Development Indicators.* Washington, DC: World Bank, July 2006.

World Economic Forum. *Global Competitiveness Report, 2004–2005.* Geneva: WEF, 2004.

———. *Growth Competitiveness Report, 2005/2006.* Geneva: WEF, 2006.

Wyplosz, Charles. "The Challenge of a Wider and Deeper Europe." In Klaus Libscher et al., eds., *The Economic Potential of a Larger Europe.* Cheltenham: Edward Elgar, 2004, 8–33.

Yost, David. "France's New Nuclear Doctrine." *International Affairs* 82, no. 4 (2006): 701–721.

Youngs, Richard. *Europe and the Middle East in the Shadow of September 11*. Boulder: Lynne Rienner, 2006.

———. "The European Union and Democracy Promotion in the Mediterranean: A New or Disingenuous Strategy?" *Democratization* 9, no. 1 (2002): 40–62.

Zaborowski, Marcin. "Between Power and Weakness: Poland—A New Actor in Transatlantic Security." *Reports and Analyses* 14/03. Warsaw: Center for International Relations, 2003.

———, ed. *Facing China's Rise: Guidelines for an EU Strategy*. Chaillot Paper 94. Paris: ISS, December 2006.

Zagorski, Andrei. "Russia and the Shared Neighbourhood." In Dov Lynch, ed., *What Russia Sees*. Chaillot Paper 74. Paris: ISS, 2005, 61–77.

Zielonka, Jan. *Europe as Empire: The Nature of the Enlarged European Union*. Oxford: Oxford University Press, 2006.

———. *Explaining Euro-Paralysis: Why Europe Is Unable to Act in International Politics*. New York: St. Martin's Press, 1998.

Zimmermann, Klaus, ed. *European Migration: What Do We Know?* Oxford: Oxford University Press, 2005.

Zourabichvili, Salomé. *Une femme pour deux pays*. Paris: Grasset, 2006.

Index

Agricultural and rural policy: expensive and disputed character of, 37; national/regional administrative control proposed for, 108; need for serious adjustments in, 108

Algeria: association agreement and work toward action plan in, 178; as successful attractor of FDI, 178

Amsterdam Treaty: environmental requirements in, 102; and member state controls and veto rights, 119; and social welfare policy, 45

Azerbaijan: and Armenia conflict, 176; oil industry development and economic impact in, 176

Balkan conflict, as test of EU capacity and regional security, 123

Balkan countries: decentralization and, 182; ENP candidates and membership perspective in, 155, 182; EU reconstruction efforts in, 182; and shared European values, 182; Stabilisation and Association Process (SAP) in, 155

Banking sector, and single market program, 24. *See also* European Central Bank (ECB)

Barroso, José Manuel, 58, 143, 198

Belarus: authoritarian government of, 174; financial and technical assistance to, 174; nonparticipation in neighborhood policy, 174; Russian relations with, 174–175; and EU's soft powers of persuasion, 175

Belgium, and constitutional negotiations, 58

Blair, Tony, 143, 198; Constitutional Treaty support of, 66, 67; and European defense policy, 128

Britain, and European unity, 67

British military and defense policy: Helsinki Headline Goal interpretation of, 128; and Iraq and Afghanistan involvements, 129; views of ESDP, 128–129

Brown, Gordon, 129

Budget and financing reform, 95–101; in areas of growth, convergence, and fund restructuring, 100; and CAP funding costs, 85; and fiscal federalism, 95–96; and fund allocation standards, 99; Lisbon process and, 47; main interest groups negotiating in, 38–39; and national cohesion funds, 99; and public goods provision, 95–98, 100; regulations emphasizing individual responsibilities, 99; three pillar approach to, 98–100; trans-European networks and Lisbon strategy for, 99–100; and transparent funding based on relative wealth of members, 100–101; and voting power of member states, 82

Bulgaria: deficiencies in infrastructure and institutional capacity, 26, 33; EU membership of, 23; potential migration from, 30; reservations about EU membership 18, 23

Bush administration, and Putin's autocratic governance, 171

Cardiff process, environmental requirements in, 102

Caucasus countries, poverty and separatist ethnic conflict in, 175. *See also* Azerbaijan; Georgia

Central Asian republics: and ENP inclusion, 183; strategic importance of, 165

Central and Eastern Europe (CEE): and German export performance, 29; fiscal system deficiencies in, 33; German FDI and job creation in, 29; jobless growth in, 35; technology sector in, 34

Central and Eastern European countries (CEECs): addressing environmental degradation in, 101; common security space for, 200; development of real GDP in, 25; and EMU criteria on inflation and interest rates, 33; and enhanced cooperation in Council deliberations, 62; EU accession tactics, 162–164; FDI flows into, 28, 30; integration of, 6, 21–22, 28, 155; Lisbon process and, 35; macroeconomic policy in, 32–33; market access of, 47; and new EU-funded projects, 108; and potential migration into EU15, 29; reconfigured as sound market economies, 21; redirected funding to promote growth in, 94; regional security in, 132; Single Market extension impacts on, 26, 27–28; social welfare policy models in, 43; and trade barriers removal, 25; transition to fully-fledged market economy in, 26

Chinese market: EU-US competition over, 142–143; political problems of dealing with, 143

Chirac, Jacques, 58, 103, 199; and European constitution, 66–69

Civilian power, EU transition from, 10; debate on EU as, 125; Germany as, 131; and EU "strategic culture," 160

Cohesion Funds: and financing reform, 99–100; for growth and employment funding (2007–2013), 94*tab*; as instrument of regional policy, 89–90; limited success of, 90; redesigned to support low-income member states, 109; as side payments to buy political decisions, 93

Cohesion policy. *See* Regional policy

Committees of Permanent Representatives (COREPERs), 8; decision-making in, 62

Common Agricultural Policy (CAP), 66, 84–88; and agricultural reforms, 86–88; bond scheme for, 86, 87; delinking of direct payments from productive capacity, 85; demand for reform or abolition of, 10; excesses and deficiencies of, 84–85, 108; innovative concepts for improving, 86; international context of, 86; market intervention of, 81; and national politics, 87–88; reforms, 85–86; subsidies of, 85; and WTO negotiations, 85

Common Foreign and Security Policy (CFSP): Athena funding mechanism for, 138; and changing global context, 10; chronological overview of developments in, 127*tab*; convergence of TEU pillars of justice and home affairs with, 145; creation and purpose of, 118–120; and EU ventures into human security spheres, 119; evaluation process on progression of, 123; and individual states' expenditures, 137; links to internal security, 144; Nice outcome and, 119; OMDIs (operations having military or defense implications) funding, 137; parliamentarization of, 117; and qualified majority voting requirement, 62; perceived as weakness component in EU, 126; and rejection of Constitutional Treaty, 119; 2005 budget for, 136–137

Constitutional Treaty (CT), 2, 20, 65–74; double majority requirement to pass, 9; and double majority voting, 9, 84; ESDP inclusion in, 125; and EU legal primacy, 69; and European integration, 65–67; French "no" vote on, 42; fusion theory and, 65; and June 2007 compromise points, 72–73; and national politics, 8–9; opposition to versus support for, 70; options for enhancing approval probability, 71; previous models and understandings of, 65; proposed changes in content, 71–72; provisions governing voting in, 62–63; public opinion on, 68–69;

referendums on, 66–70; and Reform Treaty negotiations, 3, 72–73, 84; rejection of, 9, 11, 167; revision of Nice as option for, 72; revitalization options for, 70–72, 125, 194

Corporate tax reforms, 45–46

Council of Agricultural Ministers (CoAM), and CAP reform, 86

Council of Ministers: deliberations, A- and B-point matters in, 61–62; and double majority arrangements, 63; institutional power and voting system of, 9, 11; and interinstitutional rivalry, 8; under Nice system rules, 62–63; political powers of, 57–58; predominant EU role of, 55; professionalization efforts for, 63; voting power disposition in decisionmaking rounds of, 82

Delors, Jacques, 5, 56

Democratic deficit, of EU, 12

Democratization: and increased accession pressures, 161–162; NATO and US-led military-political alliance as backing for, 160; negative incentives for, 162; problems with EU promotion of, 160–162: soft power application in, 160

Eastern enlargement, 6; and creation of democratic structures, 20–21; main objectives and stages of, 21–22; weaknesses in, 23

Eastern flank countries: EU links to, 169; EU neighborhood strategy in, 169–177; trade liberalization in, 169; as transit routes for energy supplies, 176–177; and transition obligations, 169; unconsolidated autocracies in, 170. *See also specific country*

Economic and Financial Affairs Council (ECOFIN), 198

Economic and Monetary Union (EMU), 6, 15n39, 31–34; and banking and financing reform, 100; and EU effectiveness, 17; need for consolidation of, 47; and new member states, 32–33; and political union, 32; success of, 10; and system reforms, 33; welfare and, 18

Economic integration, Heckscher-Ohlin paradigm of, 27

Economic policy, national level control over, 31

Egypt, 11, 169; country report and action plan for, 179; political importance of, 179; support for Mubarak regime in, 179

Emissions Trading Scheme (ETS), Commission review findings on, 104

Employment, failed strategies for, 10

Energy policy, 104–107; and Commission's energy objectives, 105; and energy consumption and imports, 104–105, 143–144; and energy security, 143–144; foreign and security aspects of, 105; integrated with climate change policy, 104; and international politics and security issues, 143; member disputes on, 144; and nuclear power option, 106–107, 144; pan-European energy community idea in, 105; priority areas in, 105; research and innovation needs in, 106; and security of supply, 105–106; sustainability and diversity of sources as goal of, 106

Energy resources: in Central Asian republics, 165; and durable partnerships with alternative suppliers, 165; eastern flank countries and Russia as transit routes for, 176–177; and Russia's inherited pipelines, 177; strategic dimension of, 104

Environment Action Programme (EAP), activities of, 102

Environmental policy: active pursuit of goals in, 102; climate change strategy in, 103; and international agreements, 102; principal financial instrument of, 102; weak implementation and enforcement of, 101–102

EU accession: alternatives to, 167, 169; and automatic entry, 167; and budgetary resources, 167; economic convergence measure for, 23; economic criteria for, 26; neighborhood policy as substitution for, 159; security through democratic reform as criterion for, 158. *See also specific country; region*

EU association agreements, human rights clause of, 166

EU budget: for defense and security, 135–139; policy areas covered in

(2005), 136; and financial redistribution, 38–40

EU decisionmaking, 61–63; and allocation of voting power among states, 62; argument for decentralization of, 95; based on subsidiary principle, 19; enhanced cooperation proposition for, 62; and EU's broad goals, 61; legal processes' overlap with, 69; under the Nice system, 82; on voting system revision, 84

EU deepening and widening: definitions of, 17; and eastern enlargement, 20–23, 25; and economic and political paths to integration, 18; and EMU, 31–34; and financial redistribution, 37–41; and labor market effects, 27–31; and limited market integration, 24; Lisbon objectives and, 34–37; political economy of, 17; and questions of optimal size, 18–20; social dimension effects of, 17

EU democratic legitimation, 69

EU economic policies: achievements and failures in, 9–10; assigned to national versus EU levels, 45–46; of economic liberalism, 18–19; and full integration, 24; and regional income differentials, 18; for wealth generation, 10

EU economy: and gross domestic product (GNP) and, 18; sources of growth in, 37. *See also specific member state*

EU enlargements: case for slowdown of, 195–196; comparative member states' support for, 168*tab*; Copenhagen criteria for, 11, 15*n39;* and European solidarity, 11–12; financial framework for enlarged EU, 2007–2013, 98*tab*; functionalist (Monnet system) approach to, 2, 7–8, 9; and liberal norms and values, 162–164; and limits of European state, 2; measurement of economic integration in, 23; member states' attitudes toward, 156–158; occurrence of, 2; and operational capacities, 81; optimal size of, 18–20; predicted welfare effects of, 30; problems and unresolved issues of, 11–12, 107; and questions of who or what is European, 164; and social

welfare policy, 45; and structural changes in agriculture and rural development, 85; and techniques to gain entry, 162. *See also* Eastern enlargement

EU foreign policy, 119; dissonance among member state activities and goals in, 117; flexible diplomacy in, 119; lack of cohesive institutional apparatus for, 115–116; multifaceted areas and influence of, 115, 116; obstacles to, 12; reform proposals for, 125–126

EU global posture and role: geographic zones of, 115–116; and regional/global security issues, 118; terrorism's impact on, 118. *See also* EU security and defense policy (ESDP)

EU identity, defining, 1–2

EU knowledge-based economy, Lisbon objectives for, 34–36

EU law, supremacy of, 59

EU member states: attitudes toward enlargement, 156–158; and basic integration concepts, 195; and CAP reform, 85–86; and deepening and widening of EU, 195; movement toward alignment with NATO, 142

EU neighborhood strategy: alternative to accession in, 156; association agreements in, 156; bargaining and waiting scenario of, 162; and clarity about potential members and definitive nonmembers, 156; confidence-building measures in, 156; and ENP action plans, 156, 159; expanded geographic area and associated tasks in, 155; financial assistance and phased market access as incentives in, 159; geopolitical element and military factors in, 160; internal complications in, 166–169; money as soft weapon in, 165; partnership and cooperation agreements (PCAs) in, 156; and perceived need to enhance EU security, 158; potential for instability in expanded areas, 155; pursuit of credible foreign and security policy for, 165; range of cooperative arrangements in, 155; Ring of Friends formulation and, 8; and transformation of unreliable regimes, 156

EU policies: challenge of technical application of, 108; environmental considerations and goals in, 102; qualitative evaluation of, 96, 97*tab*. *See also specific policy/policy area*

EU political process: and national-level interests, 64; public disillusion with, 64; states interests and philosophies as hindrance to, 64; and transference of domestic problems to intergovernmental forums, 64; unanimity requirements in, 63

EU security, spending on, 199–200

EU15 countries: CEECs' integration impacts on, 28; shortage of skilled labor in, 30

EU3: and EU's direction and prospects, 198; rivalry and mutual respect among, 199

Euro: maintained as hard currency, 10; political implications of, 197; success of, 31

European Aeronautic Defence and Space (EADS), 135

European arrest warrant (EAW), 118

European Capabilities Action Plan (ECAP), core principles of, 121

European Central Bank (ECB): decisionmaking power over, 31; functionality and rules of, 32; and Kohl government's insistence on hard money, 65; voting rights in, 33–34

European Commission: and CFSP domain, 119; constitutional negotiation preferences of, 58; enlargement and integration support of, 158; and environmental policy, 103; and interinstitutional rivalry, 8; and liberalization of services market, 30–31; and open markets for armaments, 139–140; quasi-executive role of, 56–57; regional policy and, 94; right of initiative, 56; state aid monitoring of, 64; supervisory role for, 99

European Convention, 59, 72, 77*n24*

European Council: and CAP reform, 86; decisionmaking in, 55; and interinstitutional rivalry, 8

European Court of Justice (ECJ), authority and capacities of, 57

European Defence Agency (EDA), 125; Capability Development Plan (CDP), 135; EU governments' 2004 formalized agreement on, 134–135

European Defence Community (EDC), 5; and European politics, 8

European Defence Equipment Market initiative, 139–140

European economic and social model, 41–47: and EU club disparities, 196; and European integration, 5; European social model, 42; limits of, 196–197; and social welfare policy, 42; typology, 44*fig*

European Economic Area (EEA), Single Market's partial link to, 47

European Environment Agency (EEA), 102

European integration: and Franco-German compromise, 5; historical overview of, 5–8; process of, 6, 7*tab*; role of bottom-up influences in, 61; spillover concept of, 7

European Investment Bank (EIB), 100

European legislative and executive powers: origins of, 57; principal institutions of, 57–59

European Neighbourhood Policy (ENP), 115; action plans of, 156, 159; and eastern flank countries, 169–177; and European Security Strategy, 159; financing instrument for, 137, 162; German initiative for partnership with former Soviet states and Central Asia, 164–165; and membership aspirations, 167; motivations and objectives of, 159–160, 162; proximity and national positions on, 164; negative incentives for, 162; popular influence on, 158, 166–167; Russian participation in, 170; as substitution for membership, 159

European Neighbourhood and Partnership Instrument (ENPI), 137; and funding to members without accession perspective, 159, 160*tab*

European Parliament (EP): authority and roles of, 9, 57; constitutional negotiation preferences of, 58; enlargement and integration support of, 158; and environmental decisions, 101; and interinstitutional rivalry, 8; state executive control in, 69

European Political Cooperation (EPC), 118

European Security and Defence Policy (ESDP), 120–126; armaments and technology of, 134–135; and Berlin

Plus arrangements, 141; chronological overview of developments in, 127*tab*; convergence of TEU pillars of justice and home affairs with, 145; and costs of military actions, 117; and diverse security threats, 10; and debate on military's relationship to broader society, 131; and enhanced cooperation, 126; and EU regional security context, 122–123; evaluation process on progression of, 123; funding, 128; and German funding and political problems, 131; and Headline Goals for deployment preparedness and increased military prowess of states, 121–122, 125; institutions and staff of, 121; intelligence information sharing in, 121; lack of discriminating rules of engagement in, 122; links to internal security, 144; and maximum sustainable deployment, 122; member state contributions of troops and equipment to, 138; military capabilities as main issue for, 128; Ministry of Defence (MOD) paper on EDP and, 128–129; missions, 124*tab*; obstacles to, 12; NATO-EU Declaration on, 141; Political and Security Committee of, 121; and possibility of single defense market, 140; and questioning of EU military ambitions, 131; role of EU3 in, 129–133; and Sarajevo tragedy, 120–121; and terrorist threats, 117–118

European Security Strategy (ESS), 200; initiation of, 120; and prospect of terrorism, 117–118

European social model: and European integration, 5; and social welfare policy, 42

European Union (EU): agenda of intensifying cooperation in, 74; alleged democratic deficit in, 12; approaches to reorganization of, 3–4, 108; as "balancer" to United States, 75; British Europe versus core Europe configurations of, 198–199; complexity and opaqueness of decision-making in, 69; conceptualized as empire, 205–206; deficient popular identification with, 8; generalized crisis in, 3; global security responsibility of, 200; hypothetical scenarios for, 201–205; as military actor versus civilian power, 125

European Union Force (EUFOR), 123

Europeanization: and normative-affective sphere, 55–56; defined, 55, 159; and democratic practices, 162; in foreign and security policies, 119–120; limits of, 59; process of, 55–56; role of institutions in, 55

Eurozone: comparative labor productivity and labor participation rates in, 34–35, 35*fig2.4*; lack of political support for, 32; Lisbon objectives and, 34; need for coordination of structural and macroeconomic policies in, 36–37

EU-Russia Partnership Agreement, 172

EU-US relationship. *See* Transatlantic relationship

Exchange Rate Mechanism (ERM), and CEE currencies, 32–33

Extended associate membership in EU, as alternative to permanent membership, 156

Factor-price equalization: and capital flows, 28–29; and economic integration of wealthier and poorer countries, 27; and inward labor migration, 29

Ferrero-Waldner, Benita, 117, 178

Financial redistribution: and budgetary negotiations and compromise on, 38–40; as central feature of EU integration, 37–38

Financial resources and funding mechanisms, 135–140; and burden-sharing arguments, 138; and CFSP funding and expenditures, 136–138; comparative expenditures, 138–139; and member states' contributions, 138; and perceived ineffectiveness of defense spending, 139; and policy areas covered in EU 2005 budget, 136–137

Financial services, Lamfalussy process for, 24, 48*n14*

Fiscal federalism, criteria for policy shift to, 95–96

Fiscal policy, national level control over, 31

Fischer, Joschka, 74, 143

France: and Anglo-French ESD transformation, 10; and CAP reforms, 86–87; constitutional negotiations in, 58; economic recovery, 4; growth and welfare effects of EU integration in, 29; Iran negotiations of, 119; and Lisbon objectives, 34–35; referendums on EU enlargements, 68; and changed context of enlarged EU, 195. *See also* EU3

Franco-German partnership, and sustained absence of economic growth, 74

French defense and security policy: activism in, 139; and ESDP survival, 138; and EU development of military capacity, 129; and Islamist-inspired terrorism, 130; motivations for, 129–130; nuclear deterrence doctrine in, 130; and regional disputes, 130

Funding distribution, 81–84; and net payer states, 82–83

General Affairs and External Relations Council (GAERC): Battlegroup Concept of, 122; political/strategic decisionmaking in, 121; secretariat, 57

Georgia: deterioration of Russian relationship with, 176; EU Rule of Law mission to, 176; Rose Revolution protest against electoral fraud and corruption, 176; security risks and threats in, 176

German defense and security policy: and *Bundeswehr* restructuring, 132; and development of EU defense and security, 130–132; and post-Cold War peace dividend, 131; reluctance to move to more interventionist policy in, 131

German unification, and European integration, 6

Germany: and Anglo-French ESD transformation, 10; "bazaar economy" characterization of, 28–29; and CAP reforms, 86–87; economic development and recovery in, 4, 91–93; EU funding to, 93; and financial redistribution, 40; Iran negotiations of, 119; and Lisbon objectives, 34; Russia first preference of, 171; and southern Lebanon peacekeeping, 200–201;

2005 federal election impacts, 198; and Ukraine accession, 174 *See also* EU3

Industrial policy, and adherence to Stability and Growth Pact rules, 64–65

Innovation (R&D): ideational convergence initiatives, 60; public spending for, 34, 36

Institutional summits, lack of substantial results in, 195

Institutions: *acquis communautaire* as criteria for, 26–27; balance of power among, 56; constructivist theory on, 59–60; and Europeanization, 55, 159; enabling and driving integration, 56; and formal democratic representation at European level, 9; and interinstitutional rivalry, 8; introspective and legalistic tinkering in, 117; lack of transparency and public scrutiny of, 9; liberalization process impacts on, 6; under member state control, decisionmaking in, 55; and policymaking, 8–10; for Single Market functioning and supervision, 96; and Single Market requirements, 26; subsidiary principle as basis for, 19; supranational, 57

Intergovernmentalism, 8, 139; "weak," 59

Internal security, terrorism and, 144–145

Iran: EU 2006 Declaration on policies of, 181; EU3 accord on nuclear program of, 181

Iraq: EU and member state aid and debt cancellation in, 181; EU reconstruction role in, 180–181

Ireland: Cohesion Fund payments to, 93; per capita GDP, 91

Israeli-EU relations: action plan in, 179; strategic shortcomings of both countries in, 179

Israeli-Palestinian conflict, EU's efforts for two-state solution to, 177

Italy, and Lisbon objectives, 34–35

Jordan: ENP action plan for, 179; ENPI finance to support modernization agenda of, 179; EU's priorities in, 179

Justice and Home Affairs (JHA), and qualified majority requirement, 62

Knowledge economy advancement, and Open Method of Coordination initiative, 60
Kohl, Helmut, 131
Kyoto Protocol, target costs for EU, 103

Labor migration: impacts of, 30; and internal competition for jobs, 29–31; predictions of inflow, 29–30; restrictions on, 30
Lebanon: association agreement and ENPI/MEDA financing for, 180; EU deployment in, 201
Libya: ENP eligibility of, 178; EU's attempt to advance relations with, 178
Lisbon process/Agenda, 47; and budget reform, 96–98; goal of, 17; and innovation spending, 34, 36; modest outcomes of, 35–37; and national labor market policies, 36; rationale for reform of, 36–37; and relevant problems in Eurozone countries, 34–35
Lukashenko, Alexander, 174–175
Luxembourg Compromise, veto option introduced by, 59

Maastricht criteria, 50n49; and fiscal deficits in CEECs, 33; and SGP framework, 31
Maghreb states: EU energy dependence on, 144; EU's failure to obtain effective regionalism in, 181. *See also* Algeria; Libya; Morocco
Mashreq countries, 178–180; lack of democratization prospects in, 178. *See also specific country*
Mediterranean states, enlargement impacts on, 195
Members of the European Parliament (MEPs), and institutional loyalty, 57
Merkel, Angela, 171, 193, 199
Middle East regime, EU's failure to obtain effective regionalism in, 181
Middle Eastern states, EU energy dependence on, 144
Migration, and social welfare benefits, 46–47
Military Staff/Military Committee of ESDP, 121
Mitterrand, François, 5, 65, 207
Moldova: action plan for, 175; conflict with Transnistria separatist region,

175; Parliament's resolution recognizing importance of, 175
Monetary policy, decisionmaking power over, 31
Monnet method, sustained attack on, 60
Morocco: ENP Action Plan for, 177; role in promoting links among Maghreb countries, 178

National Allocation Plans (NAPs), 103
National defense industries, end of the Cold War impacts on, 134
National income levels, progress toward convergence in, 91
National military forces and defense policies, enhanced cooperation in, 126. *See also specific country*
Nation-states, Europeans' identification with, 6
NATO: EDA coordination with, 135; EU Strategic Partnership with, 141; and national military forces, 128; option of anchoring EDSP in, 132–133; sole responsibility for collective European defense, 141; and stabilization exportation and democratization promotion, 160; strategic goal of balancing US power, 141–142; Turkey's important role in, 133
Neighboring states: comparative ratings for development of democracy and market economy in, 163*tab*; evaluation of political rights and civil freedoms in, 160, 161*tab*; evolution of EU policy toward, 157–158. *See also* European Neighbourhood Policy; EU's neighborhood strategy
Netherlands: and economic and social models, 42; and financial redistribution, 40–41; as net payer to EU budget, 82
Networking industries, and single market program, 24
Nice Treaty: and Constitutional Treaty revitalization, 71, 72; decisionmaking impacts of, 82; and member state controls and veto rights, 119; Jean-Claude Juncker view of, 194
North Atlantic Treaty Organization (NATO), 5
Nuclear power, use of and prospects for: in the EU, 106–107, 144; in Germany, 143; and Iran, 181

Open Method of Coordination (OMC), optimal policy design aims of, 60

Palestinian territories: action plan for, 180; EU's political and economic aid for, 179–180; permanent two-state solution proposed for, 180
Poland, CAP support benefits for, 88
Polish defense and security issues: and Poland's Atlanticism and Iraq War support, 132, 133; position on EDSP and new NATO, 132–133
Political power, critical role of state interests in, 58–59
Prodi, Romano, 8
Putin, Vladimir, 170–171, 174

Qualified majority voting (QMV), 119; and environmental decisions, 101; and European integration, 5–6; processes of, 59

Regional policy, 88–95; aims and instruments of, 89–90; and allocations conceptualized as investment, 94; appropriations for 2007–2013, 93–94; and convergence of national income levels, 90, 91–93; as demonstration of solidarity with poorer regions, 88–89; and discretionary political decisions, 81; effectiveness of, 91; EU enlargement's bearing on, 91, 93; funding to less favored regions, 89; as key component of EU's program and budget, 88; member states' financing of, 98–99; and misallocations of funds, 93; pan-EU competitiveness and convergence goals, 94; persistence of, 37–38; and regional income convergence, 91. *See also* Cohesion Funds; Structural Funds
Regional policy areas: EU funding flows into, 81; and voting power of member states, 82
Romania: EU membership of, 3*tab*, 22*tab*, 23, 169*tab*; deficiencies in infrastructure and institutional capacity, 7*tab*, 26, 33; as net receiver from EU budget, 82; nuclear reactor, 106; potential migration from, 29–30; reservations about EU membership, 18, 23; structural funding for, 91, 94

Rome Treaty, and social security regulation, 41
Russia: Iran negotiations of, 119; legitimate security interests of, 172; as possible EU member, 172;
Russia-EU relations: and autocratic governance in Russia, 170–171; cooperation and recognition of respective interests in, 170; and different conceptions of EU foreign and bilateral relations, 170; energy issues in, 171, 172; positions on terrorism and independence movements, 172; and Russia's geopolitical and military presence, 171; strategic partnership proposal for, 170

Sarkozy, Nicolas, 4, 72, 167–169, 199
Schengen rules, extension of, 207
Schröder, Gerhard, 66, 74, 143; Putin's friendship with, 171
Security policy, and EU defense identity, 10
Single European Act (SEA): and EU politics, 8; significance of, 5
Single Market (SM), 23–27, 47; as core economic project, 23; criticisms of, 24; and eastern enlargement, 25, 28; benefits for smaller and poorer countries, 96; and EU effectiveness, 17; growth effects of, 23–24; institutional requirements of, 26; labor market effects of, 27–31; need for consolidation of, 47; role of borders and geography in, 24; success of, 10; and welfare production, 18
Social security policy: Anglo-Saxon model for, 42–43, 44; in CEECs, 43; continental countries' model for, 43, 44; and European integration legitimation, 42; harmonized with highly integrated market, 41; and Mediterranean states' welfare model, 43–44; Nordic model for, 42, 44, 45; and pension reform, 44; sustainable models for, 43–44; and 2004 directive on migration and inclusion, 46
Solano, Javier, 117, 121, 125, 126, 134, 143, 181
Southern flank countries: Barcelona Process results in, 177; democratization and security prospects in, 177; EU funding and commitment to, 177; and EU neighborhood strategy,

177–181; MEDA I and II financial instrument provisions for, 177; US role in, 177; as zone of instability and conflict, 177. *See also specific country*

Spain, Structural Funds allocation in, 93

Stability and Growth Pact (SGP), 6; and Kohl government's insistence on hard money, 65; purpose and legitimacy of, 31

Structural Funds: in accession countries, 91; convergence goal in, 90; criticisms of, 90, 91; factors influencing performance of, 90–91, 92*fig4.3*; and growth promotion, 90, 91; objectives of, 90; positive appraisal of, 91; qualifying for, 90; redesigned to support low-income member states, 109; as regional policy instrument, 89–90; as side payments to buy political decisions, 93

Syria: as full participant in Barcelona Process, 180; stalled association agreement negotiations, 180

Terrorist threats: and European security system, 200; EU-US cooperation on, 142; internal security and, 144–145; and mobilization to assist member states, 118; and operations in Afghanistan, 144

Thatcher, Margaret, 5–6

Trade, EU and European, compared to North American trade, 24

Transatlantic defense and security relationship: areas of agreement and cooperation in, 142; and Cold War alliance survival, 140; and competition for Chinese market, 142–143; and differences about global economic and social models/roles, 140; and EU development of sustainable independence from US, 140–141; military and security as recurring and related issues in, 140; and NATO-led versus EU-led operations, 141–143; and respective articulations of soft power, 140; and terrorist threat, 142; and US security provision, 141

Treaty on European Union (TEU), 57; and CFSP operational expenditures,

138; environmental protection enshrined in, 101; and European politics, 8

Turkey: and Constitutional Treaty referenda, 67; and ESDP development, 133; military strength of, 134; NATO role of, 133; undemocratic politics in, 182

Turkey's accession: alternative to, 156; association agreement in, 182; democracy criterion for, 160; negotiations and indications on, 133, 182–183; and popular influence on neighborhood policy, 158

UK military forces and defense policy: and ESDP survival, 138; Helsinki Headline Goal interpretation in, 128; terrorism and, 118; and transatlantic security relations, 141; and transatlantic security relations, 141; 2001 Ministry of Defence (MOD) paper on, 128–129; view of ESDP in, 128–129

Ukraine: arguments for membership perspective, 173; democracy in, 173–174; EU balancing act in, 173; pro-West and pro-EU divisions in, 173; Russian relations with, 174

United Kingdom (UK), 128–129; constitutional negotiation preferences of, 58; CO2 emissions reductions goal of, 103–104; Iran negotiations of, 119. *See also* EU3

United States, 37, 75, 125, 132, 206; defense spending, 138–139; and Kyoto Protocol, 103; stabilization exportation and democratization promotion of, 160. *See also* Transatlantic relationship

Voting power: and double majority voting system, 84; and EU budget, 82; in EU27, net payers and recipients in, 82–84

Western Europe: defense and security policy, 120; and German reunification, 6

Yushchenko, Viktor, 173, 174

About the Book

This concise but wide-ranging work explores the major political, economic, and strategic challenges confronting the European Union in the context of a rapidly changing geopolitical environment.

Steve Wood and Wolfgang Quaisser consider the actors and issues at the center of current developments in the integration process. Beginning with some basic conceptual questions—for example, what is Europe?—they focus on the Union's increasingly complex politics and economy. Their discussion ranges from political economy, to policy reform and institutional change, to the arena of international relations. They also address the more intangible factors of European identity and common political will. An intriguing set of possible future scenarios concludes the authors' topical examination of the EU after enlargement.

Steve Wood is a research fellow and lecturer in the School of Political and International Studies at Flinders University (Australia) and associate research fellow at the Osteuropa Institut München. He is the author of, among other books and articles, *Germany and East-Central Europe: Political, Economic and Socio-Cultural Relations in the Era of EU Enlargement.* **Wolfgang Quaisser** is senior research fellow at the Osteuropa Institut München (now based at the University of Regensburg), and lecturer in economics and social policy at the Academy for Civic Education, Tutzing. His recent publications in English include *EU Member Turkey? Preconditions, Consequences, and Integration Alternatives*, coauthored with Steve Wood.